Uncle John's
BATHROOM READER®
PLUNGES INTO
National Parks

Uncle John's
BATHROOM
READER®
PLUNGES INTO

National
Parks

The Bathroom Readers'
Institute

San Diego, California

**Uncle John's Bathroom Reader
Plunges into National Parks**

For information, write The Bathroom Readers' Institute
Portable Press, 5880 Oberlin Drive, San Diego, CA 92121
e-mail: unclejohn@advmkt.com

Library of Congress Cataloging-in-Publication Data

Uncle John's bathroom reader plunges into national parks. -- 1st ed.
p. cm.
ISBN-13: 978-1-59223-784-5 (pbk.)
ISBN-10: 1-59223-784-3 (pbk.)
1. National parks and reserves--United States--Miscellanea. 2.
National parks and reserves--Canada--Miscellanea. 3. National
parks and reserves--United States--History. 4. National parks and
reserves--Canada--History.
SB482.A4U53 2007
973--dc22

2006031048

Printed in the United States of America
First printing: March 2007

07 08 09 10 11   10 9 8 7 6 5 4 3 2 1

CONTENTS

OH, CANADA!

THE NAME GAME

WAR STORIES

NATURAL PHENOMENA

WESTWARD HO!

MOVIES, MUSIC, AND MORE

THE ADVENTURERS

HISTORIES

PROJECT TEAM

Gordon Javna, Editor-In-Chief
JoAnn Padgett, Director, Editorial and Production
Melinda Allman, Developmental Editor
Sandy Ursic, Production Editor
Connie Vazquez, Product Manager

The Bathroom Readers' Institute sincerely
thanks the following additional people whose advice
and assistance made this book possible.

Jennifer Payne

Julia Papps

Dan Mansfield

Rebecca Kaiser

Lise Jorgensen

Rob Davis

Amy Miller

Sydney Stanley

Jennnifer Thornton

Nancy Toeppler

Jay Newman

Brian Boone

Mary Lou GoForth

Raincoast Books

Donna Gibbings

Kristine Hemp

Michelle Sedgewick

Shoba Grace

Mana Monzavi

Dylan Drake

Laurel Graziano

Thom Little

Chandra Teitscheid

NATIONAL PARK SCHOLARS

The Bathroom Readers' Institute sincerely thanks the following talented people who contributed selections to this work.

Toney Allman	Megan Kern
Jahnna Beecham	Andy Levy-Ajzenkopf
Joan Brandwein	Jane Lott
Myles Callum	Graham Meyer
J. Carroll	Ryan Murphy
Jeff Cheek	Ken Padgett
Taylor Clark	Debbie Pawlak
John Dollison	Joyce Slaton
Kathryn Grogman	Stephanie Spadaccini
Debbie K. Hardin	Scott Tharler
Vickey Kalambakal	Steve Theunissen
Angela Kern	Lori Hall Steele
Kerry Kern	Susan Steiner

CALLING ALL
<u>PARK LOVERS!</u>

In 2006, the U.S. National Park Service celebrated its 90th birthday. To honor the agency, the parks, and everyone who loves them, we decided on national parks as the next title in our "plunges into" series.

Deciding which parks to profile, though, was a challenge. Should we choose the big ones? The small ones? Ones outside the United States? What about historic sites, seashores, and battlefields? We started asking around, compiling lists of favorite parks and park stories from BRI members. JoAnn remembered seeing the Yosemite firefall as a child. Jen P. waxed poetic about Yellowstone and Banff. And Melinda told everyone the legend of Pele, the feisty mythical protector of Hawaii's Volcanoes National Park.

Of course, those are the big ones, the parks everyone knows, and though we were sure they deserved mention, we also wanted to investigate sites that few people had heard of. What about parks in the Arctic, monuments in the desert, treasures in the ocean? So we polled our friends, our families, even passers-by at the beach, and we found that the national park system is vast and full of undiscovered stories. Did you know . . .

- Zion's Great White Throne (not *that* kind of throne, Uncle John!) was named by a Methodist minister?
- Some of the best scuba diving and snorkeling can be found in national parks?
- There are lava beds in California?

In the end, we decided to limit our scope to U.S. and Canadian parks because they're the most accessible to our readers. We also decided to include every type of site we could find—national parks, monuments, seashores, lakeshores, battlefields, and much more—to make sure we dug deep enough to entertain and enlighten everyone from the casual park visitor to the enthusiast. So grab a map, some comfortable shoes, and a protein bar to keep up your stamina— it's time to take the plunge! As always, go with the flow . . .

HAIL THE SAVIOR
OF YOSEMITE

"Thousands of tired, nerve-shaken, over-civilized people are beginning to find out that going to the mountains is going home; that wilderness is necessary; and that mountain peaks and reservations are useful not only as fountains of timber and irrigating rivers, but as fountains of life."
–John Muir

John Muir was one of America's first conservationists. His books and essays about his adventures have influenced generations and continue to be read today. And his active lobbying efforts to protect California's Sierra Nevada mountain range led to the designation of Yosemite as a national park.

BORN TO BE WILD

The third of eight children, John Muir was born in 1838 in Dunbar, Scotland. From an early age, he roamed the countryside whenever he had the chance. At a young age, he was given a lot of responsibility by his strict father, Daniel Muir. When John was five years old, he began working from sunup to sundown, chopping wood, hauling water, and even making repairs on the family home. Sojourns into nature were his only means of escape from the physical labor. Thus, early on, Muir looked at nature as a place to relax and seek refuge from the world.

In 1849, the Muirs immigrated to the United States to start a farm in Marquette County, Wisconsin. John worked alongside his family throughout his youth to make the farm a success. Then, at his father's insistence, he attended the University of Wisconsin for several years. He never graduated, though. Instead, he left to attend what he called the "university of the wilderness." John Muir walked nearly 1,000 miles to Florida; from there, he planned to launch an exploration of South America. However, he became sick with malaria, and after spending many months recovering, he decided to go to California instead.

WORSHIPPING AT THE ALTAR OF YOSEMITE

As soon as Muir arrived in San Francisco in early 1868, he started planning a visit to Yosemite. He'd read and dreamed about the valley for years, and it did not disappoint him. On seeing Yosemite Valley for the first time, Muir wrote, "No temple made with hands can compare with Yosemite."

Although Muir stayed in Yosemite on this initial visit for only about a week, his heart remained. He immediately began looking for ways to return to the area and eventually secured a position as a sheepherder in the Yosemite foothills. Soon, Muir was exploring the mountains during his free time. He climbed Cathedral Peak and saw such places as Mono Lake and Tuolumne Meadows. He also began to wonder about how the Yosemite Valley had been formed.

OH, NOBLE EARTHQUAKE!

Josiah Whitney, then head of the California Geological Survey, had long claimed that a catastrophic earthquake had caused the valley to collapse on itself, leaving behind Yosemite's most famous rock formations: Half Dome and El Capitan. But, after studying the area and noting the U-shaped valley and the smoothly polished granite walls—phenomena that indicated something had smoothed out what would have been naturally peaked mountains—Muir came to believe that massive and slow-moving glaciers had actually scoured the valley and its surrounding areas.

Many people ridiculed Muir, but leading geologists of the time studied his theory and agreed with him. Then, in 1872, a strong earthquake centered near Muir's home rattled through the middle of the night. Nearby settlers were terrified; they believed Whitney's theory that the Yosemite Valley had been formed by an earthquake, and many expected the nearby Owens Valley to collapse on top of them in a similar fashion.

But Muir knew better. Demonstrating his somewhat eccentric personality—and his love for all things natural, even destructive forces such as earthquakes—he ran out of his cabin yelling, "Oh, a noble earthquake!" Then, by moonlight that night, he surveyed the rockslides the earthquake had created and recorded the damage, showing that the new rock formations were different from the ones in Yosemite Valley. This proved that Yosemite was not the product of an earthquake, and within a few years, most scientists accepted Muir's theory of a glacially carved valley.

CALLING FOR A NATIONAL PARK

In 1880, Muir married Louisa Strengtzel, a farmer's daughter from Martinez, California, and the couple had two daughters, Wanda and Helen. He moved in with his in-laws and, for almost a decade, managed the family's ranch. But Muir was never satisfied with his life as a ranch manager. He missed his days living in the Sierra Nevada, and spent most of his free time visiting Yosemite. He climbed Half Dome several times (without the rope lines that climbers use today) and spent weeks wandering the backcountry with nothing more than the clothes on his back and a couple of loaves of bread to sustain him. He also studied the valley's ecosystems and natural geological formations. With each passing year, Muir grew increasingly concerned that Yosemite was in danger.

Human encroachment and cattle ranching seemed to be destroying the valley's ecosystems. So Muir teamed up with an editor named Robert Underwood Johnson to try to drum up support for preserving Yosemite. The two wrote editorials and lobbied politicians in Washington. If the federal government took on the responsibility for managing the valley, the two men believed, Yosemite would be safe. Muir, especially, wanted Yosemite to be designated a national park.

Congress answered the call. In 1890, it passed a bill that officially made Yosemite a protected park. But, much to Muir's disappointment, the bill left Yosemite in state control. Muir feared California's politicians would mismanage the preserve and exploit Yosemite's natural resources for their own purposes.

So Muir kept working. In 1892, he founded an environmental organization that he named the Sierra Club, whose mission was to protect the Sierra Nevada range and other natural places in the nation and to educate citizens about what they could do to keep the wild world healthy. Muir became the club's first president, and the Sierra Club spent the next 10 years calling for a national park designation for Yosemite.

CAMPING WITH TEDDY

By the turn of the 20th century, Muir's work as a conservationist had made him famous. And in 1903, President Theodore Roosevelt, an avid outdoorsman, decided to visit Yosemite.

Muir accompanied the president and tried to convince Roosevelt that the state was mismanaging Yosemite—California was still allowing logging on the park's borders, and animals were not protected from hunters. Muir also told Roosevelt that the best way to preserve Yosemite was through federal management—by designating Yosemite, finally, as a *national* park. To bolster his argument, Muir took Roosevelt camping in Yosemite's backcountry. The two men talked for hours around the campfire about the federal government's role of natural land management, and eventually Roosevelt agreed that Yosemite ought to be a national park.

With the president firmly in their corner, Muir and the Sierra Club redoubled their lobbying efforts to Congress. In 1905, the Yosemite Valley and the Mariposa Grove of ancient sequoia trees finally became Yosemite National Park.

A BROKENHEARTED MAN

Yosemite's national park status was a victory for John Muir, but it was short-lived. Eight years later, Roosevelt's successor, Woodrow Wilson, refused to support another Muir project: protecting Hetch Hetchy, a valley in northern Yosemite that Muir described as rivaling Yosemite Valley in beauty and diversity of landscape. Instead, Wilson signed legislation that allowed the river that flowed through Hetch Hetchy to be dammed. The resulting flood reached nearly halfway up the valley's walls and became a reservoir for San Francisco.

Within a year of losing the battle to save Hetch Hetchy, Muir died at his home in northern California, many say of a broken heart. But, despite this loss, Muir continues to be revered as one of the greatest conservationists of all time. To commemorate his work, a 211-mile hike that runs from Yosemite Valley to Mt. Whitney in northern California is named the John Muir Trail, a reminder of one man's efforts to save the wilderness he loved.

To read the story of Hetch Hetchy, turn to page 116.
For some of John Muir's most famous quotes, turn to page 184.
To read about Galen Clark and the Mariposa Grove, turn to page 205.

Obsidian—volcanic glass—is so sharp it's still used today in cardiac and eye surgery.

PARK STATS

How well do you know the United States' national parks?

1. What is the only state without a national park site?
    A. Rhode Island
    B. Delaware
    C. Vermont

2. How many primary sites are there in the National Park System?
    A. 520
    B. 284
    C. 390

3. The largest protected area in the U.S. National Park System is . . .
    A. Yosemite National Park
    B. The National Mall and Memorial Parks
    C. Wrangell-St. Elias National Park and Preserve

4. The smallest site is . . .
    A. Thaddeus Kosciuszko National Memorial
    B. Carter G. Woodson Home National Historic Site
    C. Cowpens National Battlefield

5. America's deepest lake can be found in what national park?
    A. Crater Lake
    B. Yellowstone
    C. Yosemite

6. Which two protected sites are located north of the Arctic Circle?
    A. Denali National Park and Preserve and Gates of the Arctic National Park and Preserve
    B. Gates of the Arctic National Park and Preserve and Kobuk Valley National Park
    C. Aleutian World War II National Historic Site and Denali National Park and Preserve

Petrified wood was once so abundant it was used by Pueblo Indians as building material.

7. What was the first area to be protected as a "national park"?
   A. Yellowstone
   B. Acadia
   C. Hot Springs

8. When was the National Park Service established?
   A. 1906
   B. 1897
   C. 1916

9. How many major types of sites are there in the National Park System?
   A. 6
   B. 11
   C. 14

10. How many millions of acres do U.S. national park sites encompass?
    A. 84.4
    B. 103.2
    C. 25

For answers, turn to page 384.

* * *

QUOTE ME

"National parks are the best idea we ever had. Absolutely American, absolutely democratic, they reflect us at our best rather than our worst."

—Wallace Stegner, writer and environmentalist

"There is nothing so American as our national parks . . . The fundamental idea behind the parks . . . is that the country belongs to the people, that it is in process of making for the enrichment of the lives of all of us."

—Franklin D. Roosevelt

Until the 1830s, most Americans thought the Rocky Mountains were impassable.

WHY'D THEY
CALL IT THAT?

*One of the perks of being the outdoorsy type is that you get to name
your newfound landmarks whatever you want. Here's how some
of the mountains, rocks, trails, and other park features got
their unusual names.*

ZION NATIONAL PARK (UTAH)

The views in Zion were heavenly to Methodist minister and explorer Frederick Fisher. He named a grand white sandstone monolith the Great White Throne because it resembled what he envisioned as the throne of God. He also named nearby Angel's Landing—a cliff so steep and treacherous that only an angel could land on it to bow at the feet of the deity sitting on the Great White Throne. The Three Patriarchs are three sandstone monoliths named for the three Biblical patriarchs, Abraham, Isaac, and Jacob. Fisher named a sheer white cliff with red stains running down its side the Altar of Sacrifice, an Old Testament reference. The Mormon pioneers got in on the name game, too. Kolob (as in Zion's Kolob Arch) is the star at the center of the universe—the star nearest the throne of God in Mormon doctrine.

GRAND CANYON NATIONAL PARK (ARIZONA)

Grand Canyon National Park has religious references, too. The canyon's earliest American explorer, John Wesley Powell, was about to name a certain creek Silver Creek when he recalled a favorite hymn: "Shall we gather at the river, where bright angel's feet have trod…" Since that day, thousands of feet have trod along the Bright Angel Trail.

Geologist and explorer Clarence Dutton took a more ecumenical view, inspired by the religions and mythologies of the world: Vishnu Temple, Buddha Temple, Conficius Temple, Isis Temple, Wotan's Temple, Freya Castle, Hindu Amphitheater, Krishna Shrine, Apollo Temple, Zoraoaster Temple, the Temple of Ra . . . the list goes on.

GRAND TETON NATIONAL PARK (WYOMING)

The names of some park features are rooted less in the divine and more in comedy. Grand Tetons is French for big, um, *tetons*—the French word for "breasts." The rough, jagged mountains were named by French trappers who obviously had been without feminine company for much too long.

CAPITOL REEF NATIONAL PARK (UTAH)

In Utah's Capitol Reef National Park, there's a small, cone-shaped butte across from an arch. The arch is named Cassidy Arch after the outlaw Butch Cassidy, and the cone-shaped butte is called Fern's Nipple. Legend has it that Butch Cassidy named it for a favorite feature of a girlfriend named Fern.

DEATH VALLEY NATIONAL PARK (CALIFORNIA)

The map of Death Valley National Park shouts doom and gloom from every quadrant. There are the Funeral Mountains, Coffin Canyon, Breakneck Canyon, Hell's Gate, the Devil's Golf Course (an area covered with sharp spikes of salt as far as the eye can see), and Dante's View, named after Dante's description of purgatory in *The Inferno*.

Death Valley got its name from a group of pioneers who got lost there in the winter of 1849. Only one of the men actually died (and he was elderly and weak to start with); the rest were rescued. But while they were stranded, the group believed the valley would be their grave, and as they left with their rescuers, one man said, "Bye, Death Valley!" The name stuck.

YELLOWSTONE NATIONAL PARK (WYOMING, MONTANA, AND IDAHO)

Yellowstone National Park warns visitors with Death Gulch, so named because toxic gas from vents in the gulch once caused the death of six bears, one elk, and lots of smaller critters and insects. The Stygian Caves, named for the River Styx of Greek myth, killed any bird or animal that got too close to the poisonous gases that rise from their openings. Electric Peak is a reminder of the danger of lightning strikes: in 1872, surveyor Henry Gannett was ascending the peak when an electric storm came up, causing his hair to stand on end.

Michigan's Pictured Rocks National Lakeshore has 7 named waterfalls.

YOSEMITE BY THE NUMBERS

When it comes to American National Parks, Yosemite is one of the best known. Whether you visit for its impressive mountains, its numerous waterfalls, or its vast valley greenery, no discussion of the National Park System is complete without a discussion of Yosemite.

8.5 miles
Length of the trail hikers use to climb the 4,337 feet to the top of Half Dome. Arguably Yosemite's most famous landmark, Half Dome appears on the backside of the California state quarter.

17
Waterfalls in Yosemite. The tallest is Yosemite Falls; at 2,425 feet, it's also the highest waterfall in North America.

350
Miles of road in Yosemite; there are also 800 miles of hiking trails and 1,600 miles of streams.

500
Number of mature giant sequoias in Yosemite's Mariposa Grove. The grove's main attraction (and oldest tree), the Grizzly Giant, stands 209 feet tall, weighs 2 million pounds, and is about 2,700 years old.

1864
Year President Abraham Lincoln signed a bill protecting the Yosemite Valley, the first natural area to be protected by the federal government. Yosemite officially became a protected park in 1890.

3,000 feet
Height of El Capitan, the largest granite monolith in the world. The first (known) person to reach the peak was famous rock climber Warren J. "Batso" Harding (no, no . . . not the president) in 1958.

There are more than 300 known caves in the Ozark National Scenic Riverway area.

13,114 feet
Highest peak in the park: Mt. Lyell, named for Scottish geologist
Charles Lyell (1797–1875)

CALIFORNIA

Yosemite National Park
Yosemite National Park, CA 95389

Founded: 1890
Area: 761,266 acres
Average annual visitors: 3,300,000

www.nps.gov/yose

* * *

DISASTERS: NATURE CLEANS HOUSE

Heavy snows covered Yosemite National Park during the winter of
1996–1997. Then came drenching rain and sudden warm temperatures. From January 1 to January 3, 1997, Yosemite's Merced River
saw its worst flooding since gauges were installed 80 years before.
Standing water in some places was six to ten feet deep. Much of
Yosemite Lodge was underwater, and Yosemite Valley was closed
until March 14, 1997, as roads, restrooms, picnic tables, and campsites were washed away. The main entrance road could not be
opened until Memorial Day weekend. Fortunately, no human lives
were lost.

The flood washed away half of Yosemite Valley's campsites, but
the National Park Service used the disaster as an opportunity to
reduce the number of campsites (which had been built on a hazardous flood plain) and to restore those areas back to nature.
Today, many of those former campsites are forests and meadows
teeming with wildflowers and wildlife.

Invasive exotic plant species infest approximately 2.6 million acres in the national parks.

SPEAKING "TOURIST"

Here at the BRI, we have nothing but respect for park rangers. Not only do they brave bears, avalanches, and forest fires, they cope with a little-understood phenomenon called "tourists." Here are some of the silliest comments and questions park rangers have received from tourists at U.S. and Canadian national parks.

"How far is Banff from Canada?"

"At what elevation does an elk become a moose?"

"Where does Alberta end and Canada begin?"

"Do you have a glacier at this visitor center?"

"Is this a map I'm looking at?"

"We had no trouble finding the park entrances, but where are the exits?"

"The coyotes made too much noise last night and kept me awake. Please eradicate those annoying animals."

"Where does Bigfoot live?"

"When do they turn off the waterfalls [at Yosemite]?"

"How come all of the war battles were fought in national parks?"

"How many miles of undiscovered caves are there?"

"Are the national parks natural or man-made?"

"Is there anything to see around here besides the scenery?"

"Are you allowed to stay overnight in the campgrounds?"

"Is this island completely surrounded by water?"

At Glacier National Park

Tourist: How did these rocks get here?

Ranger: They were brought down by a glacier.

Tourist: But I don't see any glacier.

Ranger: Really? I guess it has gone back for more rocks.

Sorry, treasure hunters: metal detectors are not allowed in national parks.

PARKS IN THE GREAT WHITE NORTH

Canada's national park system is vast and varied. Established in 1911—and the world's first national parks agency—Parks Canada administers 155 national historic sites, 42 national parks, and two marine conservation areas. Here are six of our favorite Canadian sites.

AUYITTUQ NATIONAL PARK (NUNAVUT)

If you don't mind cold, tundra, and craggy cliffs, Auyittuq National Park in northern Canada is for you. In the Inuit language, *auyittuq* means "the land that never melts," an apt description for a park located in the eastern Arctic. Bitter winds (sometimes reaching 62 miles per hour), violent storms, and desperately cold temperatures (thermostats routinely dip below zero . . . Celsius and Fahrenheit) make this park the territory of the hardy. Auyittuq is dominated by the Canadian Shield, a U-shaped band of bedrock that stretches from the Great Lakes in the United States to the Arctic Ocean. The Shield's highest peak—Penny Ice Cap (which scientists believe was the birthplace of the last ice age)—is within the park's boundaries and is accessible to climbers.

GROSSE ILE NATIONAL HISTORIC SITE (QUEBEC)

From 1832 to 1937, Grosse Ile was a quarantine station for immigrants entering Canada through the Port of Quebec. But in 1847, it was also the site of tragedy. That year, 100,000 immigrants arrived in Canada (up from 30,000 a few years before); most were fleeing Ireland's potato famine and came west in the hopes of finding a better life. But what they discovered on arrival was that they were trapped on the cramped island (sometimes for up to a month) with little food, water, or sanitation facilities. Deadly diseases like cholera and typhus, brought with the malnourished immigrants from European ports, were rampant at Grosse Ile. Afraid that the diseases would spread to Canadian towns and cities, government officials quarantined the new arrivals. They managed to protect Canada, but at a great cost to the immigrants themselves. In 1847, thousands of immigrants (some sources say more than 3,000) died

The scenic Icefield Parkway in Alberta, Canada, takes you past three massive glaciers.

on Grosse Ile; thousands more died on the journey across the Atlantic. Over the next 80 years, the Canadians worked hard to clean up Grosse Ile; one of the most significant changes was reorganizing the immigration station to ensure that sick travelers didn't come into contact with healthy ones. Today, the former quarantine station is a national historic site, memorializing the people who never made it off the island and commemorating its important role as the primary entry point for immigrants to Canada during the 19th and early 20th centuries.

FATHOM FIVE NATIONAL MARINE CONSERVATION AREA (ONTARIO)

Beneath the chilly water at Georgian Bay (on the Canadian side of Lake Huron) is a marine park rich in history and life. Twenty-two shipwrecks rest on the bottom of the bay, and all are accessible to divers. Glass-bottomed boats will take visitors over some of the park's most impressive shipwrecks. Hikers and campers also come to explore the many islands that dot the bay. The most popular (and, many people say, most beautiful) of those is Flowerpot Island, a two-square-kilometer bit of land that boasts two rock formations that resemble flowerpots and gave the island its name.

MARCONI NATIONAL HISTORIC SITE (NOVA SCOTIA)

Love your cell phone and television remote control? Thank Canada, because in 1901, Gugliemo Marconi, an Italian engineer, received the first wireless communication at his radio station on Newfoundland's Signal Hill. That transmission was so weak that many people questioned its veracity. So Marconi tried again. In February 1902, he boarded a ship bound for England and started radioing messages back to Canada. He was able to transmit from 2,099 miles away before losing the signal. Arguments about whether or not his radio transmission company violated Newfoundland's business monopoly rules forced Marconi to leave the province, but he soon set up shop in Nova Scotia and continued his experiments. The Marconi Company operated there until 1946 and did hold a monopoly on wireless communication through the end of World War II. Today, the site of Marconi's Nova Scotia laboratory is a national historic site. Tourists can see the original transmission station and visit a museum called the Wireless Hall of Fame.

"Wetlands" include marshes, bogs, swamps, mudflats, and wet meadows.

MINGAN ARCHIPELAGO NATIONAL PARK RESERVE (QUEBEC)

Located near the Gulf of Saint Lawrence's north shore, the Mingan archipelago is a collection of 40 islands and 1,000 reefs and islets. Limestone rock formations carved by eons of ocean erosion are scattered throughout the park, and thousands of animals and plants call the islands home. Atlantic puffins come here to breed. Seals lounge on the shores. Whales swim in the distance. Wildflowers bloom, and small climbing plants take root in sea-cliff crevices. The reserve is dominated by water and accessible only by boat. From mid-June through August, private companies shuttle tourists to the islands from the nearby towns of Longue-Pointe-de-Mingan, Mingan, and Havre-Saint-Pierre. You can also kayak, scuba dive, or sail around the islands to explore them at your own pace. And 44 campgrounds are available for people who want to stay overnight.

L'ANSE AUX MEADOWS NATIONAL HISTORIC SITE (NEWFOUNDLAND AND LABRADOR)

Around AD 1000, an expedition of Vikings landed in North America. They named their settlement "Vinland," or "Wine Land," because of the fruit (grapes or cranberries) they found growing there. Although that Viking landing is well documented, just where Vinland was has long been the subject of speculation. In 1960, a Norwegian scholar named Helge Ingstad unearthed an ancient Norse settlement at L'anse aux Meadows (French for "Jellyfish Cove") in eastern Canada that may (or may not) have been Vinland. Ingstad and his team excavated the Newfoundland site and found fireplaces, cooking pits, and the walls of eight Norse buildings. They also uncovered artifacts like a bone knitting needle and a stone oil lamp. In dating their finds, they determined that the settlement was the oldest Norse site yet unearthed in North America. Today, L'anse aux Meadows in a national historic site, and Parks Canada officials have reconstructed three of the eight buildings so that visitors can get a glimpse of what life was like for the Vikings who lived there in the 11th century. Numerous hiking trails are also available for people who want to explore the bays and lakes surrounding the settlement. And keep an eye out: you might catch sight of an iceberg or two floating by.

PARKS CANADA STATS

- James B. Harkin served as Parks Canada's commissioner for 25 years. A journalist by trade, Harkin was also an avid outdoorsman and conservationist who was greatly influenced by John Muir. He became the agency's first commissioner in 1911 and retired in 1935. In 1972, the Canadian government established the Harkin Conservation Award to honor him.
- 425 wardens (equivalent to rangers in the United States) keep an eye on Canadian national parks and historic sites.
- More than 4,000 people work for Parks Canada. This includes students, interns, and full-time, part-time, and seasonal employees.

* * *

CANADA'S WORLD HERITAGE

Thirteen sites in Canada are also UNESCO World Heritage Sites.

- Kluane/Wrangell-St. Elias/Glacier Bay/Tatshenshini-Alsek (Yukon and British Columbia)
- Gang Gwaay (British Columbia)
- Nahanni National Park Reserve (Northwest Territories)
- L'Anse aux Meadows National Historic Site (Newfoundland and Labrador)
- Head-Smashed-In Buffalo Jump (Alberta)
- Dinosaur Provincial Park (Alberta)
- Wood Buffalo National Park (Alberta and Northwest Territories)
- Canadian Rocky Mountain Parks (Alberta and British Columbia)
- Historic District of Old Québec (Quebec)
- Gros Morne National Park (Newfoundland and Labrador)
- Old Town Lunenburg (Nova Scotia)
- Waterton-Glacier International Peace Park (Alberta)
- Miguasha National Park (Quebec)

The names used are the ones adopted by the World Heritage Committee, which at the time were the official names used in Canada.

THE STORYTELLER

When explorer Jim Bridger told people about the wonders and oddities he'd seen at Yellowstone, nobody believed him. Maybe it was because he told so many other tall tales.

FROM CITY SLICKER TO MOUNTAIN MAN. Bridger was born in 1804 in Richmond, Virginia, but moved with his family to an area near St. Louis in 1812. At 13, he became a blacksmith's apprentice and started acquiring outdoorsman's skills. By 1822, the 18-year-old Bridger was ready to head out to the frontier. He joined an expedition to trace the Missouri River to its source, and for the next 40 years, he was in and out of the West, trapping beaver, guiding groups, and skirmishing with Native Americans. He became one of America's most famous mountain men, a group of fur trappers who traveled through and explored the area west of the Rocky Mountains between 1810 and the 1840s.

Many of Bridger's frontier exploits took place in Wyoming, including founding Fort Bridger, a major trading post along the California and Oregon trails (now national historic trails). Today, Wyoming still shows Bridger's influence; the state is home to Bridger National Forest and Fort Bridger State Park, as well as the bulk of Yellowstone, where Bridger collected or concocted many of his famous stories.

TRUE TALES

Bridger's stories were so good they were hard to swallow. But they weren't all fictitious. Here are some that people should have believed.

- The Continental Divide is a line of elevated land that jags from Canada to Mexico and runs right through Yellowstone. On the east side of the line, all rivers flow toward the Atlantic Ocean. On the west side, all rivers flow to the Pacific. Bridger spoke of finding a river that forked into branches that ran down either side of the Continental Divide. Two Ocean Creek in Yellowstone does this.

- Bridger also said he'd seen a column of steaming water, as thick as his body and about 60 feet high, spout out of the ground. No doubt, Bridger was describing one of Yellowstone's geysers.

- Bridger told people about a river near the headwaters of the Columbia River that was cold near its source but was hot downstream. He attributed this phenomenon to friction generated by the water running over the riverbed. The Firehole River in Yellowstone does have the temperature differential Bridger described, but it's not from friction—it's from hydrothermal activity that enters the riverbed from below.

TALL TALES

For all his true stories, Bridger's specialties were completely fictitious or not-quite-true tales. Here are some of his best.

- Bridger claimed to have seen an elk in the distance one day. He said he shot at it four times, getting closer each time, without it showing any reaction. Eventually, he became so fed up that he charged the elk, planning to clobber it with the butt of his gun. But before he reached the animal, he was knocked off his feet by running into something hard. He said it was a transparent mountain made of glass and that it also was a telescopic lens, so that the elk was not where it appeared to be, but actually 20 miles away. (There is, of course, no transparent glass mountain in Yellowstone, but there *is* a glass mountain. It's made of obsidian, a black volcanic glass, and some people speculate that it may have reflected an image of an elk in the distance.)

- Another Bridger story with a loose basis in fact is of Yellowstone's famous petrified forest, where petrified trees still stand. Bridger claimed there were also petrified animals— including petrified birds that sang petrified songs—and that, in that forest, the sun and moon shone with petrified light.

- When tenderfeet asked him how long he'd been in the West, Bridger sometimes pointed to Pike's Peak in the Rockies and said, "See that mountain there? When I first came out here, that was just a hole in the ground."

- Bridger claimed that the following was his most thrilling adventure: During a beaver-trapping expedition, he and another man were at camp when they were surprised by a band of hostile Indians. The two men grabbed their rifles and leaped onto their horses, abandoning all their gear at their campsite. They traded gunfire with the Indians until it started to get dark and then hid in the woods until morning. At dawn, the chase resumed, and Bridger and his partner spotted a narrow canyon that they thought offered a better defensive position, so they headed into it. The Indians continued their pursuit, plunging into the canyon after them. The canyon became narrower and narrower as the hunters and the hunted went on, and the floor of the canyon got deeper from the top. As the Indians closed in, Bridger and his partner turned a corner and saw a 200-foot waterfall ending the canyon. They were trapped. At this point in the story, Bridger usually paused and waited for his listeners to say, "Yes? And what happened next?" Bridger always replied, "They killed us."

WYOMING

Yellowstone National Park
Yellowstone National Park, WY 82190

Founded: 1872
Area: 2,212,789 acres
Average annual visitors: 3,000,000

www.nps.gov/yell

* * *

WHAT A HUMDINGER!

South Dakota's Jewel Cave is 137 miles long, the second-longest cave system in the world. The national monument's name comes from the sparkling calcite crystals that miners and brothers Frank and Albert Michaud discovered when they first explored the cave in 1900. The Michaud brothers tried to turn the cave into a tourist attraction, constructing a lodge and organizing a dancing club. But getting to the cave was difficult in the early 1900s and few people lived in the area at the time, so they abandoned the idea.

In addition to the crystals, one of the cave's most interesting features is the strong wind that often blows through its passages. These winds are caused by changes in barometric pressure, even in places that are miles from the cave entrance. Sections of the cave where the wind is exceptionally strong or loud have names like Hurricane Corner, Whistle Stop, Exhaust Pipe, Humdinger, and Drafty Maneuver.

Over 40 NPS sites are designated as "Globally Important Bird Areas."

PROTECTING
THE WILD

The U.S. National Park Service (NPS) manages sites in nearly every state across the country—from Virginia's Shenandoah Valley to Hawaii's Volcanoes National Park. But for many years, the United States had national parks with no park service. Here's a timeline of important dates in the history of the NPS.

1832: Artist George Caitlin, who often painted Native Americans, comes up with the idea of a national park. Worried that westward expansion would destroy wilderness, wildlife, and the native way of life, Caitlin proposed that large tracts of land in the West come under government protection. The government took his suggestion to heart, and President Andrew Jackson established the Hot Springs Reservation in Arkansas. (It became a national park in 1921.) This was the first natural area to be set aside as a federal preserve.

1872: President Ulysses Grant designates Yellowstone as a park "for the benefit and enjoyment of the people." The federal government managed the park, making Yellowstone the United States' (and the world's) first national park.

1880: Frontiersman Harry Yount (called the "father of the park ranger service") becomes the first national park ranger, called a "gamekeeper" at the time. He quit after just one year, though, saying it was impossible for one man to patrol so many millions of rugged acres. He becomes the first person to propose that a special agency be created to supervise the parks.

1906: Congress passes the Antiquities Act mainly to protect prehistoric Native American ruins. The act authorizes a president to put sites of historic or scientific interest under federal protection as national monuments. Congress intends to use the Antiquities Act to make national monuments out of small, prehistoric sites in the Southwest, but President Theodore Roosevelt has different ideas.

There are 27,000 historic sites within the National Park System's 390 units.

The first monument Roosevelt created was Devil's Tower in Wyoming, a rock formation surrounded by countryside. In all, Roosevelt used the Antiquities Act to designate 18 national monuments during his presidency.

1912: Park employees begin wearing uniforms and an Alpine-style hat created by designer Sigmund Eisner. The hat was the precursor to the stiff-brimmed "Smokey the Bear" hat that rangers wear today.

1916: By now, there are 17 national parks and 21 national monuments with no government agency overseeing them. President Woodrow Wilson changes that when he signs the Organic Act, which creates the National Park Service. All the national parks and some monuments come under government control.

1917: Stephen T. Mather, a conservationist and self-made millionaire, becomes the first NPS director.

1920: Isabel D. Bassett, a Wesley College graduate with a degree in geology, becomes the first female park ranger; she works at Yellowstone.

1933: The National Park Service is officially put in charge of all national monuments and parklands, including some that had previously been managed by the War Department and the Forest Service.

1933–1941: During the Great Depression, President Franklin Roosevelt's New Deal provides jobs to unemployed young men through the creation of the Civilian Conservation Corps. Among their many duties, CCC workers construct new roads, trails, fire towers, and facilities in national parks.

1956: As America's economy booms and people have more discretionary income, they start to travel, and the country's national parks are flooded with visitors. Conrad L. Wirth, director of the NPS, begins a 10-year, billion-dollar program to upgrade national park facilities.

What's the diff? A national park is set aside by an act of Congress, but...

1961: Two national park service sites—Chickamauga and Chattanooga National Military Park in Georgia and Tennessee and Antietam National Battlefield in Maryland—begin holding weapons-firing demonstrations. These were the first living-history exhibits, and the program soon spread to other parks. In the years since, the NPS living history program has become one of the most popular attractions in the national parks.

1963: The famous "Leopold Report" is published. Ecologist A. Starker Leopold and a government-appointed committee on wildlife management report that the goal of the NPS must be to conserve parklands and keep them as close to their original condition (before they were "first visited by the white man") as possible.

1980: The Alaska National Interest Lands Conservation Act adds more than 47 million acres (an area larger than New York and Massachusetts combined) to be used for that state's national parks, doubling the size of Alaska's national park lands.

1993: Roger G. Kennedy, National Park Service director, introduces a Web site and puts the NPS on the Internet.

1997: Robert G. Stanton, who began his career as a park ranger, is the first African American to head the NPS.

2001: Fran P. Mainella becomes the NPS's first female director. Under her watch, 6,000 park improvement projects are either started or completed. (She retired in 2006.)

2006: The NPS manages 390 major sites across the country and welcomes more than 280 million visitors a year.

* * *

"The parks do not belong to one state or to one section... The Yosemite, the Yellowstone, the Grand Canyon are national properties in which every citizen has a vested interest; they belong as much to the man of Massachusetts, of Michigan, of Florida, as they do to the people of California, of Wyoming, and of Arizona."

—Stephen T. Mather, NPS Director, 1917–1929

...a national monument is created by a presidential proclamation.

FREE TO BE

A Jewish community in search of a place where it could freely practice its religion found a home in colonial Rhode Island.

STOP AND STAY A WHILE

Having been kicked out of Spain and Portugal during the Inquisition in the 1490s, some Jewish communities resettled in the New World, which generally wasn't much more hospitable. A Jewish safe haven briefly flourished in Brazil when the region was under Dutch control, but when the Portuguese recaptured Brazil in 1654, many Jewish families chose to move elsewhere.

One group of émigrés first tried to disembark at New Amsterdam (now called New York). Rejected there, they continued up the coast to Newport, Rhode Island. Roger Williams, the governor of Rhode Island, was well known for being tolerant of all religions, so the Jews settled down.

WHAT THEY REALLY NEED IS A BUILDING

Over the next 100 years, the congregation gathered for worship in private houses. But by the mid-1700s, they had a large community and a charismatic leader named Isaac Touro. So they made the first step toward constructing a synagogue: they hired an architect.

They chose Peter Harrison. Often called "America's first architect," Harrison was an amateur who designed buildings for fun after making his fortune in shipping and business. For the Jews of Newport, hiring a wealthy architect had a major advantage—the cash-strapped congregation was able to convince Harrison to design the synagogue for free.

The building was constructed between 1759 and 1763 and dedicated on December 2, 1763, making it the oldest synagogue in the United States. The congregation decided to name it after Touro.

HIDE AND SEEK

In his design, Harrison included a feature that has become the stuff of legend: a trapdoor that leads to a small compartment right underneath the reading desk in the center of the sanctuary. Although it's not clear what the space's original purpose was, there are some ideas:

First national seashore: Cape Hatteras National Seashore, established in 1953.

Theory #1: Other synagogues, including many in Isaac Touro's home city of Amsterdam, had trapdoors leading to tunnels that served as emergency escape routes. Although Jews did not face religious persecution in Amsterdam, Europe as a whole had a hostile climate toward Jews at the time, so one couldn't be too careful. The trapdoor and compartment at Touro Synagogue led nowhere, however. So some people speculate that this was the first step toward building an escape route but the congregation never finished it.

Theory #2: Others say that the compartment was used to hide fugitive slaves. It's true that the synagogue participated in the Underground Railroad, but the neighborhood around it was a free black zone, where black people didn't have to worry about being out in public. This fact makes it unlikely that escaped slaves would need to hide underneath Touro Synagogue.

Two more mundane theories about the compartment are that it was either the unfinished start of a way to access the underside of the building or that it was used for storage. (But those explanations are no fun.) The current congregation keeps mechanical controls under there.

CHURCH AND STATE

In addition to being the oldest U.S. synagogue, Touro played a role in the establishment of America's principles of religious freedom. In 1790, the Bill of Rights not yet ratified, President George Washington visited Newport. A representative of Touro wrote Washington a letter expressing the congregation's hope that the new country, like Rhode Island, would affirm religious freedom. Washington's reply assured them that it would. And Newport's Jews knew they would have a home in the United States.

RHODE
ISLAND

Touro Synagogue
National Historic Site
Newport, RI 02840

Founded: 1946
Area: .23 acres
Average annual visitors: 30,000

www.nps.gov/tosy

Some ground squirrels hibernate up to 8 months a year.

HOMES OF THE LITERATI

How and where the literary half lived.

MINUTE MAN NATIONAL HISTORIC PARK (CONCORD, MASSACHUSETTS) This park honors the minutemen who fought the British during the American Revolution, but it also includes one of the most famous writers' houses in the National Park System. Nathaniel Hawthorne was born in Salem, Massachusetts, where his ancestor John Hathorne (the original spelling of the family name) had presided over the Salem witchcraft trials. Hawthorne grew to resent the town—and its history of persecution—displaying early on the social conscience that would make him famous.

Hawthorne at Work: According to legend, Hawthorne burned his first set of short stories because publishers rejected them, and copies of his first novel when it didn't sell. In 1837, his book *Twice Told Tales* got good reviews from a tough literary critic named Edgar Allen Poe, but Hawthorne's career didn't really take off until 1850, when he published *The Scarlet Letter*.

Hawthorne at Home: In 1852, after the success of that novel, Hawthorne paid $1,500 for a house on eight acres in Concord, Massachusetts. He bought the home from professor and writer Bronson Alcott (father of Louisa May Alcott, who authored *Little Women*). In June, Hawthorne and his family moved into the home they called "the Wayside." Hawthorne lived the rest of his life in that house, writing in his sky parlor.

After Hawthorne died in 1864, the house changed hands several times, but in 1883, another author moved in: Harriett Lothrop—who wrote children's books (most notably The Five Little Peppers) under the pen name Margaret Sidney—lived there with her husband and daughter.

In 1965, the Wayside became the first literary site to be acquired by the National Park Service. Today, it's part of Minute Man

The Commandant's House at Boston National Historical Park is available for weddings.

National Historic Park. When visitors are done touring Hawthorne's house, they can go next door to Orchard House, where Louisa May Alcott lived when she wrote *Little Women*. It isn't run by the park service, but it is a museum open to the public.

LONGFELLOW NATIONAL HISTORIC SITE (CAMBRIDGE, MASSACHUSETTS)

Henry Wadsworth Longfellow grew up in Portland, Maine, as part of a distinguished American family that included generals and legislators. He taught at Bowdoin and Harvard but was eventually able to support himself and his family as the most successful American poet of his day.

Longfellow at Work: The American reading public loved Longfellow's poetry because it romanticized their lives and history; he praised working men in "The Village Blacksmith," mythologized Native Americans in "Song of Hiawatha," and turned forgotten events into patriotic legends in "The Midnight Ride of Paul Revere."

Modern critics call his writing sentimental, but Longfellow could spin a timeless tale. His 1839 "The Wreck of the Hesperus," about a skipper caught in a hurricane, inspired a 1948 movie of the same name.

Longfellow at Home: When Longfellow married Fanny Appleton in 1843, his father-in-law gave them a home in Cambridge, Massachusetts, as a wedding present. For the rest of their lives, the Longfellows lived there, raised five children, and entertained celebs of the day like Charles Dickens and Nathaniel Hawthorne.

Built in 1759 for a family who abandoned it during the Revolutionary War, the home (called "Craigie House") became a barracks for American patriots, including General George Washington, who made it his headquarters during the siege of Boston.

In 1972, the house became the Longfellow National Historic Site when it was donated to the National Park Service. Group and student tours can be arranged by appointment; the grounds and garden are open to the public year-round. And the National Park Service holds special events at Longfellow House, including concerts and poetry readings.

The Herbert Hoover National Historic Site and his birthplace are in West Branch, Iowa.

EDGAR ALLAN POE NATIONAL HISTORIC SITE (PHILADELPHIA, PENNSYLVANIA)

Orphaned at the age of two, Poe lost his beloved foster mother when he was 20; his foster father disowned him. His wife, Virginia, was an invalid for nearly half their marriage until she finally succumbed to tuberculosis in 1847. Two years later, Poe died destitute. But he was also a well-known journalist, literary editor, and critic, and the author of spooky poems and short stories that—more than 150 years later—still send shivers down readers' spines.

Poe at Work: Poe wrote comic pieces and even science fiction, but his haunted tales were definitely his most famous. His horror classics feature death by haunted mansion in "The Fall of the House of Usher," by torture in "The Pit and the Pendulum," by cholera in "The Masque of the Red Death," and by live burial in "The Cask of Amontillado." He also wrote the very first mystery novel: *Murder at the Rue Morgue.*

Poe at Home: Poe lived in Philadelphia from 1838 to 1844, when the city was America's literary center. In his last year there, he rented a house at 532 North Seventh Street, where he lived with Virginia, his mother-in-law, and a beloved cat named Catarina.

Life on Seventh Street was more cheerful than Poe's fiction; he hosted intellectual evenings with colleagues and friends in the modest brick home. This was where he wrote "The Tell-Tale Heart," "The Black Cat," and "The Gold Bug," which won a prize in a newspaper-sponsored contest. He started work on "The Raven," which was later published in New York and which made him internationally famous.

In 1980, Congress declared the house at 532 North Seventh Street in Philadelphia to be the Edgar Allan Poe National Historic Site. Self-guided tours are available through the house (which is unfurnished) and the cellar (which resembles the fictional cellar where a murderer kills his wife in "The Black Cat"). More exhibits and a short film on Poe's life and work are next door at the visitor's center. Recitations of Poe's horrific tales and spooky candlelight tours are held at various times during the year.

THE LAND OF SINKING SANDS

Two tales of sea rescue, brought to you by the Chicamacomico Life-Saving Station on North Carolina's treacherous Cape Hatteras National Seashore.

The area once known as Chicamacomico, an Indian word meaning "land of sinking sands," sits on the ocean's edge, just off of mainland North Carolina. Known as the "Graveyard of the Atlantic," it's a place of hidden shoals, violent storms, brutal waves, and strong currents that conspire to bring seagoing vessels to their doom—more than 2,000 ships have sunk in this part of the Atlantic since 1526.

LIFESAVERS

Completed in 1874, the Chicamacomico Life-Saving Station was a wooden shanty staffed by "surfmen" who patrolled the beaches on foot and on horseback, watching for signs of ships in danger. At the sound of a ship's distress whistle or the sight of a listing mast, the rescue team, led by a "keeper" or captain and usually consisting of six or seven surfmen, would launch lifeboats, row out to the ship, and load the stranded sailors aboard. Rescues were attempted in the worst of weather, including thick fog, blizzards, and during hurricanes. There were times, too, when the weather and water conditions made the use of lifeboats impossible.

INGENIOUS RESCUE

Take the late summer of 1899, for example, when seven sailors aboard the three-masted *Minnie Bergen* were stranded offshore. High surf and rough weather made launching the lifeboat impossible, but the surfmen managed to save the lives of everyone onboard using a "beach apparatus," a black powder cannon called a Lyle gun mounted on a wooden carriage that fired a 20-pound projectile attached to a rope 450 yards long. This day, their aim was true, and the projectile flew over the wrecked ship. The endangered crew grabbed it and attached it securely to the ship.

The Blue Ridge Parkway has 11 visitor centers along its 469-mile route.

Hooked underneath the rope, or hawser, was a rescue device called a "breeches buoy," a lifesaving flotation ring with pants legs in which a man could sit. One at a time, the sailors were hauled hand over hand to safety on shore.

IN WITH THE NEW
In 1911 a new, larger lifesaving station was built to house the surf-men, and the old shanty became their boathouse. Over the next few years, much of the lifesaving service was upgraded and modern-ized. The beach apparatus was replaced by powerboats—which came in handy during one especially perilous rescue incident.

THEIR MOST DARING RESCUE
On August 16, 1918, the British tanker *Mirlo* struck a mine left by a German submarine off the coast. The ship, which carried a cargo of gasoline and a crew of 51, burst into flames and started to sink.

The keeper called the alarm, and all six surfmen on duty leaped for the powerboat and headed straight for the tanker, which was now about five miles offshore. On the way, they met one of the tanker's lifeboats carrying 16 men and the captain. From them, the surfmen learned that two other boats were trapped inside a ring of fire surrounding the ship. The keeper knew that the captain's lifeboat couldn't land without help, so he directed the captain to wait and headed out after the other boats. Between two walls of flame he saw an overturned lifeboat with six men clinging to it. The surfmen ran their boat through the floating wreckage and burning gas and oil and pulled the six men into their boat. They eventually found the other boat with 19 men aboard and towed it to where the keeper had told the first boat to wait.

The surfmen successfully rescued 42 of the 51 British sailors on the *Mirlo*. Their dash into the fire was so heroic that the British government awarded them Gold Life Saving medals. And the U.S. honored each of them with an American Cross of Honor, an award that only five others have ever received in U.S. history.

VISITING CHICAMACOMICO
Chicamacomico Life-Saving Station, the only surviving station in North Carolina, is being restored to its original state. Visitors can see the original boathouse, the station itself, and a completely fur-nished home of one of the keepers that's been relocated to the site.

Cape Hatteras National Seashore has many kid-specific activities...

A museum houses artifacts and displays about the surfmen and the rescue station, and in the summer, staff members tell the stories of the history of the station and its most famous rescues.

But the most popular attraction at Chicamacomico has always been the reenactment of the weekly lifesaving drills, complete with beach apparatus: the Lyle gun is shot off, the hawser is attached to a mast erected on the beach, and a volunteer slides down in the breeches buoy to safety.

And in case you were wondering—even though the surfmen lived by the motto, "You have to go out, but you do not have to come back!" no Chicamacomico surfman's life has ever been lost at sea.

Cape Hatteras National Seashore
Manteo, NC 27954

Founded: 1953
Area: 24,470 acres
Average annual visitors: 2,250,000

www.nps.gov/caha

* * *

LIGHT THE WAY

The best-known landmark on the Outer Banks is the black and white spiral-striped Cape Hatteras Lighthouse, the nation's tallest brick lighthouse, which was built in 1870. Although it has survived some 40 hurricanes over the years and even a series of earthquakes in 1886, over time the distance between it and the ocean kept diminishing. Originally built only 1,500 feet from shore, a controversial decision to relocate the lighthouse was made when the buffer diminished to 120 feet. The National Park Service spent more than $3 million studying various options before reaching its decision. In 1999 the 4,800-ton lighthouse was moved without mishap.

The Hatteras lighthouse is one of 406 historic lighthouses over 50 years old that is still in active use as a navigational aid. However, in the near future, the Coast Guard intends to retire many lighthouses.

RED-HOT MAMA

*Gushing over geysers, hooting for hot springs, flushing out
fumaroles: it's geothermal grandeur galore!*

Geysers are the most dramatic members of the geothermal-emissions family. Their close relatives, the hot springs, are kinder and gentler and don't get as much press. The rough and smelly side of the family is represented by the fumaroles and the least-attractive members of the family—the mud pots.

RED-HOT MAGMA

Geysers form in volcanic areas where magma (molten rock) is relatively close to the surface—just one or two miles down. Of course, they need lots of hot water. The geysers in Yellowstone National Park spew a stupefying 75 million gallons of water into the air every day. The water comes from the rain and snow that have percolated down through the earth into the geyser's plumbing system. This trickle-down effect takes a long time—centuries, in fact. The water that shoots out of Yellowstone's geysers today is 500 years old. Geysers also need a special rock known as geyserite and underground channels with one or more constrictions near the top.

The magma heats the water to 500°F or more. (The water doesn't turn to steam because of the immense pressure it's under.) The pressure continues to build until the water rises, spilling some into the geyser's pool at the surface. This sudden decrease in pressure triggers a violent chain reaction. The superheated water bursts through the constriction, and the geyser erupts. Hot springs are geysers without the constriction. The boiling water gurgles to the surface into a bubbling pool. It's that simple.

WHAT A GAS, MAN

Fumaroles are basically steam vents—holes in the earth that are blowing off steam; what little water there is rises to the surface and boils away. Instead of shooting water into the air like geysers, fumaroles pass gas—hydrogen sulfide, to be exact—which produces a horrible "rotten egg" smell. Mud pots form when hydrogen sulfide bubbles up through the water and is eaten and metabolized by bacteria that convert the hydrogen sulfide to sulfuric acid. One of Yellowstone's mud pots, in fact, is as acidic as battery acid. The acid dissolves the rock into a mucky clay that boils, burps, and throws lumps of mud on unwary observers. Even when it isn't converted into sulfuric acid, hydrogen sulfide can be lethal at high levels.

LOCATION, LOCATION, LOCATION
Yellowstone National Park has the most geothermal features in the world: 300 geysers—more geysers than the rest of the world combined. New Zealand is a distant second. Geysers are found on every continent except Antarctica. Outside of Yellowstone, only Siberia, New Zealand, and Iceland have a significant number of geysers. *Geysir* is an Icelandic word meaning "spouter" or "gusher" and is actually the name of a particular geyser in Iceland. Considering that geologic time is measured in millions of years, geysers are babies. The oldest geyser in the world—thought to be Castle Geyser, just a short walk from Old Faithful—is between 5,000 and 40,000 years old (geyserology is an inexact science). Old Faithful is roughly 300 years old.

MORE GRISLY THAN GRIZZLIES
Don't get too close. At Yellowstone's altitude, water boils at 199°F; some hot springs spike up to 205°F. Lovely to look at, but lethal. At least 19 people have accidentally boiled to death in Yellowstone's hot springs—more than have been killed by its bears.

MAKING A COMEBACK
Geologically speaking, geysers don't last long. They've been known to explode, blowing out their plumbing systems and becoming mere hot springs.

But there have been cases where hot springs have suddenly become geysers due to the intervention of humans. Solitary Spring in Yellowstone was channeled many years ago to provide hot water for a swimming pool, but when the water level decreased, Solitary

Spring became Solitary Geyser. More geysers and hot springs are "spouting up" all the time. One rookie is Parking Lot Spring, discovered one day by a Yellowstone ranger in—you guessed it—a parking lot.

To read about geyser gazers, turn to page 141.

Yellowstone National Park
Yellowstone National Park, WY 82190

Founded: 1872
Area: 2,212,789 acres
Average annual visitors: 3,000,000

www.nps.gov/yell

* * *

GREAT GEYSER FACTS

- Two-thirds of the world's geysers are in Yellowstone National Park.

- Most of those, including the famous Old Faithful, can be found in Yellowstone's Upper Geyser Basin. This one-square-mile area contains about 150 geysers.

- In the early 19th century, tourists used to stuff objects such as furniture and food into thermal springs like Old Faithful, just to see them fly into the air when the geysers blew. This contaminated many of the geysers with bacteria, and some became inactive as a result.

- Want to see a geyser in the backcountry? Take a five-mile hike to Yellostone's Lone Star Geyeser Basin and catch an eruption of Lone Star Geyser, which shoots into the air every three hours or so. You can pick up the trail just south of Old Faithful.

A single brown bat can catch hundreds of mosquitoes in an hour.

LITTLE THINGS
MEAN A LOT

Don't sweat the small stuff? That may be good personal advice, but in history, small stuff can be a big deal. A little-known, split-second decision by one Confederate soldier had a powerful influence on the Battle of Gettysburg—and maybe even the course of the Civil War.

The Confederate Army was winning the war for secession when it marched into Gettysburg, Pennsylvania, in the summer of 1863. The Union Army had retreated after decisive victories by Confederate general Robert E. Lee, who was now on the offensive and pushing deep into Union territory.

That June 30, the battle-worn Southern army was hungry for Northern supplies and eager for another victory. If General Lee could push through the line of Union troops, he and his men had a clear shot at marching through Washington, D.C., and raising the Confederate flag over the U.S. Capitol.

THE RED STAIN
To stop the Confederate threat, President Lincoln had dispatched General George Meade and his men, who caught up with Lee in Pennsylvania. On July 1, two closely matched armies—75,000 troops under a Confederate flag and 88,000 under the Union's Stars and Stripes—faced off in the green hills around Gettysburg.

It was July 3 before the battle was over. More than 7,000 of those 163,000 troops were dead. Another 27,000 were wounded. And more than 48,000 were missing in action. Gettysburg was littered with body parts, exploded caissons, and dying horses. Its green hills were stained blood red.

The awful battle horrified both North and South; it also marked the turning point of the Civil War. General Lee never took that march through Washington. The Union line had held—just barely. And Lincoln knew the country had come through a close call. But even he didn't know just how close.

The "Water Gap" is where the Delaware River cuts through a mountain ridge.

DO OR DIE

By the second day of the battle, the Union army was faltering and the Confederates were poised to take Little Round Top, a strategic hill on the far left edge of the Union position. Taking the hill would allow the Confederate forces to outflank and circumvent the Union line. They could put more of the Union men in their sights, and they would have a clear, undefended path to Washington. To defend the hill, a volunteer militia—the 20th Maine—was sent to take up the southern spur of Little Round Top with orders to hold the ground or die trying.

The 308 men of the 20th Maine weren't led by a professional military man. Instead, their colonel was a scholar: Joshua Lawrence Chamberlain, a graduate of Bangor Theological Seminary and professor of rhetoric and oratory at Bowdoin College. Chamberlain was on sabbatical and could have been studying in Europe. But he'd chosen to defend his country instead. Some historians believe that it was Chamberlain's scholarship and leadership, combined with the bravery of the men of the 20th, that changed the course of the Civil War.

A STUDIED DEFENSE

The professor believed in learning and had studied everything he could about military strategy. At Gettysburg, in the thick of battle, outnumbered by the 500 Confederate troops of the 15th Alabama, Chamberlain ordered a complicated military maneuver called the "refusal of the line." The action helped the 20th Maine defend against flank attacks. Against all odds, they held their ground.

Confederate colonel William C. Oates would later say that he thought that his men nearly penetrated the Union line five times, but five times the 20th Maine turned them back. As Chamberlain would later write of his troops, "How men held on, each one knows—not I." Historians agree that the men were aided by Chamberlain's leadership. At one point, the center of the Union line opened. Determined to keep the hill, Chamberlain filled that position himself. (Remember that center position; it comes up later.)

But though the volunteers of the 20th managed to hold out, their ammunition was nearly gone. The men were tired; a third of the regiment was dead. The command was to keep control of the hill. Retreat wasn't an option. Yet Chamberlain knew there was no way that the 20th Maine could repel the 15th Alabama again.

LITTLE ROUND TOP WAS A BIG DEAL

Chamberlain went on the offensive. Because his unit was running low on bullets, he ordered his men to charge with bayonets. So the 20th Maine, in one long line, swept down the hill with bayonets at the ready. By now, they were only 200 men, but they screamed with a bloodcurdling noise that made them sound like 600. The Confederates, exhausted and suffering horrific casualties of their own, may have believed that they were outnumbered. In any case, they fled.

The 20th Maine, under the brilliant leadership of Colonel Chamberlain, had saved Little Round Top. Because the Union line was so vulnerable there, some U.S. historians give the Battle of Little Round Top credit for saving the day at Gettysburg. Colonel Oates, leader of the 15th Alabama, wrote, "Great events sometimes turn on comparatively small affairs."

Joshua Chamberlain was awarded a Medal of Honor for his service on Little Round Top. Thirty years after the battle, Chamberlain received a small package in the mail containing the medal. The citation read: "Daring heroism and great tenacity in holding his position on the Little Round Top against repeated assaults."

SOUTHERN GRACE

Chamberlain's contribution was great. But remember above when we told you that Chamberlain filled the Union's open center position himself? Years after the war, Chamberlain received a letter from a soldier of the 15th Alabama. "Twice in that fight I had your life in my hands," the soldier wrote. Describing Chamberlain's position, he explained:

> You were standing in the open behind the center of your line, full exposed. I knew your rank by your uniform and your action, and I thought it a mighty good thing to put you out of the way. I rested my gun on the rock and took steady aim. I started to pull the trigger, but some queer notion stopped me. Then I got ashamed of my weakness and went through the same motions again. I had you, perfectly certain. But that

---

First national military park: the Chickamauga and Chattanooga battle sites.

same queer something shut right down on me. I couldn't pull the trigger, and gave it up—that is, your life. I am glad of it now, and hope you are.

Today, the site of the infamous Battle of Gettysburg is a National Military Park in southwestern Pennsylvania.

Gettysburg National Military Park
Gettysburg, PA 17325

Founded: 1895
Area: 3,000 acres
Average annual visitors: 1,750,000

www.nps.gov/gett

* * *

FORD'S THEATRE NATIONAL HISTORIC SITE

This landmark is best known as the place where President Abraham Lincoln was shot by John Wilkes Booth on April 14, 1865, while attending a performance of the comedy *Our American Cousin.*

However, the events of that ill-fated day might never have happened had theater proprietor John Thompson Ford heeded the warnings of others when he was told it would be bad luck to convert the former Baptist church he leased in 1861 into a theater. Prior to Lincoln's assassination, the theater was destroyed once by fire. Later, in 1893, part of the theater collapsed, bringing down the house and injuring 68 people.

After Lincoln's death, the theater was shut down, but it reopened in 1968 as a living memorial to Lincoln. Today, Ford's Theatre is still an operating theater.

Independence National Historical Park spans 55 acres in Philadelphia.

MATHER NATURE

*Here's how a West Coast marketing whiz became the first director
of the National Park Service.*

A BITE OUT OF THE BIG APPLE

Born in San Francisco in 1867 and educated at the
University of California, Stephen Mather first sought his
fortune in New York City, where he worked as a reporter for the
New York Sun and then took a position in the advertising department of the Pacific Coast Borax Company. He settled into his
new job quickly, producing advertising campaigns that made his
bosses lots of money. In fact, it was Mather's idea to rename the
company's leading product, a laundry detergent, 20 Mule Team
Borax (a reference to the method of transporting borax out of
Death Valley, California). The name stuck and is still used today.

In 1904, after more than a decade of working for the Pacific
Coast Borax Company (in New York City and, later, in Chicago),
Mather and a friend named Tom Thorkildsen formed a company
that would allow them to mine and refine borax themselves. The
Thorkildsen-Mather Company (later known as Sterling Borax) was
a success and made Mather a millionaire by the age of 40. Mather
stayed on as the company's president until 1912 before he retired
to pursue a life of leisure.

MR. MATHER GOES TO WASHINGTON

Retirement made Mather more active and adventurous than ever:
he took up mountaineering and joined the Sierra Club. During an
expedition to Yosemite National Park in 1914, he discovered a
new calling.

Appalled by the poorly maintained roads and trails he encountered, Mather wrote a scathing letter to his friend and former
schoolmate Franklin Lane, the newly appointed Secretary of the
Interior. Lane was so impressed with Mather's vigor and insight
that he promptly offered him the position of assistant to the
secretary to oversee the parks. "I can't offer you rank or fame or
salary," he admitted to Mather at the time, "only a chance to do
some great public service." Mather accepted the job.

Only 15,000 years ago, much of North America lay under a huge glacier.

As a member of the presidential cabinet, Mather was a persistent proponent of conservation, and he pressured President Woodrow Wilson to sign a bill authorizing the formation of the National Park Service in 1916. The bill was significant because it brought the parks under a single unified authority rather than trusting their upkeep to a loose alliance of superintendents and federal agencies as had been done previously. Eight months later, Mather became the National Park Service's first director.

GETTING DOWN TO BUSINESS

With the help of his assistant Horace Albright, Mather shaped the National Park Service into one of the most efficient sectors of the government. The two men established a network of professional rangers, preserved parkland by warding off miners and loggers, and made the parks more accessible to the public by overseeing the construction of lodges, concession areas, roads, and railroads. In later years, Mather and Albright also convinced Congress to extend the National Park System to the East, resulting in the authorization of the Great Smoky Mountains and Shenandoah national parks in 1934 and 1935.

And they did it all on a shoestring budget. In fact, because the agency's annual operating budget of $20,000 wasn't enough to make all the improvements Mather wanted, the director routinely dipped into his own pockets to finance the operations. In addition to paying some of his old friends from the *Sun* to help publicize the parks in print, he used his own money to pay nearly half of the salaries of upper-level staff and to buy additional parkland.

NATIONAL PROPERTIES

By far, though, Mather's greatest personal accomplishment was making the parks available for all Americans to enjoy. "The parks do not belong to one state or to one section," he said. "The Yosemite, the Yellowstone, the Grand Canyon are national properties in which every citizen has a vested interest; they belong as much to the man of Massachusetts, of Michigan, of Florida, as they do to the people of California, of Wyoming, and of Arizona."

Mather's arduous workload and constant travel eventually got the best of him, and he suffered a debilitating stroke in 1928. Although he retained his title of director for one more year, he passed away in 1930.

There are more than 200 miles of hiking trails in Big Bend National Park.

NAME IT AFTER MATHER

Today, many places in the U.S. National Park System are named after Stephen Mather. These include Mather Point in the Grand Canyon, Mather Gorge on the border of Maryland and Virginia, and Mt. Mather in Alaska. Visitors to these and other national park sites can also find a series of commemorative bronze plaques that read:

"He laid the foundation of the National Park Service, defining and establishing the policies under which its areas shall be developed and conserved, unimpaired for future generations. There will never come an end to the good he has done."

* * *

QUOTE ME

"[Camping in Yosemite National Park] was like lying in a great solemn cathedral, far vaster and more beautiful than any built by the hand of man."

—**Theodore Roosevelt**

"The primary duty of the National Park Service is to protect the national parks and national monuments under its jurisdiction and keep them as nearly in their natural state as this can be done in view of the fact that access to them must be provided in order that they may be used and enjoyed. All other activities of the bureau must be secondary (but not incidental) to this fundamental function relating to care and protection of all areas subject to its control."

—**Stephen Mather**

"The national park idea has been nurtured by each succeeding generation of Americans. Today, across our land, the national park system represents America at its best. Each park contributes to a deeper understanding of the history of the United States and our way of life."

—**George B. Hartzog, former NPS director**

Elvis Presley's *Graceland* became a national historic landmark in 2006.

UH-OH, SHENANDOAH

This legendary sea chantey seems to memorialize Virginia's Shenandoah National Park and, for a brief shining moment, verged on becoming the state's official song. But alas, Virginians are still out of a tune, thanks to the wide Missouri.

O**UT WITH THE OLD**
Virginia lost its state song, "Carry Me Back to Old Virginia," in 1997 after the lyrics (about a slave's hope to reunite with his master in the afterlife) were declared offensive. A 12-member legislative subcommittee solicited suggestions from state residents and received 400 nominees, including many tunes scored just for the state. Famed sausagemaker and country singer Jimmy Dean and his wife wrote a song (aptly titled "Virginia"). And local musician Robbin Thompson's 1980 "Sweet Virginia Breeze" was among finalists. But lawmakers finally gave up after debating the choices for more than two years.

Then in 2006, state senator Charles Colgan Sr. revisited the subject. He approached his legislative colleagues about making the classic "Oh, Shenandoah" the state's official song. Colgan argued that "Oh, Shenandoah" and the mountains it memorialized were synonymous with the state of Virginia. Indeed, much of the fabled Shenandoah region has been preserved as northwestern Virginia's Shenandoah National Park, which includes parts of the Blue Ridge and Appalachian mountains, the Shenandoah River, 100 miles of the Appalachian Trail, and the breathtaking 105-mile-long Skyline Drive.

SHENANDOAH TO THE RESCUE . . . OR NOT

In early 2006, things were looking good for "Oh, Shenandoah." Colgan's committee approved it as an interim state song, and it needed only a majority vote in the state legislature to make it official. But then the effort hit a snag. Although Shenandoah National Park and the Shenandoah River were Virginia icons, the song never *actually* mentions the state.

The song begins "Oh, Shenandoah, I long to hear you, / Away, you rolling river." Some people believe this is a reference to the Shenandoah River. Others believe it has nothing to do with a river

Want to hear "elk bugling," bird calls, and other sounds from the parks...

at all, but is about the daughter of Native American Chief Shenandoah, who's courted by a white river trader. Still others think it's another river entirely. In one verse, the singer laments, "Away, I'm bound away, 'cross the wide Missouri," a river located hundreds of miles from Virginia.

The mention of Missouri in Virginia's state song just wouldn't work for the legislators, and ultimately they decided that "Oh, Shenandoah" wasn't appropriate after all. "That's a deal breaker," said a spokesman for then-governor Timothy Kaine. So, for now, Virginia remains in silence.

PARKS IN SONG
Songwriters have crooned over the majestic peaks and jaw-dropping vistas of America's national parks for centuries:

- Hawaii's Haleakala National Park (located on the island of Maui) is the subject of numerous tribal songs and chants.
- California's Redwood forests, located in Redwood National Park, are a central image in Woody Guthrie's "This Land Is Your Land."
- A 1963 Walt Disney children's album, aptly titled *Songs of the National Parks*, lauds national park rangers and canyons.
- Bruce Springsteen gets downright desolate in his song "Badlands," which references Badlands National Park in South Dakota.
- The 1960s bluegrass hit, "Rocky Top," refers to a peak along the Appalachian Trail in Great Smoky Mountains National Park and serves as the fight song for the University of Tennessee.

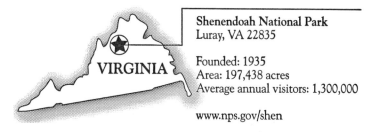

Shenendoah National Park
Luray, VA 22835

Founded: 1935
Area: 197,438 acres
Average annual visitors: 1,300,000

www.nps.gov/shen

VIRGINIA

CASTLE IN THE DESERT

Walter "Death Valley Scotty" Scott conned his way to fame, to fortune, and into the house that bears his name.

HOT PROPERTY

In a desolate canyon in Death Valley National Park sits a 33,000-square-foot Spanish-Mediterranean castle with 14 bathrooms, 14 fireplaces, 4 kitchens, a solar water heating plant, a hydroelectric generating system, a gas station, stables for dozens of horses, and a 56-foot clock tower complete with 25 chimes. The main house has a rock wall fountain, is decorated with European antiques, hand-painted tiles, and handcrafted ironwork, and features a theater organ with 1,121 pipes and a 250-foot unfinished swimming pool. The castle sits on 1,500 acres and is surrounded by a 45-mile-long fence. It cost $2 million to build in the 1920s.

Walter Scott lived there in high style for decades. He claimed the castle as his own and said that it sat atop a gold mine. But the truth was he didn't have a cent.

A DRIFTING GRIFTER

Walter Scott was born in Kentucky in 1872. He left home at 11 to become a cowboy in Nevada and, at 13, got a job working as a water boy for the Harmony Borax Works in Death Valley. By the time he was 18, he was such a skilled rider that Buffalo Bill Cody offered Scott a role in his Wild West Show. For 12 years Scott traveled and performed throughout the United States and Europe. In 1901, he arrived in New York City, where he was supposed to ride into town with the other performers. But he went out drinking instead. Buffalo Bill saw Scott standing drunk (and cheering) along the parade route and fired him on the spot.

He was out of work but not out of ideas. One winter, Scott had (unsuccessfully) worked a gold mine in Colorado, so well versed in the art of publicity from his days with the Wild West Show and a natural storyteller, Scott invented a tale about a gold mine in Death Valley, one of the most remote areas of the country at that

---

Millions of migratory birds nest in and around Mono Lake, near Yosemite.

time and the perfect place to hide a fictitious gold mine. Scott rallied several New York investors with tales of the lucrative mine and convinced them to give him money to excavate the ore in exchange for a percentage of the profits.

A PRO AT CONS

There was no mine, but Scott took the money anyway and headed to California. Once there, he lived it up in the towns around Death Valley and in Los Angeles. He stayed in expensive hotel suites and tipped in large bills.

None of the investors' money went to mining equipment. But he continued spinning his tale, and investors continued to give him money. When his investors asked why they hadn't seen any ore or profits from the mine, Scott put them off, saying there had been a mule stampede, a flash flood, or a run-in with bandits.

ENTER ALBERT JOHNSON

One investor, though, started to distrust Scott's excuses. Born in 1872, Albert Johnson had made a fortune in zinc mining but also made several bad investments. In 1906, Johnson invested in Scott's gold mine.

Three years passed before Johnson began to doubt Scott's tales, but in 1909, he traveled to California to see for himself the Death Valley Mine whose riches were always just out of reach. Scott agreed to take Johnson to the mine, believing the trip would prove too difficult for the Easterner and that Johnson would back out before Scott actually had to produce a mine. But Johnson loved the desert. Ten years earlier, he'd been injured in a train crash, and he still suffered the ill effects of a broken back. The dry climate and the adventure in Death Valley made him feel better than he had in years.

It didn't take long for Johnson to realize there was no mine, though he had so much fun in Death Valley that he didn't care that he'd been duped. He kept returning to the area and eventually bought 1,500 acres in Grapevine Canyon. When his wife, Bessie, began accompanying him on his trips and grew tired of the tents and rude shack that served as accommodations, Johnson decided to build a permanent home.

More than 1,000 species of plants live in Death Valley.

HOME ON THE RANGE
In 1925, Albert Johnson approached Frank Lloyd Wright to design the house, to be called the "Death Valley Ranch." But Wright's design wasn't grand enough for Johnson, so he hired a second architect, C. Alexander MacNeiledge. Over the next five years, the castle started to take shape. And because the home was so elaborate, its construction revived the rumors of Scott's gold strike, rumors that neither Scott nor Johnson did anything to quiet. In fact, Scott (who by this time had earned the nickname "Death Valley Scotty") bragged to reporters about the castle and said it belonged to him. Johnson perpetuated the lie and would say only that he was "Scotty's banker." So Death Valley Ranch became known as "Scotty's Castle."

In 1931, construction on the castle stopped. The 1929 stock market crash had cost Johnson most of his fortune, and he could no longer afford to keep building. The Death Valley Ranch remained unfinished.

DEATH (VALLEY) AND TAXES
In the early 1930s, the federal government began surveying Death Valley in preparation for making it a national monument and discovered that Albert Johnson didn't actually own the land on which he'd built his castle. The boundary for Johnson's land was one mile north and west of the castle site. It took four years for Johnson to get permission from the government, but in 1937, Johnson bought the land he thought he already owned for $1.25 an acre.

In 1933, Death Valley officially became a national monument, and the tourists began pouring in. Johnson, still needing money, opened up the castle for guided tours and paying guests. Albert and Bessie moved to a house in Los Angeles, but Scotty remained at the castle, where he entertained visitors with jokes and stories of the Wild West.

Scotty also continued to brag about the gold mine underneath his castle, which brought some unexpected (and unwelcome) attention in the early 1940s. The Internal Revenue Service wanted to know why Scotty had never paid any income taxes on this supposedly fabulous wealth. Finally, Albert Johnson had to admit that he owned the castle and Scott never had a gold mine in Death Valley.

Bajadas are gently rolling hills at the base of a taller mountain.

END OF AN ERA

Albert Johnson died in 1948, but Death Valley Scotty lived at the ranch until his death in 1954. After that, a charitable organization called the Gospel Foundation inherited the castle and maintained it. In 1970, the National Park Service bought the castle for $850,000.

Today, 200,000 people visit the ranch annually. Park officials wear authentic 1930s garb and regale tourists with the tale of Death Valley Scotty and the legend he built on a lie.

CALIFORNIA

Death Valley National Park
Death Valley, CA 92328

Founded: 1994
Area: 3,400,000 acres
Average annual visitors: 800,000

www.nps.gov/deva

* * *

DETERGENT IN DEATH VALLEY

Death Valley's twenty-mule teams were not the first or the only ones. In 1877, another borax producer—Francis Marion Smith (nicknamed the "Borax King")—used twenty-four-mule teams to haul borax 160 miles out of Nevada's desert. In 1890, Smith bought William T. Coleman's Death Valley borax operation, consolidated it with his own, and formed the Pacific Coast Borax Company, which made Twenty-Mule Team Borax famous. The detergent is still being sold today, and Smith Mountain in Death Valley is named for the Borax King.

THE OLD MAN
OF THE MOUNTAINS

*Park ranger Carl Sharsmith was a legend at Yosemite. Now his friends
are trying to affix his name permanently in the landscape.*

LONG-LIVED

There's a story you might hear at Yosemite about a woman
who asked a park ranger what she should do if she had only
one day in the park. "Well," the ranger replied, "if I only had one
day here, I'd sit by the Merced River and cry."

The ranger in the story is Carl Sharsmith, who was the longest-
serving and the oldest ranger in the National Park System when
he died in 1994 at the age of 91. (His friends held his memorial
service on the gravel next to a river instead of in one of Yosemite's
lovely fields because they knew Sharsmith would object to the
plants getting trampled.)

For more than 60 years, Sharsmith spent most summers in
Yosemite's Tuolumne Meadows. During the off-season, he was a
botany professor at San Jose State University, where the herbarium
is named for him. An alpine flower called "Sharsmith's stickseed"
(say that five times fast), or Hackelia sharsmithii, is also named for
him and his wife, who together discovered the first specimen in the
mountains of Yosemite.

Over his more than six decades at the park, Sharsmith's reputation as a hike leader grew to legend. He inspired plenty of hikers to
take up ecology by showing his own enthusiasm for the subject,
and they couldn't help but be charmed by him. On one hike, a
visitor asked if one of the flowers they were looking at smelled
good. "Why don't you ask the flower?" Sharsmith asked.

A LABOR OF LOVE

He lived his life with the thrift of a true nature lover, wasting
nothing. He patched his clothes instead of throwing them out and
kept the same flashlight, sleeping bag, ranger hat, and car for more
than 50 years. But even if he'd wanted to buy replacements, he

---

Why you're not supposed to touch stalactites or stalagmites in a cave:

may not have been able to on the $8.21 an hour he earned in 1985, after 54 years of service.

THE PEAK OF HIS FAME
To commemorate Sharsmith's contribution to life at Yosemite, his friends have banded together to try to convince the government to name a mountain on the edge of Yosemite after him. It's now informally known as Sharsmith Peak, and it's not as if the renaming would replace some previous notable person—the current name is Peak 12002. If Sharsmith's friends succeed, his name will live on in official maps right next to the meadows he returned to faithfully every summer.

CALIFORNIA

Yosemite National Park
Yosemite National Park, CA 95389

Founded: 1890
Area: 761,266 acres
Average annual visitors: 3,300,000

www.nps.gov/yose

* * *

DON'T TRIP ON THAT SKIRT
George G. Anderson made the first successful recorded climb up Yosemite's Half Dome. He scaled the rock's 8,842 feet in 1875. Just days later, Sally Dutcher became the first woman to make the 17-mile round-trip climb, reportedly scaling the rock while wearing a long dress.

Today, thousands of people ascend Half Dome every year. Cables secured to the rock help modern climbers on the way up. Everyone from children to senior citizens has been known to make the climb.

The oil and sweat on human hands can alter these natural formations forever.

THE CONSERVATION PRESIDENT

As a child, Theodore Roosevelt loved science, nature, and physical activity. Those childhood passions became lifelong pursuits and influenced many of his presidential decisions. Today, he is often called the "Conservation President" and five National Park Service sites are dedicated to his memory.

THE STRENUOUS LIFE

Theodore Roosevelt was born in 1858 to a wealthy family in New York City. Teedie, as his parents nicknamed him, was educated by tutors both at home and while traveling abroad. He was a sickly child afflicted with asthma, and when he was ill, he spent his time reading about faraway places, nature, and history.

When Roosevelt was 10 years old, his father told him, "Theodore, you have the mind, but you do not have the body. You must make your body." The young boy took his father's advice seriously and began a lifelong commitment to what he later referred to as "the strenuous life." The Roosevelts installed a private gym on their porch, where Teedie began lifting weights. He also enjoyed hiking, tennis, and boxing—although, as an adult, he gave up boxing after a blow to the head led to blindness in his left eye. Then at 13, Roosevelt got his first gun and soon took up hunting.

In 1876, Roosevelt went off to Harvard, where he lost the nickname "Teedie"; instead, friends called him "Ted," "Ted O," or "Teddy." Initially, he planned to study science and become a naturalist, but he didn't like the way the science professors taught the subject—in labs and not outdoors. So he studied law instead.

At Harvard, Roosevelt met his first wife, Alice; the pair married shortly after his graduation in 1880. He then started law school at Columbia University and, in 1881, began his career in public service when he was elected to the New York State Assembly.

GO WEST, YOUNG MAN

In 1883, Roosevelt took his first trip to the Dakota Territory in hopes of hunting big game. It took him 10 days to shoot his first

---

Did you know that Abraham Lincoln's birthplace was once a national park?

bison, a disappointment that showed him the bison herds he had read about as a child were quickly disappearing.

That trip was cut short in 1884 when his first child, a daughter named Alice after her mother, was born on February 12. Roosevelt returned home for her birth and to continue his political career. But when his wife and his mother both died two days later, Roosevelt again looked west. Filled with grief, he left the baby with his sister and left for the Dakota Territory again. There, he bought and worked a cattle ranch and tried to fit in with the cowboys. He once even chased two horse thieves through his ranch and, after capturing them, marched them to the sheriff.

Finally, in 1885, Roosevelt returned to New York and married a childhood friend named Edith Carow. But he couldn't stay away from the West for long. He returned in 1887 and spent most of his time ranching, riding, and writing. His books and magazine articles painted a romantic picture of the area and enticed many Easterners to travel to the Dakota Territory.

HOWDY, MR. PRESIDENT

Over the next few years, Roosevelt got more involved with conservation. He formed a cattlemen's association to address problems caused by overgrazing and in 1887 started the Boone and Crockett club, whose purpose was to conserve big-game animals and their habitat. But his political career was also heating up.

In 1900, Roosevelt became vice president and, a few months later, he became president when William McKinley was assassinated. As America's new leader, Roosevelt brought his conservationist views and love of nature with him to the White House. In fact, he considered the conservation of natural resources the be "the fundamental problem which underlies almost every other problem in our national life." So he got right to work.

FIRST ORDER OF BUSINESS: SAVE THE FORESTS

In 1891, the U.S. Congress had passed a law allowing the national government to create forest reserves—later called national forests. Prior to Roosevelt's presidency, 50 million acres had been placed in the forest reserve program. But still, by 1900, more than half of the timber in the United States had been cut down. Using the law, Roosevelt and his new chief of the Bureau of Forestry, Gifford

It was disbanded in 1939 and redesignated as a national historic site.

Pinchot (an old friend from his ranching days), added millions more acres to the program in an effort to prevent forests from being further stripped by lumber companies. By the end of his presidency in 1908, Roosevelt had increased national forest land to 172 million acres.

NEXT: SAVE WILDLIFE
When Roosevelt became president, there was no federal protection for wildlife. Animals living in established national parks were offered some protection, but that was it. So Roosevelt decided to set aside land specifically for wildlife. In 1903, he declared Florida's Pelican Island to be the first national wildlife refuge; he went on to create 50 more national wildlife refuges during his time in office.

NATIONAL MONUMENTS
In 1906, Roosevelt signed the Antiquities Act, which authorized presidents to proclaim historic landmarks and other objects of historic or scientific interest as national monuments. The act was meant to preserve antiquities on federal lands—particularly Indian ruins. However, the inclusion of the term "scientific interest" in the law led to broader use.

Three months after the Antiquities Act passed, Roosevelt declared Devils Tower, a monolith in Wyoming, the first national monument, and he kept going from there. During his presidency, he designated a total of 18 national monuments, the most famous of which—the Grand Canyon—later became a national park.

NATIONAL PARKS
In 1903, Roosevelt visited his first national park—Yellowstone—for a two-week tour. Later that year, he traveled to Yosemite with famed naturalist John Muir. Muir believed that camping was the best way to experience the grandeur of Yosemite. The two nature lovers had a great time on the trip. Roosevelt later said that Muir was a first-class cook and that the three days and two nights he spent with him were delightful.

Muir also convinced Roosevelt of the importance of establishing national parks. During his presidency, Roosevelt created five national parks: Crater Lake in Oregon, Mesa Verde in Colorado, Platt in Oklahoma (now part of the Chicksaw National Recreation

Area), Sullys Hill in North Dakota (now managed by the U.S. Fish and Wildlife Service), and Wind Cave in South Dakota. He also added land to Yosemite.

BACK TO CIVILIAN LIFE

Roosevelt left office in 1908, but he continued his outdoor adventures. Two weeks after leaving the White House, he set off on an 11-month African safari with his son Kermit. For the next 11 years, Roosevelt traveled and wrote. He also remained a dedicated conservationist until his death in 1919.

NAME IT AFTER TEDDY!

Roosevelt once said that he never would have been president if not for his experiences in North Dakota. So it was fitting that not long after his death, proposals to establish a memorial in his honor began. Ideas for national parks, wildlife refuges, scenic roads, and state parks were all suggested. Eventually, an area in western North Dakota that included land from Roosevelt's two cattle ranches became the Theodore Roosevelt National Park.

The honors didn't stop there. In all, four other national park sites are dedicated to him: the Theodore Roosevelt Birthplace National Historic Site, Sagamore Hill National Historic Site, and the Theodore Roosevelt Inaugural National Historic Site (all in New York) and Theodore Roosevelt Island in Washington, D.C. He's also one of the four presidential busts carved into Mt. Rushmore.

* * *

LAND OF ENCHANTMENT

Not far from North Dakota's Theodore Roosevelt National Park is a self-guided, 30-mile driving tour known as the Enchanted Highway. On the drive, visitors pass a collection of large metal sculptures that includes a giant grasshopper, a 150-foot-long gaggle of geese, and a 51-foot-tall sculpture of Theodore Roosevelt riding a horse.

America's first national river: the Buffalo National River in the Ozarks.

UNCOVERING PARKS CANADA

Canada offers a wealth of national parks for visitors. See if you can match sites with the features that make them famous.

1. Glacier (British Columbia)

2. Wapusk (Manitoba)

3. Cape Breton Highlands (Nova Scotia)

4. Pukaskwa (Ontario)

5. Grasslands (Saskatchewan)

6. Mt. Revelstoke (British Columbia)

7. Ukkusiksalik (Nunavut)

8. Kluane (Yukon)

9. Point Pelee (Ontario)

10. Aulavik (Northwest Territories)

A. Includes one-third of the scenic and world-famous Cabot Trail

B. The world's largest known polar bear maternity denning

C. The place to which Sitting Bull escaped after the Battle of the Little Big Horn in 1876

D. Called a polar desert

E. Home to Mt. Logan, Canada's highest peak

F. The only wilderness national park in Ontario

G. Rogers Pass

H. Protects an old-growth rain forest that contains ancient Western red cedars

I. Canada's newest national park

J. Includes the southernmost point of the Canadian mainland

For answers, turn to page 385.

Lake Superior's Isle Royale is the largest island in the largest freshwater lake.

PUTTING LIBERTY ON A PEDESTAL

Anyone who says one person can't make a difference has never heard the story of the Statue of Liberty National Monument.

I n 1865, a young French sculptor named Frederic-Auguste Bartholdi went to a banquet near the town of Versailles, where he struck up a conversation with Edouard de Laboulaye, a prominent historian. De Laboulaye, a great admirer of the United States, observed that the country's centennial was approaching in 1876. He thought it would be a good idea for France to present America with a gift to commemorate the occasion. But what? Bartholdi proposed a giant statue of some kind . . . and thought about it for the next six years.

COMING TO AMERICA

By 1871, Bartholdi had most of the details worked out in his mind: the American monument would be a colossal statue of a woman called *Liberty Enlightening the World*. The French people would pay for the statue, and the pedestal it stood on would be financed and built by the Americans.

The idea excited him so much that he booked passage on a ship and sailed to New York to drum up support for it. As he entered New York Harbor, Bartholdi noticed a small, 12-acre piece of land near Ellis Island called Bedloe's Island. He decided it was the perfect spot for his statue.

Bartholdi spent the next five months traveling around the United States and getting support for the statue. Then he went back to France, where the government of Emperor Napoleon III (Napoleon Bonaparte's nephew) was openly hostile to the democratic and republican ideals celebrated by the Statue of Liberty. They would have jailed him if he'd spoken openly of the project, so Bartholdi kept a low profile until 1874, when the Third Republic was proclaimed after Napoleon III's defeat in the Franco-Prussian War.

Bartholdi went back to work. He founded a group called the
Franco-American Union, comprised of French and American
supporters, to help raise money for the statue. He also recruited
Alexandre-Gustave Eiffel (soon to become famous for the Eiffel
Tower) to design the steel-and-iron framework to hold the statue up.

A WOMAN IN A HURRY

By now the centennial was only two years away. It was obvious
that the huge statue couldn't be designed, financed, built, shipped,
and installed on Bedloe's Island in time for the big celebration. But
Bartholdi kept going anyway.

Raising the $400,000 he estimated was needed to build the
statue in France wasn't easy. Work stopped frequently when cash
ran out, and Bartholdi and his craftspeople missed deadline after
deadline. Then in 1880, the Franco-American Union came up
with the idea of holding a "liberty lottery" to raise funds. That did
the trick.

In the United States, things were harder. There was some
enthusiasm, but not as much as in France. It was, after all, a *French*
statue . . . and not everyone was sure the country needed a French
statue, even for free. The U.S. Congress did vote unanimously to
accept the gift from France but didn't provide any funding for the
pedestal. Neither did the City of New York or the state.

By now, the Statue of Liberty's right hand and torch were
finished, so Bartholdi shipped it to the Philadelphia Centennial
Exhibition and had it put on display. For a fee of 50 cents, visitors
could climb a 30-foot steel ladder up the side of the hand and
stand on the balcony surrounding the torch. Two years later, the
statue's head was displayed in a similar fashion in Paris, giving
people a chance to climb up into the head and peek out from the
windows in the crown. But even though events like these
generated a lot of enthusiasm, they didn't raise as much money as
Bartholdi had hoped.

LADY'S MAN

In 1883, the U.S. Congress voted down a fresh attempt to provide
$100,000 toward the cost of the pedestal; the vote so outraged
Joseph Pulitzer, publisher of the *New York World*, that he launched
a campaign in the pages of his newspaper to raise the money.

"The Bartholdi statue will soon be on its way to enlighten the

world," he told his readers, "More appropriate would be the gift of
a statue of parsimony than a statue of liberty, if this is the appreciation we show of a friendly nation's sentiment and generosity."
After two months of nonstop haranguing, Pulitzer managed to raise
exactly $135.75 of the $200,000 needed to build the pedestal.

NOTHING TO STAND ON

In June of 1884, work on the statue itself was finished. Bartholdi
had erected it in a courtyard next to his studio in Paris. The original plan had been to dismantle it as soon as it was completed, pack
it into shipping crates, and send it to the United States, where it
would be installed atop the pedestal on Bedloe's Island. But the
pedestal wasn't even close to being finished. So Bertholdi left the
statue standing in the courtyard.

In September 1884, work on the pedestal ground to a halt when
the project ran out of money. An estimated $100,000 was still
needed. When it appeared that New York was coming up empty-
handed, Boston, Cleveland, Philadelphia, and San Francisco began
to compete to have the Statue of Liberty built in their cities.

IF AT FIRST YOU DON'T SUCCEED . . .

Furious, Joseph Pulitzer decided to try again. In the two years since
his first campaign, his newspaper's circulation had grown from a
few thousand readers to more than 100,000. He hoped that now
his paper was big enough to make a difference. For more than five
months, beginning on March 16, 1885, Pulitzer beseeched his readers day after day to send in what they could. No reader was too
humble, no donation too small; every person who contributed
would receive a mention in the newspaper. "The statue is not a gift
from the millionaires of France to the millionaires of America," he
told readers, "but a gift of the whole people of France to the whole
people of America. Take this appeal to yourself personally." This
time, the campaign got results: by March 27, 2,535 people had
contributed $2,359.67. Then on April 1, Pulitzer announced that
the ship containing the crated parts of the statue would leave
France aboard the French warship *Isere* on May 8. The excitement
began to build, prompting a new wave of giving. By April 15, he'd
raised $25,000, and a month later another $25,000—enough
money to restart work on the pedestal.

Then, the makers of Castoria laxative stepped forward to help.

They offered to chip in $25,000, "provided that for the period of one year, you permit us to place across the top of the pedestal the word 'Castoria.' Thus art and science, the symbol of liberty to man, and of health to his children, would be more closely enshrined in the hearts of our people." The offer of a laxative for Miss Liberty was politely declined; Castoria kept its money.

ON A ROLL

By now the race to fund the pedestal had captivated the entire country, and money really began to pour in. People sent in pennies, nickels, and dimes. They also began buying copies of the World each day to keep track of the race. By the time the dust settled, the *World*'s circulation had exploded to the point that it was the most widely read newspaper in the entire western hemisphere.

On June 19, the fund-raising passed the $75,000 mark; three days later, the *Isere* arrived in New York Harbor and began unloading its cargo, bringing the excitement—and the giving—to its peak. Finally on August 11, Pulitzer's goal was met. "One Hundred Thousand Dollars! Triumphant Completion of the World's Fund for the Liberty Pedestal." More than 120,000 people had contributed to the effort, with an average donation of about 83 cents per person.

Work on the pedestal now moved at a steady clip. By April 1886, it was finished, and the pieces of the statue itself were put into place. The internal steel-and-iron framework structure went up first; then the pieces of the statue's outer skin were attached one by one. Finally, on October 28, 1886, at a ceremony headed by President Grover Cleveland, the statue was opened to the public . . . more than ten years after the original July 4, 1876, deadline.

The statue was late—*very* late. But better late than never.

NEW YORK

Statue of Liberty National Monument
New York, NY 10004

Founded: 1924
Area: 12 acres
Average annual visitors: 4,235,000

www.nps.gov/stli

There are at least 33 species of sharks in the Gulf of Mexico.

THE MIGHTY SEQUOIAS

The majestic sequoia trees are found naturally in only one place on earth: California's Sequoia National Park. Here are six facts about the arboreal giants that might amaze you.

1. The trees got their name from a Native American silversmith.
The trees were named after Sequoyah, a Cherokee leader and silversmith. In the early 1900s, Sequoyah created a written language for his tribe after a customer asked him to sign his work the way white silversmiths did. However, the Cherokee had no written language at the time (and Sequoyah couldn't write in English). The name itself is actually a misnomer; white missionaries mispronounced his native name Sogwali and called him Sequoyah. (Sequoias are sometimes also called "Sierra redwoods" or "big trees.")

2. They're older than you might think.
Sequoias are among the longest-lived trees on earth. Rangers speculate that some of the park's sequoias may be more than 3,000 years old. Only the bristlecone pine and alerce conifer—which can reach more than 4,000 years in age—are longer-lived.

3. And bigger, too.
Sequoia evergreens are members of the redwood family. They can grow to be over 300 feet high and more than 35 feet wide at their base. The tallest tree in the park is named Hyperion and stands 378.1 feet tall, and the widest is the General Grant, with a base diameter of 40 feet. One of the most impressive sequoias, though, is the General Sherman, named after Civil War leader General William Tecumseh Sherman. Although this sequoia is neither the tallest (just 275 feet) nor the widest (only 36 feet wide at the base) in the park, its volume is staggering: the General Sherman is estimated to weigh more than 2.7 million pounds, making it the heaviest living thing on earth.

Nebraska's Scotts Bluff towers 800 feet over the North Platte River.

4. They used to be common.

Today, sequoias grow almost exclusively within a narrow, 200-mile strip on the western slope of the Sierra Nevada mountains. But 175 million years ago, they flourished worldwide and continued to do so until approximately 11,000 years ago, when the most recent ice age wiped them out.

5. They're heavy drinkers.

The trees thrive in northern California because the area offers ideal weather conditions: warm, dry summers and mild, wet winters. Sequoias need moist, well-drained soil and thousands of gallons of water each day, which they get mostly from snowmelt that has soaked into the ground from the upper plateaus of the park.

6. They're fireproof (sort of).

The trees' distinct reddish-brown bark acts as its main protector. The bark contains almost no combustible resins and can be 31 inches thick. This protects the sequoias from insect infestations and forest fires.

Sequoia & Kings Canyon National Park
Three Rivers, CA 93271-9700

Founded: 1890
Area: 865,000 acres
Average annual visitors: 1,600,000

www.nps.gov/seki

CALIFORNIA

* * *

Two of the most popular attractions at Sequoia National Park are the Auto Log, a felled giant sequoia that visitors used to be able to drive through (decomposition has made that impossible today) and the Tunnel Log, a 2,000-year-old, 275-foot-long, 21-foot-wide tree through which park officials carved a two-way tunnel.

The mountain lion is one of nature's most successful predators.

THEY SHALL OVERCOME

It's the shortest trail in the National Park System but is by far one of the most significant. Preserved by Congress in 1996, the National Voting Rights Trail from Selma to Montgomery memorializes the hundreds of protesters who walked from Selma, Alabama, to the state capital in Montgomery in an effort to ensure that all Americans, no matter their skin color, were allowed to vote.

I t's been called it one of the "last great grassroots human rights campaigns in America" and the "summit" of the civil rights movement. But for the folks who took to the streets during three separate marches in early 1965, it was a test: Would they really be able to stand up to violent Southern racists so that black voters could get their turn at the ballot box?

BLOODY SUNDAY

It didn't start out well. The first attempt was planned for March 7, 1965. Six hundred civil rights protesters—led by activist John Lewis and Reverend Hosea Williams—gathered on Highway 80 in Selma, Alabama. Their goal was to march to the state capital in Montgomery, some 54 miles away, to demand that African Americans in Selma and across the South be allowed their constitutional right to vote.

Even though the 15th and 19th amendments guaranteed everyone the right to vote, African Americans in the South were kept from the polls. Alabama and other Southern states required literacy tests or demanded taxes (called "poll taxes") from voters. But because many Southern blacks were uneducated and poor, they couldn't meet the requirements and were thus excluded from voting. Harassment and violence were also commonplace. In Selma alone, the Ku Klux Klan and local police had clashed more than once with voters and had prevented the town's black residents—almost half the population of Selma—from registering to vote.

So on that Sunday in early March, the protesters set off for Montgomery. They made it only six blocks—to the Edmund Pettus

Bridge—before they were confronted by about 200 state and local police officers. The police ordered them to turn back, but the marchers kept going.

Billy clubs raised and tear gas ready, the officers attacked the unarmed protesters, pushing them back toward Selma. The clash was fierce and violent. The protesters could do little to fight back as the officers descended on them. Seventeen marchers ended up in the hospital, and dozens of others staggered away bleeding and bruised.

What the police hadn't counted on, though, was the effect of the media. Several reporters and cameramen were also on the bridge, documenting the march. The next day, their photos of the assault appeared in newspapers and their footage showed up on television nationwide. Americans were horrified by the treatment of the Alabama protesters on what came to be known as "Bloody Sunday."

IF AT FIRST YOU DON'T SUCCEED

Civil rights leader Martin Luther King Jr. challenged those horrified Americans to get off of their couches and join the protesters in Alabama. He planned a second march for March 9, and instead of simply taking to the streets, this time the organizers decided to try to get government help. They appealed to the state court in Alabama to prevent the police from interfering during their march. What they got was a disappointment but not a defeat: Judge Frank Johnson, one of the few Southern judges who was sympathetic to their cause, issued a restraining order saying the march to Montgomery couldn't take place until he'd had a chance to hold additional hearings.

King thought a symbolic march over the bridge, though, was important. He wanted to show the country, the protesters, and most of all, the white supremacists that violence wouldn't defeat them. So on March 9, the protesters set out a second time. They gathered on Highway 80 and walked the six blocks to the bridge. Once again, they were unarmed and peaceful. And once again, they were met with violence. This time, the police left them alone but they clashed with angry residents, and a white minister from Boston was killed.

At 376 wooded acres, Fort Dupont Park is one of the largest parks in Washington, D.C.

TRY, TRY AGAIN

That was enough for the courts to get involved. Although some black leaders (in particular, activist Stokely Carmichael) were upset that it took the death of a white person to spur the government into action, many people were glad that someone stepped in. A federal judge overruled the previous state court, saying that the police had no right to interfere with the march.

So on March 21, 1965, the protesters gathered one more time in Selma—by then, they were 8,000 strong—and set out for Montgomery. They were heckled and harassed but physically left alone. They walked 12 miles each day, stopping to eat and rest at campsites set up along the way and picking up more supporters as they went. By the time they arrived in Montgomery on March 24, their numbers had swelled to nearly 25,000.

That night, there was a celebration. Hollywood stars including Sammy Davis Jr., Tony Bennett, and Harry Belafonte held a rally for the marchers, called the "Stars for Freedom" rally. And the next day, Martin Luther King led the marchers to the steps of the Alabama State Capitol where he delivered one of his most famous speeches:

> I know you are asking today, "How long will it take?" Somebody's asking, "How long will prejudice blind the visions of men, darken their understanding, and drive bright-eyed wisdom from her sacred throne?" Somebody's asking, "When will wounded justice, lying prostrate on the streets of Selma and Birmingham and communities all over the South, be lifted from this dust of shame to reign supreme among the children of men" . . . I come to say to you this afternoon, however difficult the moment, however frustrating the hour, it will not be long, because truth crushed to earth will rise again.

AFTERMATH

The marches from Selma to Montgomery were pivotal to the civil rights movement. Two months later, on May 26, 1965, President Lyndon Johnson signed the Voting Rights Act, which outlawed poll taxes, literacy tests, and all other voting restrictions. Voters could also register with the federal government, as opposed to with the states, to prevent Southerners from continuing to discriminate against voters based on race.

Some birds, such as gulls and cormorants, can drink salt water.

Today, visitors can drive the entire length of the route the marchers took to achieve that monumental ruling. All 54 miles along Highway 80 are now part of the Selma to Montgomery National Historic Trail. Museums and memorials in both cities bookend the route, offering tourists a glimpse of life before, during, and after the historic march.

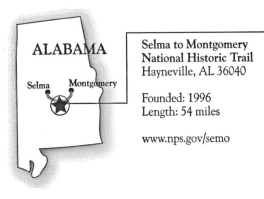

ALABAMA

Selma   Montgomery

Selma to Montgomery
National Historic Trail
Hayneville, AL 36040

Founded: 1996
Length: 54 miles

www.nps.gov/semo

* * *

HOW MANY STOPS ON THE UNDERGROUND RAILROAD?

You have to put the words "stops" and "Underground Railroad" in quotes, of course, because the Underground Railroad is a metaphorical term. It wasn't underground, it wasn't a railroad, and its "stops" weren't train stations or depots. They were sometimes churches or other buildings, but mostly they were the homes of people who helped fugitive slaves on their journey to freedom. The National Park Service lists 64 Underground Railroad locations in 21 states. They include such historic spots as the John Brown Cabin in Osawotamie, Kansas, the Harriet Beecher Stowe house in Cincinnati and the William Lloyd Garrison House in Boston.

* * *

Everglades National Park includes the largest mangrove forest and slowest-moving river in the world.

YELLOWSTONE BY THE NUMBERS

The oldest official national park, Yellowstone has long been the mainstay of the U.S. National Park System.

2
Species of bears that live in Yellowstone: black bears and grizzlies

34
Average number of Yellowstone fires that begin every year as a result of lightning strikes

96
Percentage of the park that's in Wyoming; another 3 percent of the park is in Montana, and 1 percent lies in Idaho.

204°F
Temperature of the water that erupts out of Old Faithful. Most eruptions of the geyser last for 1-1/2 to 5 minutes, shoot about 130 feet into the air, and, on average, occur at 92-minute intervals.

300
Geysers that erupt in Yellowstone every year. Old Faithful is the most famous, but Steamboat Geyser is the world's tallest. Steamboat Geyser sometimes sends water more than 300 feet into the air, and its eruptions can last anywhere from 3 to 40 minutes. Steamboat isn't a reliable geyser, though; usually, more than a year passes between major eruptions, and the longest span was 50 years.

430 feet
Maximum depth of Yellowstone Lake. On average, the lake is about 140 feet deep and has 141 miles of shoreline.

900 feet
Depth of the Grand Canyon of the Yellowstone River

The entire California National Historic Trail system covers about 5,665 miles.

1,000+
Number of earthquakes that rock Yellowstone every year

1872
The year Yellowstone became a national park

3,000
Number of bison that live in the park; Yellowstone is the only place in the world where bison have lived continuously since ancient times.

11,358 feet
Height of Eagle Peak, the highest point in the park; at 5,282 feet, Reese Creek is the park's lowest point.

Yellowstone National Park
Yellowstone National Park, WY 82190

Founded: 1872
Area: 2,212,789 acres
Average annual visitors: 3,000,000

www.nps.gov/yell

* * *

THE TRAILBLAZER
Maine's Acadia National Park was the first NPS site established east of the Mississippi River. It was born in 1916, when President Woodrow Wilson established a national monument there. Three years later, the site became Lafayette National Park (to honor the Marquis de Lafayette, a French military man who supported the American Revolution). Finally, in 1929, the area was renamed Acadia. The park preserves three islands—Mount Desert Island, Isle au Haut, and Baker Island—and part of the mainland. The Cadillac Mountains, located in the park, are a popular stop for tourists because, from October to March, they are the first place in the United States to experience the sunrise.

Alcatraz Island gets more than 1.4 million visitors a year.

DON'T CALL HIM A PIRATE

Jean Lafitte was a pirate. So why was a national park in Louisiana named after him?

A notorious pirate, Jean Lafitte, prowled the Gulf of Mexico during the early 19th century. He captured ships by threatening to attack, took their goods as booty, and occasionally sold the ships back to their owners afterward. After his death, he and his brother, Pierre, became local legends, with the stories about them growing more elaborate each time they were told. Today, his name is proudly attached to Jean Lafitte National Park in Louisiana, where they prefer to call him a "privateer."

AN OFFER HE COULD REFUSE
Near the end of 1814, Lafitte's pirating operation on the gulf coast of Louisiana was in jeopardy. His brother, Pierre, had been arrested and was facing trial for piracy, robbery, and selling stolen goods. While Jean was pondering his future, the British navy approached him, offering to buy his ships and enlist him and his crew as sailors in exchange for pardoning their crimes and giving them land in America after they won the war. Lafitte mulled over this offer but turned it down. Land was cheap, and his ships were the cornerstone of his operation. How could he be a pirate with some farmland and no ships?

But then came some bad news: the Americans had raided the Lafittes' base in Barataria Bay, 60 miles south of New Orleans. The Lafitte brothers were on the lam.

LOW ON AMMO
Meanwhile, in New Orleans, General Andrew Jackson was in some trouble himself. The British were closing in on the city, and Jackson's soldiers were running dangerously low on the flints needed to fire their guns. To make matters worse, the officer in charge of two warships guarding the city told Jackson he was facing a major manpower shortage. Jackson didn't know that the British

---

In Shenandoah National Park, ginseng roots are marked with dye to deter poaching.

had offered a deal to Lafitte, so he decided to try it himself. He and the governor of Louisiana offered to halt all legal proceedings against the pirates and to petition the president for a full pardon for anyone who volunteered. With their home base destroyed, the idea of coming into the fold was looking a lot better to the buccaneers. From all quarters, they came streaming in, including Jean and Pierre Lafitte and their much-needed gunflints.

When the British invasion force reached the city, the Americans won a decisive victory in the last battle of the War of 1812. Looking back, war historians say the contribution of the Lafittes didn't necessarily tip the balance, but the flints they brought with them helped a great deal. It's not really clear, though, what exactly Jean Lafitte was doing during the battle; no account of the battle says anything about him being anywhere nearby.

IT TOOK A FRENCHMAN

In spite of his questionable occupation, Lafitte was well loved by the French Louisianans during his life and became a folk hero after his death. His fighting for the Americans, although it was in his own interest, convinced many locals to feel like Americans for the first time. And General Jackson needed some seasoned seamen as well as the flints—and Jean Lafitte supplied them.

All of which was enough for the government to feel justified in naming a park after him, with maybe a little wink to Louisiana's famous tolerance for scoundrels. And, anyway, he wasn't a *pirate*— he was a *privateer* . . . right?

LOUISIANA

Jean Lafitte National Historic Park and Preserve
New Orleans, CA 70130

Founded: 1978
Area: 14,475 acres
Average annual visitors: 500,000

www.nps.gov/jela

REMEMBER THE *ARIZONA!*

When the USS Arizona was sunk in December 1941, it became a symbol of mourning for its fallen soldiers and the triumph of the American spirit that followed.

THE ATTACK

In the early morning hours of December 7, 1941, the USS *Arizona* rested at anchor in Pearl Harbor, Hawaii, the soldiers onboard unaware of the Japanese warplanes humming toward them from the north. The planes zeroed in on the warships and aircraft that were clustered together in the harbor, prepared for possible deployment if diplomacy between the United States and Japan broke down. The Japanese, on the other hand, saw war with America as inevitable, and with a sneak attack on Pearl Harbor, they hoped to grab a huge advantage in the Pacific.

The Japanese planes came closer, following a signal from an American radio station. The American battleships—all lined up only 50 to 100 feet apart in an area called "Battleship Row"—were easy targets. Planes were parked in a tight formation to minimize the risk of sabotage. American radar did pick up the Japanese planes, but the radar operators were expecting a group of American bombers to arrive, so they assumed the blips were friendly. By the time anyone realized otherwise, it was too late. The Japanese flew over the island of Oahu and split apart to dive-bomb the American navy.

Bombs dropped all over the harbor. Midget submarines that had sneaked in fired at the parked warships. The USS *Arizona* was hit by one torpedo and eight bombs. One of the bombs barreled through the deck and into a powder magazine, causing a massive explosion. Half of the ship was destroyed, and the battleship started sinking. Hundreds of sailors were trapped inside. Of a crew of 1,400, more than 1,100 men died aboard the *Arizona.*

The San Andreas fault is visible in California's Pinnacles National Monument.

LEFT TO RUST

The *Arizona* was too damaged to be salvaged. Many of the other ships sunk at Pearl Harbor were raised, repaired, and sent back into battle, but the *Arizona* was a lost cause. Some of her parts were scavenged and put to other uses, including two gun turrets that were redeployed by the time of the Japanese surrender in 1945.

The place where the *Arizona* sank was out of the main channel, so there was no need to move it. Useless, but not in the way, the ship sat there, part of its superstructure peeking out of the water at low tide.

The sunken battleship was a reminder of the importance of being prepared for the unexpected and was also a grave marker for the thousands who died in the attack. But truth be told, it was also a bit of an eyesore. No one was taking care of it. One veteran named Tucker Gratz said that, one year, he took a wreath to leave at the ship on the anniversary of the attack and saw the previous year's wreath still lying there. Something had to be done.

FUND-RAISING

A group called the Pacific War Memorial Commission headed the charge to create an appropriate remembrance. Even though the U.S. Treasury oversaw the commission, it ran into some problems convincing the government to fund anything, so it pledged to build the memorial solely with private donations and worked to get a law passed that allowed it, as a government body, to build using nongovernment funds. As with many government enterprises, negotiating conditions and shepherding a new law through Congress was slow going. The law finally passed in March 1958, more than 16 years after Pearl Harbor.

Now the commission had to find $500,000 in donations. In addition to soliciting gifts from some obvious places like the Hawaii state legislature and veterans' groups, the commission came up with a few unusual ideas:

- *This Is Your Life* was a long-running TV show of the 1950s and early 1960s in which a celebrity's relatives and old friends told stories from offstage while the celebrity listened, and then they'd all have an emotional reunion. The memorial commission arranged an episode in which the *Arizona* was the "celebrity." A phone number appeared onscreen periodically throughout the program, and the commission raised $95,000.

- The editor of the *Honolulu Advertiser*, Hawaii's main newspaper, sent letters to the editors of other newspapers, asking them to help the fund-raising effort. One that ran an editorial supporting the memorial was the Los Angeles Examiner, which happened to be read by Elvis Presley's manager, Colonel Tom Parker. Presley was going to be in Hawaii filming a movie soon, so Parker scheduled a charity concert. It raised $64,696.73.

BUILDING OVER

The money raised, the commission turned to architect Alfred Preis for a design. The navy still controlled the ship and stipulated that the memorial had to be in the form of a bridge and could not touch the *Arizona* itself. Also, it had to accommodate at least 200 people.

Jewel-encrusted burial crypts of the Austrian Hapsburg emperors inspired Preis's first design. He envisioned a passage leading down into a viewing area that would show the battleship from below the surface of the water; the rust and the marine organisms on the hull of the ship would resemble jewels. But everyone except Preis thought this idea was morbid.

Preis's second idea was to have an open deck for assembly in the middle of a bridge that cut transversely across the sunken ship and rested on two concrete piles off to port and starboard. The bridge arced downward and became narrower in the middle, going from 21 feet high at the ends to 14 feet at the center (and 36 feet to 27 feet in width). Preis also designed a shrine room at one end of the bridge to display the names of the dead. At the center of the bridge, seven holes on either side would allow visitors to look at the ship in the water, and seven holes in the ceiling let in natural light. This became the existing memorial.

Many people loved this design. They said that the way the roof rose to a high point at the ends was like the fortunes of the United States in the war, starting at a low after Pearl Harbor and rising to victory in 1945. (Preis said the curved roof made for better weight distribution.) They said the 21 openings in the middle of the bridge evoked a 21-gun salute. (Preis said the holes kept the center of the bridge from getting too heavy.) The completed memorial was dedicated in May 1962.

THE ARIZONA TODAY

The memorial was a huge hit. Within a few years, it was over-whelmed with visitors. Because it's out in the middle of the harbor, the navy was shuttling visitors over as fast as it could, but there were still long waits on shore. Worse, there was no visitor center to keep people occupied while they waited or to keep them dry when it was raining. Another building was called for.

But again, no one wanted to pay for the building. The navy wanted the National Park Service to do it, and the NPS wanted the navy to do it. Finally, they reached an agreement that the navy would build the complex and the park service would operate it.

And so it is today. If you visit, look for the fuel leak that's still oozing from the hulk near the #3 turret foundation. It releases a few quarts of oil a day from a store that might still have as much as 500,000 gallons remaining, a still-bleeding wound from one of the darkest days in American history.

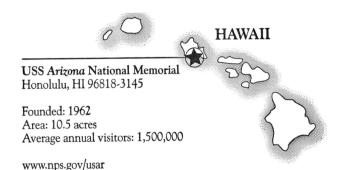

HAWAII

USS *Arizona* National Memorial
Honolulu, HI 96818-3145

Founded: 1962
Area: 10.5 acres
Average annual visitors: 1,500,000

www.nps.gov/usar

* * *

A BARGAIN AT ANY PRICE

Until 1917, the U.S. Virgin Islands were owned by Denmark. During World War I, the U.S. government feared that Germany would use the islands for U-boat bases and bought the islands from Denmark for $25 million, the highest price the United States had ever paid for land. The United States took possession of the islands in 1917 and granted citizenship to all their residents 10 years later.

Booker T. Washington National Monument is 25 miles from Roanoke, VA.

TALES OF THE TRAIL: PART I

The Appalachian Trail and the people who've trekked it

The Appalachian Trail stretches through 14 states: Georgia, North Carolina, Tennessee, Virginia, West Virginia, Maryland, Pennsylvania, New Jersey, New York, Connecticut, Massachusetts, Vermont, New Hampshire, and Maine. No one knows its exact distance, but the National Park Service figures that it's about 2,174 miles long. However, the exact mileage isn't important to the members of the "2,000-mile club," the few inspired and dedicated people who've walked the entire trail.

FORGING A PATH

The Appalachian Trail began with a conservationist named Benton MacKaye. In 1921, he came up with an idea for a trail from Georgia to Maine that connected farms and towns along the way. By 1923, the first section of the trail—from Bear Mountain State Park in Georgia to Harriman State Park in New York—was completed. The rest was finished in the 1930s.

Today's Appalachian Trail is no manicured footpath. It's rocky, wet, and dangerous. Hikers must climb Clingmans Dome in Tennessee (the trail's highest peak) and cross the Hudson River in New York (the lowest point). They also have to deal with dramatic weather: snow, rain, ice, and high winds are common.

Most of the thousands of people who travel the trail are back-packers and weekend hikers who explore small sections, following the wooden markers and white blazes on trees that point the way and enjoying the wilderness. A small percentage of the hikers—approximately 2,400 a year—set out to make it the whole way, but only 10 to 20 percent of those succeed. Many have to abandon the effort due to blisters, falls, broken bones, exhaustion, loneliness, the stifling heat, the bitter cold, or the misery of unending spring-time rain and mud.

Fifty-five mammal species live in the Ozarks' Buffalo National River area.

A VERY EXCLUSIVE CLUB

Since the Appalachian Trail was completed in 1937, only about 8,000 people have reported hiking it from beginning to end. Some have accomplished that feat in one season—generally taking four to eight months, beginning in April, and leaving the trail periodically for a rest stop at a hotel, a hot meal, a resupply of equipment, or a phone call home. The people who conquer the trail in a single year are known as "thru-hikers." Other hikers may complete the trail over a period of several years, instead of in just one season. Even if it takes years, these "section-hikers" are still considered "2,000-milers."

THE ROUTES MOST OFTEN TAKEN

Most aspiring thru-hikers begin at the generally accepted start of the trail, Springer Mountain in Georgia, and try to hike straight through to Mt. Katahdin in Maine. Others do a "flip-flop" and hike half the trail, say from Georgia to Pennsylvania, and then fly or drive to Maine and hike back south to the point where they left the trail. Flip-flops avoid the crowds of hikers on the trail in spring and ensure that the hike of Katahdin is completed by the time fall approaches. At an altitude of 5,267 feet, Katahdin is so remote and dangerous (it gets slippery with ice and snow) that the Park Service closes it between October 15 and May 15. Flip-flop or not, any thru-hike is considered a tremendous accomplishment.

A REWARDING EXPERIENCE

The Appalachian Trail Conservancy, a nonprofit organization dedicated to preserving and maintaining the trail, keeps records of every 2,000-miler who reports finishing the trail, adds his or her name to their list of 2,000-milers, and awards the hiker a certificate of completion and a rocker patch that reads "2000-MILER."

The Appalachian Trail Conservancy's Web site provides some interesting information about those who've become 2,000-milers:

- The first thru-hiker of the Appalachian Trail was Earl V. Shaffer, who completed the hike in 1948.
- The oldest thru-hiker was Lee Barry, who was 81 when he completed his second hike in 2004. His trail name was "Easy One."
- The youngest thru-hiker is a six-year-old boy who did a flip-flop hike with his parents in 1980. Another six-year-old made the trek with his family in 2002.

Cypress trees have mysterious upright growths called "knees."

- About 30 people have reported hiking the entire trail three or more times, including Emma Gatewood, who completed her third hike in 1964 at the age of 76. Her trail name was "Grandma Gatewood."
- Bob Barker (not the TV show host) hiked the Appalachian Trail three times during the 1980s despite having to navigate the trail on crutches due to multiple sclerosis.

See pages 243 and 382 for thrilling real-life stories of two people who overcame terrific odds to become official "2,000-milers" of the Appalachian Trail.

Appalachian National Scenic Trail
Harpers Ferry, WV 25425

Founded: 1925
Length: 2,175 miles
Annual average visitors: 3,500,000

www.nps.gov/appa

* * *

PRETTY AS A PICTURE

The artist most often associated with Yosemite is Ansel Adams, but the first published image of the park was created in 1855 by a man named Thomas Ayres. Ayres's lithograph print is a magnificent representation of steep cliffs, a roaring Yosemite Falls, and animals grazing and people camping in the valley below. Ayres made the print after a trip to Yosemite Falls, which he describes as "gleaming like a silver thread from the dark precipice."

At 208 feet, Cape Hatteras Lighthouse is the tallest lighthouse in the United States.

LET THE FIRE FALL!

*For many years, visitors to Yosemite National Park enjoyed a
spectacular show of sparks and flames hurtling over a cliff at Glacier
Point—and all the while, Smokey the Bear was nowhere in sight.*

Even before Yosemite achieved national park status, hotel
proprietor James McCauley, who owned and managed the
Mountain House Lodge, started tossing things over
Yosemite's cliffs just to see how long it took for them to disappear
out of sight—and as a gimmick to attract attention to his establishment. First McCauley tossed over a chicken, much to the dismay
of onlookers. He reassured his audience that the chicken was never
harmed, and many people later reported that the same chicken
could be seen climbing up the summit trail every morning, heading
for home.

It wasn't long before McCauley found bigger and better things
to launch over the cliffs, including a giant bonfire he sent tumbling
over the edge at Glacier Point. Witnesses in the Yosemite Valley
below were treated to a shower of sparks and glowing embers that
looked like a waterfall made of fire. McCauley enjoyed the favor-
able response to this act so much that he decided to repeat the
"firefall" nightly. Every evening at nine o'clock, he started a large
fire of red fir bark (because red fir bark burned out quickly and,
thus, lessened the hazard of starting an unwanted blaze below).
Then he shoved it over the edge, turning an ordinary cliffside into
an unforgettable 1,000-foot spectacle.

HELLO, GLACIER POINT!

This practice outlived McCauley's tenure at Yosemite; he and his
family sold the lodge in 1897. Two years later, David and Jennie
Curry opened Camp Curry in the Yosemite Valley (the precursor to
what is now known as Curry Village) and took over the Yosemite
firefall, hoping to attract more visitors to the park. The National
Park Service even got in on the act, and rangers were assigned to
the show. Every night at nine, someone from Camp Curry would
call up from the valley floor, "Hello, Glacier Point!" and a ranger
stationed at the top of the cliff would call down, "Hello, Camp
Curry!" Then the Curry representative hollered, "Let the fire fall!"

Do you know the name of President Herbert Hoover's rustic vacation home?

The ranger above answered by pushing the blazing pile of fir bark over the cliff.

THE TRADITION FIZZLES OUT

For many years, the Yosemite firefall was a wildly popular attraction—so popular that it led to congested thoroughfares as excited drivers stopped to watch and parked their vehicles in the middle of the park's only road. Congestion leaving the valley also increased after the firefall was over for the night and people tried to make their way home. Plus, to get a good vantage point, many spectators strayed off of designated trails, trampling meadows, destroying fragile ecosystems, and disturbing nocturnal animals.

Because of these problems, in the 1960s, environmentalists and other conservationists began to criticize this kind of artificial entertainment. They also argued that the firefall had nothing to do with the park's natural wonders and so detracted from the wilderness experience and went against the sentiment of preserving the park in the first place. Curators of Yosemite eventually agreed, and in 1968, the Yosemite firefall was discontinued. But visitors to Yosemite can still see traces of the firefall in the form of a white burn streak visible on the face of the cliff beneath Glacier Point.

CALIFORNIA

Yosemite National Park
Yosemite National Park, CA 95389

Founded: 1890
Area: 761,266 acres
Average annual visitors: 3,300,000

www.nps.gov/yose

* * *

Arizona's Petrified Forest National Park is the only national park to include a stretch of historic Route 66.

Rapidan Camp, a precursor to Camp David, is in Shenandoah National Park.

THE MODOC WAR

*In 1873, the Modoc tribe used an ancient, cave-ridden lava flow
to hold off the U.S. Army. The site of that battle is now
Lava Beds National Monument.*

HE AIN'T MY NEIGHBOR!
For centuries, the Modoc had lived east of the Cascade
Mountains on either side of the border between Oregon
and California. The tribe numbered around 500 people in the
1860s, when white settlers began arriving in the area. The new-
comers wanted to build homes and towns on land where the tribe
lived, and they expected the U.S. government to protect them
from angry Indians who didn't want to move.

The government made an effort. Federal agents convinced the
Modocs to try reservation life—but the agents sent them to an
Oregon reservation populated by the Klamath tribe, the Modocs'
mortal enemy. Not surprisingly, the shared reservation didn't suit
either group. So in 1870, a Modoc leader named Kintpuash (called
Captain Jack by the Americans) led most of the Modocs away from
the reservation and vowed never to return.

For the next two years, Kintpuash and his tribe lived near white
settlers. Many pioneers, suspicious of all Native Americans, complained to the government. They claimed the Modocs stole cattle
and "insulted the femail inmates of our sacred Homes," one worried farmer wrote to the governor of Oregon.

PLAN A: FORCE

In late November 1872, a 31-man unit of the U.S. Cavalry tried to
round up the Modocs. Shooting broke out, and one man was killed
on each side. That same day, other Modoc camps were ambushed
by both civilian and army forces, who shot and killed a woman and
several children. The Modoc War had begun.

The Modocs retreated to California's lava beds. Located outside
of Tule Lake in northern California, the lava beds are a collection
of ancient lava rocks that formed craggy cliffs, irregular paths, and
plenty of hiding places. Having lived in the area for many years,
the Modoc knew the beds well; the U.S. soldiers did not. Still, the
army followed, and by mid-January 1873, 400 armed soldiers and

volunteers had gathered at the lava beds to attack Kintpuash's stronghold. But a heavy fog settled in, making an assault difficult. Instead, the Americans sneaked toward the Modoc camp, undetectable in the fog . . . until a nervous volunteer accidentally fired his gun and gave them away.

Bullets flew from the lava beds—from crevices and caves and from the tunnels beneath the sprawling lava flows. One by one, the soldiers and volunteers were hit until the men left standing retreated. No Modocs were shot, but the army lost 37 men.

Despite the victory, Kintpuash did not actually want to continue fighting the army. He told his warriors, "The white men are many. No matter how many the Modocs kill, more will come each time, and we will all be killed after a while." The warriors, though, refused to lay down their arms.

PLAN B: PEACE

Back in Washington, the Modoc "problem" had reached the attention of President Ulysses S. Grant. He appointed a Peace Commission to negotiate a deal, but the members of the commission came from both military and civilian ranks, and they distrusted each other. And civilians in California wanted the Modocs tried for murder.

The Modocs weren't interested in a peace deal either. The warriors knew that they faced prison or hanging due to the skirmishes with the settlers. And the only thing the government offered—life on a reservation far from their home—wasn't appealing.

On April 11, 1873, members of the Peace Commission met with the Modocs, but the tribesmen had prepared an ambush. Kintpuash shot and killed Brigadier General E. R. S. Canby, head of the Peace Commission; other warriors attacked Reverend Eleasar Thomas, another commission representative, and wounded a third negotiator. The Modoc War continued.

SOLD OUT BY HIS OWN

The army's second assault on Kintpuash's stronghold was no more successful than the first. But this time, the Modoc abandoned their caves and moved south during the night. Days later, the warriors trapped 66 soldiers, killing or wounding two-thirds of them while suffering only one casualty themselves. But they were cut off from freshwater and were running low on ammunition; they couldn't continue for long.

In May, the army made some progress. They ambushed the Modocs, killed one man, and pushed the tribe backward. In order to escape, the Modocs had to abandon critical supplies. Many of the warriors blamed Kintpuash for this defeat. No longer willing to trust him, some decided to follow Hooker Jim, a Modoc warrior and Kintpuash's rival. Jim led the group away from Kintpuash's encampment, and within a few days, they surrendered to the U.S. Army. To avoid hanging, Hooker Jim and his followers made a deal with the soldiers: they would lead the army to Kintpuash's band in exchange for money and pardons. The commander accepted the offer, and Hooker Jim delivered.

DEFEAT

As the army closed in around him, Kintpuash continued to fight back. Although he managed to escape capture for several days, he was finally caught on June 1, 1873. The army planned an immediate execution, but California's attorney general intervened, declaring that civilian courts could not hang the Modocs for murders committed during a war with the United States.

In the end, Kintpuash, three other men, and two youths were tried by a military court. Since they'd attacked the army during peace negotiations, Kintpuash and the three men were hanged for murder; the youths got life sentences at Alcatraz prison. Kintpuash's band of Modocs were sent to the Quapaw Reservation in Oklahoma, where about 200 of their descendants live today. The rest of the Modoc tribe remained in Oregon. In 1925, the site of the Modoc War became Lava Beds National Monument. Thousands of tourists visit every year, and one of the most popular volcanic formations is called "Captain Jack's Stronghold."

Lava Beds National Monument
Tulelake, CA 96134

Founded: 1933
Area: 46,560 acres
Average annual visitors: 109,000

www.nps.gov/labe

Take Old Job Trail for an easy hike at Vermont's White Rocks National Recreation Area.

ROCK STAR

*A sculptor with a storied past creates a national monument
that pays homage to America's presidents.*

In 1927, Gutzon Borglum was one of America's foremost sculptors. He was 60 years old, had been fired from his last job, was a
fugitive from justice, and was deeply in debt. But that summer,
work began on Borglum's masterpiece, a sculpture designed to last
for millennia.

AT HOME WITH MOM AND DAD...AND MOM
He'd been born in a log cabin in Idaho, the son of three Mormon
parents—Borglum's father was married to two sisters. That was fine
in Idaho, but when the family moved to Nebraska, the situation
became embarrassing. So Borglum's father sent his son's mother
away; the boy never saw her again.

His unconventional childhood was so painful that Borglum
never spoke or wrote of it. The entire subject was a Borglum
family taboo.

THE THINKING MAN'S SCULPTOR
At 23, Borglum married Lisa Putnam, an artist he'd met in Los
Angeles. She helped him develop important contacts in society
and the art world, and they moved to Paris.

Gutzon's younger brother, Solon, was also an artist. At first,
Gutzon concentrated on painting while Solon took up sculpture.
At the 1900 Paris Exhibition, Solon's sculpture was the toast of
Paris. Soon after, perhaps due to sibling rivalry, Gutzon abandoned
painting and began sculpting. Shortly thereafter, he also aban-
doned his first wife, leaving her in Europe while he shipped back to
the United States. On shipboard, he met his second wife, Mary
Montgomery.

Borglum became a huge success as a sculptor. As a measure of
his success, Borglum has more statues in the U.S. Capitol's
Statuary Hall than any other sculptor. Commissions came in
steadily from the wealthy and influential people Borglum cultivated,
among them Teddy Roosevelt, which explains in part how Teddy
joined Washington, Jefferson, and Lincoln on a mountainside.

The National Park Service administers 245 miles (13%) of the U.S.-Mexico border.

HERE COMES TROUBLE

In 1915, an elderly Confederate widow, president of the Atlanta chapter of the United Daughters of the Confederacy, contacted Gutzon about sculpting a Confederate memorial on the great granite face of Stone Mountain, Georgia. Gutzon surveyed the site and proposed a colossal spectacle—Lee and his army marching across the cliff. He had no idea how he would project the image onto the rock, how the workers would carve on the steep face, or how he would remove the thousands of tons of granite. And for their part, the Daughters had no idea how they would raise the millions of dollars in projected costs.

Enter the Ku Klux Klan, which had reorganized itself in 1915 on top of Stone Mountain. The Klan raised money for the memorial. Why Borglum joined the Klan is unclear, but self-promotion may have been the primary reason. His political views were as erratic as his personality. At times, he wrote poisonously anti-Semitic diatribes, but as soon as Hitler came to power and took measures against the Jews, Borglum was one of the first to speak out against it. Borglum had no trouble befriending anyone so long as they were wealthy or influential, preferably both. (He also had no difficulty making enemies due to his arrogance and temper.)

HAPPY BIRTHDAY, GENERAL LEE!

Robert E. Lee's portrait was unveiled on Stone Mountain in 1924 on what would have been his 100th birthday. Carving had already begun on Stonewall Jackson's portrait, and the space was cleared for Jefferson Davis. But a faction of the Klan wanted Borglum off the Stone Mountain project, mostly because he was also planning a "great Union memorial in South Dakota."

THE GREAT ESCAPE

Borglum was fired. Enraged, he ordered his crew to break up the model for the memorial and drop it over the cliff. The Stone Mountain Association raised a posse and chased Borglum through the back roads of Georgia with an arrest warrant for "willful destruction of association property." After an all-night chase, Borglum slipped across the border into North Carolina, out of reach of the Georgia law.

Augustus Lukeman, the sculptor who was hired to complete Stone Mountain, blasted away most of Borglum's work (the head of

Lee). By 1928, he had completed only Lee's horse Traveler, the heads of Davis and Lee, and the outlines of their bodies. Two more sculptors were hired before the memorial was completed in 1972.

FOUR PRESIDENTS GET STONED IN SOUTH DAKOTA

Meanwhile, South Dakota needed a tourist attraction. Easterners cruised through the state on their way to Yellowstone, but they weren't stopping and spending. Doane Robinson, head of the South Dakota Historical Society and its poet laureate, wanted to borrow the idea of Stone Mountain—and its original artist. What would suit South Dakota? Frontiersmen carved into one of the cliffs of the Black Hills? Gutzon Borglum had far grander notions.

A national theme was needed, not only to suit Borglum's grandiose dreams, but for a far more practical reason: to attract national funding. Borglum proposed George Washington as the country's father, Abraham Lincoln as the savior of the nation, and Thomas Jefferson and Theodore Roosevelt as embodiments of national expansion for the Louisiana Purchase and the Panama Canal, respectively. The Roosevelt choice was controversial— Borglum's old pal had been dead for only a few years, and history hadn't had time to weigh in. But Congress had been discussing a Teddy Roosevelt memorial, and Borglum grabbed the chance to get some federal money for his project.

After touring the Black Hills for an appropriate site, Borglum chose Mt. Rushmore for the quality of its granite and for its south-eastern exposure. Work began in the summer of 1927. Money turned out to be a continual problem—exacerbated by the onset of the Great Depression. The project got federal funding, but this was accompanied by politics. Southerners wanted Abraham Lincoln removed; Democrats wanted Woodrow Wilson added; Eleanor Roosevelt wanted Susan B. Anthony. Borglum stood firm.

MOUNTING RUSHMORE

Experienced miners did the sculpting while Borglum and his son, Lincoln, supervised. The miners jackhammered and dynamited 400,000 tons of rock to within three inches of the final surface. Structural problems developed. Jefferson was originally to have been on Washington's right, but a bad cut ruined that head and it had to be blasted off. The second Jefferson is tilted upward, giving him a dreamy look. It wasn't intentional; it was necessary to avoid cracks in the rock. Washington's nose was deliberately left one foot longer than scale because Borglum thought it would add another 100,000 years to the life of the monument. (The National Park Service estimates the figures will last for 20,000 years.)

UNFINISHED BUSINESS
The presidential portraits were to have been busts, but the plans to complete Mt. Rushmore died with Borglum in 1941. War was looming in Europe, and the government decided not to appropriate any more money to the project. Lincoln Borglum cleaned up the site, packed up his materials, and left. Like many of the men who blasted and carved Rushmore, Lincoln's lungs were scarred by granite dust. He continued working as a sculptor but died in 1986. The visitor's center at Mt. Rushmore is named for Lincoln Borglum, not his father.

Mt. Rushmore had cost just $900,000. And South Dakota got its wish. Tourism is now second only to agriculture in the state's economy.

To read more about Mt. Rushmore, turn to page 238.

Mt. Rushmore National Memorial
Keystone, SD 57751-0268

Founded: 1925
Area: 1,278 acres
Average annual visitors: 2,000,000

www.nps.gov/moru

* * *

WHAT'S IN A NAME?
Mt. Rushmore is named for a New York City lawyer, Charles Rushmore, who was sent by his British clients to investigate their mining claims in the Black Hills in 1885. Years later, Rushmore donated generously to the monument that would immortalize "his" mountain.

Alcatraz Island is now part of the Golden Gate National Recreation Area.

BANFF BY
THE NUMBERS

*It began with the discovery of a hot spring in an Alberta, Canada, cave.
Today, it's the country's oldest and most famous national park.
Welcome to Banff.*

1

Prisoner-of-war camp set up at Banff during World War I and
World War II. The camp was located at what is now the Cave and
Basin National Historic Site and was one of 14 such camps in
Canada. Part of the detainees' workload included building the Ice
Palace for the 1917 Winter Carnival and improving local toboggan
and ski runs.

3

Number of times the Canadian government bid for (and lost) the
right to hold the Winter Olympics at Banff: 1964, 1968, and 1972.
The last attempt was the most controversial because the bid was
backed by an oil company (Imperial Oil) and conservationists
fought hard to keep the Olympics out of the park. Ultimately, the
president of Parks Canada withdrew the bid, and the 1972 Winter
Olympics were held in Sapporo, Japan.

4

All-day hikes in Banff (meaning they will take more than five
hours). The most difficult of these is the Cory Pass Loop, a gain of
about 3,000 feet (915 meters) on an eight-mile (13-kilometer) trail.
There are also nine shorter hikes for less-experienced travelers.

6 inches

Safe thickness of ice for skating. Visitors can skate on Banff's
frozen ponds and lakes, but they do so at their own risk. So make
sure the ice is at least six inches thick, and if you really want to be
safe, choose one of the park's three free skating rinks instead.

National historic landmarks include *Priscilla,* an oyster-dredging sloop in Long Island.

$7.40
Cost for an adult to take a dip in the Banff Upper Hot Springs, a restored 1930s bathhouse whose pools are filled with warm mineral water. If you don't want to share, you can rent the whole pool for $272.40 an hour (Canadian, of course).

24
Wildlife crossings (bridges or tunnels) on the Trans-Canada Highway through Banff. Access from the wilderness area to the road is restricted by a fence in an effort to protect the bears, cougars, and other animals that live in the park from being killed on the highway. Parks Canada estimates that more than 70,000 animals have used the crossings.

1883
Year three workers building the Canadian Pacific Railway discovered Banff's Cave and Basin Hot Spring. William McCardell, Tom McCardell, and Frank McCabe hoped to buy the land, open a resort, and make millions. Instead, they got wrapped up in a legal battle with each other and the Canadian government over who really owned the land. Two years later, the government took over the area and established Rocky Mountains National Park. It wasn't until 1930 that the park was officially called Banff. That year, the Canadian government passed the National Parks Act, which afforded the park more land and renamed it after Banffshire, Scotland, the hometowns of two directors of the railway company.

ALBERTA

Banff National Park
Banff, AB T1L 1K2

Founded: 1930
Area: 1,641,026 acres (6641 sq km)
Average annual visitors: 3,900,000

www.pc.gc.ca/pn-np/ab/banff

Want to see a peregrine falcon or cougar? Try California's Pinnacles National Monument.

UNCLE SAM BATHES THE WORLD

*The national parks are filled with the artifacts of civilization—
ghost towns, prisons, leper colonies, and the largest collection of
bathhouses from the golden age of the spa.*

In 1944, Bill "Bojangles" Robinson tap-danced for two miles through downtown Hot Springs, Arkansas, followed by 1,000 revelers. The dancer was on a mission to save a bathhouse, and he tapped right on through the fantastical Bathhouse Row—perhaps the only land in a national park that's considered a medicinal resource.

FOUNTAIN OF YOUTH?

The 143-degree waters of Hot Springs National Park have been rejuvenating people since ancient times; there's evidence that Native American tribes frequented the springs 10,000 years ago. Spanish explorer Hernando de Soto and his troops were the first Europeans to discover the youth-giving waters, followed by French traders and trappers. Settlers flocked to the springs, which were believed to cure an array of maladies including sore joints, aching muscles, and even sorrow. In 1832, the federal government took the unprecedented step of setting aside a portion of the springs as a national reserve.

INDOOR PLUMBING

The first bathhouses were canvas tents. Later, the springs were channeled, and elaborate structures were erected around them, promoted by slogans like "The Nation's Health Sanitarium" and "Uncle Sam Bathes the World." Water from some of the area's 47 hot springs was piped into bathhouses and cooled before use in a variety of drinks, baths, and treatments.

The eight spas in today's Bathhouse Row are the largest collection of spa-era bathhouses in the nation. Most were built during the golden era of spas—from the turn of the 20th century through the 1940s—in architectural styles like Spanish, Italianate, Neoclassical, and Renaissance Revival.

The Wright Brothers National Memorial is at Kill Devil Hills, North Carolina.

BATHHOUSE BIGWIGS

The rich and famous flocked to Hot Springs. Al Capone had a suite in the Arlington Bath House and reportedly used secret underground tunnels to access a speakeasy across the street. Babe Ruth, Harry Truman, Andrew Carnegie, and F. W. Woolworth took to the waters of Hot Springs, and heavyweight champ Rocky Marciano and major league baseball teams trained there.

WATER WORKS

The healing water is 4,000-year-old rainfall that seeps through cracks in Hot Springs Mountain, travels 8,000 miles down into the earth, and then percolates back up, producing about 850,000 gallons a day. The water is packed with minerals, but unlike the hot springs at other parks, it's not driven by volcanic action, so there's no sulfur smell.

Bathers often arrived at the baths with detailed instructions from doctors for certain water temperatures, exercises, and water pressure. At one bathhouse, rooms made of marble are still lined with tubs, needle showers, hot-wrap and cold-wrap lounges, sitz baths, hydrotherapy rooms with high-pressure hoses, and steam cabinets and tubs (through which passed mild electric currents during therapy sessions). At least one former park employee admits that the setup looks like a "chamber of horrors."

DIFFERENT SOAKS FOR DIFFERENT FOLKS

At bathhouses, men and women bathed separately, and when Jim Crow laws were passed after the Civil War, the bathhouses also became racially segregated. African American attendants were sometimes allowed to use the spas after they closed, but most chose not to. (At the time, doctors believed the optimal bathing time was 10 a.m. to noon, and that it would be a health risk to walk home in the cool evening or morning air after bathing.)

The first bathhouse for African Americans, the Crystal, opened in 1904. Built about 10 years later, the Woodmen of the Union was an impressive complex with a bathhouse, hotel, gym, and a 2,000-seat theater that attracted celebrities like Count Basie, Pegleg Bates, and Joe Louis. It also served as the primary health-care facility for the city's African American community, housing a hospital and medical and dental offices. This was the bathhouse that Bojangles had come to save.

Monument to Bill? No. Castle Clinton is a national monument in lower Manhattan...

TAPPING INTO HEALTH

When he tapped through town that day, the *Sentinel-Record* reported that "the day was hot and Bill [Bojangles] was 66, but he had the 'pep' of a man of just half that age." He performed that night to a capacity crowd to help raise money to reopen the Woodmen of the Union, then auctioned off his shoes for $100 and donated the money to pay for a paralyzed woman in town to have thermal-bath treatments.

The African American National Baptist Convention bought the Woodmen of the Union Building in 1948 and continued the tradition with a hospital, nurses' training school, doctors' offices—and thermal treatments. The Woodmen is closed today, as are most of the original bathhouses—victims of modern plumbing (many homes didn't have hot water in the early 20th century), modern medicine, and in-home spas.

ARKANSAS

Hot Springs National Park
Hot Springs, AR 71901

Founded: 1832
Area: 5,550 acres
Average annual visitors: 1,300,000

www.nps.gov/hosp

* * *

GHOST STORIES

Canada's Nahanni National Park and Reserve in the Northwest Territories was established in 1972 to protect the South Nahanni River from development. But the region has long been the subject of legend. First, the Naha people, thought to have settled the area 10,000 years ago, mysteriously disappeared (though archaeologists speculate that they may be the ancestors of the Navajo). Then, in the late 1800s, as prospectors descended on the region looking for gold, the rugged terrain and fierce rivers (along with the legends of the vanished Naha) led to stories of haunted valleys. Today, this history is reflected in the names of some of Nahanni's park features, including Headless Range, Funeral Range, and Deadman Valley.

GET ON THE BUS!

If you really want to get a good look at Glacier National Park,
take a trip on a red bus.

Since its completion in 1933, Glacier National Park's Going-to-the-Sun Road has provided visitors with the opportunity to travel into the Rocky Mountains and across the Continental Divide. But the road is also rife with hairpin turns and roadside cliffs that make it hard to sightsee while driving. Additionally, during the early 20th century, many visitors arrived at the park by train and thus needed a way to get around while they were visiting. So in the late 1930s, in an effort to solve both of these problems, the National Park Service started operating a fleet of red tour buses that took visitors on drives along the Going-to-the-Sun Road.

BUS BRIGADE

Initially, Glacier was not the only national park with tour buses. As part of an effort to standardize transportation services in the parks, the National Park Service introduced a fleet of more than 500 buses to several Western parks in the 1930s. Each park got to choose its buses' color: Yellowstone chose . . . well . . . yellow, Yosemite picked white, and Glacier asked for bright red—the color of the mountain ash berries that grow in the park.

For many years, the buses were well used, but as rail travel to parks decreased and visits in private cars increased, demand for bus tours waned. By the 1950s, most tour bus operations had ceased, including those in Yellowstone and Yosemite—but not in Glacier.

THE RED BUSES ROLL ON

Glacier's fleet of 17-passenger, 25-foot-long bright red tour buses became a highlight of visits to the park. The buses' canvas tops could be rolled back during good weather to allow passengers an open-air view. And red-bus drivers—called "jammers" because those early buses required that they do a lot of gear jamming while climbing mountainous roads—provided tourists with a safe ride and colorful and entertaining narration. With the exception of three years during World War II, the red buses were on the road continuously until . . .

Want to see what an old trading post really looked like? The Bents Old Fort National...

LOSS OF THE BUS CREATES A FUSS

In 1999, after a mechanical failure in one bus, all of Glacier's red buses were inspected and discovered to have serious problems. The buses had worn metal parts, cracks in their frames, and, after more than 60 years of service, more than 600,000 miles each. They were declared unsafe and were taken off the road.

A nearby tour operator quickly purchased some white vans to keep tours running, but the vans lacked the charm of the old red buses—plus there was no convertible top. Many people believed the red-bus era had come to an end as the Park Service considered replacing the buses with a new, safer, cleaner running fleet. But traditionalists wanted the old buses to be renovated, not replaced—an expensive proposition. Soon, a volunteer group called the Glacier Park Foundation and a fleet of avid red-bus supporters became determined to save the old red buses.

Eventually, the two sides compromised: one bus was kept in its original condition to be used as a museum piece, and the rest went in for renovation.

BUSES GET GUSSIED UP

In 2000, the Ford Motor Company agreed to renovate the fleet. The buses' traditional interior and exterior looks were maintained. The body, seating, and running boards were restored. Windows and doors were replaced. Plywood floors were traded for aluminum; heat and ergonomic driver's seats were added. Each bus got a new a chassis and an engine that ran on a cleaner propane-and-gasoline fuel system.

Then, on June 8, 2002, twenty of the buses returned to Glacier National Park. The rest arrived by the end of the summer, and today visitors can, once again, take a trip down the Going-to-the-Sun Road in a canvas-topped, jammer-driven—but now safer and cleaner—renovated red bus.

Glacier National Park
West Glacier, MT 59936

Founded: 1910
Area: 1,013,572 acres
Average annual visitors: 2,000,000

www.nps.gov/glac

TRUTH LAID BEAR

The how and why of close encounters.

Probably the most feared (and the most troublesome) animal in the national parks is the bear. Whether it's grizzly bears in Yellowstone or black bears in the Great Smoky Mountains, bear attacks are of great concern to many park visitors. In reality, though, bears attack humans far less frequently than one might think. Since Yellowstone was established in the late 19th century, only five of the millions of people who have visited the park have been killed by bears. Of more concern is the harm tourists do to the bears themselves.

AVOIDING BEAR ENCOUNTERS
The National Park Service offers the following advice to visitors about what to do if they encounter a bear.

While hiking:
- Don't approach bears; the farther away you stay, the less likely the bear will attack. Plus, approaching bears is illegal. In Yellowstone, hikers must stay 100 feet away from all bears; the Denali hiking guide says people should stay 1/4 mile away.

- Hike in groups, and make noise to alert bears of your presence. Bears don't like being surprised.

- If you do happen to surprise a bear on the trail, don't run away. Back away slowly. Bears can run up to 35 mph; that's faster than an Olympic sprinter. If you run away, the bear may instinctively see you as prey and give chase.

- Avoid hiking in the early morning, evening, or after dark, when bears are most active.

- Don't take any pets into the backcountry. It's illegal and could prompt a bear attack because, to a bear, your rambunctious retriever looks like lunch.

In camp:

- Store all food out of bears' reach. At campgrounds in bear country, that means a bear box or bear-resistant canister. And to a bear, "food" is anything with a scent, including perfume, sunscreen, and even the clothes you wore when you roasted hot dogs over the fire. Trash is also food to a bear, so be sure to dispose of it in proper receptacles. And remember, improper food storage is a federal offense that can result in fines of up to $5,000 and six months in jail.

- Remove all food, crumbs, and trash from your car. To a bear, cars are metal cans with food inside, and bear claws make handy can openers. In fact, bears in national parks are so adept at breaking into cars that they can do it in seconds. They insert their claws between the door frame and the body of the car and rip the door off in one movement. Then they tear through the backseat to get into the trunk. Bears have even learned that, by jumping up and down on the tops of minivans, they can pop the doors open. In Yosemite National Park in 1997, bears broke into 1,000 cars and caused $580,000 in damage. Between 1997 and 2002, bears in Yosemite caused $1.6 million in damage to vehicles. Yosemite rangers joke that the best place to see bears is in the parking lot at night.

BEAR PAUSE

These guidelines aren't just for visitors' benefit. They're also important to maintaining healthy bear populations in the national parks. Garbage dumps in Yellowstone used to be bear buffets. Every evening, the bears came to dine; park officials even set up bleachers so visitors could enjoy the show. Bears also prowled Yellowstone's roads, panhandling for snacks that tourists tossed from their cars. But all this bear/human interaction encouraged the animals to see humans as sources of food and was actually harmful. Bears that ate human junk food were fatter than bears that ate natural food, and they didn't live as long. Bears also died from ingesting plastic and other food containers. Plus, bears standing so close to the road meant that more of them were being hit by cars.

In 1970, Yellowstone instituted a bear management program that put the animals back on their natural diet. Feeding bears is now strictly prohibited. The dumps were closed, and garbage cans are now bear-proof. By 1980, garbage-dependent bears were gone

---

Cape Cod National Seashore includes more than 2,500 acres of salt marshes.

from Yellowstone. Similar programs began in other national parks where bears lived. Bear boxes for food storage were placed at the parks' campgrounds and can be opened only by humans. Park officials teach visitors how to bear-proof their cars and campsites, and will ticket violators. This has dramatically reduced the number of bear/human incidents and property damage.

BRAINIACS

Even with all these regulations, the bears still sometimes get themselves into trouble. They're incredibly smart animals that adapt quickly to new surroundings. In Great Smoky Mountains National Park, bears even learned how to distinguish the vehicles used by park rangers from those of visitors. The bears sometimes beg for food by the roadside until a park ranger drives up—and then they scoot off into the woods, only to return when the rangers have left.

BEAR BITES

Here are some interesting facts about bears:

- Bears can detect the scent of humans on a trail for up to 14 hours after the humans have left.
- A bear's metabolism slows so much during hibernation that its kidneys and bowels stop functioning, and it doesn't urinate or defecate.
- Grizzly bears used to be found throughout California, but the last California grizzly bear was shot near Sequoia National Park in 1922. Today, only black bears live in the state.
- Black bears on the East Coast are black, but those in the West are usually shades of brown.
- Black bears can run 30 miles per hour. Even a fast sprinter with a 100-foot head start would be caught by a black bear in less than six seconds.

* * *

HOW SYMBOLIC

The National Park Service's emblem is an arrowhead with a sequoia tree, a buffalo, mountains, and a stream inside to represent vegetation, wildlife, scenic values, and historical values.

Boaters might see nesting osprey at Utah's Flaming Gorge National Recreation Area.

ANSEL ADAMS AND THE SIERRA NEVADAS

In the early 20th century, a photographer's black-and-white images of the Sierra Nevadas became iconic of Yosemite and helped save the big trees of Kings Canyon.

AN ARTIST IS BORN

Ansel Adams was born in 1902, the only child of an affluent San Francisco family. His doting parents lavished attention on him, exposing him to literature, art, and music from an early age. In response, young Ansel taught himself how to play the piano and how to take photographs—activities at which he excelled quickly.

Despite these accomplishments, he had a difficult time in school. His parents attributed this to hyperactivity, so they pulled him out of his traditional academic setting and homeschooled him. He had a relatively solitary childhood as a result and spent many hours taking long walks in what was then the wilderness surrounding the San Francisco Bay, photographing the natural world and indulging his love of the outdoors. He spent the rest of his free time practicing to become a concert pianist (his first career choice).

YOSEMITE MAKES AN IMPRESSION

Ansel's parents also loved nature and regularly took him to the nearby Sierra Nevadas to camp. The family especially loved Yosemite National Park, and it was here that Ansel first learned about John Muir (a person he came to admire a great deal) and about the conservation and environmental movement that Muir helped to found.

Ansel Adams was drawn to environmental activism, and in 1919, the teenager joined Muir's Sierra Club. For four summers, Adams cleaned up trails and acted as steward of the club's LeConte Memorial Lodge in Yosemite Valley. The Sierra Club also turned out to be integral to Adams's success as a photographer; his first photographs were published in the club's 1922 bulletin, and he held his first photography exhibition at the club's San Francisco headquarters in 1928. Then, when he was 28 years old, the Sierra Club chose Adams to be its official artist. He was paid well enough for this job that he abandoned his plans to be a pianist and concentrated on photography.

A TRIP TO WASHINGTON

Although Yosemite National Park was Adams's first love, he made his mark as an environmental activist on behalf of another park. Thanks to the earlier efforts of Muir and the Sierra Club, Sequoia National Park had been established in 1890. This was supposed to ensure the protection of the park's giant sequoias. But by 1900, logging had decimated more than half of those trees. Nearby Kings Canyon was one of the few groves left intact, and Muir and the Sierra Club pleaded with Congress to expand Sequoia National Park to protect this grove. Congress didn't listen.

It wasn't until 1936 (22 years after Muir's death) that Congress finally held hearings to address protecting Kings Canyon. Ansel Adams went to Washington as the spokesperson for the Sierra Club. He was armed with a famous photograph, one he'd taken of the giant sequoias of Kings Canyon, and with a voluminous knowledge of the area. But there were strong forces opposing the establishment of Kings Canyon National Park. Politicians wanted to harness the natural resources of the Kings River to create reservoirs for southern California and to use the Giant Sequoia forests for logging and profit. But thanks to both Adams's artwork and his eloquent arguments, the senators and representatives at the 1936 hearings were finally convinced that Kings Canyon should be preserved. And there the effort stopped. It was still not enough to make the park a reality—yet.

IT'S WHO YOU KNOW

The year after he testified before Congress, Adams sent his a copy of his book, *Sierra Nevada: The John Muir Trail* (which featured photographs of the giant sequoias in Kings Canyon) to then-Secretary of the Interior Harold Ickes. Ickes was so impressed that he, in turn, presented the book to President Franklin D. Roosevelt. Both men were enchanted by the photographs and intrigued by Kings Canyon, and they joined in the fight to protect the area.

With Ickes and Roosevelt on board, Kings Canyon was finally included in the National Park System in 1940 as an add-on to

Sequoia National Park. Together the two parks comprise 863,741 acres. The giant sequoias that remain in the Sierra Nevada range are protected by law for generations to enjoy. And Adams's enduring photographs of the big trees—and of his beloved Yosemite— still speak to the majesty of the Sierra Nevadas.

CALIFORNIA

Yosemite National Park
Yosemite National Park, CA 95389

Founded: 1890
Area: 761,266 acres
Average annual visitors: 3,300,000

www.nps.gov/yose

* * *

IT'S A GRAND OL' TREE

Although it may be low on the Christmas radar for most of us, the massive General Grant Tree, located in California's Kings Canyon National Park, has been America's official Christmas tree for 80 years.

When Charles Lee of Sanger, California, visited the mammoth tree in the mid-1920s, he overheard a little girl say, "What a wonderful Christmas tree it would be." Liking the idea, Lee wrote to the president of the United States about it. Calvin Coolidge designated it the nation's Christmas tree in 1926. Since then, a small group of hardy hikers have made their way to the tree each year for an annual Trek to the Tree celebration. The celebration includes Christmas music and speeches, and a large wreath is placed at the base of the tree.

The General Grant Tree serves a dual purpose as both the national Christmas tree and the only living national shrine dedicated to the memory of soldiers who have died in any U.S. war (a distinction it received in 1956).

...the first decisive victory in the American Revolution. It's a unit of Fort Sumter.

THE LAZY MAN'S WAY TO SEE PARK FEATURES

Mountains, panthers, redwoods, eagles—those are just some of the hundreds of beauties you might run across in America's national parks. Alas, you probably won't have time today to see several dozen parks, so here's the easy way to do it: find 44 features in this word search. Hint: they're hidden in the arrowhead shape of the National Park Service logo. Happy trails!

ACTIVE
VOLCANO
ANTELOPES
ARCHES
BADLANDS
BALD EAGLES
BEARS
BIRDS
BISON
BOGS
CANYONS
CAVES
CLIFF
DWELLINGS
DESERT SCENERY
ENDANGERED SPECIES
FALCONS
FJORDS
FOSSILS
GLACIERS
HOT SPRINGS
ICE CAPS
KARST

KIVAS
LIMESTONE CAVERNS
MARSHES
MEADOWS
MOUNTAINS
MUD FLATS
PANTHERS
PARK RANGERS
PERMAFROST
PETROGLYPHS
PONDS
PUEBLO RUINS
REDWOODS
ROCK SPIRES
SAND DUNES
SEA OTTER
SEQUOIAS
SHARK
SNAKES
STALACTITES
SWAMPS
WETLANDS
WILDCATS

In Hawaii, traditional bowls, baskets, and mats are often made from...

```
                  S  D  D  A  P  S  F  E  T  S
               V  B  M  A  R  S  H  E  S  Y  F  L
               M  M  U  P  O  F  Z  T  I  I
               K  Q  D  O  R  N  A  P
         Q  D  X  F  W  U  G  Q  F  R  N  L  O  J  J  F  U  E
      R  B  O  G  S  S  B  D  U  B  C  L  S  A  N  D  D  U  N  E  S  I
   V  M  Q  Z  S  D  N  A  L  D  A  B  Z  A  C  D  C  X  D  V  I  E  K  L
F  S  E  A  O  T  T  E  R  B  V  L  F  A  P  T  S  R  A  K  Y  N  Q  Y  E  H
N  W  Q  V  Z  F  T  F  L  E  B  D  V  C  A  I  S  N  I  A  T  N  U  O  M  Q
S  R  E  H  T  N  A  P  S  I  V  E  D  T  R  T  G  W  M  P  E  Q  O  O  W  J
S  K  K  X  I  E  W  L  D  Z  R  A  C  I  K  E  N  E  E  J  L  G  I  Q  Y  R
   S  N  O  S  I  B  L  C  R  G  G  C  V  R  S  I  T  A  S  P  M  A  W  S
   M  L  D  T  I  S  M  B  O  W  L  J  E  A  D  R  L  D  I  U  D  S  G  T
   N  G  P  R  I  R  J  S  D  N  E  D  V  N  O  P  A  O  J  E  E  N  N  W
      A  D  G  L  A  C  I  E  R  S  I  O  G  O  S  N  W  N  B  I  S  E
      S  N  A  K  E  S  R  S  P  K  O  L  E  W  T  D  S  A  L  N  P  A
      Y  P  T  R  B  V  O  E  K  I  Y  C  R  D  O  S  M  L  O  E  R  A
      Q  A  E  B  K  C  R  B  P  Z  A  S  E  H  Z  E  Y  R  B  I
      R  K  C  L  I  K  T  H  F  S  N  K  R  E  W  N  M  U  X  S
      N  P  E  O  S  S  M  I  T  O  A  F  D  A  A  U  I  L
      K  S  X  C  P  C  Q  S  A  K  K  F  C  F  J  K  N  L
      R  N  Q  I  E  Z  R  C  T  F  A  R  C  H  E  S
      A  Q  R  N  S  J  D  I  O  O  R  U  R  D
      H  E  E  U  F  L  G  S  D  Q  L  R
      S  R  Z  C  I  T  S  E  E  O
      Y  X  T  W  U  I  O  J
      U  N  M  X  L  F
      Q  T  L  S
      L  Z
```

For answers, turn to page 387

...leaves collected and stripped from the puhala tree.

A COLD WAR

Alaska's Aleutian World War II National Historic Area pays homage to a little-known battle during the war: the fight in the northern Pacific for the American-occupied Aleutian Islands, where terrible weather and miserable isolation made a bad situation even worse.

NOT UNLIKELY ENOUGH

Neither Japan nor the United States really believed they could mount a large-scale invasion of the Aleutian Islands. The terrain was terrible, the weather was worse, and there weren't enough harbors. Most of the tiny islands weren't even that close to each other, much less the mainland or any cities. Gale-force winds regularly blew across the archipelago from west to east, occasionally clearing away the fog that hung over the region. (Pilots trying to land in that fog had to rely entirely on radar to keep from slamming into the mountains.) In the Aleutians, it only stopped snowing in midsummer, and the cold in the winter was almost unbearable. But neither side was willing to take the risk that the other was crazy enough to try to set up an encampment. So both planned invasions.

For their part, the Japanese also thought that creating a distraction in the Aleutians might draw American forces away from Midway Island, an important strategic plot of land in the South Pacific. Japan's first salvo in the campaign for the far north was a raid on the American military base at Dutch Harbor, Alaska.

DOUBLE DUTCH

On June 3, 1942, Japanese planes discovered a break in the fog over Dutch Harbor; the momentary clarity revealed the U.S. base to them, and they dove down to attack. The planes strafed key locations on the base, damaging several oil tanks and destroying a barracks, a hospital, a radio station, and some planes. Two days later, the Japanese commanders decided to bomb Dutch Harbor again. They swooped in a second time and finished off the oil tanks. The Aleutian campaign had begun.

ATTU! (BLESS YOU!)

While the bombers attacked Dutch Harbor from the air, another group invaded two U.S.-occupied islands: Attu, the westernmost

Aleutian Island, and Kiska, located slightly farther east. The Japanese occupied Attu on June 5 (taking two American missionaries and an Aleut villager prisoner) and Kiska on June 7 (capturing ten American weather-station workers). However, the United States didn't realize their islands had been occupied until June 10, when they started to wonder why they hadn't gotten any weather data from Kiska for five days. Plans to retake the islands began immediately.

U.S. commanders thought that an air raid would be the best approach. But no aircraft stationed at Dutch Harbor had a long enough range to reach Attu and return to base—the trip was more than 1,000 miles each way. Kiska was within range, but two bombardments scheduled for July had to be canceled because of the weather. The Americans also tried some naval bombardments, but they weren't effective.

PUTTIN' ON THE SQUEEZE

The United States needed to get closer to Attu to have any chance of retaking it. So the army threw together a base, including an airstrip, on an unoccupied island nearby, and started moving closer to the Japanese position. The U.S. military then started a blockade of the two Japanese-occupied islands. On March 26, the two sides came to blows.

Neither had any submarines or air power nearby, so it was an old-fashioned surface naval battle, the only one of World War II. In terms of damage, the United States took more significant hits, but in the end, the Japanese turned around. From then on, the Japanese were only able to send small supply shipments via submarine to Attu and Kiska. The occupying forces were almost completely isolated.

ATTU PART II

The United States planned to take back Attu on May 7, 1943. On that day, the soldiers were armed, locked, and loaded—ready to go. But the weather was too bad for an invasion, so they waited.

Four days later, the Americans landed. Initially, the Japanese had the advantage: they holed up and compelled the attackers to move forward slowly. But eventually, the American force, with its greater numbers and better support, overpowered them. The Japanese made a final, suicidal banzai charge on May 29. They

---

...designated wilderness. It's located in Arizona's Sonoran Desert.

took out a medical station and two command posts before they were cut down. Attu was back in American hands. More than 600 Americans and 2,300 Japanese soldiers had been killed in the battle.

ARCTIC GHOSTS I
The Japanese stationed on Kiska learned a lesson from the invasion of Attu: they started a slow evacuation by submarine. Still, the Americans kept a close watch on the island and attacked any retreating vessels.

The U.S. military was prepped for an invasion of Kiska, but a bizarre incident derailed the plan. On the night of July 26, an American patrol reported seeing on radar seven boats 200 miles southwest of Attu. Fearing a Japanese onslaught, the U.S. ships patrolling Kiska charged down to add support for the coming battle. When they arrived, they started firing.

More than 1,000 rounds later, the shooting stopped and the men realized that there were no enemy ships. No ever found out what caused the ghostly pips to appear on the radar, though some people speculated that they were caused by the radar bouncing off of faraway mountains. The event was named the Battle of the Pips.

ARCTIC GHOSTS II
Still, Kiska loomed as the last Japanese holding on the Aleutians. The Americans amassed 34,000 Allied troops (the Canadians contributed 5,300 of the total) and 100 ships and prepared for an invasion. On August 15, they landed in Kiska's tiny harbor; troops streamed onto the beach and disappeared into the fog.

In the cold rain, strong winds, and thick fog, the Allies combed Kiska. They met no resistance. Shots were fired, but there were never any confirmed enemy sightings. Little by little, the Allies inched onward. They heard shots and explosions, but they never spotted the Japanese.

Soon the soldiers realized that there were no Japanese on the island. Later, the U.S. government found out that the Japanese had evacuated all 5,000 of their troops while the American fleet was refueling after the Battle of the Pips.

THE REMNANTS

Today, the site of these battles is the Aleutian World War II National Historic Area, and it's a pretty rugged place. Its Web site offers more of a warning than an advertisement:

> This site preserves bunkers that are still in excellent condition; however, tunnel entrances leading into the bunkers are not stable or have caved in. Many of the floors were constructed of wood that has rotted over the years . . . and the underground buildings and tunnels are dark. Entrances into these tunnels and bunkers are at the visitor's risk. Cliff edges and collapsed tunnels may be hidden by dense fog. Please remain on roads and trails.

The remains of the Dutch Harbor base are the central attraction of the site. There's also a visitors' center with newspaper articles, artifacts, and films. It's within walking distance of the Unalaska Airport and the cruise-ship dock.

What's remarkable, though, is not necessarily what's at the Aleutian World War II National Historic Area, but just *where* it is. In the middle of the Pacific, far from anything but salt water and volcanoes, the place gives a sense of how lonely the Second World War's Aleutian campaign really was.

Aleutian World War II National Historic Area
Unalaska, AK 99685

Founded: 1996
Area: 134 acres

www.nps.gov/aleu

WILD HORSES

One of the few places in the country where wild horses still roam free is on an island that straddles the Maryland/Virginia border just a few hours from the nation's capital.

Assateague, a barrier island off the coast of Maryland and Virginia, and less than 200 miles from Washington, D.C., is shared by both states. Designated the Assateague Seashore National Park in 1965, it boasts 37 miles of pristine beach and 18,000 acres of marshes, scrubland, and dunes, and it is home to more than 300 migratory and resident birds for at least part of the year. But it's the island's wild horses that have made Assateague famous.

TAX EVASION, 17TH-CENTURY STYLE
Folklore has it that the horses are descendants of shipwreck survivors: a 16th-century Spanish galleon carrying horses as cargo sank off the Virginia coast, and the horses that survived the wreck swam to shore. Others think early colonists may have brought horses to the island. But most historians agree that horses were likely abandoned on the island in the late 17th century by mainland owners who didn't want to comply with the fencing laws of the day and who were trying to avoid paying taxes on their livestock.

Today, the approximately 300 wild horses on Assateague are divided into two main herds, separated by a fence that cuts the island almost down the middle. The National Park Service manages the Maryland herd; the Chincoteague Volunteer Fire Department owns and manages the Virginia herd, each of which includes about 150 animals.

THE ANNUAL PONY SWIM
On the last Wednesday in July, the Virginia herd—known as the Chincoteague ponies—is rounded up and made to swim across the Assateague Channel to nearby Chincoteague Island. The "wild pony swim," famously mentioned in Marguerite Henry's novel *Misty of Chincoteague*, pulls in more than 40,000 spectators. It's a short swim of about three minutes, and takes place at low tide for the safety of the spring foals. After the swim, a festival is held

---

Gumbo limbo trees like the ones at De Soto National Memorial in Bradenton, Florida...

during which the horses are corralled for a few days to give visitors and residents a chance to admire them. A small percentage of the ponies are auctioned off during this time, in part to keep population numbers manageable. The auctions also raise money for the Chincoteague Volunteer Fire Department, which started the event back in 1925 to fund the purchase of new equipment. Two days after the auction, the remaining horses are herded back across the channel to Assateague.

DON'T FEED THE ANIMALS
Visitors throughout the year can see the horses running or grazing along the shoreline. But the park upholds strict no-feeding, no-petting rules; animals who learn to look to humans for food are at risk of getting too close to roads, which puts them in danger of getting hit by cars. In addition, they are a risk to humans. Cute as they are, the ponies have been known to bite, kick, and charge after park visitors who don't keep a safe distance.

MARYLAND

Assateague Island National Seashore
Berlin, MD 21811

Founded: 1965
Area: 51,000 acres
Average annual visitors: 2,000,000

www.nps.gov/asis

* * *

HONORING JOHN MUIR
The father of America's national parks, John Muir is memorialized in two NPS sites: the John Muir National Historic Site in Martinez, California, and the Muir Woods National Monument in Marin County, north of San Francisco.

Muir's name shows up in many other places around the world, too. There's the John Muir Wilderness in California's Sierra Nevada National Forest; John Muir High School in Pasadena, California; the John Muir College at the University of California, San Diego; and John Muir Country Park in Scotland.

...are called "tourist trees" because they stand in the sun, turn red, and peel.

DEATH VALLEY
BY THE NUMBERS

*The lowest, hottest, driest place in North America, California's
Death Valley National Park is a lesson in extremes.*

2
Years during which no rain was recorded in Death Valley: 1929 and
1953

6.44 inches
Record rainfall in Death Valley during the 2004–2005 rainy season

15°F
Record low temperature in Death Valley (January 8, 1913)

23
Years that *Death Valley Days* was on the air. The longest-running
syndicated television show in history—it ran from 1952 to 1975—
Death Valley Days began as a 1930s radio Western and then moved
to television. It was filmed in and around Death Valley, starred a
young Ronald Reagan, and was sponsored by none other than 20
Mule Team Borax.

95 percent
Amount of the park that is designated as "wilderness"

134°F
Record high temperature (July 10, 1913)

140 miles
Length of Death Valley

282 feet below sea level
Location of Badwater Basin, the lowest point in North America

---

700 feet
Height of the Eureka Dunes, the highest sand dunes in California

1994
The year Death Valley became a national park; it had been a protected site since February 1933, when President Herbert Hoover designated the area as a national monument.

1996
Hottest summer on record in Death Valley. That year, 40 days recorded temperatures of 120 degrees or more and 105 days reached 110 degrees or more.

5,000 feet
Height of Dante's View, the park's most popular (and, some say, most breathtaking) overlook

11,049 feet
Height of Telescope Peak, the highest point in the park

1.8 billion years
Age of the oldest rocks in Death Valley

CALIFORNIA

Death Valley National Park
Death Valley, CA 92328

Founded: 1994
Area: 3,400,000 acres
Average annual visitors: 800,000

www.nps.gov/deva

The Pine Barrens aquifer holds 17 trillion gallons of fresh, drinkable water.

WELCOME TO AMERICA

From 1892 to 1954, Ellis Island was the premier immigration station in the United States. More than 12 million people passed through on their way to new lives in America. But there's more to the island's history than just the immigration years. Here are some things you might be surprised to learn about Ellis Island.

THE EARLY YEARS

- The island has had at least three names. Native American tribes called it Kioshk (Gull Island), and early Dutch and English settlers gave it the moniker Oyster Island because there were so many oyster beds there. Then, during the Revolutionary War, merchant Samuel Ellis set up a tavern on the island. His name stuck even after his family sold the island to New York State in 1808 for $10,000.

- During the War of 1812, Ellis Island was a key strategic position. Ships from Great Britain had passed unhindered through New York Harbor during the American Revolution, so at the outset of the War of 1812, the U.S. government decided to set up fortifications in the harbor. The government bought Ellis Island from New York State, established Fort Gibson, and outfitted it with 20 guns and a barracks in order to protect the city from invasion.

- Originally a 3.3-acre sandbar, Ellis Island expanded over the years to 27.5 acres. The landfill for the island came from many sources, but mostly from ships' ballast and earth generated by the building of New York City's subway system.

IMMIGRATION

- In 1890, the federal government took over the handling of immigration to the United States. Before that, the states had admitted their own immigrants individually. But a huge jump in immigration in the late 19th century (due primarily to economic and religious persecution in Europe and Russia) over-

---

Arrowheads made from Alibates flint, a multicolored stone, can be seen at...

whelmed state facilities, and the federal government stepped in. A $75,000 wooden immigration station opened on January 1, 1892, and the first person to pass through was 15-year-old Annie Moore from Ireland. It was also her birthday, and she received a $10 gold coin to get her started in her new home.

- In June 1897, the wooden immigration station on Ellis Island caught fire. No one was injured, but the structure and many immigration papers were destroyed. This led to a regulation that all future buildings on Ellis Island had to be fireproof.

- There were strict rules for entering the United States during the Ellis Island period. Prostitutes, criminals, illiterates, political radicals, and those considered "lunatics" and "idiots" were some of the categories of people who were deported immediately.

- First- and second-class passengers to arrive at Ellis Island around the turn of the 19th century were exempted from processing unless they had obvious medical or legal problems. Their papers and belongings were inspected cursorily, and then they were sent on their way. All third-class passengers, however, were required to take part in processing. If they were healthy and had the proper immigration papers (this group made up about 80 percent of travelers), processing took three to five hours, and then they were released. The remaining 20 percent endured much more rigorous and invasive procedures, and about 2 percent of these were denied entry due to medical or political problems. This led to Ellis Island getting the nickname "Island of Tears."

- The peak year for immigration through Ellis Island was 1907, when 1.25 million immigrants arrived. On April 17 of that year, officials processed 11,747 people.

THE END OF AN ERA

- During World War I, Ellis Island acted as an Army hospital, a Navy way station, and a detention center for enemy aliens. In World War II, it was used primarily as a detention facility for enemies. At the war's end, about 7,000 Germans, Italians, and Japanese (both American citizens and noncitizens) were held there.

- In November 1954, a Norwegian man named Arne Peterssen was the last immigrant to pass through Ellis Island.

STATS:

- Ellis Island became part of the National Park System in 1965, when President Lyndon Johnson declared it to be part of the Statue of Liberty National Monument.
- Visitors began coming to the island in 1976, but in 1990, after a massive renovation, the Ellis Island Immigration Museum opened. Today, more than 2 million people visit annually.

NEW YORK

Ellis Island National Monument
New York, NY 100004

Founded: 1965
Area: 27.5 acres
Average annual visitors: 2,000,000

www.nps.gov/elis

* * *

A WOMAN OF FEW WORDS

The verse most closely associated with the Statue of Liberty—"Give me your tired, your poor, / Your huddled masses yearning to breathe free"—wasn't added to the pedestal until 1903 . . . and then only after officials realized what an inspiration the statue had become to the waves of immigrants arriving at nearby Ellis Island.

The verse is part of "The New Colossus," a sonnet composed in 1883 by New York poet Emma Lazarus. She donated it to an auction at the New York Academy of Design to raise money for the statue's pedestal.

TRAILS AND TRAILBLAZERS

Congress passed the National Trails System Act in 1968, establishing a framework for a nationwide system of scenic, recreational, and historic trails.

JUAN BAUTISTA DE ANZA NATIONAL HISTORIC TRAIL
Established: 1990

Route: 1,200 miles from Nogales, Arizona, to San Francisco, California.

The Anza Trail commemorates the 1,200-mile journey undertaken by a group of Spanish colonists led by Juan Bautista de Anza, a captain in the Spanish army. From 1774 to 1776, while Americans on the East Coast were working on winning independence from British rule, Anza and his group were traversing the deserts of the Southwest on their way to the Pacific coast, where they ultimately established a mission and a presidio, or military fort, at what became San Francisco. The group started out from the presidio in Tubac (now in Arizona) and ended up at the Golden Gate, where San Francisco's Presidio stands now.

Today: You can follow the Anza Trail and visit historic sites along the way that bear the imprint of Spanish colonization: forts, missions, parks, and historic monuments, including Tubac Presidio State Historic Park, Arizona's famous Painted Rocks State Park, El Pueblo de Los Angeles Historic Monument, Santa Monica Mountains National Recreation Area, El Presidio de Santa Barbara State Historic Park, Mission San Luis Obispo, and the Presidio of San Francisco.

CALIFORNIA NATIONAL HISTORIC TRAIL
Established: A work in progress, parts of it awaiting official passage by some of the states it traverses.

The California National Historic Trail commemorates the greatest mass migration in American history. In the 1840s and 1850s,

---

Shad have made a comeback in the Delaware River, thanks to pollution control.

more than 250,000 gold prospectors, farmers, and others took this route from the Midwest to California, in search of fortune, fertile fields, and adventure.

Route: 2,000 miles through 10 states, from Missouri to California.

Today: In the wilderness along the way, you can still see more than 1,000 miles of trail ruts left by the wagons and stagecoaches of a century ago. State-by-state interpretive guides will eventually be available for the entire trail.

OVERMOUNTAIN VICTORY NATIONAL HISTORIC TRAIL
Established: 1980

Route: 330 miles through four states, from Abingdon, Virginia, to Kings Mountain, South Carolina.

This trail marks a 14-day trek in 1780 across the Appalachians. A militia formed of local patriots from Virginia, Tennessee, and North Carolina and followed the trail for one reason: to drive the British from the southern colonies.

After three victories in South Carolina in 1780, the British army was getting closer to taking the rest of the South. Assuming that the local populace would be loyal to England and join its troops in the next step—taking Virginia, America's largest colony—Major Patrick Ferguson, Inspector of Militia for South Carolina, tried to recruit loyalists to the British cause. But when the colonists didn't join up, he took a different approach. In an attempt to intimidate settlers, he threatened to "lay waste to the country" and march his troops into the mountains where the colonists lived if they didn't lay down their arms and pledge allegiance to King George III.

The patriot militia opposed Ferguson. It formed in Tennessee and grew as it marched east, until nearly 1,000 men met up with British troops on October 7 in South Carolina. The one-hour battle, in which every British soldier was killed or captured, was the turning point in the Revolutionary War.

Today: Most of the trail is now road and highway; the only foot trail that remains is a 20-mile portion across the mountains. A vol-

---

American Samoa is the only U.S. territory south of the equator.

unteer group called the Overmountain Victory Trail Association (OVTA) cooperates with the park system to preserve and interpret the original route. Every year since 1975, the OVTA has reenacted the original "march" in full costume.

PONY EXPRESS NATIONAL HISTORIC TRAIL
Established: 1992

Route: 1,800 miles through eight states, from St. Joseph, Missouri, to Sacramento, California.

The Pony Express had been operating for only 18 months—from April 1860 to October 1861—when it was made obsolete by the telegraph and the transcontinental railroad. But in its prime, the 1,800-mile route from Missouri to California supported riders who carried the mail in the unprecedented time of 10 days in good weather. It also became a symbol of the energy of America and the taming of the West. The Pony Express National Historic Trail follows the primary route taken by the young riders who braved deserts, mountains, bandits, and other dangers to carry the mail across the country.

Today: Except for short segments in Utah and California, most of the original trail has been obliterated over time. Eventually, the park service hopes to make 120 historic sites along the route available to the public, including about 50 Pony Express stations or their ruins. For each state that the trail passes through, the National Park Service is developing interpretive guides that will approximate the historic route and will point visitors to the actual remnants of the trail.

TRAIL OF TEARS NATIONAL HISTORIC TRAIL
Established: 1987

Route: 2,052 miles from Georgia to Oklahoma.

The Trail of Tears commemorates the forced march of 16,000 Cherokee from their home in Georgia to exile in the Oklahoma Territory. As the population of Georgia grew—it increased six-fold between 1790 and 1830—the new settlers pushed the Cherokee Nation farther west toward the frontier. Finally, acting under a controversial treaty (opposed by as the likes of Daniel Webster,

Henry Clay, and Davy Crockett), a U.S. Army division led by General Winfield Scott marched 16,000 Cherokee 1,000 miles from their homes to the Oklahoma Territory. With General Scott's permission, the principal Cherokee chief, John Ross, broke the party into smaller groups so that they could move separately through the wilderness and forage for food along the way. The routes they traveled became known as the "Trail Where They Cried," or the "Trail of Tears," because by the time the exiles arrived in Oklahoma, during the winter of 1838–39, 4,000 Cherokees had died.

Today: The designated trail follows two of the main routes: an 826-mile overland trail from Chattanooga, Tennessee, to Tahlequah, Oklahoma, and a 1,226-mile water route along the Tennessee, Ohio, Mississippi, and Arkansas rivers.

ALA KAHAKAI NATIONAL HISTORIC TRAIL
Established: 2000

Route: To be determined.

Created for the preservation, protection, and interpretation of traditional native Hawaiian culture and natural resources, the Ala Kahakai (Trail by the Sea) will be a 175-mile walking trail on the island of Hawaii.

The exact route hasn't yet been determined, but as proposed, it will follow the coastline from Upolu Point in North Kohala, through both urban Kona and rural South Kona, down to South Point (the southernmost point in the United States and a National Historic Landmark District itself), then up to the eastern boundary of Volcanoes National Park. The trail will wind through hundreds of ancient Hawaiian settlement sites, *heiau* (temples), fishponds, fishing shrines, petroglyphs, sacred places, *pali* (cliffs), shore reefs, and estuarine ecosystems—passing the habitats of migratory birds, native sea turtles, and several threatened and endangered endemic species of plants and animals.

Today: Finalization of the route is awaiting consultation with native Hawaiians, landowners, the Na Ala Hele Statewide Trail and Access System, the National Park Service, and other key stakeholders.

The Ice Age National Scenic Trail winds nearly 1,200 miles through Wisconsin.

FEAR FACTOR

*Visitors to the national parks have little to fear from wildlife.
Statistically, tourists are much more likely to be injured or killed in a
motor vehicle accident, by falling on rough terrain, or by drowning.
Nevertheless, many people fear animal attacks, and perhaps for good
reason—after all, the creatures that live in the parks are wild, running
around loose, and they aren't all cute and cuddly.*

BISON: GORING OFF ON TOURISTS

In Yellowstone, bison are the most dangerous animals; they injure about four visitors every year (more than bears). In July 2000, a bison bull suddenly charged up the sidewalk near the Old Faithful visitors' center. People managed to get out of the way—most of them climbed a nearby log fence. But an elderly Australian man couldn't move quickly enough and was gored in the upper thigh.

Usually, though, bison charge people who are harassing them in some way. Many people approach the animals and try to pet them, maybe believing they're gentle. But bison are unpredictable, weigh up to one ton, and can run at 30 miles per hour. For these reasons, Yellowstone park officials have instituted regulations that require visitors to stay at least 25 yards away from bison.

MIGHTY MOUNTAIN LIONS

In recent years, attacks by mountain lions (also called cougars or pumas), although still rare, have been rising, including attacks within the national parks. In 1995, a mountain lion stalked a photographer in Rocky Mountains National Park; the man climbed a tree and used a branch to keep the cat from following him. In 1997, a four-year-old boy was attacked by a mountain lion in Mesa Verde National Park. And in 2001, a cross-country skier was attacked and killed by a mountain lion in Canada's Banff National Park, the first fatal mountain lion attack in that park's history.

To avoid being attacked by a mountain lion, the National Park Service offers these warnings for tourists:

- Always hike in groups. And they mean hike, not run. Running or jogging through mountain lion territory makes a person look like prey and may trigger an attack.

Badlands National Park contains rich fossil beds from 28 to 37 million years ago.

- Don't run if you spot a mountain lion. Hikers who see one of these animals should never turn their backs or run away. Instead, back away slowly, raising your arms to make yourself look bigger and more threatening.
- Dogs attract mountain lions and are not permitted on national park trails.
- Keep children close; don't let them lag behind. More than half of all people attacked by mountain lions are less than four feet tall.

SNAKES ALIVE

Snakes are common in national parks across the United States. The western diamondback rattlesnake makes its home in Arizona's Saguaro National Park. Prairie rattlesnakes often appear in Badlands National Park in South Dakota. And Great Smoky Mountains National Park is home to two venomous snakes: the copperhead and the timber rattlesnake. Yet very few snakebites are reported by park visitors.

Perhaps this is because tourists take the following warnings to heart:

- Leave snakes alone; don't try to get a good look at them or kill them.
- Don't handle dead snakes; even when they're deceased (or just a decapitated head), snakebites can still occur because bite reflexes and muscle contractions in the snake's head remain functional for a short time after death.
- When hiking, wear sturdy leather hiking boots, stay out of tall grass, keep to the trail, and don't put your hands or feet anywhere a snake could be hiding.

BEWARE OF BAMBI

Whether inside the national parks or out, one of the most dangerous woodland creatures is the deer. (Really!) Deer attacks are rare, but the animals cause many car accidents when they step out into traffic. In fact, deer-related car crashes kill 130 Americans annually. According to the U.S. Department of Transportation, deer cause 1.5 million accidents every year.

Minute Man National Historical Park is located in Massachusetts. It's where...

SOME BITING REMARKS ABOUT ALLIGATORS

Unlike many animals, alligators don't bite in self-defense. Instead, alligators bite people in order to eat them. Fortunately, alligators don't eat much. A 180-pound alligator eats only 1 percent of what a 180 pound man eats over a year. And alligators don't eat during the winter; the cooler weather slows their metabolism so that they can't digest food.

This may be one reason that there have been no fatal alligator attacks in Florida's Everglades National Park . . . even though rangers report that they've seen tourists harass the park's alligators by running over them on bicycles, poking them with sticks, and even putting children on the alligator's back for a picture!

To read about bears, turn to page 90.

* * *

MAMA BEARS DOWN ON THE CROWD

Pit bull terriers have a reputation for being twitchy, vicious bite machines. But as anyone who has ever owned any infamous breed of dog knows, most of the time the dog's actions have more to say about the intelligence of the owner than the dog's disposition.

With that in mind, consider this story from the Great Smoky Mountains National Park in Tennessee. One July weekend a bunch of sightseers created what the locals call a "bear jam"—which means that they all stopped their cars and got out to ooh and aah at a mother bear and her three cubs. Among these sightseers was a man named Stanley, who was visiting from Georgia with his pit bull terrier.

The Great Smoky Mountains National Park requires that dogs in the park be restrained. But Stanley apparently forgot about that, which would explain what happened next. His pit bull sized up one of the cubs, decided he could take it, and bolted from the road. Naturally, mama bear didn't take kindly to this, so she went after the dog and chased it back into the crowd. Generally speaking, being pursued by a 1,000-pound angry bear would be enough for most dogs to take the hint, but this particular pit bull was persistent—or particularly dim—and needed to be chased back into the crowd several times before it got the hint.

...the American Revolution started with "the shot heard 'round the world."

OH, DAM

How did Yosemite's twin end up underwater?

Twenty miles north of Yosemite Valley, in Yosemite National Park, is another glacier-carved valley with majestic cliffs and waterfalls. The valley, sometimes referred to as Yosemite's "twin," is called Hetch Hetchy, a Miwok Indian phrase that means "grass-seed valley" or "acorn valley." Hetch Hetchy is about half the size of Yosemite Valley, and today it's submerged under 300 feet of water.

SIERRA CLUBBED

In the late 1800s, San Francisco legislators began searching for more water sources to support the city's booming population. The narrow-mouthed Hetch Hetchy valley with its roaring Tuolumne River looked like an ideal reservoir because of its abundant, rushing waters and narrow mouth. The expanse across which a dam needed to be built was short, making dam construction easier than in other places.

The plan to dam Hetch Hetchy had critics; the most vocal was John Muir, founder of the Sierra Club, who saw the valley as a natural wonder, a sister to Yosemite Valley, and a pristine wilderness that should be preserved, not altered. Muir and other conservationists took their fight to Washington, where they battled San Francisco city leaders. Initially, the environmentalists were successful: the city abandoned the dam idea in January 1906.

Three months later, everything changed. On April, 18, 1906, San Francisco was rocked by an earthquake that measured 8.3 on the Richter scale. In the aftermath, fires devastated the city, and the lack of easily accessible water to put them out rekindled the crusade to dam Hetch Hetchy.

That same year, Yosemite was made a national park, and President William H. Taft, an ally of John Muir, was against damming Hetch Hetchy. But in 1913, President Woodrow Wilson, who believed the environmental impact of damming Hetch Hetchy would be small compared to the good it would do for the public, signed the Raker Act, which gave the City of San Francisco control over Hetch Hetchy's fate.

Greer Garson's Forked Lightning Ranch is now part of Pecos National Historic Park.

DAWN OF THE DAM

Construction began on the O'Shaughnessy Dam in 1919; it was completed in 1923. The dam created an eight-mile-long reservoir holding 117 billion gallons of Tuolumne River water. Over the next 11 years, engineers built the tunnels and aqueducts needed for the water to travel from the reservoir to San Francisco homes. Finally, in 1934, the first Hetch Hetchy water reached the city after traveling 167 miles from Yosemite. San Francisco also got its electricity from Hetch Hetchy hydroelectric power plants.

BACK TO NATURE?

John Muir died in 1914, but the quest to save Hetch Hetchy didn't go with him. For the next 70 years, the Sierra Club continued working to restore the valley to its pre-dam splendor. Their pleas were ignored for many years, but in 1987, Don Hodel, Secretary of the Interior under President Ronald Reagan, proposed removing the dam, draining Hetch Hetchy, and restoring the valley. A government report argued that newer reservoirs made Hetch Hetchy unnecessary for San Francisco's water supply and that other plants also would provide the city with enough electricity.

But losing the reservoir meant losing money for San Francisco and California. The city sells the excess energy acquired by Hetch Hetchy's hydroelectric plant, and costs of restoring the valley were estimated at $1 billion to $8 billion. Plus, the process could take as many as 100 years. So for now, Yosemite's twin remains underwater.

To read more about John Muir, turn to page 1.

* * *

"Dam Hetch Hetchy! As well dam for water-tanks the people's cathedrals and churches, for no holier temple has ever been consecrated by the heart of man."

—John Muir

PRESIDENT CUSTER?

Today, the site of the Battle of the Little Bighorn is a national monument in Montana. But more than a century ago, the area was home to a bloody clash between the United States military (led by General George Armstrong Custer) and the Sioux. Why did Custer rush recklessly into that battle? Could it be that he thought a well-timed victory would sweep him into the White House?

On the morning of June 25, 1876, the men of Custer's Seventh Cavalry were exhausted. They'd raced for three days to be the first to reach the Sioux camp along the Little Bighorn River. Their orders were to wait until June 26, when all three groups of an expeditionary force would meet and take action together. But Custer didn't want to wait. He thought he had a chance to be the Democratic Party's nominee for president that year, and the national convention was just two days away. He was ready to gamble the lives of his soldiers against 3,000 Sioux and Cheyenne warriors on a long shot.

THE GOOD, THE BAD, AND THE UGLINESS

Custer had made a name for himself 10 years earlier. Even though he'd graduated at the bottom of his class at West Point, his Civil War record earned him a wartime promotion to general at the age of 23. In fact, Custer was the youngest man ever to wear a general's star—and still is. But after the war, this temporary rank was removed and he reverted to his permanent grade of lieutenant colonel. He'd also been court-martialed on a variety of charges that included going AWOL.

Still, he was a popular figure in the press, and he had influential friends. Even better than that, he had some very unpleasant information that would mortally wound the already scandal-plagued administration of the Republican president, Ulysses S. Grant.

It seems that Grant's secretary of war, William Belknap, and Grant's own brother, Orvil, were involved in skimming money on goods sold to the Indians and to the troops stationed on the frontier. Custer gave the story to the *New York Herald*, and before long, Democrats in Congress were calling for Belknap's impeachment—so loudly that Belknap decided to resign.

EAT MY DUST, MR. PRESIDENT

Custer had been required to testify before a congressional committee and was still in Washington, but his career plans were elsewhere. A campaign against the Sioux was planned for that summer, and Custer wanted to return to his command in the West.

President Grant struck back by refusing to permit Custer to return to his post. (Grant may also have been holding another grudge against Custer, who'd had Grant's son, Fred, arrested for drunkenness while he was attached to the Seventh Cavalry.) This might have stymied someone with lesser ambitions, but Custer just packed up and left Washington anyway. Grant retaliated by having him arrested. The press cried foul, and Grant relented. Custer returned to the Seventh Cavalry.

GREAT WHITE FATHER-TO-BE

No one knows what backroom deals and promises the Democrats made to Custer regarding the nomination for president. What is known is that shortly before the Battle of the Little Bighorn, Custer told his trusted Indian scouts that if he gained even a small victory over the Sioux, he would become the "Great White Father" in Washington.

It's not as far-fetched as it sounds. The Democrats wanted a general of their own to run against the Republicans, and a lot of Democrats weren't happy with their frontrunner, New York governor Samuel B. Tilden. Custer had made himself a hero by testifying against graft and corruption; his star was on the rise. All he needed now was a victory over the Sioux to clinch the deal.

DYING TO BE PRESIDENT

The Democratic convention was scheduled to begin on June 27 in St. Louis, Missouri. But the Little Bighorn was days away from the nearest telegraph office, so Custer would have to attack by the 25th if Washington was to receive news of his victory in time. He also wanted to attack the Sioux alone so that no other general would share the credit. He took the gamble and would either become a martyr or the president.

He lost. According to legend, Sitting Bull, a Sioux medicine man, reported that when the end came and Custer knew he had been defeated, Custer died laughing. But it's doubtful that the more than 200 soldiers who died with him thought it was all that funny.

Cape Cod National Seashore has six beaches and 11 self-guided walking trails.

WHEW! THAT WAS A CLOSE ONE!

Samuel Tilden got the nomination. The election of 1876 was so close that it was thrown into the House of Representatives to be decided. Tilden lost by one electoral vote to Rutherford B. Hayes. Afterward—and for the rest of his life—he maintained that he'd been robbed.

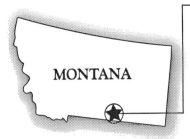

MONTANA

Little Bighorn Battlefield
National Monument
Crow Agency, MT 59022

Founded: 1879
Area: 765 acres
Average annual visitors: 350,000

www.nps.gov/libi

* * *

HERNANDO DE SOTO

Spaniard Hernando de Soto and crew had been exploring on either side of the Mississippi River—in an area that is now Tennessee, Arkansas, and Louisiana—when he was stricken with a fever and died. The local Native Americans lived in mud houses, so there was a large hole (the source of the mud) just outside their village. De Soto's men buried his body there but then remembered that their captain had told the natives that Christians were immortal.

This presented a problem. What if the Indians discovered the body? They hadn't been all that friendly to begin with. And if they found de Soto's body, they might decide they'd been lied to and do something nasty. So the sailors dug up the body, put it in a hollowed-out tree trunk, and sank it in the Mississippi River. It was fitting that de Soto got a burial at sea (sort of), but it's unlikely that this would have been exactly what the explorer had in mind.

A speleothem is any kind of cave formation. Spelunkers (cavers) call them "pretties."

GOLD!

Today, the Lost Horse Mine is a four-mile hike in California's Joshua Tree National Park. But at the turn of the 20th century, it was the site of horse stealing, gold mining, and a search for buried treasure.

WELCOME TO CALIFORNIA

In 1890, a Texan named Johnny Lang traveled with his father to a valley just east of California's Little San Bernardino Mountains. The Langs had come to California hoping to strike gold and get rich. But on his first morning in the valley, Johnny discovered that his horses were gone. He went looking for them and came upon the camp of the McHaney brothers, a well-known gang of cattle rustlers and horse thieves. The McHaneys denied knowing anything about Lang's horses—though Johnny didn't believe them—and then ran him out of their camp, threatening that they'd kill him if he came back.

Johnny left without his horses but soon came upon another camp, this one belonging to Frank "Dutch" Diebold. He too had been threatened by the McHaneys, and thus, he was afraid to develop the claim he'd set up in the desert. (Dutch had found gold on his claim, and he feared that if he turned the place into a full-blown mine, the McHaneys would kill him to get the riches.) Diebold offered to sell the Langs the claim for $1,000, and Johnny accepted. He and his dad moved in, and Dutch moved on.

THE LOST HORSE

The Langs called their claim the Lost Horse Mine after the lost horses that had led them to the place. To protect themselves from the McHaneys, they brought on three partners—five men working and protecting the claim were stronger than two and would be harder for the McHaneys to attack.

In 1893, the partners started mining. They set up a two-stamp mill, diverted water from wells nearby to power the steam engines, and began crushing ore to extract gold. The mill operated 24 hours a day, and Lost Horse became the most successful gold mine in the area. Between 1894 and 1905, miners extracted 16,000 ounces of silver and 10,000 ounces of gold from it.

The Mississippi River is only about three feet deep at its headwaters in Minnesota.

MINER '95-ER

A wealthy Montana rancher named J. D. Ryan kept tabs on emerging gold claims in the California desert, and in 1895, he bought out Johnny Lang's father and partners and became a senior partner in the Lost Horse. Johnny stayed on, and in 1896, the two increased the mine's productivity by installing a 10-stamp mill, which allowed them to crush five times more ore than the two-stamp mill did. (The new mill needed lots of wood to fuel the steam engines, though, and Lost Horse workers cut down so many trees in the area that the surrounding hillsides were laid almost bare. To this day, hikers note the lack of trees in the vicinity.)

Ryan and Lang worked together for many months, but Ryan began to see discrepancies between the mine's output during the day shift (which he managed) and the night shift (which Lang managed). The day shift produced gold/mercury amalgams the size of baseballs, but the night shift produced amalgams that were only the size of golf balls. So Ryan hired a private investigator to look into the matter and discovered that Lang was reporting only half of the gold from the nightly intake process; the rest he kept for himself. Lang wouldn't admit his involvement or reveal where he'd hidden his stash (though most people believed he'd either buried it in the desert or on the mill grounds). Ryan confronted Lang and gave him an ultimatum: sell his share of the mine or go to jail. Lang sold Ryan his share for $12,000 and set off to prospect elsewhere.

BACK TO THE SCENE OF THE CRIME

Between 1905 and 1931, the Lost Horse shut down because miners hit a fault line and lost sight of the original ore-bearing vein; thus, they declared the mine "dry." During this period, Johnny Lang returned to the desert several times to retrieve his stash bit by bit. Exactly how much gold he took over the years is unknown, but on at least three occasions, he sold off pure gold bullion, which allowed him to buy food and supplies.

Then, in 1925, during one of these trips, Lang died at his camp. He was 75 years old by then, too old and infirm to survive the harsh conditions in the California desert. A local resident named William F. Keys found the body and buried it across from the access road to the mine. The grave site is still there today, outlined with rocks and marked with a tombstone.

"There are two ways to get to Chaco Canyon [NM]. One is bad and the other is...

BURIED TREASURE

Lang took the location of his stash with him to the grave. To this day, hikers and adventurers speculate that Lang's ill-gotten gold still lies somewhere near the Lost Horse Mine, though it's never been found. And treasure hunters better not look too hard. The Lost Horse Mine came under the stewardship of the National Park Service in 1936 with the creation of the Joshua Tree National Monument; it became a national park in 1994. And it's illegal for anyone to dig in an NPS-protected site. So where Lang's treasure lies, it will likely remain.

CALIFORNIA

Joshua Tree National Park
Yucca Valley, CA 92284

Founded: 1936 monument status
         1994 national park status
Area: 800,000 acres
Average annual visitors: 1,300,000

www.nps.gov/jotr

* * *

THE HIGHS AND LOWS
OF NATIONAL PARKS

At 14,494 feet, Mt. Whitney is the tallest mountain in the contiguous 48 states. It was first scaled in 1873 by three fishermen: A. H. Johnson, John Lucas, and Charles Begole. In the years since, thousands have followed. Most use the popular 22-mile Mt. Whitney Trail.

Seventy-six miles to the east is Death Valley, the lowest point in the United States at 280 feet below sea level. Both are in California.

THE CELEBRI-TREE

The rise and fall of a beloved Yosemite landmark.

In August 2003, the world mourned the passing of one of California's most-photographed celebs—a famous and beautiful profile snapped by professional photographers and amateur shutterbugs alike. But this wasn't a Hollywood star. This photo subject was a wind-twisted pine tree, and for more than a century, its appearance atop Yosemite's Sentinel Dome thrilled nature lovers who made it one of the most-photographed trees in the world.

ON THE ROCKS

Yosemite Valley is famous for the soaring granite peaks that rim its edges. Once named "Sakkaduch" by the Native Americans, Sentinel Dome is a granite monolith, the second highest point of Yosemite National Park. With an elevation of 8,122 feet (about 1.5 miles), Sentinel Dome rises high above Yosemite Valley and Yosemite Falls and overlooks Half Dome, El Capitan, and the Sierra Mountain Range.

Few places are less hospitable to trees. Open and exposed, the dome experiences fierce winds, lightning strikes, and freezing winter storms. Yet, at the very top, one tree grew for more than 400 years. The 12-foot conifer was gnarled and bent into twisted shapes, its limbs growing sideways, but it survived by drawing water through tiny cracks in the granite while seeming to grow out of barren rock. The tree atop Sentinel Dome was a Jeffrey Pine, a variety named for Scottish botanist John Jeffrey, who discovered the first one in 1852.

TAKING THEIR BEST SHOT

From Yosemite's early days, visitors flocked to the tree, and by 1900, the Sentinel's pine was a popular destination for sunset dinners. Some visitors even dressed for the occasion in formal tuxedos and ball gowns! For the next 70-plus years, most of the pine's admirers were more casual in their attire, but they were just as impressed with the tree.

In the 1860s, Carleton Watkins (who became one of the Pacific Coast's most famous photographers) set up camp on the Sentinel

---

A hummingbird egg is the size of a Tic-Tac breath mint.

Dome. There, he took and developed the first well-known photos of the Sentinel pine. In the years that followed, other professional photographers documented the tree; the most famous was Ansel Adams, who, in 1940, produced a black-and-white portrait entitled *Windswept Jeffrey Pine*. Adams's photo became a classic; its image was reproduced on thousands of postcards and posters, and it made the Sentinel Dome's Jeffrey Pine a symbol of Yosemite.

Professional photographers weren't the only ones who appreciated the tree. So many tourists took their own snapshots of the pine that they made it one of the world's most photographed trees.

A TREE FALLS IN YOSEMITE
In 1976, Northern California suffered one of its worst droughts ever. Worried visitors assisted park rangers by carrying buckets of water up to the top of Sentinel Dome to water the pine. But despite their efforts, it died that year. The pine remained standing as a park icon, however, and people still came to view and photograph its twisted trunk and limbs, though they were now bare of foliage.

Then, in August 2003, after a series of heavy thunderstorms, the Jeffrey Pine finally fell. Its remains still lie atop Sentinel Dome.

CALIFORNIA

Yosemite National Park
Yosemite National Park, CA 95389

Founded: 1890
Area: 761,266 acres
Average annual visitors: 3,300,000

www.nps.gov/yose

* * *

Fundy, established in 1948, was the first national park in Canada's New Brunswick province.

Hummingbird nest? The size of a walnut shell.

I AM A ROCK

Everybody knows that Alcatraz (also known as "the Rock") was a federal prison. But it wasn't always just the dungeon of the notorious.

GOLDEN OPPORTUNITIES

When gold was discovered near San Francisco in 1848, word spread like a virus. Seemingly overnight, the sleepy western town turned into a full-fledged city. The population exploded from about 800 people in 1848 to 25,000 at the end of 1849. The federal government, which granted California statehood in 1850, saw the rising importance of the port of San Francisco and the need to defend it. Alcatraz—positioned near the Golden Gate, the entrance to San Francisco Bay from the Pacific Ocean—was the perfect place for the main military installation.

The first order of business was building a lighthouse, the first on the Pacific shoreline; it was built between 1852 and 1853, stood 166 feet high, and could be seen from 14 miles away. The light became operational in 1854, and right away, lighthouse keepers found it unpleasant to work on the island. The isolation—Alcatraz is more than a mile from San Francisco, across the frigid, frequently choppy bay—made it a lonely and boring place to live.

Meanwhile, the military set to work converting the island to the first permanent fortification on the Pacific coast. They blasted off the top of the hills to create a plateau and installed 111 cannons around the island's perimeter. In 1864, the army added three gigantic cannons with 15-inch shells that weighed 440 pounds apiece. (Each of the cannons weighed 50,000 pounds.) The last line of defense for Alcatraz was a citadel, a fort in which soldiers could hunker down in the case of a prolonged siege. The citadel held four months' worth of supplies for 200 men. Work on the fort finished in 1859, just in time for the outbreak of the Civil War in 1861.

ALL QUIET ON THE WESTERN FRONT

Although, San Francisco was the 12th-largest urban area in the country in 1861, its distance from the main conflicts of the Civil War meant things at Alcatraz were fairly low-key.

Petroglyph National Monument in Albuquerque, NM, contains more than 15,000...

In March 1863, the Union government learned of a plot hatched in San Francisco to start up a Confederate privateering ship, which would loot and steal on behalf of the secessionist South. The ship, the *J.M. Chapman,* made it no farther than Alcatraz. The navy stopped the ship before it ever made it out of the bay. The privateers were arrested and brought to Alcatraz to be held until the end of the war.

Throughout the Civil War, Alcatraz was used as a military prison. In 1861, four Navy sailors who refused to swear an oath of loyalty to the Union were held there. And just after President Lincoln was assassinated, 39 citizens who spoke positively about the president's death were hustled off to Alcatraz's basement as safekeeping against a possible riot or insurrection.

WE STILL KEEP BAD GUYS HERE

Alcatraz continued as a military installation after the end of the Civil War, but it quickly became apparent that the buildings were showing their age. The government tried to modernize the island during the 1870s, but it was clear that Alcatraz's time as defender of the Pacific coast was petering out . . . less than two decades after it opened.

Alcatraz's biggest contribution became its prison. Nineteen Hopis from Arizona were shipped there in 1895 for refusing to let their children attend public schools. In 1898, the prison was filled to capacity with detainees from the Spanish-American War. Finally, Alcatraz officially became a military prison in 1907 when the active army troops left the island.

BIGGER, BUT NOT BETTER

During its time as a military prison, Alcatraz underwent expansion. A new cell block was planned, but because it was going to be so tall that it would block the lighthouse, a new lighthouse had to be built, too. The new electric light opened in 1909. The new cell block accommodated 600 prisoners, and it was a minimum-security facility, in contrast to the supersecure federal prison that was the next (and most famous) occupant of Alcatraz.

But, as with the fort, the military prison didn't last long. It was expensive to maintain a facility on an island; everything had to be shipped over on boats. Alcatraz's biggest problem was that it had no freshwater source, so it was dependent on enormous cisterns

---

...petroglyphs—images carved in rock, some from prehistoric times.

that collected rainwater or on water sent from shore. In 1933, the army gave the compound to the Federal Bureau of Prisons, leaving behind 32 unlucky prisoners who became the Rock's first inmates.

TO PRISON AND BEYOND

For 30 years, Alcatraz was the most notorious federal prison in the United States. Criminals from Al Capone to Robert Franklin Stroud (better known as the Birdman of Alcatraz) were incarcerated there. Escape attempts from Alcatraz are legendary—one (that of Frank Morris, who'd managed to escape from several other prisons before coming to Alcatraz) even inspired the film *Escape from Alcatraz*. Most inmates, though, served out their sentences on the Rock. Attorney General Robert Kennedy closed the prison in 1963.

Nobody really knew what to do with Alcatraz after that. A number of proposals were suggested, but none took hold. For a while, it looked like the government might build a memorial to the United Nations, which had been established in San Francisco, but the State Department didn't like the idea of associating the UN with a former prison. The city tried to slate Alcatraz for commercial development, but San Franciscans didn't go for it. They wanted the National Park Service to take control of the place.

In the midst of this squabbling, on November 20, 1969, a group of 90 Native Americans landed on Alcatraz and announced they wanted to buy it for $24 worth of beads and red cloth, referring to the price paid to a local tribe for Manhattan Island in 1626. (They actually considered this a generous offer, because an 1868 treaty between the Sioux and the United States stated that "surplus land," which is how Alcatraz was classified, reverts to the Native Americans.) The government wanted them off, but they refused to leave unless the government agreed to build a Native American cultural center and university.

The government had no such plans. Both sides dug in their heels, and there was no progress for a long time. The occupation became a cause célèbre. Jane Fonda and Ethel Kennedy visited, winning sympathy for the Native Americans. Hippies from San Francisco moved in. Graffiti appeared everywhere. The occupiers announced that they would give tours to raise money for supplies, but the government countered by saying that anyone going to Alcatraz was trespassing and would be prosecuted. Neither side would budge.

Remember Longfellow? "Gitchee Gumee" was the Ojibwa name for Lake Superior.

But then the leader of the occupation, Richard Oakes, left the island in January 1970 after his daughter died in a fall. Without him, the movement foundered. Negotiations went nowhere, so the government tried to force the protesters from the island by cutting off the electricity and stopping water delivery to the island. Three days later, fires broke out. The lighthouse keeper's quarters, the warden's house, the prison doctor's home, and the social hall were destroyed. The government blamed the Indians for the fire; the Indians blamed undercover government agents. People moved off the island slowly but steadily. By June 1971, the occupiers numbered only 15. Deciding that enough was enough, federal marshals went to the island and removed the remaining Native Americans.

The National Park Service has been in charge of Alcatraz since 1972 and started giving public tours the following year. Today, more than 1 million visitors a year see the remnants and ruins of the island's different eras.

CALIFORNIA

Alcatraz Island,
Golden Gate National Recreation Area
San Francisco, CA 94123

Founded: 1972
Area: 18.86 acres
Average annual visitors: 1,300,000

www.nps.gov/alca

* * *

MISNOMER

Martin Luther King Jr. (for whom a national historic site in Georgia is named) was christened Michael Luther King Jr. in 1929. Five years later, his father, Michael King Sr., returned from a trip to Europe and changed his and his son's names to honor the 16th-century German church reformer, Martin Luther.

North America has the greatest diversity of freshwater mussels in the world—297 species.

THE GRAND CANYON BY THE NUMBERS

First protected in 1893 as a forest reserve, the Grand Canyon became a national park in 1919. It's not the deepest canyon in the world (Hell's Canyon in Idaho and Mexico's Barranca del Cobre are deeper), but it is one of the most famous. More than 5 million people visit the Grand Canyon every year to marvel at its unique landscape and size, which made us wonder—just how "grand" is it, anyway?

0
Number of easy hiking trails into or out of the Grand Canyon; the shortest trail to the bottom of the canyon is 6.5 miles long and includes a vertical drop of about 4,400 feet.

2 days
Time it takes to travel to the bottom of the canyon and back by mule or on foot

3 days
Time it takes to hike from the North Rim to the South Rim (one way)

18 miles
Width of the canyon at its widest point

56°F
Average temperature at the North Rim; at the South Rim, the average temperature is 62°F.

277 miles
Length of the Grand Canyon

400
Average number of medical emergencies that occur within the canyon every year. Most of these are the result of visitors taking on hikes that are too difficult for their skill level.

1,450 miles
Length of the Colorado River, which flows through (and carved) the canyon

$2,000
Minimum cost of a helicopter rescue in the canyon; this is at the injured party's expense, so be careful!

6,000 feet
Height from rim to river at the deepest point of the South Rim, the most accessible part of the park. The average height from rim to river is 5,000 feet.

8,200 feet
Height (above sea level) of the North Rim

5 to 6 million years
Age of the carved canyon. Rocks at the bottom of the canyon (its oldest point) may be as much as 2 billion years old.

ARIZONA

Grand Canyon National Park
Grand Canyon, AZ 86023

Founded: 1893
Area: 1,218,375 acres
Average annual visitors: 4,000,000

www.nps.gov/grca

* * *

The Anasazi Indians once lived in the Grand Canyon, and remains of the storage rooms they used for corn and beans have been found in the national park's cliffs. But around 1150 AD, the Anasazi abandoned their Grand Canyon digs and moved south to what is now New Mexico. No one really knows why, but archaeologists speculate that a drought sent them looking for a new water source and a new place to live.

...lost their footing on a local trail and spilled a load of whiskey into a nearby ravine.

TAKE A HIKE!

On Canada's west coast, outdoorsy types can venture into the wilderness . . . and follow in some historical footsteps along the way.

Located in British Columbia's Pacific Rim National Park, the West Coast Trail is a 47-mile (75-kilometer) hiking trail along southwestern Vancouver Island. Today, experienced backpackers, day hikers, and campers traverse the trail, but 100 years ago, it served a different purpose: it was constructed to help shipwreck survivors.

FOR SAFETY'S SAKE

Pacific Rim National Park's shoreline is part of a section of the Pacific coast called the "Graveyard of the Pacific," which stretches from Oregon to the northern tip of Vancouver Island. It's so named because during the 19th century, more ships were destroyed there than anywhere else in the Pacific Ocean. The weather is brutal: fog, cold, wind, and storms are common. And a sand bar called the Columbia Bar marks the place where the Columbia River empties into the ocean. It's the site of many wrecks because the bar's quickly changing currents make its waters particularly dangerous.

Around the turn of the 20th century, the Canadian government decided to do something about all the wrecks. Officials built the Pachena Point Lighthouse to help ships navigate the craggy shore-line (visitors to Pacific Rim can still see the structure), and, per-haps more importantly, they constructed a trail—then called the Dominion Life Saving Trail—that included a telegraph line and cabins. Shipwreck survivors could more easily pass through the Canadian wilderness, use the telegraph to call for help, and find shelter in the cabins while awaiting rescue. For their part, rescuers could more easily reach the survivors and better communicate with each other using the telegraph.

A WALK IN THE WOODS

These days, the renamed and revamped West Coast Trail is a trek for only the hardiest hikers. It generally takes five to seven days to travel the length of the trail, and hikers will pass through thick forests and mud, bogs, and streams. They'll climb wooden stairs and ladders and traverse boardwalks. You'll also need a permit to hike the trail, whether for a day hike or for an overnight excursion, and Parks Canada allows only a certain number of hikers to venture onto the trail each day. Most hikers take to the trail during the peak season (June 15 to September 15), but it's open from mid-March to mid-October and there's usually plenty of space available then.

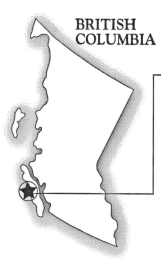

BRITISH COLUMBIA

Pacific Rim National Park Reserve
Ucluelet, BC V0R 3A0

Founded: 1970
Area: 123,406 acres
Average annual visitors: 1,000,000

www.pc.gc.ca/pn-np/bc/pacificrim

* * *

SURF'S UP!

Canada's Pacific Rim National Park is also well known for another kind of outdoor sport: surfing. Called Canada's most popular surfing destination by Parks Canada, Pacific Rim offers up the waves at Long Beach to rival great breaks around the world.

The water at Long Beach is cold—generally a steady 50°F, though temperatures sometimes reach 58°F in the summer. But no matter the season, the waves are pristine . . . 12-foot sets are common. An added plus: anyone can surf Long Beach; there are even four surf schools for beginners in the area. Just make sure to bring a wetsuit and booties . . . brrr!

THE FRINGES OF SOCIETY

*The islands that make up Boston Harbor Islands National Park have a
rich history—of murder, disease, piracy, shipwrecks, and ghosts.*

Boston Harbor Islands National Park Area comprises a
collection of islands in the sheltered harbor just east of the
city's downtown, some with sinister-sounding names like
Hangman, Ragged, and the Graves. The islands aren't well known,
even among Bostonians, possibly because in their history; they've
housed all kinds of things that Boston would rather not remember:
quarantine hospitals, prisons, glue factories, and sewage-treatment
facilities. The sizes of the 34 islands can change drastically according to how high or low the tide is. Moon Island, for example,
measures 54 acres at high tide; at low tide, it's 269 acres—and it's
attached to the mainland.

Each island has its own past, all of which is bound up in the
history of Boston, of Massachusetts, and of the United States. But
the stories aren't always ones of great men; more often they're
about the wretched, the marginal, and the fringes of society. Here
are 10 of them.

ARRGH, MATEY!

At one point, Nixes Mate was as large as 12 acres. In 1726, pirate
chief William Fly was hanged in Boston and then "gibbeted"—that
is, put on public display as a warning to other buccaneers who
might pass by. Fly (and two other pirates) were then buried on the
island. Legend has it that the island is named for the mate of one
Captain Nix, who was murdered. Nix's mate was convicted of the
crime and hanged on the island. The mate's last words included
the prediction that the island would someday disappear and that
this would be a mystical sign of his innocence. Whether the story
has any basis in fact or not, most of the island has indeed disappeared due to slate quarrying and erosion. All that's left now at
high tide is a channel marker; at low tide, there's a small spit
of sand.

First national lakeshore: Pictured Rocks National Lakeshore on Lake Superior.

LIGHT MY WAY
Little Brewster Island is the home of Boston Light, the oldest light-house site in the United States. The original was built in 1716, more than 30 years before any other American lighthouse. After being partially destroyed by fleeing British soldiers in 1776, it was rebuilt in 1783. Another renovation in 1859 included the installation of a Fresnel lens, a large piece of intricately cut glass that boosts the intensity of the light. In 1998, the light became the last lighthouse in the United States to be automated.

THIS ONE'S A WRECK
Lovells Island is best known for two major offshore shipwrecks. One was the most famous wreck in Boston Harbor history—when the French warship *Magnifique* sank in 1782, taking with it a large quantity of gold and silver coins that supposedly financed the retirement of a light keeper's assistant in the early 20th century. The second shipwreck, in 1786, led to 13 deaths, including a couple who made it to shore but died of exposure, huddled together in a small shelter now called Lover's Rock. This disaster led the Massachusetts Humane Society (for people, not animals) to establish "huts of refuge" along treacherous shorelines. The small shelters were stocked with a few necessities to help the stranded survive until the weather improved enough to escape. The first hut of refuge was built on Lovells Island.

ROTTEN EGGS
Deer Island houses the main wastewater-treatment facility for the city of Boston. Its most prominent features are 12 enormous, egg-shaped "sludge digesters" that metabolize Boston's sewage. Technically, Deer Island hasn't been an island since 1938, when Hurricane Edna closed a strait that separated it from the mainland. In its checkered past, Deer Island has been home to a quarantine hospital that treated Irish immigrants during the potato famine, an almshouse for paupers, a reformatory for juvenile delinquents, a prison, and the largest of several sites where Native Americans were interned in 1675 and 1676 during the colonist-native conflict known as King Philip's War.

WHAT A DUMP
Spectacle Island has a history of undesirable tenants. Like Deer

---

Historic site: Montana's Grant-Kohrs Ranch was once a 10-million-acre cattle empire.

Island, it was also the site of a quarantine hospital, from 1717 until 1737, when the hospital was moved to Rainsford Island (see below). In the 1800s, two hotels that operated gambling dens made it a popular spot. The hotels were closed down by the police, and a big, stinky horse-rendering facility that turned old, broken-down horses into glue opened its doors in 1857 and stayed open until the horse was supplanted by the automobile as a means of transportation. Then, from 1921 to 1959, the island became a solid-waste dump. More recently, the city's leaders dumped dirt excavated during the Big Dig, the massive highway project in downtown Boston, on top of the garbage dump. Now it's open to visitors—and is not smelly.

STRANGE BEDFELLOWS
Rainsford Island is the third Boston Harbor Island that once had a quarantine hospital. Strangely enough, there was a summer resort operating there at the same time.

GLORY DAYS
Gallops Island has seen flurries of activity during wartime. Most recently, during World War II, it was the site for a maritime radio school with 325 students and a cooking school with 150. During the Civil War, the island housed 20 barracks with a total capacity of 3,000 troops. The most famous former residents of those barracks are the 54th Massachusetts Volunteer Regiment, the soldiers dramatized in the movie *Glory*.

A GHOST OF A CHANCE
Georges Island is home to Fort Warren, a military installation that the United States started building in 1825, planning to have 300 guns that (the government thought) would repel even a large offensive. By the time the fort was finished in 1847, military strategy had already outpaced it. It was still useful for training and as a military prison, especially during the Civil War, when Confederate Vice President Alexander H. Stephens was held there for five months. Fort Warren is also supposedly haunted by a ghost: the Lady in Black, a Civil War prisoner's wife who was hanged after getting caught trying to break him out.

Louisiana's Jean Lafitte National Historic Park celebrates Cajun food, music, and culture.

ISLANDS OF WAR

Peddocks Island, the island with the longest coastline, was once the site of Fort Andrews, a military installation that held 1,000 Italian prisoners of war during World War II. Many of the buildings from Fort Andrews still exist on the island, along with a few summer cottages that remain in private hands. The owners of these cottages were grandfathered in when the islands became parkland, and the residents were allowed to keep their houses for life. When they die, the government will take over the cottages.

NOWHERE'S-VILLE

World's End isn't really an island; it's connected to the mainland by a man-made causeway. In the late 1800s, legendary landscape architect Frederick Law Olmsted was hired to develop the land on World's End for residential housing. He prepared plans for roads, landscaping, and subdivisions. The roads were built and the landscaping done, but no houses were ever built. So all the beautifully sculpted and arbored streets lead . . . nowhere.

MASSACHUSETTS

**Boston Harbor Islands
National Recreation Area**
Boston, MA 02110

Founded: 1996
Area: 3,100 acres at low tide
Average annual visitors: 1,600,000

www.nps.gov/boha

* * *

WHEN WOMEN GOT THE NEEDLE

One of the unfortunate results of the French and Indian War is that it left many women widows. They still had to support their families, but few occupations were open to them in the mid-1700s. In 18th-century Boston, one of the few jobs a woman could get was owning a shop to sell sewing supplies. By 1770, more than 70 women owned such shops in Boston. They were called "She-Merchants."

Though only inches deep in places, the Everglades swamp is the widest river on earth.

BLACK SATURDAY AND BEYOND

In 1988, Yellowstone National Park was engulfed by fire.
But was it a blessing in disguise?

UNCONTROLLED BURN

June 1988 was the driest summer on record in Yellowstone. There was no rain to counterbalance the more than 1,000 lightning strikes that occur every summer and fall. To make matters worse, hot, dry, 60- to 80-mph winds blew in from the south. It was prime fire season, and the park's trees and brush were just waiting for ignition. The spark came in July when a bolt of dry lightning—a strike that occurs without rain—hit one of the park's pine forests.

At first, park officials left the fire alone. Since the 1970s, Yellowstone and other parks had been ruled by a controlled-burn policy, meaning that fires started by lightning would be allowed to burn. This encouraged forest growth by clearing out old brush to make room for new plants. But by July 21, more than 8,000 acres were ablaze.

FIGHTING THE FIRE

Firefighters mobilized, but they were no match for the firestorm. Within three weeks, more than 200,000 acres had burned.

Then came the worst day, August 20, called Black Saturday by locals. That morning, 80 mph winds whipped up a nearly dead fire and pushed it 10 miles in just three hours. The forest exploded, creating walls of flames that rose thousands of feet from the ground; the smoke pushed even higher. In all, more than 165,000 acres of Yellowstone burned that day alone.

And it kept going. On September 6, the flames came within feet of the park's historic Old Faithful Inn; the log structure was saved only by a new sprinkler system on its roof and a fortunate shift in wind direction.

As local firehouses battled the blazes, they recruited help from around the country. Yellowstone National Park was closed.

The Utes near Mesa Verde have their own version of Sadie Hawkins Day...

People who lived in surrounding areas were evacuated. And still the fires burned. Finally, on September 11, 1988, the weather changed: rain and snow began to fall, and by October, at a loss of millions of dollars and after the work of 25,000 fire fighters, the fires went out.

AFTER THE BLAZE

Politicians called it a disaster. Reporters called for investigations. People around the country were outraged that the fires had been allowed to get out of control. Yellowstone's controlled-burn policies came under close scrutiny. It was true, the fire had done horrific damage:

- 793,880 acres had burned.
- The fires caused about $3 million in property damage and destroyed several park structures, including 16 cabins near Old Faithful.
- 333 elk, nine bison, and six black bears died, most from smoke inhalation.
- Two firefighters also died: one was struck by a falling tree; the other was killed while piloting a small plane.

Most people were afraid that Yellowstone would never bounce back.

THE UPSIDE?

But botanists thought something else. They argued that even though the area had suffered a great loss, it would also reap future rewards.

The fire that cleared meadows of brush and old trees, making them more accessible to the sun; today, wildflowers thrive in those meadows. Pinecones glued shut by resin opened when the fire melted the resin; winds from the fire blew the seeds to different parts of the park, preparing new pine groves. Ash and burned bark mulched into the soil, providing nutrients for new plants.

After much study and investigation, the scientists won out . . . sort of. In 1992, Yellowstone National Park reinstated its controlled-burn policy, but the guidelines were much more strict than they had been, necessities for protecting homes and other buildings in the Yellowstone area.

To this day, park managers continue to believe that fire is an essential natural force, and they theorize that Yellowstone hasn't seen the last of the firestorms. They expect large fires like the one in 1988 to occur every 250 to 400 years.

WYOMING

Yellowstone National Park
Yellowstone National Park, WY 82190

Founded: 1872
Area: 2,212,789 acres
Average annual visitors: 3,000,000

www.nps.gov/yell

* * *

DISASTERS: QUAKE LAKE

At 11:37 p.m. on August 17, 1959, one of the strongest earthquakes in North America's history struck Yellowstone National Park. Measuring 7.5 on the Richter scale, it caused panic among the guests in the Old Faithful Inn when the dining room's fireplace chimney fell over. But that was nothing compared to what was happening just 15 miles north along the Madison River canyon.

There, the earthquake created 20-foot waves in Hebgen Lake that overtopped Hebgen Dam. A wall of water rushed down the Madison River Canyon. Further down the canyon, 80 million tons of rock—half of a 7,600-foot mountain—came crashing down at 100 miles per hour. In the path of the landslide was the Rock Creek Campground, where 19 people were killed by the massive slide. The slide also blocked the Madison River, forcing the surging water from the overtopped dam back up the canyon. A total of 28 campers lost their lives in the canyon that night.

In the end, though, the earthquake helped scientists study the relationship between seismic activity and Yellowstone's geysers and hot springs. The quake caused 200 known geysers to erupt and new ones sprang to life overnight. Hot springs changed temperature and color. Today, the quake is commemorated with a visitor center and a memorial to those who lost their lives.

GEYSER GAZERS

If you've been to Yellowstone, you've probably seen Old Faithful erupt at least once. But for some visitors, once isn't enough.

DON'T SET YOUR WATCH BY IT

Yellowstone National Park is home to the Old Faithful geyser, a spectacular erupting thermal feature that most visitors to the park see as the highlight of their trip. But Old Faithful is not the only game in town. Yellowstone boasts approximately 10,000 thermal features, including several hundred active geysers. Although it is the most famous, Old Faithful is neither the biggest geyser (at 90 to 180 feet, it is dwarfed by Steamboat, the largest geyser in the world, which is three times larger) nor the most regular. Despite legends that claim you can set your watch by Old Faithful, intervals between eruptions range from 35 minutes to 120 minutes, and predictions can be off by as much as 10 minutes. (Daisy Geyser, also in Yellowstone, is actually the most predictable geyser in the world, with eruptions every 110 and 130 minutes, and predictions are generally accurate within a few minutes.)

ADDICTED TO ERUPTIONS

Each year, close to 5 million visitors come to Yellowstone to watch Old Faithful and the other geysers. Among this number is a growing group of people who call themselves "geyser gazers." These folks have become so fascinated with geysers that they return to Yellowstone year after year to observe the park's geysers and monitor their ever-changing patterns.

Most geyser gazers spend the majority of their time at Upper Geyser Basin, the area in Yellowstone that has the greatest concentration of predictable geysers (including Old Faithful). But watching the geysers isn't all they do. Geyser gazers also help out the National Park Service by sharing their observations of eruption times with rangers via walkie-talkies, which in turn helps the rangers make accurate predictions of future eruptions. The gazers also sometimes act as stewards of the park by picking up trash as they make their rounds through the geysers.

Author Eudora Welty's house in Jackson, MS, is a national historic landmark.

MAKE FRIENDS, FIND MATES

Gazers are self-taught experts from all walks of life. You can generally spot a gazer by looking for a person sitting near an inactive geyser for a long period of time. It is a lucky thing to find a geyser gazer, because they keep in contact with one another via short-wave radio and, thus, are generally knowledgeable about impending eruptions—often more so than the rangers, who cannot be in the geyser basins for long periods of time.

Camaraderie among the geyser gazers has blossomed into an active community, who keep in touch via e-mail and 'blogs and sometimes take part in social events. The Old Faithful Inn, located just steps from its namesake geyser, has hosted several weddings for geyser gazer couples who have met at Yellowstone. There's even a Geyser Observation and Study Organization (GOSA), founded by a group of gazers. GOSA's mission is to study geysers and disseminate information about them and other thermal features in Yellowstone and throughout the world (other geyser basins exist in Iceland, Russia, and New Zealand, although in much less concentrated areas than Yellowstone). Founded in 1983, GOSA maintains a database of predicted eruption times, records of recent geyser activity, and detailed descriptions of Yellowstone geysers. GOSA also maintains links to a geyser gazer e-mail list, designed to help gazers get to know one another. So the next time you're in Yellowstone, keep your eyes open for geysers and gazers alike: both are unique features of Yellowstone National Park.

To read about how geysers are formed, turn to page 30.

WYOMING

Yellowstone National Park
Yellowstone National Park, WY 82190

Founded: 1872
Area: 2,212,789 acres
Average annual visitors: 3,000,000

www.nps.gov/yell

Alaska's Glacier Bay didn't exist 200 years ago. It lay beneath thousands of feet of ice.

THEIR MUSE

This trio of poets was inspired by America's national parks.

ADELAIDE CRAPSEY (1878–1914)
Born in Brooklyn, the daughter of an Episcopal priest, Crapsey made her living teaching classical studies. But for fun, she dabbled with a new form of poetry—the cinquain (a five-line, 22-syllable verse inspired by Japanese haiku). Crapsey's poems showed her love of the natural world; among her chosen topics are trees, fall leaves, and clean snowfalls. She also penned verses about national parks, including one entitled "The Grand Canyon" that refers to the national park as a home for characters from Greek mythology.

Crapsey died of tuberculosis in 1914, and the following year her first book of poetry, *Verses*, was published. Carl Sandburg—whose own home is now part of the National Park System—helped make her a mini-icon in his 1918 homage to her, titled simply "Adelaide Crapsey."

MARIANNE MOORE (1887–1972)
In 1922, Moore visited Washington's Mt. Rainier National Park, where she photographed Nisqually Glacier, took close-ups of alpine flowers, and explored the park's ice caves. When she returned to New York, Moore began working on an epic poem about Adam and Eve in Paradise. The result was "An Octopus." The piece was inspired by Mt. Rainier—she even referred to the peak as "an octopus of ice." In the poem, Moore used language from national park brochures and included glowing descriptions of lush meadows, chipmunks, and flowers, all existing within the shadow of a glacier. In the end, Moore concluded that happiness meant being unaware of the colossal dangers of being alive (like the animals and plants at Mt. Ranier were unaware of the possible danger posed by the glacier).

GARY SNYDER (1930–)
In the early and mid-1950s, beat poets Gary Snyder and Jack Kerouac served as fire lookouts in Washington's North Cascade Mountains (now a National Park Service complex). Kerouac

---

Wild mustangs roam Pryor Mountain Wild Horse Range on the Wyoming-Montana border.

reportedly couldn't wait to leave the remote area, but the land-scapes and isolation inspired Snyder to explore Buddhism and Eastern attitudes toward nature—and also to write. The most famous poem to come of out that experience was "Paiute Creek," a piece that talks about the Zen-like emptiness Snyder experienced while on his watches.

Today, many people consider Snyder to be the "laureate of deep ecology." This Pulitzer Prize–winning poet is nationally known as an environmental writer, poet, and activist.

* * *

U.S. WORLD HERITAGE SITES

UNESCO World Heritage Sites are those whose cultural and environmental histories the United Nations deems particularly important to humanity. There are 19 such sites in the United States, and 16 of them are administered by the National Park System:

- Carlsbad Caverns National Park
- Chaco Culture National Historic Park
- Everglades National Park
- Glacier National Park
- Grand Canyon National Park
- Great Smoky Mountains National Park
- Hawaii Volcanoes National Park
- Independence Hall (part of Independence National Historic Park)
- Mammoth Cave National Park
- Mesa Verde National Park
- Olympic National Park
- Redwood National Park
- Statue of Liberty National Monument
- Wrangell-St. Elias National Park
- Yellowstone National Park
- Yosemite National Park

The American alligator derives its name from the Spanish *lagarto*, or "lizard."

FROZEN IN TIME

*In a park in northeastern Arizona, prehistoric fossils and remnants of
ancient civilizations reveal what life was like thousands—
even millions—of years ago. Here are six things you may not know
about Petrified Forest National Park.*

1. ITS TREES MORPHED INTO COLORFUL STONE.

As they fossilized over hundred of millions of years, the forest's
trees turned to stone, and today, many of the logs lie where they
fell eons ago. They're also better preserved and more colorful than
those found anywhere else in the world. Southwest historian
Charles F. Lummis described the Petrified Forest as "an enchanted
spot…to stand on the glass of a gigantic kaleidoscope, over whose
sparkling surface the sun breaks in infinite rainbows."

2. IT WAS ONCE UNDER WATER.

In prehistoric times, the area of northeastern Arizona where the
Petrified Forest is located was closer to the equator and was not a
desert. It was a floodplain, swollen with streams and rivers. Cycads,
horsetails, and ferns dominated the landscape. Coniferous trees
were plentiful and large—a much as 200 feet tall and nine feet in
diameter. When those trees fell, rivers carried them away, and
before they could decompose, some were buried under clay, mud,
sand, and volcanic ash. Gradually, minerals in the water leeched
into the wood, filling the cracks and crevices of the logs and form-
ing the vivid fossilized logs we have today. Different minerals, of
course, made different colors: quartz produced white; manganese
oxides made blue, purple, black, and brown; and iron oxides turned
the wood yellow, orange, and red.

3. IT WAS HOME TO NORTH AMERICA'S OLDEST DINOSAUR. (We think.)

The Petrified Forest is home to all kinds of fossils, so many that
scientists are still discovering new (extinct) species there. Remains
of small dinosaurs, mammal-like reptiles, prehistoric crocodiles,
amphibians that weighed as much as one ton, and unusual fish
have been exhumed, along with the large predatory amphibian
Koskinonodon. With its flat head and upturned eyes,

Washington State's North Cascades Mountains are often called the "American Alps."

Koskinonodon probably stalked fish and small animals from a comfy spot in the mud at the bottom of ponds. But perhaps the park's most famous fossil is of a seven-foot-long carnivorous dinosaur nicknamed "Gertie." When Gertie's bones were discovered in 1984, they were estimated to be 225 million years old—at the time, the world's oldest dinosaur remains (older ones have been found since). Scientists tentatively classified her as a *Staurikosaur*, a smaller relative of the *Tyrannasaurus rex*, but when they examined Gertie's ancestry more closely, they discovered something surprising. She was a sort of prehistoric hybrid, possessing characteristics of both reptiles *and* dinosaurs. So the scientists gave her a new classification: *Chindesaurus*. And even though the experts continue to debate Gertie's age, many paleontologists classify her as the earliest dinosaur species in North America.

4. PEOPLE LIVED THERE, TOO!

Humans populated the Petrified Forest as early as 8000 BC and left behind many relics of their civilizations. The most remarkable are collections of petroglyphs dating to at least AD 1000. Anasazi Indians produced these rock carvings by scratching or chipping at dark rock to unveil its lighter surface underneath. Despite being exposed to hundreds of years of harsh sunlight, desert winds, and monsoon rains, many engravings remain intact.

The petroglyph art found in the Petrified Forest includes squiggles, stick figures, scenes, and complex geometric patterns. Their meanings generally confound archaeologists, but many believe the Anasazi—who had no other written records—used the pictures to communicate important information about their village and its residents. Many scientists speculate that the carvings may be maps, prayers, or even warnings that say, "Hey, foreigners, this is *our* village."

Two scientists—astronomer Robert Preston and his wife, Ann—think that some of the petroglyphs function as solar calendars. The Anasazi relied on the angle of the sun's light to tell them of impending season changes. When sunlight intersects with certain spirals and other carvings on the rocks, it acts like a sundial, letting the Anasazi know when the days would become longer or shorter and when they could start planting crops.

5. IT INCLUDES PART OF THE PAINTED DESERT.

The Painted Desert is made up of about 7,500 square miles of land in northern Arizona, from the Grand Canyon to the Petrified

Forest. It's a stretch of cliffs, hills, and hardened sand dunes that are "painted" with bright red, green, and yellow bands; many of the rocks also become red, purple, or blue at sunrise and sunset. The colors are the result of mineral deposits left behind by fossilized trees and animals and shaped by wind and water. As the cliffs erode, the fossils and minerals are exposed, changing the desert's colors.

6. THE HARVEY GIRLS ONCE WORKED THERE.

In the early 20th century, Route 66 was the best way to travel from the Midwest to California. The road stretched more than 2,000 miles from Chicago to Los Angeles, and by car, the trip took about one week each way. But this was a case of the journey being as exciting as the goal; for many people, the drive was a big part of the fun. As more people traveled along Route 66, gas stations, motels, and restaurants sprung up along the way to cater to travelers. Businessman Fred Harvey managed several of the restaurants. He began his career in the late 1800s, setting up restaurants along the Santa Fe Railway for travelers to the West. When automobile travel and Route 66 supplanted the railroad, he adapted. At first, Harvey hired young men to wait on customers. But those waiters turned out to be rude and rowdy, so Harvey decided to staff his establishments with a more civilized bunch: unmarried young women looking for adventure along the historic highway. They were called "Harvey Girls" and, between 1883 and 1968, hundreds of them served customers in Harvey's restaurants. One of those establishments was the Painted Desert Inn (today a visitor's center and gift shop at the Petrified Forest National Park). In 1947, Harvey Girls went to work in the inn's dining room, serving up milk shakes, burgers, coffee, and banana splits with a smile.

Petrified Forest National Park
Petrified Forest, AZ 86028

Founded: 1906
Area: 93,532 acres
Average annual visitors: 600,000

www.nps.gov/pefo

...32 species of reptiles, 26 species of land mammals, and at least 14 species of bats.

NATIONAL PARK
IQ TEST

Test your National Park IQ by matching the icons below to their parks.

A. Mesa Verde National Park

B. Zion National Park

C. Yellowstone National Park

D. Yosemite National Park

E. Hawaii Volcanoes National Park

F. Grand Canyon National Park

G. Denali National Park

H. Redwood National Park

I. Bryce Canyon National Park

J. Carlsbad Caverns National Park

K. Glacier National Park

L. Sequoia and Kings Canyon National Park

1. **Thor's Hammer:** This tall, skinny spire of a rock is called a "hoodoo" by the Paiute Indians, who believed that it and other similarly shaped hoodoos were ancient "legend people" who had been turned to stone for their bad behavior.

2. **Half Dome:** The 8,842-foot-tall granite cliff was sculpted into its unique shape about 70,000 years ago, when a passing glacier knocked out part of what was then a dome-shaped chunk of rock, causing it to split.

3. **Spruce Tree House:** A cliff dwelling constructed in the 13th century by the Anasazi of the Southwest, Spruce Tree House has approximately 130 rooms and is thought to have been home to about 80 people.

Bandelier National Monument (NM) has several thousand ancestral Pueblo dwellings.

4. Old Faithful: The famous geyser erupts every 35 to 120 minutes, spouting 200°F water 90 to 180 feet in the air. Eruptions last from a minute and a half to five minutes and release between 3,700 to 8,400 gallons of water.

5. General Sherman: If the General Sherman—one of the oldest giant sequoias alive today and the largest tree by volume in the world—were laid horizontally on a football field, with the top of the roots on the goal line, the top of the tree would stretch all the way to the nine-yard line on the opposite end.

6. Havasu Falls: These secluded 60-foot-tall twin falls in Havasu Canyon are accessible only by foot, horseback, or helicopter. Even though they're within the national park boundaries, the land actually belongs to the Havasupai Reservation. Nearly 650 Havasupai (People of the Blue-Green Waters) live inside the park.

7. Going-to-the-Sun Road: Completed in 1932, the road winds through 52 miles of high country in Montana, crossing the Continental Divide at Logan Pass, 6,646 feet above sea level. The road is open only from about mid-June to mid-October. Plows start clearing the heavy snow from the road as early as April, but it often takes two months to push away some drifts, which can be 100 feet tall.

8. Giant Dome: This 62-foot stalagmite was formed more than 750 feet below the surface of the earth in the Hall of Giants. The limestone rock that surrounds it is packed with ocean plant and animal fossils, left behind from the time before dinosaurs, when New Mexico was submerged beneath the sea.

9. Kolob Arch: The largest freestanding arch in the western hemisphere, at approximately 310 feet tall, Kolob Arch was carved out of the Navajo sandstone cliffs by centuries of wind and water erosion. The arch is accessible only via a 14-mile round-trip trail or by way of the Ice Box Canyon hike up and over steep surrounding cliffs.

Utah's Timpanogos Cave National Monument has three spectacularly decorated caverns.

10. **Devastation Trail:** This one-mile footpath runs through a forested area that was devastated by cinders falling from the lava fountains—as high as 1,900 feet—created by the Kilauea Iki crater eruption in 1959.

11. **Mt. McKinley:** The highest mountain in North America rises to a summit of 20,320 feet. Permanent snowfields cover more than half the mountain, which is so far into the clouds that it can only be seen from a distance one out of five days on average.

12. **Lady Bird Johnson Grove:** This ridgetop forest of old-growth redwoods was named after Mrs. Johnson by President Richard Nixon in 1969. In fact, he signed the proclamation dedicating the grove on a table made from redwood trees.

For answers, turn to page 387.

* * *

DELAWARE WATER GAP NATIONAL RECREATION AREA

Notable Achievement: Creating America's most expensive publicly funded outhouse

The recreation area, which is administered by the National Park Service, needed a new outhouse. The Park Service assembled more than a dozen designers, architects, and engineers and assigned them to the project—which took two years to complete. The final result: A beautiful "two-holer" (one for men, one for women) with a gabled Vermont slate roof, cottage-style porches with Indiana limestone railings, earthquake-proof cobblestone- and-concrete walls, and custom-built composting toilets that cost $24,000 each. Total cost for the two-hole privy: at least $333,000, which comes to $166,500 per hole. Portable outhouses used elsewhere in the park cost $500 each.

"We could have built it cheaper, yes," former park superintendent Roger Rector says, "but we wanted someone coming up the trail to encounter a nice restroom facility."

The Statue of Liberty's face was said to be modeled after the sculptor's mother.

SAVING THE TURTLES

In 1996, two Kemp's ridley sea turtles returned to Padre Island National Seashore to lay their eggs. The turtles, of course, remained calm and focused on the task at hand, but the marine biologist and park personnel who discovered them were overjoyed: the creatures were the first success stories in a decades-old attempt to rescue the endangered turtles.

L ocated off the southeast tip of the Texas panhandle, Padre Island became a national seashore in 1962. At 130,434 acres, it is the longest remaining undeveloped barrier island in the world and is home to hundreds of animals, including five of the seven endangered sea turtle species in the Gulf of Mexico: the leatherback, hawksbill, green, loggerhead, and Kemp's ridley. As humans develop the turtle's natural habitat along the U.S. and Mexican gulf coast, the animals' numbers have dwindled. Without safe habitats, the turtles have nowhere to lay their eggs, a fact that further threatens their survival.

LET'S HEAR IT FOR THE KEMP'S RIDLEY
The most endangered of the five species is the Kemp's ridley. In 1947, Mexican authorities counted 40,000 of them nesting in eastern Mexico in an area called Tamaulipas. Sixty years later, there were fewer than 4,500. So the folks at Padre Island decided to do something to save the animals.

Although the Kemp's ridley's primary nesting area is in Tamaulipas, the turtles sometimes come ashore on Padre Island. Because the area is protected by the U.S. government, it's a safe beach for the turtles to set up nests. Between 1978 and 1988, Texas scientists collected 2,000 turtle eggs each year from Tamaulipas and incubated them in a Galveston laboratory until they hatched. When they were big enough, they'd be released at Padre Island.

FREEBIRDS! (ER...TURTLES!)
The turtles spent several months at the lab. They lived in enclosures filled with Padre Island sand, because researchers think that turtles might recognize the chemical composition in the sand at their birthplace. (Turtles usually return to their own nesting

---

Visiting Maine's Acadia National Park? Whale-watching trips are offered in Bar Harbor.

grounds when it comes time to lay their eggs, though researchers are unsure why.) Because the chemical composition of the water also might play a role, the hatchlings took a dip in the gulf during their first days of life too.

When the turtles were between 9 and 11 months old, the researchers decided to release them into the gulf. At that age, they were big enough to avoid most predators and strong enough to survive on their own in the wild. Each baby was tagged, and then they were all carefully placed on the beach at Padre Island and guided toward the sea.

SWEET SUCCESS

No one knew if the project would work or if the turtles would come back to Padre Island. Plus, it takes turtles 5 to 15 years to reach sexual maturity, so the researchers were in for a long wait. Every year, the scientists hoped, and from 1983 onward, they had some circumstantial evidence that turtles were nesting on the island—researchers found 17 nests but didn't find the mother turtles. Then, in 1996, they got some hard evidence. That year, two Kemp's ridleys with tags (one from 1983 and one from 1986) were found nesting on Padre Island.

In the years since, more turtles have returned to Padre Island. In 2005, scientists found 28 tagged Kemp's ridleys making their nests on Padre beaches.

VISIT THE BEACH, SAVE A TURTLE

Today, park officials and scientists still protect and release Kemp's ridley turtles, and the visiting public is encouraged to help. Although rangers stress that tourists should not touch or otherwise interact with turtles they see (not only does this interrupt the animals' natural lifestyle, it's a felony), visitors can help the park service keep track of and protect the Kemp's ridleys by following several tips:

- People who see turtle tracks or live (or dead) turtles on the beach should tell a ranger.
- If you see a turtle nest, protect it from traffic. People walking along the beach can easily trample a nest, so place an identifying marker about one foot away to show visitors and rangers where it is.

- If you see hatchlings crawling toward shore, don't help them, but do protect them from traffic and other animals. If you can videotape or photograph them for rangers, all the better.

Scientists collect most of the eggs they find on the island's beaches and incubate them in a facility on-site until they're ready for release. Park visitors can watch these hatchlings return to the sea. Typically, releases take place on early summer mornings. You can even call ahead to find out release days and times, though these aren't guaranteed and park officials note that they do change the times if the turtles are ready for release sooner or later than planned.

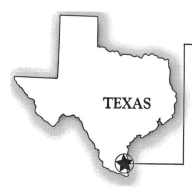

TEXAS

Padre Island National Park
Corpus Christi, TX 78480-1300

Founded: 1962
Area: 130,434 acres
Average annual visitors: 660,000

www.nps.gov/pais

* * *

HOW DID THE VIRGIN ISLANDS GET THAT NAME?
According to legend, in the 4th century, British Saint Ursula was on a pilgrimage. Her entourage included 11 ships, each filled with 1,000 virgin acolytes. However, Ursula was martyred when she refused to marry a Hun leader. (The exact number and fate of her followers in not recorded.) A church was built in their honor in Cologne, Germany. And the story goes that Columbus, who discovered the Virgin Islands during his second voyage in 1493, was reminded of Ursula and her virgins and, as a result, named the islands the Virgins.

THE BIG ONE

What is the largest volcano in the world?
Yellowstone National Park

SUPERVOLCANO

Beneath Yellowstone's meadows, hot pools, and mountain peaks lurks a molten monster. The entire park is a supervolcano, a volcano with the potential for massive eruptions.

Yellowstone's caldera, or crater, is one of the largest in the world. It encompasses 1,500 square miles. (By comparison, the Mt. St. Helens caldera is only two square miles.) The magma chamber that sits beneath the park and fuels its geysers, mud pots, and pools is three times the size of New York City. Bulges in the earth form and subside yearly, raising and lowering the elevation of the park's center. One bulge under Lake Yellowstone spilled water into a nearby meadow. The crater also leeches poisonous gases into the air—in 2004, those gases killed five bison near one of the geyser basins. "The beast," as geologists call the volcano's magma, is stirring.

APOCALYPSE NOW . . . OR LATER

In 2005, the U.S. Geological Survey said that Yellowstone had a high threat for volcanic eruption and ranked it 21st out of the 169 most dangerous volcanoes in the United States. This means that Yellowstone could erupt in the next few years—or not for 100,000 years. It may never erupt. Predicting volcanic activity is a tricky science. But the researchers do say this: Current geologic evidence suggests that Yellowstone erupts every 600,000 years. The last eruption was 630,000 years ago. Think about that the next time you take a walk by Old Faithful.

WYOMING

Yellowstone National Park
Yellowstone National Park, WY 82190

Founded: 1872
Area: 2,212,789 acres
Average annual visitors: 3,000,000

www.nps.gov/yell

The reddish color sometimes seen on snow at California's Lassen Volcanic National Park...

THANK
THE SHEEP

Denali might never have become a national park if it were not for a hunter's favorite species.

S AVE THE DALL!
Alaska's Denali National Park and Preserve is a wilderness area comprising almost 6 million acres—an area larger than Massachusetts. It's home to spectacular Mt. McKinley, which stands 20,320 feet high and is the tallest mountain in North America. There are more than 650 species of flowering plants and shrubs in Denali; expansive white and black spruce forests; miles of deciduous taiga forests; 39 species of mammals, including the endangered grizzly bear; and 166 species of birds, including the Alaskan ptarmigan and the golden eagle. More than 17 percent of the spectacularly scenic land is covered with eye-catching aqua-blue glaciers.

But these were not the wonders that motivated Charles Sheldon, the conservationist who led the campaign to preserve the land that is now Denali. Although Sheldon wrote appreciatively of the awe-inspiring natural beauty of the region, he was moved to convince the U.S. Congress and the Alaskan people to protect this pristine wilderness for one reason: the Dall sheep.

MOUNTAINS OF THE DALLS

Dall sheep are indigenous to the mountains of northwest Alaska, and today several thousand of the once-threatened species make their homes in Denali. But when Sheldon visited the area for the first time in 1906, he saw that the sheep's habitat was in danger. Population growth throughout Alaska was driving the sheep from their longtime habitats and forcing them to find new places to live. There weren't many homes that would work for the sheep, though. They need high, rocky precipices where they can hide from their numerous predators—grizzly bears, wolves, and coyotes—that can't negotiate the steep mountains the way the sheep can. Sheldon was afraid that, without those mountains, the sheep would eventually become extinct.

PRESERVING A SPORT

Sheldon was an avid hunter. It was his love of tracking big mammals that motivated his conservationism. With this spirit of outdoorsmanship, Sheldon began contacting legislators in Congress, appealing to them in person and via letters and newspaper editorials to save the Dall sheep and their habitat. Sheldon also marshaled the influence of his hunting group, the Game Committee of the Boone and Crockett Club, of which he was chairperson, to call on congressional representatives to save the Dall sheep.

A PARK BY ANY OTHER NAME

In 1917, Congress finally gave Sheldon what he wanted, naming the new park McKinley National Park after the popular president William McKinley who had been assassinated in 1901. The locals, however, called the region Denali, a native word meaning "the high one" (referring to Mt. McKinley). Sheldon pushed for the native name to be used for the park instead, but Congress refused.

For the next 60 years, environmentalists and native tribes continued to lobby to have the park's name changed to reflect its Alaskan heritage. Finally, in 1980, President Jimmy Carter signed the Alaska National Interest Lands Conservation Act. This act expanded the area of the original park and officially renamed it Denali National Park and Preserve. The growth in acreage (from the original 4,690,866 acres to the current 6,028,754 acres) increased the protected range of the Dall sheep, as well as the other species that call the park home.

A RECLUSIVE BUNCH

Most visitors to Denali will never see the animal that was the inspiration for the park, except maybe as white spots on a distant mountain range. Because of the harsh weather (snow sometimes falls in August) and the limited access to the park's interior (there is only one road that stretches a mere 90 miles into the park), most visitors never get close to the sheep's steep, rocky habitat.

The largest living mahogany tree in the United States is in the Everglades.

This is exactly as the curators of the park intend: as many as 5,000 Dall sheep continue to live and thrive in harmony with the Alaskan wilderness, undisturbed by Denali's more than 400,000 annual visitors.

Denali National Park
Denali Park, AK 99755-0009

Founded: 1917
Area: 6,000,000 acres
Average annual visitors: 400,000

www.nps.gov/dena

* * *

BUSY BEAVERS

In 1970, scientists at Quebec's Forillon National Park discovered a problem: only seven beaver colonies remained in the park, down from several hundred a few centuries before. Since the 1600s, beavers had been prized for their pelts. But uncontrolled trapping through the end of the 19th century caused serious declines in the number of beavers living in North America.

Today, Canadian beavers in general are protected by strict hunting regulations, and that has really helped the animals living in Forillon National Park. From just seven colonies in 1970, the beaver population grew to 46 colonies in 1996. With an average of four to six beavers per colony, the park's beaver population is 180 or more.

This is great news for the beavers and the other animal species that depend on them. Birds nest in beaver dams, brook trout thrive in areas where beavers clear away trees and brush, and predators like kingfishers and minks feed on the brook trout. But for park visitors, beavers can pose problems: in particular, dams built near trails or roads sometimes damage the paths. So park officials in Forillon spend a lot of time managing (and sometimes relocating) the park's beaver colonies. Busy, busy.

An episode of *The West Wing* was filmed in Catoctin Mountain Park, site of Camp David.

BETWEEN A ROCK
AND A HARD PLACE

Thinking of visiting Hawaii? Make sure that photos and memories are all you take home with you. Pele's watching . . .

Thousands of tourists visit Hawaii's scenic Volcanoes National Park every year, and every year a little bit of the park leaves with them. Many visitors can't resist taking a few of the park's unique lava rocks or a handful of dark black sand as a reminder of their visit to the island. No harm done, right?

Try telling that to Timothy Murray, one of many who have suffered terrible luck since taking home a memento from the park. "My life literally fell apart," says Murray, who naively scooped black sand into a soda bottle during a 1997 trip.

On returning home to Florida, Murray's luck took a sharp turn for the worse. He lost his job. His fiancée dumped him without warning. He began hitting the bottle. His pet died. FBI agents—who had received a tip from someone in Hawaii—arrested him for a minor computer copyright infringement violation. "The FBI agents said they never arrest people for what I did," says Murray. "They told me, 'You really must have pissed someone off.' After some research, I figured out who it was."

It was Pele.

LEGEND HAS IT

Here's the legend: Of all the deities in Hawaiian lore, the most well known—and most feared—is Pele, the fiery-tempered volcano goddess whom Hawaiians believe created their islands. Pele is the daughter of the earth goddess Haumea. According to myth, Pele spent most of her youth learning to make and control fire. But she was wild, and the sea goddess, Namaka, had to put out many of her mistakes. Haumea knew that Namaka would hunt Pele down and punish her, so she sent Pele to find a secluded home, where she could make as much fire as she pleased without disturbing anyone. Pele chose Hawaii—then only a tiny atoll—which she made to rise out of the sea in a storm of volcanic activity. But Namaka tracked

Mineral seepage creates the colors at Pictured Rocks National Lakeshore (MI)...

Pele down and confronted her. Fire and water clashed in a violent brawl. Namaka got the upper hand and banished Pele to Hawaii's volcanoes forever.

The hot-tempered goddess jealously guards her domain and takes out her anger at Namaka on the hapless humans who dare cross her. Hawaiians say that before every major eruption, Pele appears as a withered old woman walking along remote back roads. Those who pass her by find their homes destroyed by hot magma. However, those who offer her a ride find that a river of molten lava has stopped inches from their property. Many park visitors have reported meeting an old woman who asks for a cigarette, lights it with a snap of her fingers, and then vanishes mysteriously. Though Pele may like to tease humans playfully at times, she is dead serious about one thing: don't steal her stuff.

HAWAIIAN PUNCH

The stories of Pele's revenge on the tourists who make off with her rocks are many. Since pinching a few rocks, Denver business owner Larry Bell has needed emergency heart surgery, his marriage nearly fell apart, his daughter was plagued by mysterious health problems, and he had to relocate his business. One Los Angeles lava thief who was building a house watched helplessly as her basement floor caved in, her interior walls bent peculiarly, a worker drove a nail through his wrist, and her father-in-law fell off the roof and broke several ribs—all in the weeks following her return from the park. According to such "victims," Pele has made cars break down, brought down stock prices, torn Achilles tendons, and even steered lawn mowers over toes.

HOMEWARD BOUND

Can this horrible luck be reversed? Every day, shipments of contraband lava rocks, shells, and even old shoes filled with sand are delivered anonymously to the post offices and park stations around Volcanoes National Park. The packages come from all over the world, sometimes containing debris taken from the park decades earlier. Some former visitors are so terrified of Pele's curse that they return to the park in person just to make sure that their rocks are put back in the exact spot from which they were taken. One letter contained a single grain of sand, which the writer found in the cuff of a pair of pants he had worn while walking on the

...red and orange are copper, green and blue are iron, black is manganese, white is lime.

beach. In another letter, addressed to "Queen Pele, Hawaii," the writer's plea was simple: "Oh, please stop punishing me!"

ROAD TO RECOVERY

Most park rangers insist that there is no curse of Pele, that it's only natural that a small percentage of the many people who go through the park every year will suffer some misfortune after leaving. But there's no fooling Timothy Murray. "You may have your doubts about Pele," he says. "But let me tell you, when these things happen, you are willing to be on your knees in front of anyone or anything. Since I sent the sand back, I've started getting my life back. That's all I know." Murray's message to future park visitors: Beware Pele's wrath. Leave the rocks alone.

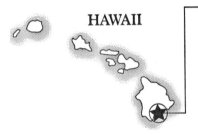

HAWAII

Hawaii Volcanoes National Park
Hawaii National Park, HI 96718

Founded: 1916
Area: 333,000 acres
Average annual visitors: 2,600,000

www.nps.gov/havo

* * *

ETERNAL FLAME

The only hotel at the Kiluea volcano is a lodge that has been open since 1846, when Benjamin Pitman Sr. built a grass shack on the Kiluea crater and named it the Volcano House. Over the years, the structure was enlarged and improved, and today it's built of wood and stone. But the most unique feature of the Volcano House is its lobby fire—called the "everlasting fire"—which has been burning continuously since 1877. George C. Jones, who owned the hotel at the time, lit the fire as a symbol of hospitality and the aloha spirit. When the hotel burned down in 1940, rescue workers salvaged embers from the everlasting fire; when Jones rebuilt the hotel the following year, the embers went into the new fireplace and the everlasting fire blazed again.

Porcupine babies are called porcupettes. They can climb trees within an hour of birth.

WHAT'S IN A NAME?

Just how do they go about naming those National Parks? A little history, some ingenuity, and a whole lot of imagination.

BRYCE CANYON NATIONAL PARK (UTAH)

Unka-timpe-wa-wince-pockich (or "red rocks standing like men in bowl-shaped canyon") was the name early Native Americans gave to Bryce Canyon National Park. According to legend, a coyote, angered by local residents, turned the citizenry into stone, resulting in the unusual rock formations found throughout the park. This changed when Ebenezer and Mary Bryce, a Mormon couple, traveled to Utah in 1875. They settled near the canyon, prompting their neighbors to call it Bryce's Canyon. Despite these names, modern geologists insist it's not actually a canyon at all, but a series of horseshoe-shaped amphitheaters.

CAPITOL REEF NATIONAL PARK (UTAH)

Even though most people considered south-central Utah a desolate wasteland, brothers-in-law Ephraim P. Pectol and Joseph S. Hickman saw beauty in the area's colorful canyons and sandstone cliffs. The men called the place "Wayne Wonderland," after the county in Utah where the site is located, and then lobbied hard to persuade the U.S. government to recognize the spot as a national monument. Finally in 1937, President Franklin D. Roosevelt complied. Geologists, however, soon replaced the name after studying the park's 90-mile reeflike chain of tall, dome-shaped cliffs. The scientists thought that the white sandstone peaks resembled the U.S. Capitol and renamed the park accordingly. But before Pectol, Hickman, or the government got involved, the Navajo had their own name for the area—"The Land of the Sleeping Rainbow"—because of its dramatic white and pink cliffs.

CITY OF ROCKS NATIONAL RESERVE (IDAHO)

As early as 1843, the City of Rocks was a landmark for pioneers looking for adventure and new lives in the American West. As they traveled along the California Trail, the men and women welcomed the sight of more than 100 granite rocks (some dating back 2.5 billion years) that signified they had almost finished their

The entire city of legendary Deadwood, SD, is a national historic landmark.

long journey. They called the place the City of Rocks. Located in southern Idaho, just two miles north of the Utah border, City of Rocks National Reserve still embraces adventurers: the 14,000-acre reserve is considered one of the premier rock-climbing sites in the world.

CUYAHOGA VALLEY NATIONAL PARK (OHIO)
Ohio's Cuyahoga Valley National Park got its name from the Native Americans. The Mohawk word *cuyahoga* means "crooked river." The 33,000-acre park located between Cleveland and Akron, Ohio, is named for the winding Cuyahoga River that meanders through the state. The river formed more than 10,000 years ago as glaciers receded, and it's so curvy that, even though it's 100 miles long, it covers only about 30 miles of land.

HALEAKALA NATIONAL PARK (HAWAII)
This park can thank the Hawaiian demigod Maui for its unusual name tag. In Hawaiian, *haleakala* means "house of the sun." According to legend, Maui believed that the people of Hawaii needed more daylight to live and work by. So he emerged from his hiding place underneath the roots of an ancient tree and lassoed the sun. Maui then took the sun prisoner, placing it inside a volcano in the hopes that daylight would last a little longer. Now dormant, that volcanic crater is called Haleakala, and visitors to its summit get spectacular sunrise views, as well as a panoramic view of the other islands.

SLEEPING BEAR DUNES NATIONAL LAKESHORE (MICHIGAN)
The Chippewa tribe of northern Michigan told a tale of Mother Bear, who lived with her two cubs in Wisconsin on the shores of Lake Michigan. Forced into the lake by a forest fire, the three bears swam for miles, with Mother Bear in the lead. When she finally reached the state of Michigan, at what is now Sleeping Bear Dunes National Lakeshore, she climbed a bluff to wait and watch for her cubs. But they never made it to shore. Mother Bear's heartache at the loss of her cubs so touched the Chippewa's Great Spirit that he created two islands to mark the spots where the cubs had disappeared. Blowing sand then covered the sleeping Mother Bear. Thus were created the dunes at Sleeping Bear and the North and South Manitou islands in the lake.

Minnesota's 47-mile Edge of the Wilderness Scenic Byway passes 1,000 lakes.

VOYAGEURS NATIONAL PARK (MINNESOTA)

Minnesota's Voyageurs National Park is a series of waterways that connects about 900 islands. The park was named after French Canadian canoe-men, known as *voyageurs*, who, during the 1800s, routinely traveled those waterways to get to Canada. The voyageurs were fur traders—mostly beaver—who sang songs as they rowed their canoes. This area, called the "Voyageurs Highway," was so well known that the treaty ending the American Revolutionary War recognized it.

YOSEMITE NATIONAL PARK (CALIFORNIA)

Before Yosemite Valley became Yosemite, it was called "Ah-wah'-nee" by Native Americans who lived in the area. (They called themselves Ah-wah'-nee-chees.) As settlers encroached on the tribe's land, many members left the area. One, Chief Teneiya, stayed and fought with the settlers until he was driven out of the area. He also named the valley Yosemite. According to Teneiya, a young brave was going fishing when a grizzly bear attacked him. He fought the bear with a tree limb until he finally killed it. Awed by the brave's prowess, his peers called him Yosemite, or "grizzly bear." Teneyia then adopted the moniker for the northern California valley where his tribe once lived.

HONORABLE MENTION: VALLEY OF TEN THOUSAND SMOKES (ALASKA)

In 1912, Novarupta, a volcano in southern Alaska, erupted. It was the largest eruption of the 20th century, and the volcano spewed ash as far as 100 miles away. In the days after the eruption, thousands of fumaroles—small openings in the earth's crust—vented steam and gases over a 40-square-mile valley covered, in some spots, in 700 feet of ash. When botanist Robert F. Griggs came to the valley in 1916 to survey it for the National Geographic Society, he wrote, "The whole valley as far as the eye could reach was full of hundreds, no thousands—tens of thousands—of smokes curling up from its fissured floor." The smoke finally stopped, but it took several years. In 1918, Congress declared the valley to be part of Katmai National Monument (it's now Katmai National Park and Preserve), in an effort to preserve the valley and its unique volcanic landscape. Today, the valley remains a barren vista of ash and volcanic rock, but it has proved useful over the years: in the 1960s, U.S. astronauts trained there for moon landings.

Fastest animal in the Western Hemisphere: the pronghorn antelope (up to 60 mph).

PARK LINGO

You can get along fine in the national parks with plain English, but some of the parks have their own jargon that's funny, slangy, or specialized. For instance: if you decide to hike part of the Appalachian Trail while a car carries your gear to a later meet-up spot, that's not backpacking— it's "slackpacking." Fill in the blanks here to find four more examples of colorful park lingo.

ACROSS
1 Discounted by
5 Carnival attraction
9 Midshipman
14 Most eligible, in a way
15 Work on copy
16 Asian noodles
17 Nervous
18 What to do when in doubt?
19 They turn blue litmus red
20 Slangy nickname for the mysterious sliding rocks in Death Valley
23 Genetic material
24 Org. that awards the Sullivan Trophy

Number of glaciers in Washington State's North Cascades National Park: 317.

25 Nickname for long, hollow pipes in Carlsbad Caverns

31 How Katie Couric is often described

35 Civil rights gp.

36 Word repeated in "Ring-around-the-rosey"

38 Diarist Anaïs

39 Bone: prefix

40 School subj.

41 Mambo cousin

43 Lilliputian

44 Old silo missile

46 Words of resignation

47 Old U.S. gas brand

49 Yellowstone GPS gadget named after a local slang term for tourists

51 South-of-the-border uncle

53 Cockney's abode

54 Climber's aid on some steep cliffs in Acadia National Park

62 Preminger and Klemperer

63 Cash register part

64 1934 Chemistry Nobelist Harold

65 Prepared to be knighted

66 To ___ (just so)

67 Give a hoot

68 Prescribed quantities

69 Take seriously

70 Noah count?

DOWN

1 "Stay" singer Lisa

2 Opposite of ecto

3 Utah's state flower

4 Prepare to break bread

5 Come up again, like onions

6 "___ thee . . ." (words to one kneeling)

7 Flintstone pet

8 Comment to a backstabber?

9 *The Devil Wears* ___ (2006 film)

10 Prepare to ice-skate

11 Middle East potentate

12 Nap sacks

13 USN rank

21 Place to be

22 Give off coherent light

25 Maine senator Olympia

26 Safari stops

27 Goes out with

28 Reggae fan, often

29 Songwriter's org

30 Kvetch

32 Utter boredom

33 Unbending

34 Govt. security

37 Blemish

42 Bridgelike water channel

45 Munsters bat

48 Lawrence portrayer

50 Like some oats

52 MIT and RPI

54 Pay-mind link

55 AAA's marked lines

56 Zion National Park's state

57 TV's Nick at ___

58 High spirits

59 Stalemate

60 Architect Saarinen

61 Deli loaves

62 Initialed

For answers, turn to page 388.

Grand Lake, in Colorado National Monument, is Colorado's largest natural lake.

THE COLTER STONE

*Does a carved stone found near Grand Teton National Park
clear up the mystery surrounding the travels of one of
the West's most famous mountain men?*

In 1931, while a farmer named Will Beard and his son Dick were plowing their hay fields near Tetonia, Idaho, they spotted an unusual-looking stone jutting out of the ground. "That rock looks like a head," Dick said. The Beards picked up the stone; it had a name and a date scratched into it: "John Colter" and "1808."

The Beards didn't know it, but John Colter was a mountain man, explorer, and fur trapper who'd traveled with Lewis and Clark on their exploration of the West. And the route he took during the trip that may (or may not) have given birth to the Colter Stone has long been the subject of debate and speculation.

ENTREPRENEURSHIP, WESTERN-STYLE

After Colter's job with Lewis and Clark ended, he fell in with a band led by Manuel Lisa, a Spaniard who was planning to set up a permanent fort and trading post in the Northwest for fur trappers. Lisa and his men, including Colter, established their base at the intersection of the Yellowstone and Bighorn rivers, near present-day Custer, Montana. But it was too late in the fall to start any beaver trapping, so they were left with just the trading post . . . and a problem—no customers.

Lisa sent three men into the winter wilderness to tell the American Indians who lived nearby that the post was open. One of them went south and east to the plains. Another went to a Crow lodge and stayed there all winter. The third, Colter, went north and west into the mountains. The journey took him 500 miles into the area that is now Wyoming, Idaho, and Montana.

Years later, Colter described that trip to his old boss, William Clark, while they were finishing up a map of the Northwest. Colter claimed to be the first white man to see the Grand Teton Range and what later became Yellowstone National Park, but he was fuzzy about the details. Historians think that claim was true and have long wanted to know exactly where Colter went that winter—which is where the Colter Stone comes in.

Utah's Rainbow Bridge National Monument is the world's largest natural bridge...

BACK ON THE FARM

One hundred years later, the Beards found the stone about 20 miles outside Grand Teton National Park and from the Teton Pass, which is where most people thought Colter crossed the mountains. At first, the Beards didn't know they had anything special. They kept the stone on their front porch for a while, until one of their neighbors, Aubrey Lyon, expressed an interest. Dick Beard had always liked Lyon's boots, so they swapped. A year later, Lyon donated the stone to Grand Teton National Park, where scientists examined it for authenticity. It was a 13x8x4-inch piece of rhyolite, a volcanic stone. The letters and numbers carved into the stone were weathered, proving that the stone hadn't been carved recently.

The Beards were interviewed, and it turned out they'd never heard of John Colter, so it was unlikely that they'd have forged the stone. Plus, they'd kept it on their front porch for two years, which doesn't make it seem like they thought they had something worth much. So historians formulated a theory that seemed reasonable: Colter, bored, sitting at the foot of the Grand Tetons, spent a little time carving a stone into a head shape and then signed it.

THE PROBLEM OF PROOF

Of course, that doesn't prove it's real. Most skeptics accept that the Beards didn't carve the stone, but they also think it's possible that someone other than Colter had carved it and left in on the Beards' property. We'll probably never know if the stone is authentic or not, but if you'd like to take a look for yourself, stop in at the Teton Valley Museum in Driggs, Idaho. In 2006, the folks at Grand Teton National Park donated the Colter Stone to the museum, and it's on display there every summer.

WYOMING

Grand Teton National Park
Moose, WY 83012

Founded: 1929
Area: 300,000 acres
Average annual visitors: 4,000,000

www.nps.gov/grte

...it's 275 feet wide and 290 feet tall. Native American tribes consider the site sacred.

MORE HOMES OF THE LITERATI

Thanks to the park service, you can always find these literary gents "at home."

C ARL SANDBURG NATIONAL HISTORIC SITE (FLAT ROCK, NORTH CAROLINA)
Born in Illinois in 1878, Sandburg quit school after the eighth grade to work at everything from milk deliveries and shoe shining to soldiering. Wanderlust took him across the West on freight trains before he eventually settled into a career as a journalist, writing poetry on the side. Published in 1914, his poem "Chicago" catapulted him to international fame.

Sandburg at Work: Sandburg's volumes of poetry, including *Chicago Poems*, *Smoke and Steel*, and *Good Morning, America*, were plainspoken free verse; his themes were the joys and struggles of the nation's working people. He found the common man's tragic hero in Abraham Lincoln, and wrote a six-volume biography of the frontier-born president. The last four volumes, *The War Years*, won Sandburg the 1940 Pulitzer Prize (he won a second Pulitzer in 1951).

Sandburg at Home: In 1945 Sandburg, his wife, Lillian, and their three daughters moved to an estate called Connemara on 240 acres in Flat Rock, North Carolina. They took along Lillian's herd of champion dairy goats and a library of more than 10,000 books. Sandburg, who'd written the definitive Lincoln biography, now lived in a home built in 1883 for Christopher Memminger, the secretary of the treasury for the Confederacy.

In 1968, Connemara became the Carl Sandburg National Historic Site, and today the public can experience what Sandburg called a "bracing clarity of mountain air" as they walk its five miles of hiking trails. The descendents of Mrs. Sandburg's goats still live in the dairy barn, but they're for petting rather than milking. A tour through the Sandburg home reveals simple furnishings, a homey kitchen, and, of course, a library containing thousands of books.

Picturesque pioneer homestead: the Faraway Ranch at Chiricahua National Monument.

EUGENE O'NEILL NATIONAL HISTORIC SITE (DANVILLE, CALIFORNIA)

Born in a Broadway hotel, Eugene O'Neill was the son of a Shakespearean actor and a mother who was still grieving over the loss of Edmund, the younger of Eugene's two older brothers. Edmund's death and the family's on-the-road life (Eugene's father spent most of his career touring with a play) threw the family into unhappy chaos and fed the "family curse" of addiction.

After O'Neill's own battles with alcoholism ended his education at Princeton, he worked at odd jobs and traveled the world as a sailor until tuberculosis forced him into a sanatorium. While he recuperated, he studied plays and tried his hand at writing them.

O'Neill at Work: In 1920, O'Neill's first three-act play, *Beyond the Horizon* (the story of two brothers in love with the same woman), opened on Broadway and won the Pulitzer Prize. He won the Pulitzer Prize again two years later for *Anna Christie* and a third time in 1928 for *Strange Interlude*. In 1936, he became the first and only American playwright to win the Nobel Prize.

O'Neill at Home: He may have been born in and spent much of his life in hotel rooms, but O'Neill always hated them. In 1937, with his Nobel Prize money, he and his third wife, Carlotta Monterey O'Neill, built Tao House (named for the Chinese philosophy and religion that influenced his work) near Danville, California. Spanish adobe on the outside, it was what Carlotta called "pseudo-Chinese" on the inside: Asian furniture, red doors, deep-blue ceilings, and black-stained floors. O'Neill wrote his best plays here, including the one that re-created his family tragedy: *Long Day's Journey into Night*.

In 1976, Tao House and its acreage became the Eugene O'Neill National Historic Site. Guided tours are available, but visitors have to take a National Park Service van to the site from Danville. Tao House holds an annual four-day festival in October celebrating O'Neill's life and work.

DAYTON AVIATION HERITAGE HISTORICAL PARK (DAYTON, OHIO)

Although it's primarily meant to honor the contributions of the Wright brothers, the Dayton Aviation Heritage Historical Park

---

Maryland's National Colonial Farm is a living history example of a 1770s tobacco farm.

also includes the final home of African American poet Paul Dunbar. Born in 1872 in Dayton, Ohio, Dunbar was the child of former slaves. His parents separated when he was very young, and his mother worked as a laundress to pay the bills. The family was poor, but Dunbar's mother, Matilda, stressed the importance of education. Despite her lack of schooling, she had taught herself to read, and she encouraged her son's interest in books and his dream of becoming a poet. With his mother's support, Dunbar went on to graduate in 1891 from Central High School at a time when many boys—black or white—didn't make it past the sixth grade. During his high school years, Dunbar was the editor of the school paper, was president of the literary society, and saw his poetry published in Dayton's newspaper, the *Journal*.

Dunbar at Work: After graduation, Dunbar took a job as an elevator boy in a local hotel. He sent out poems for publication but found that there were few literary opportunities for young African American men in the late 1800s. So he saved up and self-published his first volume of poetry, *Oak and Ivy*, in 1893. He sold the books to elevator passengers for a dollar each and used that money to pay for his second self-published book of poetry, *Majors and Minors*, in 1895.

That book contained two types of poems: the "major" poems were written in standard English, and the "minor" poems were written in an African American dialect. Dunbar considered the major poems to be his most important, but the minor poems delighted critics and the public and brought him his first taste of nationwide fame. His next book, *Lyrics of Lowly Life*, was a huge hit and made Dunbar America's first successful black writer.

Despite this success, Dunbar was never fully satisfied; he was disappointed that his serious poems were never fully appreciated during his lifetime. In the decades after his death in 1906, though, Dunbar's poems (the major and the minor) greatly impacted American literature. Poems like "The Haunted Oak" (portraying the horror of lynching) or "We Wear the Mask" (about victims of racism who hide their bitterness) are common reading in many college classrooms, and modern African American poets still look to Dunbar for inspiration—Maya Angelou took the title of her most famous book, *I Know Why the Caged Bird Sings*, from his work.

First president to call his Washington residence the White House: Theodore Roosevelt.

Dunbar at Home: In 1904, Dunbar bought a brick home in Dayton for himself and his mother. Matilda Dunbar lived there until her death in 1934, and she kept all of her son's possessions after he died of tuberculosis in 1906—including a bicycle that he'd bought from his Dayton pals, Orville and Wilbur Wright. In July 1936, the home became the Paul Laurence Dunbar State Memorial, the first state memorial to honor an African American. And in 2004, it was made a part of the NPS's Dayton Aviation Heritage Historical Park.

Visitors to the Paul Laurence Dunbar House can still see the poet's desk and the Remington typewriter he used to produce finished drafts. There are also 100-year-old scraps of paper covered with scrawled ideas and early versions of Dunbar's poems and stories.

* * *

SETTLING NICODEMUS

In 1877, with Reconstruction in full swing in the American South, an African American pastor from Kentucky named W. H. Smigh teamed up with a white land developer, W. R. Hill, to form the Nicodemus Town Company. Their goal: relocate African American Kentuckians to an all-black town in Kansas. Of course, they first had to establish and build the town.

Kansas was a logical choice: it had been a free state and the home of abolitionist John Brown. Plus the U.S. government was offering free land on the plains. By the summer of 1877, Smigh and Hill had convinced 300 African Americans to move to 161 acres in northwestern Kansas. They named their new town Nicodemus.

By the mid-1880s, Nicodemus was a small but thriving town. Although there were many white-owned businesses in the town center, several others were owned and operated by black residents. By the 1920s, more than 600 people lived in the town.

Today, Nicodemus is still populated predominantly by African Americans. It became a national historic site in 1996 and holds the distinction of being the only town west of the Mississippi River that was founded for and by former slaves.

BATTLEFIELD ANGEL

She was a Civil War nurse, the founder of the Red Cross, and the person responsible for the United States signing the Geneva Convention. Today, her former home—also the first Red Cross headquarters—is a National Historic Site in Glen Echo Park, Maryland.

Clarissa Harlowe Barton, born in 1821, was the youngest of five children. She was shy and timid, but events would soon draw her out. Her aptitude for nursing emerged early; when she was 11, one of her brothers was seriously injured in a fall, and she devoted two years to his care and recovery. Since most of Clara's education came from her older siblings, it must have seemed natural to her at age 15 to start a school at her father's Massachusetts mill and teach the workers' children. Over the next 15 years, Clara taught in many schools throughout the Northeast.

IT'S THE PRINCIPAL OF THE THING

In 1851, some businessmen persuaded Clara to open a school in New Jersey. When enrollment topped 600, the city fathers decided to hire a man as principal because they believed it was too much for a woman to handle. Clara quit in disgust but shortly thereafter suffered a nervous breakdown. She soon recovered and moved to Washington, D.C., where she was hired as a recording clerk in the U.S. Patent Office. Clara was the first woman hired by the Patent Office, and she received the same salary as the men working there.

CLARA GETS HER WINGS

When the Civil War began in 1861, the first major confrontation between the Confederate and Union armies took place at Bull Run, just outside Washington. The battered Union army was forced into a headlong retreat. Casualties began arriving in Washington hospitals, and it became clear that the Union army hadn't allocated adequate resources to treat them.

Clara decided to help alleviate the shortages by advertising for donations of food, clothing, and medical supplies. The response was overwhelming, so Clara set up a warehouse and began distributing the supplies. Although women were not allowed anywhere near the battlefields, a year into the conflict, Clara received permission from the surgeon general to travel wherever the troops went; this made her the first woman on the front lines of battle in a major conflict. She was granted a general pass "for the purpose of distributing comforts for the sick and wounded, and nursing them." Clara often rendered assistance to wounded soldiers during the heat of battle. Once, while giving water to a wounded soldier, a bullet passed through her sleeve and killed the soldier. The number of casualties overwhelmed doctors, and the wounded had to wait hours, sometimes days, for treatment. Clara helped wherever she could; once, she removed a bullet from a soldier's face using only her pocketknife.

CIVIL SERVANT EXTRAORDINAIRE

In 1864, Clara was made superintendent of nursing for the Union army. Clara helped care for the wounded of both sides, though, and even visited Confederate field hospitals to provide them with supplies and assistance. One newspaper called her "the true heroine of the age, the angel of the battlefield"—a phrase that was used to describe her for the rest of her life.

After the war, President Lincoln asked Clara to set up an office to help locate missing soldiers. She was the first woman to head a government bureau and ran the Missing Soldier's Office for four years, answering more than 63,000 letters and determining the fate of more than 22,000 men. She interviewed returning soldiers to obtain information about the missing and succeeded in reuniting many soldiers with their families. She compiled lists of the killed, wounded, and missing, and had those lists published in newspapers. She even traveled to the infamous Confederate prison at Andersonville to identify and mark the locations of buried soldiers. Nearly 13,000 graves were identified and the prison was transformed into a national cemetery.

The sign and files from Clara's office were recently found in the attic of a building scheduled for demolition. The artifacts now reside in the Lincoln Museum at Ford's Theatre.

HOW CLARA SPENT HER SUMMER VACATION

Clara had worked very hard during and after the Civil War, and her health was failing. In 1868, she suffered another nervous breakdown. Her doctor advised her to rest, so she went to Europe in 1869 for a vacation. While in Geneva, Switzerland, she was contacted by the International Red Cross, who wanted her to help persuade the United States to sign the Geneva Convention of 1864, which, among other things, provided protection to those who cared for the sick and wounded during wartime.

Clara was also asked to aid in the Franco-Prussian War. She distributed supplies and provided relief in war-torn areas of France and Germany and was awarded the Iron Cross by Kaiser Wilhelm. By the time she returned home, she was more exhausted than she had been before her departure. She suffered a third nervous breakdown, and this time, she temporarily lost her eyesight.

CRUSADES AND CROSSES

By 1877, Clara was able to begin the fight to have the 1864 Geneva Convention signed by the president and ratified by the Senate. She wrote articles, made speeches, and lobbied Congress. It was an uphill battle because of the Monroe Doctrine, which prohibited treaties and alliances with Europe. President James Garfield promised to sign it, but he died before he got the chance.

In 1881, Clara created the American Red Cross. She organized a national office and local chapters in cities across the United States. President Chester Arthur finally signed the 1864 Geneva Convention in 1882, and the United States officially became a member of the International Red Cross.

Clara ran the Red Cross for 23 years, during which time she expanded its role to help civilians in war as well as victims of natural disasters. She was often at the forefront of relief efforts for epidemics, tornadoes, droughts, floods, fires, and hurricanes throughout the United States. She also stressed the importance of educating victims to look after themselves. This evolved into what became known as "first aid" and helped create the original first-aid kits. She established first-aid training as one of the core responsibilities of the Red Cross.

CLARA STARTS TO SLOW DOWN

When Clara was 77, she went to Havana, Cuba, at the start of the Spanish-American War to care for sick and wounded soldiers and to provide relief to civilians. She worked 16-hour days delivering supplies by mule wagon and providing medical care to soldiers living in camps rife with dysentery, typhoid, malaria, and yellow fever.

She wrote several books, including *History of the Red Cross* (1882) and *The Red Cross in Peace and War* (1899), as well as a famous poetic tribute to Civil War nurses, "The Women Who Went to the Field."

RED CROSS REBEL

Clara was outspoken and self-reliant. She refused government funding for the American Red Cross because she didn't want to relinquish any control to bureaucrats. Many of her subordinates criticized her authoritarian management style and accused her of mismanaging Red Cross funds.

Finally, after the attacks became too much to bear, Clara Barton resigned as president of the Red Cross in 1904. She was bitter about her treatment, saying, "The government I thought I loved and loyally tried to serve has shut every door in my face." In 1912, she died of pneumonia at the age of 91. It's not surprising that her last words were purported to be "Let me go! Let me go!"

The American Red Cross currently has eight regional centers and more than 800 local chapters that collect, process, and distribute blood and blood products to hospitals and medical centers through the efforts of 35,000 employees and nearly 1 million volunteers. The American Red Cross supplies nearly 50 percent of the blood and blood products used in the United States. Quite a legacy for a shy girl from Massachusetts.

A HISTORIC SITE

Barton's Maryland home became a National Historic Site in October 1974, the first National Historic Site dedicated to a woman. Today, 11 of the house's 38 rooms have been restored, including Barton's bedroom and the original Red Cross offices, and visitors to the site can take a guided tour to learn how Clara Barton lived, what kind of work she did during her lifetime, and what contributions she made to humanitarian causes around the world.

MARYLAND

Clara Barton National Hisoric Site
Glen Echo, MD 20812

Founded: 1974
Area: 8.59 acres
Average annual visitors: 13,000

www.nps.gov/clba

The Buffalo National River (AR) is one of the nation's few remaining unpolluted rivers.

GOLD IN THEM THAR RAILS

In Promontory, Utah, a golden spike completed the
transcontinental railroad . . . or did it?

T**HE RACE IS ON!**
Abraham Lincoln had two major goals for the Union: to preserve it, of course, but also (as a former railroad lawyer) to connect the country from coast to coast by rail. On July 1, 1862, President Lincoln signed the Railroad Act, which launched the "Great Railroad Race," placing two companies in competition to lay the most railroad track west of the Missouri River.

Laying track across miles of rugged frontier, however, seemed a risky proposition to most investors of the day. Willing to take the risk were California's "Big Four": Charles Crocker, Collis Huntington, Mark Hopkins, and Leland Stanford. Collectively, they formed the Central Pacific Railroad; Oliver Ames and Thomas Durant headed the Union Pacific Railroad in the Midwest.

The Railroad Act granted the builders a 400-foot right-of-way and financed the construction with 30-year loans for each mile laid. The Union Pacific (UP) would start in Omaha, Nebraska, and work its way west; the Central Pacific (CP) would run from Sacramento, California, to wherever the two lines met.

MISSION IMPOSSIBLE

A lot of people thought that Lincoln had funded a lost cause. The railroad required nearly 2,000 miles of track, and each mile would take at least 100 tons of rails and two to three tons of spikes—not to mention carts, shovels, axes, and blasting powder. The CP had its materials shipped by boat from the East Coast around the tip of South America; the UP had to import 2,500 wooden railroad ties for each mile and haul them to the treeless prairies of the Midwest until the line reached the Black Hills of Wyoming.

Central Pacific work crews had to tunnel through solid granite in the Sierra Nevada. Rotating shifts worked 24 hours a day, but on

The perforated rock walls of Natural Bridges National Monument are in southeastern Utah.

some days—as they blasted or hand drilled through the rock—progress could only be measured in inches. The UP work crews faced a guerrilla war against the Plains Indians who were defending their bison hunting grounds. Sioux and Cheyenne regularly attacked workers and supply lines and sabotaged the "iron horses" by removing railroad tracks or laying barriers across them to derail locomotives.

Even the weather worked against the project. In the Sierras, railroad workers died in blinding snowstorms and killer avalanches. In the Wyoming desert, they collapsed in 110-degree heat. But the crews kept going, and in 1867, after the Central Pacific conquered the Sierras, the railroad race really heated up. Both companies constructed two to four miles of track a day as they headed for Utah.

WHERE THE HECK IS PROMONTORY SUMMIT?

As the two railroads got closer, they ignored the original goal. Trying to claim as much of Utah as they could, each company graded about 200 miles of *parallel* railroad near the Promontory Mountains. At this point, President Ulysses S. Grant ordered the railroad executives to decide where the railroads could meet—before the government did it for them.

After some intense wrangling, UP and CP decided to meet at Promontory Summit, an obscure area populated by sagebrush and scrub cedar, giving the CP 960 miles of track and the UP 1,086 miles.

GOOD PR

On May 10, 1869, America was ready to celebrate perhaps the greatest technological feat of the century. The desolate countryside near Promontory Summit filled with crowds of sightseers and newspaper reporters. Government and railroad officials arrived—by train, of course—and the CP's Jupiter locomotive faced the UP's No. 119, only one rail apart.

Leland Stanford of the CP brought to the ceremony a railroad tie made of laurel wood and a silver-plated sledgehammer. The famous golden spike was one of four spikes that were made for the occasion.

Telegraph wires were wrapped around the spike and sledgehammer so that the signal from the blows would be transmitted instantaneously. Cannons in San Francisco and New York would be fired when the signal came in.

The three main bridges have names: Kachina, Owachomo, and Sipapu.

It was the country's first international media event, but some players weren't ready for prime time. Up until a few moments before the ceremony, Stanford and Durant squabbled over who would drive in the last spike. Since the UP had more miles of railroad line, Durant wanted the honor of driving in the last spike; Stanford argued that the CP was first to begin construction on the railroad and should finish it. Eventually they settled things: Leland Stanford drove in the golden spike, the telegraphs sent out the message "Done," and the railroads were united from coast to coast.

Well, not exactly.

MYTH TAKE ONE
Once the golden spike (which was really 17-carat gold alloyed with copper) was pounded in, the laurel tie and the four spikes were immediately pulled up and distributed among the executives; an ordinary wooden tie and iron spikes were put in place. Both Durant and Stanford swung at the last iron spike and missed. The crowd roared with laughter, and that's when the telegraph operator sent out the message "Done!" The country celebrated the joining of the railroad while two construction supervisors pounded in the last spike.

MYTH TAKE TWO
However, the "coast-to-coast" railroad wasn't quite finished. There was no railroad bridge across the Missouri River until three years later, so travelers from New York were ferried across the river from Council Bluffs, Iowa, to Omaha, Nebraska, where they could continue by rail to California.

HE HAD A DREAM
Lincoln's dream of uniting the country by rail had come true. The Pacific railroad's passenger service cut the time for a trip between San Francisco and New York from more than four months to one week. By 1880, the railroad carried $50 million worth of freight annually.

GOLDEN SPIKE HISTORIC SITE
In 1957, Congress created the Golden Spike National Historic Site to preserve and restore the Promontory Summit area. Replicas of Jupiter and No. 119 (both scrapped in the early 1900s) were intro-

duced to the park in 1969 on the centennial of the railroad's completion. Every Saturday during the summer, the locomotives face each other once again as volunteers in costumes reenact the ceremony of the Golden Spike. (The actual spike is on display in California at the Stanford University Museum.)

Golden Spike National Historic Site
Brigham City, UT 84302

Founded: 1957
Area: 2,735 acres
Average annual visitors: 40,000

www.nps.gov/gosp

UTAH

* * *

SING, SING A SONG
"Oh, Shenandoah" is one of America's most easily recognized folk tunes and has been recorded by more than 250 artists, including Bob Dylan and the Mormon Tabernacle Choir. Although they don't know for sure, many people (mostly guys and gals who study folklore) think that "Oh, Shenandoah" was originally a sea chantey composed by French-Canadian voyagers. By the 19th century, it had achieved widespread popularity on land and at sea, and its lyrics first appeared in print in an 1882 *Harper's New Monthly* magazine article titled "Sailor Songs."

* * *

"A visit [to the national parks] inspires love of country; begets contentment; engenders pride of possession; contains the antidote for national restlessness . . . He is a better citizen with a keener appreciation of the privilege of living here who has toured the national parks."

—**Newton B. Dury, former NPS director**

Chiricahua National Monument (AZ) has spectacular balanced rocks, spires, and pinnacles.

THE GREAT PIG WAR

San Juan Island National Historic Park is one of many islands that dots Puget Sound, which separates Washington and Canada. Today, it's a popular tourist destination, most notably for whale watching. But more than a century ago, it was a pig that thrust San Juan Island to the center of the world stage.

RUDE AWAKENING

In 1859, Lyman Cutlar was a potato farmer living on San Juan Island. On the morning of June 15, he was startled out of bed by the sound of grunts coming from his potato patch. He got up, grabbed his rifle, and went to investigate. What Cutlar saw incensed him: in the middle of his field was a giant black boar munching on his newly planted tubers. And next to the fence stood a man laughing at the spectacle. Cutlar raised his rifle, took aim, and shot. The pig fell dead; the man ran into the woods.

That would be the only fatality in a tense standoff that nearly brought the United States and England into a full-scale war.

THIS LAND IS OUR LAND

After winning the Revolutionary War against England in 1783, the United States started expanding west, embracing the belief that Americans had a divine right to all lands from the Atlantic to the Pacific. The Louisiana Purchase of 1803 added more than 800,000 square miles extending from the Mississippi River to the Rocky Mountains. The Mexican-American War of 1846 further expanded the nation all the way to California.

That same year, America and Great Britain signed the Oregon Treaty, which set the international boundary between the United States and western Canada, which was governed by the British at the time. According to the treaty: "The boundary shall be continued westward along the forty-ninth parallel of north latitude to the middle of the channel which separates the continent from Vancouver's Island, and thence southward through the middle of said channel, and of Fuca's Straight, to the Pacific Ocean."

Although this wording may sound thorough, it wasn't—especially the phrase "in the middle of the channel." San Juan Island sat in the middle of that channel, and there were two

---

The ocean off the Outer Banks has been called "the Graveyard of the Atlantic."

navigable channels on opposite sides of it: the Haro on the west and Rosario to the east. Britain claimed Rosario as the border, making the island British territory. The Americans claimed it was the Haro, making the island American territory.

TENSION MOUNTS

While the diplomats argued, both sides staked their claims. Hudson's Bay Company, owned by England, turned the 55-square-mile island into a giant sheep ranch. Sixteen Americans also settled on San Juan, including Lyman Cutlar. The governor of Oregon Territory had (mistakenly) assured him that San Juan belonged to the United States. Therefore, as an American citizen, Cutlar (mistakenly) thought he was entitled to 320 acres of free land under the Donation Land Claim Act of 1850. But because the ownership of the island was under dispute, the Claim Act did not apply.

Cutlar's nearest neighbor was Charles Griffin, an Englishman who managed Hudson's Bay's giant sheep ranch. Griffin also owned a few pigs, which he allowed to roam freely. After all, as far as he was concerned, the island belonged to the British.

The two sides shared an uneasy peace for a few years . . . until Cutlar killed Griffin's pig. The American farmer offered $10 compensation for the deceased pig, but Griffin scoffed at the paltry price and demanded $100. Cutlar wasn't about to pay such a huge sum for a pig that trespassed on his land. He replied, "Better chance for lightning to strike you than for you to get a hundred dollars for that hog!" Both men took their complaints to their respective governments.

SETTING THE PIECES

Griffin called on Sir James Douglas, governor of British Columbia, who sided with his countryman. Years earlier, Douglas had publicly opposed the Oregon Treaty, believing that the Columbia River—which lies many miles to the south and now separates Washington from Oregon—should have been the border between the two countries. Unhappy with the upstart Americans living on "his" island, Governor Douglas ordered Cutlar to pay the $100.

Cutlar told the governor where he could stick his order and walked away. He was, after all, an American citizen, and San Juan Island was in the United States of America! Douglas issued a warrant for the potato farmer's arrest.

The grim total of vessels lost near Cape Hatteras is estimated at over 2,000.

Cutlar ignored the warrant (he was never arrested) and complained to General William S. Harney, commander of the U.S. Army's Department of Oregon. Harney was a hothead, and he hated the British as much as Governor Douglas hated the Americans. Harney sent his best officer, Captain George Pickett, to occupy the island. Pickett landed on San Juan in July 1859 with 461 soldiers. They built a fort, brought in their artillery, and prepared for battle. Pickett proclaimed the island United States territory and appointed himself the sole authority. Meanwhile, Governor Douglas warned the British Foreign Office, "The whole of San Juan Island will soon be occupied by a squatter population of American citizens if they do not receive an immediate check."

CHECK

The British sent five warships and 2,000 soldiers. Undeterred, Harney ordered Pickett to stop the British from landing, and to open fire if they tried. Pickett pledged that he would fight to the last man.

Governor Douglas ordered his navy to take San Juan by force, but British Rear Admiral Robert L. Baynes, who commanded the British fleet, was the only one of the bunch with a knack for diplomacy: "I refuse to involve two great nations in a war over a squabble about a pig!" So Baynes kept his men on the ships, their guns pointed at the American fort. Both sides were ready to fight, but neither wanted to fire the first shot. So there they stayed, waiting.

Back in Washington, D.C., the standoff—now more than two months old—was treated with the utmost importance. With the threat of a civil war looming, no one wanted to go to war with England again. President James Buchanan dispatched his best negotiator, General Winfield Scott, who had previously mediated two disputes over the U.S.–Canadian border, one at Aroostook, Maine, and the other at Niagara Falls.

TO THE RESCUE

General Scott arrived in October to find Captain Pickett and his men tired, anxious, and with itchy trigger fingers. He met with General Harney and told him, "Resign or get fired." Disgraced, Harney left the island.

Next, General Scott met with Governor Douglas. They came to a stalemate as to the true ownership of San Juan Island but agreed on a joint occupancy until an international arbiter could be

---

The Pony Express operated for only 18 months, from April 1860 to October 1861.

brought in to settle the matter. The British fleet sailed away, and most of the American troops withdrew, as did Lyman Cutlar, who found that living on San Juan Island was far more trouble than it was worth. Each side left a symbolic token force, who shared an uneasy peace for more than a decade.

THE FINAL OINK

Thirteen years passed before the matter was finally settled. Who did England and the United States get to solve the problem? Kaiser Wilhelm I of Germany. He agreed to serve as their neutral arbiter and appointed three experts to examine the evidence. In October 1872, the German leader finally rendered his verdict: "The boundary line shall be drawn through the Haro Channel." The kaiser gave San Juan Island to the United States.

As for the wayward pig that started the whole fiasco . . . it's assumed he ended up on either Cutlar's or Griffin's dinner table.

WASHINGTON

San Juan Island
National Historic Park
Friday Harbor, WA 98250

Founded: 1966
Area: 1,725 acres
Average annual visitors: 250,000

www.nps.gov/sajh

* * *

WHY DID THE CRICKET CROSS THE ROAD?

If they're Mormon crickets, they're probably just trying to get to the tasty crops on the other side. "Mormon crickets" are actually insects called katydids—large, flightless grasshopper-like insects that swarm across roads through the summer in the western states. These agricultural pests can form such large swarms that the road appears to move and change colors where they cross.

Amistad National Recreation Area is near Del Rio, Texas. *Amistad* means "friendship."

MUIR MUSINGS

Often called the "Father of the National Parks,"
John Muir had a lot to say about himself,
the American people, and the natural world
he wanted to protect.

"I have always befriended animals and have said many a good word for them. Even to the least-loved mosquitoes I gave many a meal, and told them to go in peace."

"God has cared for these trees, saved them from drought, disease, avalanches, and a thousand straining, leveling tempests and floods; but he cannot save them from fools; only Uncle Sam can do that."

"Most people are on the world, not in it—have no conscious sympathy or relationship to anything about them—undiffused, separate, and rigidly alone like marbles of polished stone, touching but separate."

"Pure wildness is the one great want, both of men and of sheep."

"In every walk with Nature one receives far more than he seeks."

"One touch of Nature makes the whole world kin."

"After a whole day in the woods, we are already immortal."

"Most people who travel look only at what they are directed to look at. Great is the power of the guidebook maker, however ignorant."

"I might have become a millionaire, but I chose to become a tramp!"

World's largest urban national park: the Golden Gate National Recreation Area.

BORN A SLAVE

*In February 1988, the National Park Service declared the
Washington, D.C., home of famous orator Frederick Douglass to be a
National Historic Site to honor a man who was a hero to slaves and
an inspiration to abolitionists.*

Frederick Douglass, born Frederick Baily in 1818 in Easton,
Maryland, saw his mother only a few times in his life. They'd
been separated early, and the little boy was raised by his
grandmother, Betsy Baily. He never met his father, though it was
rumored that it was his white owner, Aaron Anthony.

HOOKED ON READING
When he was six, Frederick's grandmother brought him up to the
"big house" to work. His engaging personality got him assigned to a
cushy house position at the home of Hugh and Sophia Auld,
relatives of his owners. The bright-eyed boy managed to charm his
new mistress, too: seeing how excited Frederick got when she read
the Bible to him, Sophia taught him to read. Her husband put a
stop to the lessons, but by then it was too late—Frederick was
hooked. He used the little money he earned doing odd jobs to buy
tracts that denounced slavery. By age 13, Frederick knew he had to
fight for his freedom.

BREAKING A SLAVE BREAKER
When Aaron Anthony died, his "property" was divided up, and
that meant Frederick's entire family was split up. Worst of all, since
the grandmother Frederick loved above anyone else was considered
too old to work, the slavemasters pushed her out of her little cabin
in front of Frederick's very eyes. They built her a tiny mud cabin in
the woods and left her there to die alone. Witnessing his grandmother's banishment added more fuel to Frederick's antislavery fire,
and as he became more rebellious, his masters were determined to
break his spirit.
    They sent him to Edward Covey, who was known as a "slave
breaker." On one hot August afternoon, after months of continual
whippings, Frederick lost his patience. As Covey prepared to whip
him after tying him to a post, Frederick grabbed the slave breaker

by the throat. Two hours of hard fighting later, Covey gave up. At age 16, Frederick had discovered a great truth. "Men are whipped oftenist who are whipped easiest." Never again would he let himself be abused without a fight.

ANNA VS. FREEDOM
Frederick was eventually sent back to work for Hugh Auld, and he also began to meet secretly at night with free blacks to read and debate. It was here that he met Anna Murray, fell in love, and experienced his first moments of true happiness. But it wasn't enough; he'd already decided to run away. An earlier escape attempt had landed him in prison. If he was caught again, he'd surely be hanged or sold into what he called a "living death"—as a slave in the Deep South, from which there was little hope of escape.

TRAVELING THE OVER-GROUND RAILROAD
No matter. He was determined to make it to the free state of Pennsylvania. Not an easy task—professional bounty hunters patrolled the free state borders, and free blacks had to carry official papers. Frederick charmed a friend into loaning him his documents and boldly bought a train ticket to Philadelphia. He boarded his train to freedom and quivered as a railroad official checked his documents. Even though he didn't fit the description on the official papers, he was allowed to cross over into Philadelphia and then New York City in 1838.

A friend with the Underground Railroad gave him shelter in New York and helped Anna Murray travel east, where the pair was married. To make it more difficult for his former masters to find him, he took on a new last name—Douglass.

Frederick and Anna soon settled in the port city of New Bedford, Massachusetts, where Frederick immediately got involved in abolitionist causes. When the famed white abolitionist William Lloyd Garrison saw Douglass speak at a meeting, Garrison realized Douglass's potential and hired him. For the next 10 years, Douglass toured for the American Anti-Slavery Society, transferring the magnetic power of his personality into passionate antislavery lectures that would sway thousands to his cause.

$700 AND CHANGE
But Douglass wasn't convinced that his audiences truly understood the horror of slavery. He needed to tell people exactly what it was

like, so—despite the near-certainty that it would result in his recapture—he published his autobiography in 1845. The book, called *Narrative of the Life of Frederick Douglass*, was a huge success. Douglass was invited to speak all over America and in England about abolition. He was so popular in England that a group of fans collected enough money to buy his freedom—$714. Frederick Douglass was free at last.

PEACE, BUT NOT AT ANY PRICE

Among his most impressive exploits—and there were plenty— Douglass convinced President Lincoln to make emancipation a moral cause of the Civil War. Under his urging, Lincoln refused to sign a peace accord with the Confederacy during the Civil War that would leave slavery intact. Instead, Lincoln chose to continue the fight and to allow African American soldiers to fight for the Union Army—setting into motion a chain of events that would finally see slavery abolished in America.

But nothing he did for the abolitionist cause would make him as famous as when he married his white former secretary, Helen Pitts, in 1884, after Anna died. The interracial marriage—not even 20 years after the Civil War—set off a storm of controversy, which Douglass shrugged off. He'd honored his mother's race by marrying Anna, he said. All he was doing by marrying Helen was paying homage to his father's race.

Frederick Douglass died of a heart attack in 1895, a great American writer, speaker, and thinker to the end.

Frederick Douglas National Historic Site
Washington, DC 20020

Founded: 1988
Area: 8 acres
Average annual visitors: 23,000

www.nps.gov/frdo

...says one visitor, but the 2,040-acre park is "peaceful and pretty."

A BOY AND HIS BUS

*In 1992, an abandoned bus on the Stampede Trail just outside
Denali National Park became the final resting place of
Christopher Johnson McCandless. But the bus (and McCandless)
traveled a long road to that infamy.*

A ROAD TO NOWHERE

A miner named Earl Pilgrim blazed the Stampede Trail in the 1930s. Originally, it led to claims Pilgrim had staked at Stampede Creek, located at the foot of the Kantishna Hills just inside Denali's boundary. As Pilgrim's mining business became more successful—he was the state's primary producer of antimony, a chemical used in flameproofing, paints, ceramics, and enamels— he realized that he needed a reliable way to transport goods to the Parks Highway (which runs from Fairbanks to Anchorage) and beyond.

Fortunately, the State of Alaska intervened and, in 1961, hired a building and construction company called Yutan Construction to turn the primitive Stampede Trail into a road. This proved impossible. Bogs along the route and flooding from melting permafrost made the road impassable during the spring and summer. So in 1963, Yutan and the state abandoned the project. To their credit, Yutan workers managed to construct a 50-mile, unpaved backcountry road that extended about 30 miles beyond Denali's entrance. But they failed to build permanent bridges over the primary waterways—the Savage, Teklanika, and Sushana rivers. This made Pilgrim's mines nearly inaccessible, and he closed them in 1970. With the mines no longer in operation, the land was reclaimed by locals, who used it to hunt bear and moose in the fall and to snowmobile and ski in the winter.

IF YOU LEAVE IT, THEY WILL COME

Yutan, however, did leave behind a reminder of its construction days. A bus, called Fairbanks bus #142, had housed construction workers on the project. When Yutan left the area, the company also left the bus near the end of the Stampede Trail (just 25 miles west of Healy, Alaska) to serve as an emergency shelter for hunters and trappers. Thirty years later, it became the resting place of a young traveler named Christopher Johnson McCandless.

Two-thirds of Americans can't see the Milky Way from their yards. But you get a great view...

MCCANDLESS GOES INTO THE WILD

McCandless gained fame in the mid-1990s when author Jon Krakauer chronicled his story in an article for *Outside* magazine and later a book called *Into the Wild*. But when he took off for Alaska, McCandless was just a recent college graduate with a desire to get back to basics. The 24-year-old set out on a cross-country trek in 1990. His travels began in Georgia, where he'd gone to college. He packed up his old yellow Datsun and headed west with few supplies and little knowledge of life in the wilderness. When his car broke down, McCandless walked or hitchhiked, eventually arriving at Denali in April 1992. He set off on the Stampede Trail and got to bus #142 on April 28. His intentions, he wrote to an acquaintance, were simple: "To live this life for some time to come. The freedom and simple beauty of it is just too good to pass up."

Unprepared for the Alaskan wilderness, McCandless ran into trouble right away. It was cold on the trail, even in the spring, but he'd brought only a small supply of clothing, a handmade sleeping bag, and a thin tent to keep him warm. He also carried a .22-caliber rifle and a backpack containing 10 pounds of rice and several books. He had no map and no compass.

IN THE BUSH

He also had a journal, and for the next 113 days, McCandless kept detailed records of his life in bus #142. According to his notes, he hunted and foraged for food, surviving off of rose hips, berries, squirrels, spruce grouse, ducks, and porcupines. Once, he managed to poach a large caribou, but the animal succumbed to maggots before he could preserve it.

By July 3, McCandless was ready to return to civilization. But he was in a bind. The Teklanika River, which he'd easily crossed in April while it was frozen, had become a torrent, flowing heavily with glacial water that prevented him from following the same route out as he had coming in.

Uncertain of where to go, McCandless returned to the bus and waited for help as his meager supplies continued to diminish. He got weaker by the day, and the entry for his 100th day was bittersweet. He wrote, "DAY 100! MADE IT! But in weakest condition of life. Death looms as serious threat. Too weak to walk out."

McCandless died soon after. One month later, on September 6, 1992, hikers traveling the Stampede Trail found his body and the

---

...from Nevada's Great Basin National Park, one of the darkest parts of the country.

bus that had served as his home. Doctors said he'd died from starvation around August 18. But many wilderness experts agree that he likely wasted away after consuming either poisonous vegetation or hallucinogenic plants. Krakauer believes McCandless died from eating the poisonous seeds of the so-called Eskimo potato, a fleshy green-and-white plant with colorful flowers about one inch across. Although the tubers of this plant are edible, they have to be boiled first, a wilderness technique most people agree McCandless wouldn't have known.

BACK AT THE BUS

Today, bus #142 remains a popular hiking stop and has become an unofficial shrine to McCandless. Outside the rusted vehicle, the ground is littered with bones from the game he killed to survive, and the inside still contains his boots, patched jeans, and books. Visitors can also see a suitcase his parents left behind when they came to pay their respects; it's filled with survival gear. Those who pass through take what they need and leave behind what they can spare.

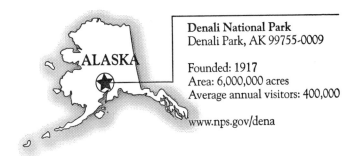

Denali National Park
Denali Park, AK 99755-0009

Founded: 1917
Area: 6,000,000 acres
Average annual visitors: 400,000

www.nps.gov/dena

* * *

The original 1917 designation of Denali National Park included only a portion of Mt. McKinley within the boundaries. In 1978, President Jimmy Carter declared the mountain itself a separate national monument, and reverted to the native name, calling it Denali National Monument, even though U.S. maps today label the peak as Mt. McKinley.

Herbert Hoover's expertise as a mining engineer made him a millionaire by age 40.

ORIGIN OF
THE WHITE HOUSE

The White House (which the National Park Service calls "President's Park") is more than just a building—it's an important national symbol and one of the most recognizable structures in the world. How much do you know about its history? Here's an introduction.

BOOM TOWN

When the Founding Fathers began making plans for the nation's capital city in 1789, they couldn't agree on a location. The northerners wanted a northern city to serve as the capital; the southerners wanted a southern city. Finally, they compromised: instead of establishing the capital in an existing city, they'd create a new one.

On July 12, 1790, President George Washington signed a law declaring that on "the first Monday in December 1800," the government would move to a new Federal District "not exceeding ten miles square . . . on the river Potomac." Philadelphia would serve as a temporary capital until then.

LOCATION, LOCATION, LOCATION

But the act didn't say exactly *where* on the Potomac the new city should be. A lot more arguing took place before the government finally agreed on a 69-square-mile area of farmland and swamps in Maryland just over the Potomac from Arlington, Virginia.

Maryland and Virginia donated the land, and President Washington hired an engineer to lay out the new city and appointed three federal district commissioners to oversee the work. One of their first decisions was to name the new city "Washington, D.C."

Since the idea of a president was so new—most European countries were still ruled by royalty—nobody really knew what a president's house should look like. So in 1792, Thomas Jefferson took out a newspaper ad offering $500 to the architect who came up with the best design for a president's house (George Washington would make the final decision).

Big Bend, Texas, is mountain lion country, especially around the Chisos Mountains.

A LITTLE HOME IN THE COUNTRY

George Washington admired the work of architect James Hoban, an Irish immigrant who had designed South Carolina's state capitol. Washington encouraged Hoban to enter the contest . . . and then chose his design.

Hoban imagined a three-story mansion and included plans for wings that could be added on later when the time came. (They were never built.) He set the dimensions of the presidential palace at 170 feet long, 85 feet deep, and three stories high. Washington thought Hoban's building was beautiful but too small. He suggested increasing its size by about 20 percent. But that was too expensive, so his suggestion was politely ignored.

HOUSE PAYMENTS

Hoban estimated that the president's house would cost about $400,000 to build, but no one knew how to pay for it. Washington thought he could raise the money by selling lots in the federal district. But building an entire city from the ground up, in the middle of farmlands and swamps, for a republic barely 10 years old, seemed such an impossible undertaking that many people doubted whether the city would ever really be built. In fact, the new city was the laughingstock of New York and Philadelphia; the state of Pennsylvania had even begun building its own permanent federal buildings in the expectation that Washington, D.C., would eventually be abandoned.

In the face of such skepticism, the few lots that sold were at much lower prices than anticipated. So planners had to cut corners. The third floor of the president's house was eliminated, as were the north and south porticoes (large, columned overhangs planned for the front and rear of the building). The marble fireplaces were replaced with ones made of wood. The "presidential palace" was becoming less palatial.

BUILDING THE HOUSE

The cornerstone for the president's house was laid on October 13, 1792 (nobody knows for sure where—the exact location wasn't recorded), and work on the four-foot-thick outer walls began. They were built by masons and slave laborers, all of whom lived in shanties on the property because there was no other place for them to live. (At one point, a brothel was even set up on the White House grounds for their "convenience.")

The exterior would be faced with freestone, a form of sandstone that can be cut like marble. But freestone is also porous and susceptible to water damage, so the masons sealed the stone with a wash of salt, rice, and glue. It was the building's first coat of white paint; soon it would be nicknamed the "White House."

STOP AND GO

Work on the White House had more than its share of problems. Despite all the cuts that had been made, it was still way over budget, and when Congress learned in 1798 how much money had been spent, it refused to pay any more. When the roof was finished, the building was sealed up and abandoned. It sat empty for more than a year until new funds could be raised to pay for the interior.

THE WET HOUSE

When work resumed, an architect named Benjamin Henry Latrobe examined the building and found that the structural timbers had been exposed to so much cold, dampness, and rain during the seven years of construction that they were now dangerously decayed. But there was no money to replace them, so Latrobe repaired them as best he could and work on the house continued.

By now the White House was hopelessly behind schedule. "We do not believe it will be possible to prepare the building for the reception of the President until October or November next," the commissioners wrote in February 1800.

FIRST NIGHT

George Washington didn't live to see the White House completed. He left office in 1797 and died two years later, at about the same time the exterior walls were finished.

The White House was still unfinished when Washington's successor, John Adams, moved in on November 1, 1800. The rest of the federal government—which consisted of 130 employees—moved to the new capital a month later.

A WORK IN PROGRESS

"Unfinished" is the polite way to describe the condition of the White House. The roof leaked, the ceilings were crumbling, and the windows were so loose that rain and wind blew into just about every room. "Not one room or chamber is finished," First Lady

Nine U.S. parks, preserves, and recreation areas have geysers and hot springs.

Abigail Adams wrote. "It is habitable only by fires in every part . . . This is such an inconvenience that I know not what to do!" The White House didn't even have an enclosed yard, so Abigail hung her wet laundry in the unfinished East Room.

The exterior looked even worse. There was trash everywhere, the workers and slave laborers were still living in shanties on the lawn, and it would be nearly a month before the White House had an outhouse.

IN AND OUT

But the Adamses would suffer for only four months. In 1800, Adams lost the presidential election to his political rival, Thomas Jefferson, who preferred to stay at Monticello (his Charlottesville, Virginia, estate) whenever possible. But still, Jefferson did a lot to improve the White House. He removed the shanties, landscaped the grounds, installed a fence, and filled the mansion with fashionable furniture.

By the time Jefferson left office in 1809, the White House was a comfortable home, though not by today's standards—there was no electricity, no telephone, no central heating, no air-conditioning, and only the most primitive system of running water. There weren't even any closets (in those days, few people owned more than a cedar chest full of clothes, and built-in closets were unheard of).

But by 19th-century standards, the White House would do just fine . . . though not for long. In 1814, British soldiers burned it to the ground, leaving the mansion's white stone walls an empty shell. President John Madison quickly had the home rebuilt just as it had been before the war. Though it has been improved in the nearly 200 years since then, the White House has for the most part retained the same look and feel of its initial construction.

WHITE HOUSE FACTS:

- It's 55,000 square feet and six stories high; most of this is underground.
- There are 35 bathrooms inside the White House.
- It takes 570 gallons of paint to cover the building's outside walls.

FromMaine to Georgia, the Appalachian National Scenic Trail passes through 14 states.

- The White House was one of the first federal buildings to be made wheelchair accessible—to accommodate President Franklin D. Roosevelt.

- In June 2006, a 100-year old elm tree that had been planted during Theodore Roosevelt's presidency was destroyed in a thunderstorm. The tree appears on the back of the $20 bill.

To read more about the White House, turn to page 248.

To read more about the White House, turn to page 248.

Presidents Park (White House)
Washington, D.C. 20242

Founded: 1790
Area: 82 acres
Average annual visitors: 1,200,000

www.nps.gov/whho

* * *

SID MEIER'S GETTYSBURG!

Yes, yes, the exclamation point in the title is a little much (it makes it seem like a bad Broadway musical, with Robert E. Lee played by Nathan Lane), but this is one of the very best examples of the historical genre. Creator Meier (who was already a legend to historical game buffs via his "Civilization" series), has painstakingly re-created the circumstances of the Battle of Gettysburg, a pivotal clash during the American Civil War. Players can take either side to seize the high ground and hold it, re-living select battles or the entire Gettysburg campaign. (If you play as the Confederates, mind you, additional and fictional storylines open up if you win.) Can't get enough? There's a sequel that takes on Antietam.

Pinnacles National Monument is a release site for the endangered California condor.

SERVING IN
THE SIERRAS

*The Buffalo Soldiers were an elite fighting group that earned more than
20 Medals of Honor, the most of any U.S. military unit. Their bravery
when fighting in Cuba during the 1898 Spanish-American War made
them national heroes. But few people know that these veterans also
made their mark as peacetime protectors of America's national parks.*

On July 28, 1866, the post–Civil War Congress established
six all-black regiments in the U.S. Army: two cavalry units
(the 9th and 10th Cavalry Regiments) and four infantry
divisions (consolidated in 1869 into the 24th and 25th Infantry).
Civil War veterans, freemen, and former slaves formed the regiments, and despite racism (which often left black military units
underequipped, ill housed, and poorly fed), these troops served
with distinction in several American wars.

They were nicknamed the "Buffalo Soldiers" by Native
Americans who fought the 9th Cavalry in 1871 during the Indian
Wars. The Kiowa tribe thought the soldiers' black, curly hair and
fierce fighting style emulated buffalo on the open prairie, and the
nickname stuck.

THE BUFFALO HUNT FOR SHEEP

In 1890, when Congress created Sequoia and Yosemite national
parks, there was no National Park Service, and there were no park
rangers to protect the wilderness and its visitors. So from 1891 to
1914, rotating regiments of the U.S. Cavalry patrolled Yosemite,
Sequoia, and General Grant (later Kings Canyon) National Parks.
For three of those years (1899, 1903, and 1904), the Buffalo
Soldiers got the assignment. They built and maintained roads and
trails, protected the fragile grasslands from ranch sheep and cattle,
and guarded native animals from poachers and forests from loggers
and fire.

Few historic records remain to document the day-to-day work of
the Buffalo Soldiers' national park assignments, but one faded
black-and-white photograph exists that shows five uniformed 24th

Infantry soldiers in Yosemite. The men are wearing slouch hats and sport rifles slung over their shoulders as they pose in the Yosemite wilderness. Reproductions of this photo are among the most popular in the park's historic collection.

THE FIRST BLACK SUPERINTENDENT
In 1903, the 9th Cavalry guarded both the Yosemite and Sequoia parks. Its mission was to enforce Department of the Interior regulations that the park be protected from "injury and depredations."

In April, some troops from the 9th Cavalry were sent to Yosemite. Others, led by Captain Charles Young (one of only a few black U.S. Army officers at that time), were assigned to Sequoia and General Grant, but the arrival of President Theodore Roosevelt delayed their departure. While Roosevelt was in San Francisco, Young and his men became the first black troops to serve as an American president's Guard of Honor. Six days later, the soldiers began a 16-day, 323-mile journey to Sequoia National Park. There, Captain Young became the acting superintendent of Sequoia and General Grant National Parks, making him the first and only African American to hold that position.

PEACETIME GLORY
Like all the military regiments stationed in the parks, the 9th was responsible for building and maintaining roads and trails. In 1903, Sequoia was already 13 years old, but its roads and trails were still so underdeveloped that few tourists were able to visit. Since 1900, the Army had been building a wagon road to the Giant Forest, home to four of the five largest sequoias in the world. But they'd made little progress: only five miles of that road had been constructed. That changed when the Buffalo Soldiers arrived.

Like his troops, Captain Charles Young met tough challenges with determination. The son of former slaves, Young was only the third black cadet to graduate from West Point, a school where African Americans were so unwelcome that 47 years passed before another black student was admitted and graduated. In Sequoia, Young set his disciplined soldiers to work and recruited local civilians to help. That summer, they laid more road than in the three previous years combined. By mid-August, wagons were carrying visitors up a new winding road that led to the giant sequoias and ended at the famous Moro Rock. Automobiles soon

---

...a 123-foot sand dune on the southern shore of Lake Michigan.

followed. The cavalrymen also built a fence around the General Sherman Tree (the world's largest tree) to protect its roots from being trampled by the tourists. Today, the road that Young and the Buffalo Soldiers built is still used by visitors as the Sequoia hiking trail.

In 1904, another group of cavalrymen went to work in Yosemite. They established a 75-acre arboretum (that has since merged with the forest around it) with trails that led to 36 different kinds of trees. By the time all the Buffalo Soldiers left the Sierras that summer, their efforts had greatly improved California's parks.

REDISCOVERING THE SHADOW SOLDIERS

For more than 80 years, the Buffalo Soldiers' stint as park rangers was forgotten. That changed in 1999 when Shelton Johnson, an African American park ranger, found the now-famous photograph of the Buffalo Soldiers in the Yosemite research library. Inspired, he researched historical documents and decided to bring the men to the public's attention.

Today, Johnson performs reenactments that detail the life of a Buffalo Solider working in Yosemite National Park. His program, called *Yosemite Through the Eyes of a Buffalo Soldier*, is presented throughout the year. Johnson has been praised, not only for highlighting a nearly forgotten part of American history but because that history encourages minorities to recognize and enjoy their connection and contribution to the American wilderness.

CALIFORNIA

Yosemite National Park
Yosemite National Park, CA 95389

Founded: 1890
Area: 761,266 acres
Average annual visitors: 3,300,000

www.nps.gov/yose

Most mountainous state in the U.S.: Nevada, with more than 300 mountain ranges.

LET 'ER VIP!

*In this case, a VIP is a "Very Important Person" who
works as a national park volunteer.*

The Volunteers-In-Parks (VIP) program invites people from
all over the United States to help the National Park
Service protect and preserve America's national treasures—
in many cases doing jobs that wouldn't be done at all otherwise.
Since Congress established the program in 1970, millions of
volunteers have performed essential services for the parks. Job
descriptions include helping build or maintain trails, planting trees,
greeting the public, teaching about exhibits at museums, doing
archaeological fieldwork, or dressing in costumes for living-history
demonstrations—jobs for all ages and for any talent or skill.

VIP ARTIST
Take Donald Davidson of Washington, D.C., who's been putting
his talent as a botanical artist to use for the National Park Service
since 1999. Davidson hikes into areas like Shenandoah National
Park, White Sands National Park, Big Bend National Park, and
Big Thicket National Preserve, where he paints spring and fall
wildflower blooms. Many of his illustrations are on permanent
display at the parks.

VIP RESCUERS
Volunteers at Mt. McKinley—with skills in emergency medicine,
rock climbing, winter camping, and mountain rescue—help Denali
National Park rangers maintain a permanent station on the
20,320-foot mountain during peak climbing season. Jennifer Dow,
a medical doctor and volunteer medical director at Denali, is just
one of the VIPs who go out on search-and-rescue missions and also
educate the public on safety.
 Another Denali VIP and an expert mountain climber, John
Roskelly, participated in the rescue of three South Korean park
visitors in May 1992. The three campers were out in a blinding
blizzard in an area of the mountain known as the West Buttress
when a snow hill collapsed and sent their campsite into a 60-foot-
deep crevasse. The one member of the party who escaped the fall

---

Women's Rights National Historical Park is at Seneca Falls, in upstate New York.

hiked down to the rangers' station for help. Roskelly was the volunteer member of the rescue party who climbed down ropes to dig out one of the trapped men and then discovered the other under the snow. All members of the party made it out alive.

NO EXPERIENCE NECESSARY

Most volunteers don't have the abilities of Dow or Roskelly, but their services are just as appreciated. At the Petrified Forest National Park in Arizona, for instance, volunteers can work at the visitors' center, the Rainbow Forest Museum, or in the wilderness areas. The VIPs are provided with housing and can explore the park when it's closed to visitors.

Parks that don't provide housing do provide campsites with RV hookups. One couple camped at the Platte River for six weeks while working at Sleeping Bear Dunes National Park, registering campers, doing head counts, patrolling the trails and beach, and canoeing in the river to patrol for illegal fishermen. During another season, the two worked in a part of the park known as South Manitou Island, giving lighthouse tours.

THE NSS VIPs

The National Speleological Society (NSS) helps restore caves throughout the park system. Before Mammoth Cave—the longest known cave system in the world, with more than 300 miles of underground rivers, rooms, and tunnels—became a national park, it had been built up as a tourist attraction, complete with electric lights, metal fencing, and wooden walkways. In 2001, a team of volunteer spelunkers started dismantling and removing the old eyesores. The work was hard, dangerous, and cold. Volunteers trekked as far as two miles into the caves and often worked while standing in underground water in pitch-black darkness, cutting up rotten wood into manageable pieces, bagging debris, and hauling it out. They pulled down fences and removed long-unused cables and light fixtures. Their work saved an estimated $250,000 that the National Park Service wouldn't have been able to afford in the first place.

ARE YOU VIP MATERIAL?

Whether they're restoring the environment by cleaning up a cave or washing graffiti off petroglyphs, or cataloging archive material,

VIPs know they're making a difference. In 2005, the National Park Service reported that 137,000 volunteers had contributed time and effort worth $92.1 million. Since its inception, the VIP Program has encouraged interested individuals, clubs, and organizations to come help save America's treasures.

You can explore VIP opportunities at the National Park Service's Web site at www.nps.gov/volunteer.

* * *

GOLD BEYOND THE TRAIL

In 1896, a Native American named Skookum Jim Mason discovered gold in the Klondike River in Canada's Yukon Territory. The discovery sparked a frenzy in the United States the next year as prospectors packed up and headed for Canada.

Many prospectors traveled overland or by sea to the town of Skagway, in southern Alaska. There, they began a 600-mile trek to the Yukon's Dawson City, the spot near the confluence of the Yukon and Klondike rivers where gold was being panned. To get there, though, they had to traverse the rugged Chilkoot Trail, a 33-mile pass through the Coast Mountains that border Canada and Alaska. The Chilkoot Trail was the most direct route from the United States to the Klondike, but it wasn't an easy one. The pass through the mountains was nearly a vertical climb, and 1,500 steps were carved into the ice to help travelers reach the top. Pack animals couldn't navigate the steep, rocky terrain, so prospectors had to carry all their gear and supplies themselves; often they made several trips. Starvation and hypothermia were common problems along the trail, and of the nearly 100,000 people who tried to make it through the mountains, only about 30,000 actually succeeded.

Today, the Chilkoot Trail is a hiking route for adventurers wanting to retrace part of the prospectors' path. It's managed jointly by the National Park Service and Parks Canada and, in the United States, is part of the Klondike Gold Rush National Historic Park in Skagway, Alaska. The trail begins in the town of Dyea (about three miles from Skagway), travels over the Chilkoot Pass, and into Canada. It's a difficult hike, reserved primarily for experienced mountaineers, requires a permit (available at the Trail Center in Skagway), and takes three to five days to complete.

A MONUMENTAL TASK

*What weighs 80,000 tons, towers 555 feet over the nation's capital,
has 897 steps to the top, is made of 36,491 stones, and can boast with
certainty that George Washington never slept there?
The Washington Monument National Memorial!*

Surrounded by flags at its base, one for each of the 50 states,
the white marble obelisk is the jewel in the crown of the
National Mall—but it took a surprisingly long time for the
nation to build it.

DESIGN DEBATES

After the War for Independence, the Continental Congress made
plans to honor General George Washington. As early as 1783,
there was a plan for an equestrian statue of Washington to be
placed near the Capitol building—once they figured out where the
capital city was going to be. But the capital moved several times,
making it difficult to find a good spot for a tribute.

After Washington died in 1799, Congress again made noises
about erecting a monument in his honor and settled on a tomb in
the Capitol building. But Washington's heirs did not want to move
his remains, which stayed firmly planted in his tomb on the
grounds of Mount Vernon, his home in Alexandria, Virginia.

As the 100th anniversary of Washington's birth approached,
there was a push to memorialize the first president. Congress
coughed up $5,000 in 1832 for a marble statue intended for the
Capitol rotunda. However, artist Horatio Greenhough's creation—
a 20-ton seated seminude figure—wasn't exactly what most folks
had in mind. This statue ended up at the Smithsonian Institution
in 1908.

In 1833 George Watterson, a former Librarian of Congress,
formed the Washington National Monument Society, whose
purpose was to finally erect a fitting memorial. The society held a
design competition, won by architect Robert Mills. His plan was
much more elaborate than the current simple obelisk. Mills wanted
an even bigger obelisk surrounded by a colonnade, which was to be
interspersed with statues of other Revolutionary War heroes and
capped by a classically inspired statue of a toga-clad Washington

The two most endangered mammals in North America...

driving a chariot. There were even plans to entomb the remains of these heroes in underground catacombs. But money—and enthusiasm—were short-lived. In 1848, the society decided to just build the obelisk and worry about the colonnade later. Excavation was begun later that year, and the cornerstone was laid on the Fourth of July.

BUILDING AND STUMBLING BLOCKS

The society encouraged all states and territories to donate memorial stones to be used in the interior walls of the monument. Donations poured in from other sources as well, including blocks from Native American tribes, private businesses, and even foreign countries. Perhaps the most well-known memorial stone came in the early 1850s from Pope Pius IX: a marble stone that had been part of the Temple of Concord in Rome. In March 1854, however, members of the Know-Nothings (an anti-Catholic, anti-immigrant political party) stole the stone and allegedly threw it into the Potomac River.

Donations to the society began to dry up in 1854, and Congress was reluctant to help. The nation was embroiled in controversy over slavery. Social turmoil and economic uncertainty stalled the plans. The monument would stand unfinished for more than 20 years as the country went to war with itself and then struggled to put itself together again.

MONUMENTAL MAKEOVERS

After the Civil War ended, Congress appropriated $200,000 to resume construction of the Washington Monument. Plans for the colonnade were finally scrapped, and the size of the obelisk was changed to make it conform more to classical Egyptian proportions. Construction began again in 1879. The new architect, Thomas L. Casey of the U.S. Army Corps of Engineers, incorporated the original donated memorial stones in the interior walls. The first memorial stone to be placed was the Alabama stone. The last two stones to be placed were installed in 1882: the Alaska stone, which is made of solid jade, and another stone donated by the Vatican to replace the original that was pilfered. The monument was opened to the public on October 9, 1888. It typically has more than 800,000 visitors each year.

...are the black-footed ferret and the Florida panther.

In 1997, the Washington Monument closed down to undergo a huge restoration effort. Scaffolding enfolded the exterior so the outside could be cleaned and repaired. On the inside, the masonry and historic donated stones were restored. On the practical side, the elevators, heating, and cooling systems were upgraded. The new elevator cab features glass panels so riders can view the commemorative stones on the 180-, 170-, 140-, and 130-foot levels. The elevator takes viewers to the top in only 70 seconds, but the ride down takes 138 seconds so people can see the stones in more detail.

DID'JA EVER NOTICE?

Because the monument was left unfinished (at about 150 feet tall) for so long, it is actually two colors. Even though the same type of stone was used after construction resumed, it had to be mined from a different quarry, and the white shade could not be matched exactly. If you look closely, you can see the change in color about a third of the way up.

**Washington Monument
National Memorial**
Washington, DC 20024

Founded: 1884
Area: 106 acres
Average annual visitors: 467,000

www.nps.gov/wamo

* * *

PENNY FOR YOUR THOUGHTS?

Did you know that there are 56 steps to the top of the Lincoln Memorial, one for each year that Lincoln lived? Most Americans have a picture of this memorial in their desk drawer: it is depicted on the back of the penny, but you might be hard-pressed to count the steps there.

Into spelunking? You can find caves to explore in 19 different U.S. parks and preserves.

THE ORIGINAL
TREE HUGGER

In the 1850s, a miner and mountain man named Galen Clark set up a homestead in the Yosemite Valley and began a life as one of the area's most ardent advocates.

GO FOR THE GOLD

Galen Clark journeyed to California's Mariposa County in 1853 after hearing stories of miners who found gold in the state's northern hills. But like so many before and after him, prospecting for gold never panned out, so he supplemented his meager income by surveying government land on the west side of the San Joaquin Valley.

Mining wasn't only a bust when it came to riches; the cold, damp conditions of the underground caverns also made Clark sick. In 1855, doctors diagnosed him with tuberculosis and gave him only six months to live. Hoping to heal his lungs (or at least live out his days in what he believed was America's most beautiful valley), Clark headed for Yosemite.

In 1857, he settled along the Merced River and built a modest cabin. Away from the mines and surrounded by fresh air, Clark's health improved dramatically and his tuberculosis went into remission.

THE BIG DEAL ABOUT BIG TREES

Clark explored the area around his homestead extensively and soon stumbled on the Mariposa Grove. Then, as now, this grove near Yosemite's south entrance was home to approximately 365 giant sequoia trees, the oldest trees on earth—some are more than 2,000 years old. Although Clark certainly wasn't the first person to see the giant sequoias, he was the first to explore the grove extensively. He counted the trees and measured each one, and he was the one who called it "Mariposa," after the county where the trees are located (and where he lived).

The big trees soon became Clark's passion. He'd always been an avid outdoorsman; Sierra Club founder and Yosemite champion

---

Estimated erosion rate of Mt. Rushmore: one inch every 10,000 years.

John Muir called him "the best mountaineer I'd ever met." But Clark's dedication to the grove was unwavering. He began offering up his homestead to travelers who wanted to see the trees. For a small fee, nature enthusiasts could sleep in his log cabin (which was called "Galen's Station" and later became the site of the Wawona Hotel) and follow his horse trail to the grove.

Clark also lobbied the federal government on behalf of the Mariposa Grove and Yosemite Valley. In the 1850s, Yosemite hadn't yet been set aside as a national park. So Clark, Muir, and others who wanted to preserve the valley wrote letters to Congress asking that the area be protected from logging and other commercial interests. Their efforts were successful. Congress created—and President Lincoln approved—the Yosemite Grant in June 1864. Although the grant didn't technically make Yosemite a national park (in 1872, Yellowstone was the first area to be called a "national park"), it did protect the Yosemite Valley and the Mariposa Grove for "public use, resort, and recreation . . . to be left inalienable for all time." And it laid the foundation for the National Parks System.

THE GUARDIAN GETS TO WORK

With Yosemite and the Mariposa Grove protected by the government, the new preserve needed an overseer, someone who knew the valley well and felt passionate about its well-being. President Lincoln chose Clark. He became the "Guardian of the Valley," a job that required him to keep roads, trails, and bridges in good repair and to relocate homesteaders who encroached on the area. Clark served in this position for 24 years, and under his watchful eye, bridges were built, roads were constructed, and trails were connected to local points of interest, improvements that made Yosemite and the Mariposa Grove accessible to visitors from all over the world.

Clark also wrote three books about his beloved trees and their valley home: *Indians of the Yosemite Valley and Vicinity* (1904), *The Big Trees of California* (1907), and *The Yosemite Valley, Its History* (1910). Although each volume is small, they all helped to promote the beauty and history of the area and encouraged tourism, which helped pay for upkeep.

George Washington lost his first tooth at 22. Over the next 35 years he lost all but one.

AT HOME IN THE BIG WOODS
Galen Clark died on March 24, 1910, after battling a severe cold.
He was just four days shy of his 96th birthday and had recently
been crowned "Mariposa County's Oldest Citizen," an impressive
feat for a man doctors had written off 50 years before.

Clark had also spent the previous 24 years planning his own
grave site. He planted and nurtured about a dozen sequoia
seedlings in the Yosemite Valley Cemetery and is buried there
beneath a simple headstone. He's also memorialized by the
Mariposa Grove's Galen Clark Tree, one of the grove's largest trees
and, some think, the first sequoia Clark saw when he arrived there
in the mid-19th century.

CALIFORNIA

Yosemite National Park
Yosemite National Park, CA 95389

Founded: 1890
Area: 761,266 acres
Average annual visitors: 3,300,000

www.nps.gov/yose

* * *

WILD AMERICA
Thirty-eight percent of the land in the United States is wilderness.

Giant sequoias are also called "Sierra redwoods," but they are a
different species of tree from the famous redwoods that grow along
California's central and northern coast.

The Big Bend region of southwestern Texas and the national park
located there were named for a sharp turn in the Rio Grande,
which flows through the area.

WOOD BUFFALO BY THE NUMBERS

Known for its forest landscape, numerous sinkholes, salt flats, and, of course, the bison that gave it its name, Wood Buffalo is Canada's largest national park.

-7°F (-21.7°C)
Average high January temperature in Wood Buffalo National Park. The park's location in northern Canada (along the border between Alberta and the Northern Territories) ensures that winters are long, cold, and dark—daylight lasts only about seven hours in December and January—and summers are short.

2
Protected wetlands within Wood Buffalo's boundaries: Peace-Athabasca Delta (the world's largest inland delta) and the whooping crane nesting area—the only remaining natural whooping crane nesting area in the world.

3
Native American tribes that inhabited the area before Europeans arrived: Beaver, Slavey, and Chipewyan. The Beaver and Slavey tribes moved after fur trading dwindled during the 1800s, and today, three other tribes remain in the park's vicinity: Cree, Chipewyan, and Metis.

8 miles (13 kilometers)
Length of Lane Lake Trail, the longest hike in the park. The hike is classified as "moderate" and winds through the forest on the way to a translucent sinkhole lake. The park's most challenging trail is called Sweetgrass Station; it's a 7-1/2-mile (12-kilometer) hike that follows a rough path to an old animal management station used during the 1950s and 1960s. Only the corrals remain, but many hikers report seeing bison grazing in the distance along this trail.

Feeling a little crabby? A popular activity at Florida's Canaveral National Seashore is...

1922

Year the Canadian government established Wood Buffalo National Park. Initially, the effort was largely an attempt to protect dwindling herds of free-roaming bison. In fact, many of the original bison were imported from Alberta, where they were being over-hunted. Because the bison herds promptly moved out of the park to an area south of the Peace River, the park was expanded in 1926 to include the new range. Today, Wood Buffalo National Park is home to three at-risk animal species: peregrine falcons, wood bison, and whooping cranes.

10,000

Estimated number of wood buffalo living in Canada—about 2,000 of these live in the park. Two hundred years ago, more than 168,000 wood buffalo roamed throughout the country.

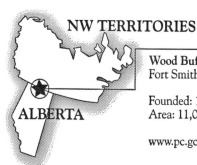

NW TERRITORIES

ALBERTA

Wood Buffalo National Park
Fort Smith, NWT X0E 0P0

Founded: 1922
Area: 11,072,050 acres (44,807 sq km)

www.pc.gc.ca/pn-np/nt/woodbuffalo

* * *

ANSEL'S ACCIDENT

When famed Yosemite photographer Ansel Adams was four years old, an aftershock tremor from the great 1906 San Francisco earthquake knocked him to the ground so violently that his nose was broken in the fall. For the rest of his life, his nose remained slightly crooked.

SCENE ON SCREEN

*Location, location, location . . . when the back lot just won't do,
filmmakers hike out to the national parks.*

MOUNT RUSHMORE NATIONAL MONUMENT (SORT OF)

Alfred Hitchcock had long imagined filming a chase scene on the sculpted presidential busts of Mount Rushmore. So, for the 1959 thriller *North by Northwest*, the director sought permission to film there. He got it but only on the condition that no violent scenes be filmed on or near the sculpture or in any of the memorial's public-use areas or by using any re-creations of the memorial. That was a problem, though, since the scenes Hitchcock imagined involved an attempted murder. So, despite the park's stipulations (and because the "attempted murder" was actually staged and part of the story), he went ahead with the filming. The scene in which Eva Marie Saint pretends to shoot Cary Grant takes place in the visitor's center cafeteria. Grant's "body" is hauled away through a Mount Rushmore parking lot. And various views of the memorial were shot from the monument's terraces. But Hitchcock shot the famous chase scene (of Grant and Saint being persued by bad guys) in front of mock-ups of Mount Rushmore that were built on an MGM soundstage in Hollywood.

YOSEMITE NATIONAL PARK

Yosemite has been the backdrop for several Hollywood films.

- Most of *The Caine Mutiny* with Humphrey Bogart takes place aboard ship. But in a subplot, one of the Naval officers takes his girlfriend on a weekend shore leave to Yosemite's Ahwahnee Hotel. They discuss marriage while viewing Yosemite Falls and the now-discontinued firefall off Glacier Point.

- In the opening scene of *Star Trek V: The Final Frontier*, it appears that Captain Kirk (William Shatner) is climbing the treacherous 3,500-foot rock face of Yosemite's El Capitan. Actually, he's climbing a rock wall set up in the parking lot at Tunnel View, an overlook that provides great views of the

California's Fresno Sanitary Landfill is a national historic landmark. Hmmm.

park's granite cliffs and domes. Clever camera angles make it look as though Shatner is climbing the real thing.

- In *Maverick*, the Indian village where Mel Gibson visits Graham Greene was set up at Leidig Meadow, next to the Merced River and under Yosemite's Sentinel Falls, the third-highest waterfall in California. The *Maverick* scene in which Mel Gibson swindles the Russian archduke was shot on Washburn Point, on the Glacier Point Road near the Glacier Point overlook.

DEATH VALLEY NATIONAL PARK
The sun-baked desolation of Death Valley has also been used for many movies. The 1970 film *Zabriskie Point* was shot at . . . of course . . . the park's Zabriskie Point, which also doubled as the Libyan mines where Peter Ustinov selects a slave (Kirk Douglas) for his gladiator school in *Spartacus*. The sand dunes at Stovepipe Wells appear in *King Solomon's Mines* with Stewart Granger and Deborah Kerr, *Three Godfathers* with John Wayne, *Yellow Sky* starring Gregory Peck, and *Star Wars Episode IV: A New Hope*.

CASTING CALL OF THE WILD
- As the boy cries "Come back, Shane," Alan Ladd rides off into Grand Teton National Park in *Shane*.
- In *The Greatest Story Ever Told*, Max Von Sydow as Jesus delivers the Sermon on the Mount facing the Green River in Canyonlands National Park.
- Devil's Tower National Monument in Wyoming was where Richard Dreyfuss went looking for the space aliens in *Close Encounters of the Third Kind*.
- Badlands National Park provided the colorful eroded cliffs for the background in *Dances with Wolves* as Kevin Costner rides from Fort Hays to Fort Sedgwick.
- The Middle Fork of the Flathead River in Glacier National Park was used for some of the river rafting scenes as Meryl Streep outwits and outpaddles Kevin Bacon in *The River Wild*.
- Although it was set mostly in Los Angeles, the film *Grand Canyon*, starring Kevin Kline and Danny Glover, included some scenes shot in Grand Canyon National Park.

There are four national lakeshores in the National Park System, all on the Great Lakes.

- The climactic battle in *The Hulk* was filmed near Pear Lake in the high Sierra backcountry of Sequoia National Park. (Visiting the site where mutant Eric Bana slugged it out with Nick Nolte requires a six-and-a-half-mile hike, uphill.)

HONORABLE MENTION: THE GRAND CANYON

In a bit of film trickery, the final scene of *Thelma and Louise* makes it look as though Susan Sarandon and Geena Davis take a plunge over the edge of the Grand Canyon. The scene looked so real that the year after *Thelma and Louise* was released on home video, three copycats committed suicide by driving their cars off the rim at Grand Canyon National Park. But those folks must not have known that a "stunt double" actually played the role of the Grand Canyon. Dead Horse Point State Park near Moab, Utah, was the real site of the ladies' slo-mo suicide.

* * *

GREAT MIGRATIONS

If you're looking for a place to see migratory animals on the move, these U.S. and Canadian national parks are where you want to be:

What: Gray whales
Where: Cabrillo National Monument (California)
When: Mid-December through March (mid-January is the peak.)

What: Elk
Where: Grand Teton National Park (Wyoming); specifically, along the 16-mile Teton Park Road
When: Summer

What: Monarch butterflies
Where: Point Pelee National Park (Ontario)
When: August

What: Robins and sparrows
Where: Gros Morne National Park (Newfoundland and Labrador)
When: Spring (May is usually the peak.)

Oregon's Hell's Canyon is the deepest canyon in North America. Take that, Grand!

BEYOND THE
<u>50 STATES</u>

*Think the U.S. national park sites are all contained in the
50 states? Think again! America's national parks are all over the map.*

AMERICAN SAMOA

The National Park of American Samoa is unique not only
because of its South Pacific location, but also because it's
the only national park that the United States rents. Located more
than 2,000 miles southwest of Hawaii, American Samoa is part of
French Polynesia and is a territory of the United States. In 1988, the
U.S. government cut a deal with local village chiefs for
permission to lease their land. More than 9,000 acres (1,000 of them
underwater) later, a distinctive national park was born. The park
encompasses four Samoan Islands: Tutuila, Ofu, Olosega, and Tau
and is home to several coral reefs and almost 900 species of fish.

PUERTO RICO

The San Juan National Historical Site is located on the Caribbean
island of Puerto Rico. This 75-acre area of the old city of San Juan
is surrounded by stone walls approximately 2.5 miles long. Within
these walls are bastions, powder houses, and forts built more than
400 years ago by Spanish troops. El Morro, a fort designed to
protect San Juan from attacks by sea, still stands on the western
side of the city. San Cristobal, which comprises 27 acres and is the
biggest fort the Spanish built in the Americas, protected the
eastern side from land attacks. Visitors to the forts today can take
in incredible views and examine the cannons soldiers once used to
guard the harbor.

GUAM

During World War II, the island of Guam saw some of the conflict's fiercest fighting. Today, it's home to the War in the Pacific
National Historical Park. Located in the western Pacific Ocean
about 3,300 miles southwest of Hawaii, Guam first became an
American possession in 1898 after the Spanish-American War. On

Kayaker? The lower stretch of Georgia's Chattahoochee River is great for kids and novices.

December 8, 1941, Japanese forces invaded and took control of the island. Three years later, the United States reclaimed it. In 1978, the U.S. Congress set aside 1,928 acres (926 of which are under water) on and around the island of Guam to honor the memory of all who fought in the Pacific during World War II. Battlefields, trenches, aircraft guns, and other sites allow visitors to learn about the battles that took place there during World War II, and the Memorial Wall (engraved with more than 16,000 names) honors the people who died during the conflict.

CANADA: ROOSEVELT CAMPOBELLO INTERNATIONAL PARK

The United States and Canada share two national park sites. The first, Roosevelt Campobello International Park, pays tribute to American president Franklin Delano Roosevelt, who often vacationed on Canada's Campobello Island (located near Maine and the Canadian province of New Brunswick) with his family. Today, an international agency called the United States/Canadian Commission supports the park. Five historical homes remain on the grounds, but Roosevelt's 34-room cottage is the centerpiece. This home was built in 1897 and the president's mother bought it in 1909 for $5,000. The cottage boasts 18 bedrooms, 76 windows, seven fireplaces, and six bathrooms. President Lyndon B. Johnson established the park on January 22, 1964, with an agreement signed by himself and Canadian Prime Minister Lester B. Pearson.

CANADA: SAINT CROIX ISLAND INTERNATIONAL HISTORIC SITE

The second joint United States/Canada park venture is the Saint Croix Island International Historic Site. This 6.5-acre island off the coast of Maine (and part of the international boundary between the United States and Canada) marks the place where French nobleman Pierre Dugua de Monts and explorer Samuel de Champlain established a North American settlement in 1604, 16 years before the pilgrims landed at Plymouth Rock. The winter of 1604 proved hard for the 79 settlers, and 35 of them died (probably from scurvy). The next spring, after the survivors' health had improved, they packed up and moved to Nova Scotia. Today, there aren't any physical structures left on St. Croix to commemorate that early settlement; the survivors dismantled everything before

Into whale-watching? Take yourself to California's Point Reyes National Seashore.

they left. But visitors can see a model of the settlement, walk the trails those men used, and take in beautiful views of the St. Croix River. The U.S. National Parks Service and Parks Canada jointly maintain the site.

THE VIRGIN ISLANDS

Located in the eastern Caribbean, the Virgin Islands came under U.S. control in 1917, when the United States bought them from Denmark for $25 million. Since then, the National Park Service has established five sites on the three largest islands: St. John, St. Croix, and St. Thomas.

- The Christiansted National Historic Site, dedicated to the Danish culture that flourished there from 1733 to 1917.

- Buck Island Reef National Monument, home to one of the Caribbean's finest reef systems, deep coral grottoes, colorful tropical fish, hawksbill turtles, and brown pelicans.

- Salt River Bay National Historic Park and Ecological Preserve, which boasts the largest mangrove forest in the Virgin Islands.

- The Virgin Islands Coral Reef National Monument, which was established by President Bill Clinton in 2001, is a delicately balanced tropical aquatic environment that supports whales, dolphins, sea-grass beds, coral reefs, and other underwater life.

- The 15,000-acre Virgin Islands National Park, protected in 1956 and known for its white sand beaches, blue-green waters, and thriving marine environment. Laurence J. Rockefeller donated 5,000 acres to get this park started.

* * *

DESIGNING MAN

The man who designed the U.S. Capitol building (adjacent to the National Mall) was William Thornton, a sugar planter from the tiny British Virgin Island of Jost Van Dyke. Thornton also helped Thomas Jefferson design the buildings of the University of Virginia.

Abraham Lincoln's birthplace, a national historic site, is in Hodgenville, Kentucky.

DRAWN TO
THE WILD WEST

Yellowstone fever was contagious, and lots of people caught it from landscape artist Thomas Moran.

In 1871, *Scribner's Monthly* published an article called "The Wonders of Yellowstone," illustrated by Thomas Moran, who by that time had caught "Yellowstone fever." He'd been supporting himself as an illustrator, but his passion was painting landscapes. When he'd read descriptions of a wild landscape with deep chasms, sulfurous springs, and smoke belching out of the earth, he knew he had to go to Yellowstone, the land "where Hell bubbled up."

GO WEST, YOUNG MAN
Born in Lancashire, England, in 1837, Moran grew up in Philadelphia, the son of immigrants. On trips to Europe, Moran studied the romantic landscapes of Turner in England, Lorraine in France, and Corot in Italy.

While working for *Scribner's* in New York, Moran went as far west as Lake Superior. When he found out that the U.S. Geological Survey Team was planning to map the headwaters of Yellowstone, Moran applied for a post. There was no money set aside to pay him, so Jay Cooke, a fellow Philadelphian and the president of the Northern Pacific Railroad, came to the rescue with a loan of $500. Moran left to join the survey party in the summer of 1871.

STRANGER IN A STRANGE LAND
The artist made dozens of watercolor sketches trying to capture the remarkable colors of Yellowstone and confided worriedly to geologist Ferdinand Hayden that the land's fantastic colors just might be "beyond the reach of human art."

Moran was especially thrilled with the view of the Lower Falls tumbling off high cliffs into the deep gorges of Yellowstone Canyon. He spent hours studying the canyon's geology, its patterns of light and shadow, and its vibrant color. (Today, a point on the north rim of the canyon is called Moran Point.) When he returned home, he went to work on a panoramic 8 x 14-foot canvas in his New Jersey studio: *The Great Canyon of the Yellowstone.*

IN LIVING COLOR

While Moran was painting, Congress was being asked to consider preserving Yellowstone as the first national park. The main pressure came from Moran's benefactor, Jay Cooke, who planned to run the Pacific Railroad from Minnesota through Montana to an area near North Yellowstone. Americans were becoming wealthy enough to travel, and Cooke wanted to entice the moneyed crowd westward—on *his* railroad, of course. The fabulous sights in Yellowstone would make for a major tourist attraction.

But the Yellowstone bill wasn't a sure thing. Some congressmen didn't want the federal government to limit development in the territories or get into the business of managing wilderness. Few people had even seen Yellowstone; those who had were skeptical about the place being a fantastic "wonderland."

Late in 1871, proponents of making Yellowstone a national park lobbied Congress for their cause. Ferdinand Hayden gave geological testimony about Yellowstone's unique properties. But the turning point for the bill came when Congress got a look at Moran's watercolors of hot springs, geysers, and mountains. The legislators were dazzled—and convinced. On March 1, 1872, Congress passed a resolution that more than two million acres of Yellowstone were to be preserved in perpetuity as a national park "for the benefit and enjoyment of the people."

THOMAS "YELLOWSTONE" MORAN

Two months later, Moran exhibited *The Great Canyon of the Yellowstone* in New York, where it created a sensation. Congress bought the painting for $10,000 and sent it on a multicity tour before returning it to Capitol Hill to hang in the Senate lobby. (The painting has been at the Department of the Interior since 1950, and it comes out only on special occasions, like the department's 150th anniversary in 1999.)

After seeing *The Great Canyon of the Yellowstone*—or Moran's watercolor sketches in *Scribner's Monthly*—many Americans caught Yellowstone fever, too, and were inspired to make the trip to the park.

...Mt. Ballyhoo, a peak in Dutch Harbor, Alaska.

For Jay Cooke, it turned out that lending money to Moran for a trip to Yellowstone was one of the best investments he'd ever made. Moran continued to paint the West: his panoramic *Chasm of the Colorado* introduced the American public to the Grand Canyon and helped influence Teddy Roosevelt to preserve it as a national park in 1908.

But Yellowstone always held a special place in Moran's life and art, so special that he signed his paintings with the stylized monogram "TYM"—Thomas "Yellowstone" Moran.

WYOMING

Yellowstone National Park
Yellowstone National Park, WY 82190

Founded: 1872
Area: 2,212,789 acres
Average annual visitors: 3,000,000

www.nps.gov/yell

* * *

"I looked at the Alps, but they are nothing compared to the majestic grandeur of our wonderful Rockies. I have painted them all my life and I shall continue to paint them as long as I can hold a brush."

—**Thomas Moran**

* * *

WHO'S BATTY NOW?

If you're in South Dakota's Black Hills near Jewel Cave National Monument at night and see bats flying around, give thanks. Vacationers and locals alike should appreciate bats—they're one of the best forms of natural insect control. All Jewel Cave bats are insect-eaters, feeding on beetles, moths, flies, and mosquitoes. They also eat cockroaches, termites, crickets, katydids, cicadas, and night-flying ants. A single brown bat can catch hundreds of mosquitoes in an hour.

Got elk? Oregon's Hell's Canyon hosts the largest free-roaming elk herd in the U.S.

THE REAL STAR-SPANGLED BANNER

In 1939, Maryland's Fort McHenry became a national memorial and shrine—the only one in the United States—to memorialize the place where Francis Scott Key first imagined "The Star Spangled Banner." Here's the story of the flag, the battle, and the fort that inspired Key to write that anthem.

THE WAR OF 1812

When England and France went to war in 1803, each country tried to prevent the other from trading with neutral countries such as the United States. As the conflict dragged on, England's powerful navy interfered with American shipping to such a degree that the new nation's entire economy was threatened. On June 18, 1812, seeing no other recourse, the U.S. Congress declared war on England.

As the war began, the port city of Baltimore, Maryland, then the third largest city in the United States, was a likely target for attack. And if such an attack ever did come, Fort McHenry, which guarded the entrance to Baltimore Harbor, would be one of the first targets, a fact that prompted the fort's defiant commander, Major Armistead, to ask for an American flag so big that "the British would have no trouble seeing it from a distance."

PUTTING IT TOGETHER

Two military officers paid a visit to the Baltimore home of Mary Young Pickersgill, a widow and "a maker of colors," and hired her to sew the flag. Mrs. Pickersgill and her 13-year-old daughter, Caroline, spent the next several weeks measuring, cutting, and sewing the 15 stars and 15 stripes that comprised the American flag at that time. They used more than 400 yards of English wool bunting, cutting stars that were two feet across from point to point, and eight red and seven white stripes, each of which were also two feet across.

Adams National Historical Park in Massachusetts includes two presidents' birthplaces.

The flag would measure 30 feet by 42 feet, much larger than the bedroom the Pickersgills were sewing it in. So they brought the pieces to the nearby Claggett's Brewery, where they laid them out on the floor and sewed them into the flag. The completed flag was delivered to Fort McHenry on August 19, 1813. Pickersgill charged the military $405.90 for her services.

BY THE ROCKETS' RED GLARE

It was a year before the flag saw any action. In August of 1814, British warships entered Chesapeake Bay, landed in Benedict, Maryland, and attacked Washington, D.C. It wasn't much of a battle—American soldiers ran and the British set fire to the Capitol, the White House, and other public buildings.

From Washington, the British moved north to mount an attack on Baltimore. But Armistead was ready with a strong defense and the British had to rely on their most formidable weapon, the bomb vessel, to try to take Fort McHenry.

At 6:30 a.m. on September 13, they started bombarding the fort. The battle lasted 25 hours, with aerial bombs and rockets exploding through the night, showering sparks and shrapnel on the fort. (A young American lawyer and amateur poet named Francis Scott Key watched in wonder from the deck of one of the British ships.) But in the end, the British couldn't dent the American defense and had to withdraw. According to Robert Barrett, a midshipman on the British frigate *Hebrus*, "As the last vessel spread her canvas to the wind, the Americans hoisted a splendid and superb ensign on their battery."

American Private Isaac Munroe saw it, too. He later wrote, "At dawn on the 14th, our morning gun was fired, the flag hoisted, 'Yankee Doodle' played, and we all appeared in full view of a mortified enemy, who calculated upon our surrender in 20 minutes after the commencement of the action." The "splendid ensign" was the Star-Spangled Banner, the largest battle flag ever flown.

FAMILY FLAG

Sometime prior to his death in 1819, Armistead acquired the flag. How he got it is unknown—he probably just took it. But he was a hero, so no one protested. It passed to his widow and remained in his family until 1907, when his grandson, Eben Appleton, donated it to the Smithsonian Institution.

If you've ever seen Mrs. Pickersgill's flag at the Smithsonian, you may have noticed that a significant portion of the flag is missing. Some of this was due to the damage it received during the bombardment of Fort McHenry, but not all of it. After the battle, a soldier's widow asked for a snippet of the flag to bury with her husband, and Armistead himself cut off a piece for her. He granted numerous similar requests, as did Mrs. Armistead and her daughter, Georgiana Armistead Appleton, after his death. Mrs. Appleton wrote in 1873, "Pieces of the flag have occasionally been given to those deemed to have a right to such a memento. Had we given all that we had been importuned for, little would be left to show."

Still, Georgiana Appleton continued giving away fragments of the flag—including one of the stars—and by the time it was brought to the Smithsonian, eight feet of material were missing from the end.

PUTTING IT TOGETHER

In 1924, the Smithsonian hired a team of 11 "needlewomen" to sew a linen backing on the flag so that it could be hung up for display. It took 1.7 million stitches.

For the next 70 years, the flag hung in the Smithsonian. Then, in 1998, curators took it down, moved it to a lab, and began an $18 million, 3-year restoration of the flag. Using forceps, scissors, and tweezers, six restorers—lying on their stomachs on a platform suspended a foot above the flag—proceeded to surgically remove the linen backing. Then they started analyzing the fabric, along with some of the snippets, which the museum had actually been able to purchase at an auction. Their conclusion, two years into the project: the material was in worse shape than they had first thought. The flag would have to be displayed in a gas-filled case and at a slight incline so as not to stress the fabric. But the Star-Spangled Banner couldn't ever be hung again.

MARYLAND

Fort McHenry National Monument and Historic Shrine
Baltimore, MD 21230-5393

Founded: 1939
Area: 43 acres
Average annual visitors: 620,000

www.nps.gov/fomc

...largest, most hotly contested battle of the Revolutionary War's southern campaign.

ROCKS ON THE GO

They say that the desert can play tricks on you. If that's the case, then California's Death Valley is the trickiest of them all.

MOVE ON OVER
While traveling through the hot California desert in 1915, a mining prospector named Joseph Crook made a startling discovery: the rocks had trails behind them—as if they had slid across the desert floor all by themselves. That portion of desert is now known as Racetrack Playa in northwestern Death Valley National Park, and curious people travel from great distances to witness one of nature's most puzzling mysteries: the moving rocks of Death Valley.

HAPPY TRAILS
These otherwise ordinary rocks are somehow transported across a flat desert plain, leaving erratic trails in the hard mud behind them. The stones come in every size and shape, from pebbles to half-ton boulders. The tracks they leave also vary. Some rocks travel only a few feet; others go for hundreds of yards, although they may have started right next to each other. The trails go every which way, crossing and looping, even doubling back on themselves. Many rocks carve zigzag paths along the *playa* (Spanish for "beach"), and some have even made complete circles. But nowhere is there a trace of what propelled the rocks—no footprints or tire tracks, nothing to reveal what force pushed the hundreds of pounds of rock.

WEIRD SCIENCE
Although geologists have yet to prove the method of movement, they've offered quite a few theories—most of them having to do with wind, rain, and, in some cases, ice. (Some people contend that aliens are to blame.) Even recent GPS studies of the rocks fail to give a concrete explanation. The fact of the matter is that Death Valley is the deepest hole in the Western Hemisphere and one of the warmest places on earth—a literal "hotbed" of strange phenomena. All scientists know for sure is that yes, the rocks move—a lot. But to this day, no one has ever seen one in motion.

Visitors to Maryland's Catoctin Mountain Park may gather morel mushrooms for...

CALIFORNIA

Death Valley National Park
Death Valley, CA 92328

Founded: 1994
Area: 3,400,000 acres
Average annual visitors: 800,000

www.nps.gov/deva

* * *

A MONUMENTAL HOAX

Every student election seems to have a joke candidate, and the 1979 student body president election at the University of Wisconsin was no exception. Jim Mallon and Leon Varjian campaigned on a unique platform: to purchase and relocate the Statue of Liberty to Madison, Wisconsin. Amazingly, they won. But voters didn't take the pledge seriously—Mallon and Varjian couldn't actually pull the stunt off. Or could they?

One winter morning, the instantly recognizable head and torch of the Statue of Liberty appeared, poking out from nearby Lake Mendota. Varjian told the UW student paper that he and Mallon tried to fulfill their campaign promise—but the cable transporting the statue via helicopter broke and, tragically, dropped the statue, partially submerging it. It wasn't the real statue, of course—it was plywood papier-mâché and chicken wire. Mallon and Varjian had been secretly overseeing its construction for months. (The two insisted that it *was* the real Statue of Liberty.)

The student newspaper later revealed that $4,500 of student money had been used to make the statue. Mallon and Varjian's response: they offered to write checks to any interested students for their individual share of wasted funds—10¢ each. The statue was destroyed by unknown arsonists three weeks later, but the prankster duo won again next year and rebuilt the statue (this time they spent $6,000). That one was removed by the Wisconsin Department of Natural Resources. It now lives in a shed on campus.

RED RUN AT WILSON'S CREEK

*When the Civil War split the country in April 1861, no state was
more bitterly divided than Missouri. Missouri tried to stay neutral,
hoping that would ensure peace, but pro-Union and pro-Confederate
factions fought so hard for control that, within months, their power
struggle led to the second major battle—and one of the bloodiest
confrontations—of the Civil War.*

THIS MEANS WAR!

After war was declared, President Lincoln ordered Governor
Claiborne Jackson to send four Missourian regiments to
help put down the Confederacy. Jackson not only refused, he
armed the pro-secession Missouri State Guard. Captain Nathaniel
Lyon, head of the U.S. 2nd Regiment Infantry, formed armed
militias (called "Wide Awakes") to fight for the Stars and Stripes.
A month after war was declared, Missouri was occupied by two
armed camps. One was in St. Louis led by the newly promoted
General Lyon. The other was in the state capital of Jefferson City,
commanded by Major General Sterling Price, who reported to
Governor Jackson.

General Lyon, well known for his hatred of the Confederate
cause, considered Jackson a traitor to his country. Governor
Jackson considered Lyon a tyrant imposing martial law on free
citizens. Even so, on June 11, the two estranged leaders agreed to
hold negotiations in St. Louis. Jackson proposed keeping
Confederate troops out of Missouri if Lyon disbanded the Wide
Awakes and brought no more Union troops into the state. Instead
of making a counterproposal, the general was so offended at any
weakening of the U.S. military that he jumped to his feet yelling,
"This means war!"

Jackson feared for his life. He fled to Jefferson City by train,
burning all the bridges behind him. The enraged general gave
chase across Missouri. The capital was abandoned by the time
Union troops arrived. Governor Jackson, Major General Price, and
the Missouri State Guard had marched off, seeking reinforcements.

White Sands National Monument (NM) is in the world's largest gypsum dune field.

SURPRISE!

Lyon pursued his enemies into southwest Missouri, establishing Union control as he went. Camped at Springfield with 6,000 tired troops, Lyon wrote to his superiors for more men and supplies to help him finish the job of keeping Missouri out of the Confederacy. By August, Lyon had received no reinforcements, but Confederate generals Ben McCulloch and N. Bart Pearce had crossed the Arkansas border to defend the Missouri State Guard. And 12,000 battle-ready Confederate soldiers were camped only 10 miles away at Wilson's Creek.

On August 9, General McCulloch (a former Texas Ranger and seasoned military leader) ordered a surprise attack on Springfield at nine o'clock that night. His eager troops were ready to ride when the attack was called off because rain threatened and could destroy their precious stores of ammunition. The rebels went to bed disappointed that they'd missed out on a fight . . . but woke up in the middle of one. At sunrise on August 10, the Federals made a surprise attack on Wilson's Creek.

General Lyon was outnumbered, though, and feared retreat because Confederate troops could easily surround his fleeing forces. So he devised a two-pronged attack: Major General Siegel and about 1,200 soldiers stormed the Confederate flank from the south while Lyon charged in from the north with the rest of their forces. Aided by surprise, they hoped to damage the rebels so they couldn't follow when the Union retreated—or better yet, drive the rebels off in confusion.

BLOODY HILL

At first, the plan succeeded. Siegel and his men opened fire on unsuspecting rear regiments causing chaos and retreat in Confederate ranks. At the same time, Lyon's troops opened fire from the north, pushing the unprepared enemy back. By early that morning, the Federals had taken the high ridge on Oak Hill; from there, they fired down on what was left of the Confederate army hoping to force it back to Arkansas.

Mistaken identity threw an early hitch in Lyon's battle plan, however. The Civil War was only a few months old, and neither side had standard uniforms. After routing the enemy, Siegel saw men in gray uniforms advancing toward him and thought they were friendly Federal reinforcements from Iowa. Instead the gray-clad Confederates, led by General McCulloch launched a bold attack that scattered Siegel's troops and sent the general on a hasty retreat to Springfield. With Siegel gone, Lyon's troops on Oak Hill had no support as the Confederates (who had recovered and regrouped) charged with an advantage of twice as many men.

That morning, so many men were wounded or died on Oak Hill that it became known as Bloody Hill. For most soldiers, this was their first major battle experience, and both sides refused to give ground. As the hours wore on, with Confederates attacking and Federals defending the ridge, Wilson's Creek became one of the deadliest battles ever fought on American soil.

The worst blow for the Union came when a bullet struck General Lyon in the chest and killed him. The general (already wounded twice that day and still fighting) was rallying his men for a countercharge against the enemy when he fell. The counter-charge was forgotten, and for some time, the Union troops had no leader. Finally, Major Samuel Sturgis was alerted that Lyon was dead, but by the time he took over, the Confederates were attacking the hill for a third time while the Federals, demoralized by the loss of Lyon, were almost out of ammunition. Sturgis ordered a retreat.

The Confederates took Bloody Hill, where hundreds of soldiers on both sides lay dead or dying. More than 2,000 men were buried at Wilson's Creek. The casualties were closely divided—1,317 Union and 1,222 Confederate.

A DIVISIVE VICTORY

The Confederates won a hard victory, but to Major General Price's dismay, McCulloch wouldn't chase after the retreating Union troops and establish Confederate control in Missouri. For one thing, in those early days of the war, the Confederate government could defend the state, but it couldn't invade and hold Missouri. For another, the experienced General McCulloch didn't order his men into battle when they were nearly out of ammunition.

In the end, General Lyon's attack at Wilson's Creek kept Missouri in the Union. The Federals were able to retreat to Rolla in central Missouri, and their near annihilation convinced President Lincoln that more troops and arms were needed to keep Missouri in the Union camp.

The battle divided ordinary Missourians even further. Neighbors and even families had been on opposite sides of the guns. On Bloody Hill, Cary Gratz of the Union infantry died fighting against a Missouri State Guard that included his stepbrother, Joseph Shelby. The deaths at Wilson's Creek inflamed Missouri's own civil war. For the next three-and-half years, gangs of raiders robbed and killed neighbors with different political sympathies.

WILSON'S CREEK NATIONAL BATTLEFIELD

Despite its violent history, today the 1,750-acre area of Wilson's Creek National Battlefield is a peaceful national park in the scenic Ozarks. Nature lovers can enjoy hiking, horseback riding, or bird watching in beautiful surroundings. The Wilson's Creek Foundation began the preservation of Wilson's Creek and Bloody Hill with the purchase of 37 acres in 1951. The National Park Service purchased the battlefield from the foundation in 1960. Today, the park includes 80 percent of the battlefield, and except for small changes in buildings and vegetation, it still looks a lot like it did 145 years ago.

Civil War buffs can tour historic sites like the Ray House, which was used as a Confederate field hospital, the area where McCulloch's troops forced General Siegel's retreat; and of course Bloody Hill where General Lyon and so many others fought and died. Displays across the battlefield explain the details of the battle. The battlefield also has the largest Civil War library in the National Park Service. And it recently acquired the General Sweeney Museum Collection, a collection of artifacts from the Civil War.

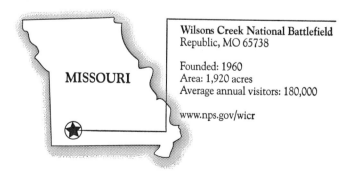

MISSOURI

Wilsons Creek National Battlefield
Republic, MO 65738

Founded: 1960
Area: 1,920 acres
Average annual visitors: 180,000

www.nps.gov/wicr

...in Danville, California, is a national historic site, but reservations are required.

AVOIDING THE PLAGUE

Think the bubonic plague died out with the Dark Ages? Think again.

In May 2006, when a chipmunk was found dead at Balcony House, a cliff dwelling at Mesa Verde National Park in Colorado, park service officials donned protective gear, gathered up the critter, and shipped it off for testing. Cause of death? None other than the bubonic plague.

THE PLAGUE SPREADS WEST, THEN EAST

The plague's heyday was the Middle Ages, when rats, which carried the disease, were heavily concentrated in cities. The bacterial toxin *Yersinia pestis* was carried by fleas from rats to humans. The black death, a form of bubonic plague, wiped out a fourth of the population of Europe in the 14th century, most of whom died after high fever, weakness, and the formation of buboes—swollen lymph glands—particularly in the groin and armpits.

As pest control improved, the incidence of epidemics waned, but the disease never went away completely. It first arrived on U.S. soil in 1899 aboard a ship that docked in San Francisco, and it slowly spread eastward to the Great Plains, largely via the squirrel population. The last urban bubonic plague epidemic in the United States was in 1924 in Los Angeles. Today the disease is mostly found in the Four Corners area of Colorado, Utah, New Mexico, and Arizona, as well as in northern California, eastern Nevada, and southern Oregon. The 1,000 to 3,000 cases of bubonic plague reported annually to the World Health Organization include 10 to 15 human infections in the United States. These days, about one in seven people who contract bubonic plague dies from it.

BATTLING BUBOES

Back in Mesa Verde, when the dead chipmunk tested positive for plague, the park quickly closed the Balcony House cliff dwellings and treated the area with delta dust, or Deltamethrin, an odorless insecticide that kills fleas. No human infections were reported.

Park officials say the plague is endemic to the park's rodent population and outbreaks occur cyclically (2005 was a particularly bad year). The disease was also discovered recently at Colorado National Monument and Natural Bridges National Monument in Utah.

THE BEST DEFENSE

Keep in mind that it's the fleas that carry the disease. Use insect repellent, especially in the backcountry, steer clear of small, dead animals, and avoid walking or camping near burrows of prairie dogs, field mice, and other little creatures, however cute they are. Also don't let pets (or kids) roam in unmonitored areas—they might just want to investigate that curious prairie dog hole where plague-carrying fleas can congregate. Park officials also urge visitors to report any dead mammals to rangers.

* * *

JOHN BROWN'S RAID

Today, Harper's Ferry, West Virginia, is part of the Harper's Ferry National Historic Park. But in 1859, it was just a town in Virginia and part of a slave state. Abolitionist John Brown wanted to change that, so he organized 18 supporters and attacked a Confederate armory at Harper's Ferry. At first, the raid went well. Brown and his allies met with no resistance when they entered the town. They quickly cut the telegraph wires and gathered a group of hostages. But after Brown opened fire on a passing train, the townspeople rose up and the local militia cornered the raiders inside a small building near the armory. The fighting lasted only one day before Brown was caught by soldiers led by Robert E. Lee. Brown was ultimately hanged for treason against the State of Virginia. But his dying words prophesized the Civil War two years later:

> I wish to say furthermore, that you had better—all you people at the South—prepare yourselves for a settlement of that question [slavery] that must come up for settlement sooner than you are prepared for it.

Family ties: The grandmother of acclaimed Harlem Renaissance poet Langston Hughes was married to one of John Brown's Harper's Ferry raiders.

Nevada, the most mountainous state, has 42 named summits over 11,000 feet.

SETTING THE WORLD ON FIRE

*Visit the woodlands where young George Washington
started a world war.*

I n May 1754, Lieutenant Colonel George Washington set up
camp in the Great Meadows in what is now southwest
Pennsylvania. Washington called the place "a charming field
for an encounter" and built Fort Necessity. On July 4, as he
retreated from the stockade with more than 100 of his own soldiers
killed or wounded, the young leader wasn't so charmed.

Fort Necessity was the site of George Washington's first defeat
and his only surrender. And the battle there fueled a global conflict that became known as the Seven Years' War.

THE STAKES
The Fort Necessity story began with Robert Dinwiddie, Virginia's
lieutenant governor, who, along with other investors, hoped to
make money from furs and real estate in the Ohio Valley. In 1749,
the English government gave 200,000 acres of land near present-
day Pittsburgh to the governor and his partners to settle in the
name of Britain and to build a fort to protect the territory. Britain
would control important trade routes through the heart of the new
frontier, and the Virginians would have a profitable development
scheme. There was only one problem—the French military.

The French had already laid claim to the Ohio Valley. They'd
established trade relations with the Native Americans and built
forts. In the winter of 1753, Governor Dinwiddie made a talented
young woodsman named George Washington his ensign and sent
him to the French fort Le Boeuf (at what is now Waterford,
Pennsylvania) to inform the French commander, Jaques Legardeur
de Saint-Pierrthe, that the English were ordering the French to
leave the Ohio Valley at once. The commander politely declined,
and when Washington returned to Virginia, he gave Dinwiddie bad
news: Washington had scouted out a strong French military presence in the valley and learned of plans for reinforcements in

spring. Concerned, Dinwiddie sent Washington back to the Ohio Valley, this time with orders to defend British interests.

SHOTS FIRED

On May 24, 1754, Washington and his men were building a wagon road from Alexandria, Virginia, through the forest into the Ohio Valley to make it easier for Virginia to send settlers and soldiers into the frontier. They made camp in the Great Meadows, where there was fresh water from streams and enough grass for their animals. While awaiting reinforcements and supplies, they got a tip from a friendly Seneca chief that there were hostile French soldiers nearby. Chief Tanaghrisson, whom the British called Half King, wanted the French out of the valley, too—partly because he believed that the British would do more for his people, but mainly because the French had been responsible for his father being boiled to death and eaten by enemy tribesmen.

On May 28, Tanaghrisson guided Washington and 40 of his militia to what is now known as Jumonville Glen. There, they surprised a sleeping French colonial militia. (It's still debated whether the French were a hostile force or only emissaries sent to warn Washington that he was in their territory.) No one knows who fired the first shot, but when the musket smoke cleared, 10 French soldiers were dead and 21 others, including the commanding officer, Ensign Jumonville, were British prisoners. Then, according to most reports, Tanaghrisson took revenge on the French and scalped Jumonville.

THAT LITTLE THING UPON THE MEADOW

Jumonville had been under Washington's protection as an officer and prisoner of war, and Washington expected French reprisals for his death. In the low-lying, marshy clearing of the Great Meadows, his men hastily constructed a palisade, a stockade fence made of white oak posts driven into the ground. Inside the fence were swivel guns—small cannons mounted on posts that could be turned in various directions—along with a shed to hold provisions. Washington notified Dinwiddie about constructing Fort Necessity and claimed that it would hold off at least 500 men.

Tanaghrisson, however, was unimpressed with "that little thing upon the meadow." Seeing that the fort was ringed in by higher ground and dense forest, he decided that the 22-year-old

Washington, while a good-natured fellow, lacked experience in war. Washington got reinforcements from Virginia and South Carolina on June 12 and was made a full colonel, but Half King and his men refused to defend the fort. Without Native American allies, the Virginians had less than 400 men to hold off the enemy.

On the morning of July 3, 600 French troops and 100 Native Americans led by Captain Louis Coulon de Villiers—the half-brother of the scalped Jumonville—fired on the fort from the cover of trees. Holding the higher ground, the French and their allies were able to take deadly aim on the troops trapped in the meadow. Washington soon knew he'd made a mistake. Even the weather worked against Fort Necessity: heavy rain swamped the Great Meadow making it nearly impossible for the militia to keep their gunpowder dry and their muskets firing.

LOST IN TRANSLATION

By nightfall, almost a third of Washington's troops were dead or wounded. Needing liquid courage to face what seemed like certain death, some soldiers attacked the fort's supply of rum and were too drunk for battle. That evening, when the French sent a surrender offer, Washington knew he couldn't refuse. Captain Jacob Van Braam, a Dutchman who was literate in both French and English, translated the French terms, and Washington wearily signed the surrender document.

On July 4, 1754, Washington and his men retreated from the Great Meadow. They left Fort Necessity to the victorious French, who burned it down to blackened stumps. It was a bleak day for Washington, but it would have been worse if he'd known that his translator had missed translating an important clause and that he'd signed an admission to assassinating Jumonville.

That charge of assassination haunted Washington, who resigned from the militia before he could be demoted. The French government used the signed surrender as propaganda until the "Jumonville affair" ignited passions that led to the Seven Years' War in Europe (known as the French and Indian War in North America). The conflict eventually involved all the major powers of Europe—including France, Great Britain, Austria, Prussia, the Russian empire, Sweden, Spain, Portugal, and the Netherlands—as well as their colonies. The theaters of the conflict spanned the globe from Virginia into Canada and Europe all the way to India. British

The giant saguaro cactus is grows slowly. Studies in Saguaro National Park show...

statesman Horace Walpole later wrote, "The volley fired by a young Virginian in the backwoods of America set the world on fire."

The British won the French and Indian War in 1763, but the conflict still influenced history. The American colonists who'd fought for King George's lands wanted their rights as proud British citizens. Meanwhile, the king found the defense of the territories a drain on the treasury, and he hit the colonists with high taxes to foot the bill. Taxation became the major cause of the American Revolution, ably led by a more experienced General George Washington, who never surrendered again.

RETURN TO FORT NECESSITY

In 1931, Congress set aside 900 acres, including the Great Meadow and Jumonville Glen, to create the Fort Necessity National Battlefield. Located on U.S. 40, about 11 miles east of Uniontown, Pennsylvania, it's open year round from sunrise to sundown. Visitors can hike to the woods where Washington surprised the French or visit the Great Meadows to tour the reconstructed fort. Tours and historic weapons demonstrations are offered during the summer months. Visitors can also see an interpretive center that showcases historic artifacts and life-size cast figures from the era of the French and Indian Wars. And the center gives audio and video presentations that tell the tale of Fort Necessity and how it helped bring democracy and the English language to North America.

PENNSYLVANIA

Fort Necessity National Battlefield
Farmington, PA 15437

Founded: 1931
Area: 900 acres
Average annual visitors: 100,000

www.nps.gov/fone

* * *

California's Pinnacles National Monument (once a volcano) originally erupted about 195 miles south of its present site. Over time, it has moved about 2 centimeters per year along the San Andreas fault.

...that a saguaro grows between 1 and 1.5 inches in the first eight years of its life.

THE SMOKIES BY THE NUMBERS

Located on the North Carolina-Tennessee border, Great Smoky Mountains National Park (nicknamed the "Smokies") is America's most-visited national park.

0
Number of motels or rental cabins in the park. There are 10 maintained campsites and one lodge, however.

2
Number of peak seasons at the park. About 1.3 million visitors come to the Smokies during the July 15 to August 15 summer season, and another 1.1 million arrive in October to see the fall colors.

30
Species of salamanders living the park. The Smokies are home to the most diverse salamander population in the world.

95 percent
Amount of the park that's forested—that comes out to about 500,000 acres. Twenty-five percent of that hasn't been touched by logging or agriculture.

100 feet
Height of Ramsey Cascades, the highest waterfall in the Smokies

135 feet
Height of the world's largest red maple, which is located in the Smokies. The tree also has a circumference of 23 feet.

270
Miles of road in the park

Texas's Big Thicket National Preserve has four different kinds of insect-eating plants.

850
Miles of hiking trails in the park. The famous Appalachian Trail runs for 70 miles through the park's center.

1,600
Approximate number of black bears living in the park

1934
Year the Great Smoky Mountains became a National Park (President Franklin Delano Roosevelt officially dedicated it in 1940.)

6,643 feet
Height of Clingman's Dome, the highest peak in the Smokies

6,800
Acreage of Cades Cove. More than 2 million people visit this valley every year, making it the most popular stop for travelers to the Smokies.

TENNESSEE

Great Smoky Mountains National Park
Gatlinburg, TN 37738

Founded: 1934
Area: 521,085 acres
Average annual visitors: 9,000,000

www.nps.gov/grsm

* * *

ROCKIN' ART
What's the difference between a petroglyph and a pictograph? Petroglyphs are images pecked into rock, whereas pictographs are painted images. Dinosaur National Monument, in Colorado, preserves both forms of Native American rock art.

The 444-mile Natchez Trace Parkway runs through Mississippi, Alabama, and Tennessee.

PAINTING THE
TOWN PINK

*Eliza Ruhamah Scidmore isn't memorialized anywhere, but her vision
and persistence helped beautify the dump heap that
Washington, D.C., was 100 years ago.*

When wayward beavers began using the landmark cherry trees of Washington, D.C. to build a dam in 1999, the story was front-page news in the *Washington Post*. The National Park Service eventually captured and moved the varmints. The message was clear: the United States takes its cherry trees very seriously. But that wasn't always the case.

SPRUCING UP THE "OLD DUMP HEAP"

In the 1800s, Washington, D.C., was a rancid and deathly swamp. The Potomac lowlands were rife with malaria and yellow fever until U.S. Army engineers pumped mud from the swamp, creating an artificial peninsula that would become the 724-acre East and West Potomac parks. They did it just in time for Washington travel writer and author Eliza Ruhamah Scidmore to launch a crusade that would take up the next 24 years of her life.

Scidmore had been smitten by the delicate cherry blossoms she'd seen in Tokyo during a tour of Asia. In 1885, she approached Colonel Spencer Cosby, the national grounds superintendent, suggesting the planting of Japanese cherry trees in "the great stretch of raw, reclaimed ground by the river bank to hide those old dump heaps . . ." But the colonel wasn't interested. The next time she tried it, with the city's grounds superintendent, she brought along some pictures . . . and struck out again.

For the next 24 years, Scidmore brought her cherry blossom pictures to each new superintendent. She even had the idea of raising the money herself and donating the trees to the city. But it was the inauguration of President William Howard Taft in 1909 that put her scheme over the top.

AN IDEA BLOSSOMS

Knowing the Tafts had lived for several months in Japan and were

---

The Big South Fork area (Tennessee/Kentucky) has over 150 miles of hiking trails.

already familiar with the flowering cherry trees, Scidmore sent a letter to the new first lady asking for her help. Three days later, Helen Taft wrote back, thanking Scidmore and saying, "I have taken the matter up and am promised the trees." In fact, the Japanese consul had suggested the cherry trees be donated in the name of Japan's capital city, Tokyo.

The following January, 2,000 trees arrived in Washington, but on inspection they were found to be infested with disease and insects. The Japanese took the problem in stride and even sweetened the deal: they replaced the trees with 3,000 new ones.

PLANTING SEASON

The cherry trees played perfectly into Helen Taft's hopes to transform the nation's capital from what she called "a mosquito-infested swamp, rendezvous of tramps, and a hiding place for criminals" into a place of beauty befitting the young, vibrant nation.

On March 27, 1912, Scidmore attended a ceremony at which Helen Taft and the Japanese ambassador's wife, Viscountess Chinda, planted the first trees between Potomac Drive and the Tidal Basin.

THE BLOOMING CAPITAL

There are approximately 3,750 cherry trees in the care of the National Park System today, 2,763 of which are Yoshino cherry, the earliest blooming variety. If you want to see the flowering cherries for yourself, the average date of the three-day blooming period is April 4, but keep an eye on the weather: depending on how warm, cold, or rainy it is, it could be anywhere from March 15 to April 18.

Eliza Scidmore died in 1928. Her ashes were buried in Japan at the request of the Japanese government.

National Mall & Memorial Parks
Washington, D.C. 20024

Founded: 1965
Area: 146 acres
Average annual visitors: 6,000,000

www.nps.gov/mall

Bald eagles and osprey hunt along the Anacostia River in Washington, D.C.

BEFORE IT WAS MOUNT RUSHMORE . . .

On page 79, we told you about building Mount Rushmore. But that granite bulge didn't always have faces on it. Before the carving began . .

- It was magma, formed 1.6 billion years ago. The molten rock rose from the earth's depths and melted layers of older rock but never broke through the surface as a volcano. Instead, it lay beneath sandstone and rubble for more than 1.5 billion years.

- It was a granite mountain. Tectonic plate movements deep in the earth shoved up Mount Rushmore and the rest of the Black Hills some 70 million years ago. The slow uplift continues to this day. Once exposed to air, wind, and cold, you might expect erosion to occur. And it does—but the ancient granite of Mount Rushmore is so hard that it erodes at less than one inch per 10,000 years.

- It was known as Six Grandfathers to the Sioux. All of the Black Hills, or *Paha Sapa* (which means "black hills" in the Sioux's Lakota language), were given to the tribe by the Treaty of Fort Laramie in 1868. This treaty, signed by President Ulysses S. Grant, was supposed to end war between the Sioux and the United States forever. It didn't. Within three years, both sides complained that the others cheated.

- It caused a gold rush. Six years after the Treaty of Fort Laramie was signed, George Armstrong Custer (the same Custer who died at Little Bighorn) led 1,200 men into the Black Hills. Officially, he was on a reconnaissance mission; unofficially, he sought gold. A month after Custer's men found a few flecks, newspapers carried the headline: "GOLD!" The rush was on, and the Treaty of Fort Laramie was forgotten.

- Pioneers called it "the needles near Harney Peak." Later, the mountain got its modern name as a joke. In 1885, New York attorney Charles E. Rushmore was paid to investigate mining claims in the Black Hills. He asked guide Bill Challis the name of a mountain as they passed it. Challis said the peak had no name and added, "We'll call 'er the Rushmore, by Jingo!" Years later, Mr. Rushmore proudly donated $5,000 to help fund Gutzon Borglum's monument on his namesake.

SOUTH DAKOTA

Mt. Rushmore National Memorial
Keystone, SD 57751-0268

Founded: 1925
Area: 1,278 acres
Average annual visitors: 2,000,000

www.nps.gov/moru

* * *

GHOST DANCES IN THE BADLANDS

In the late 1800s, as the U.S. government and settlers moved west, the country's Native Americans were having a terrible time. They were confined to reservations, the abundant buffalo herds that once roamed the plains were disappearing, and tribesmen were dying from disease and starvation. Enter Wovoka (also called Jack Wilson), a Paiute medicine man who led a new religious movement that he claimed would bring about a peaceful end to white settlement and the natives' troubles. It was called the Ghost Dance and incorporated traditional Native American tribal dance rituals, primarily the circle dance, which involved participants dancing in a circular pattern while religious leaders prophesized. According to Wovoka and his supporters, participating in the dances would repel white settlers peacefully and would usher in a new age in which the tribes lived heathfully and richly.

It didn't work. In the end, of course, the Native American tribes were overrun by white settlers and mistreated by the U.S. government. But before it waned, the Ghost Dance movement spread throughout the Native American community and was a catalyst for the pivotal 1890 Battle of Wounded Knee, in an area that is now part of South Dakota's Badlands National Park. The battle began when leader Sitting Bull was arrested by U.S. soldiers for refusing to force his tribesmen to stop participating in a ghost dance.

MAKE IT OLD AND RUSTIC

If you've been to the Grand Canyon, you may have noticed the buildings around the South Rim. If you didn't, that's because they were designed not to stand out. Architect Mary Colter used a style she developed, called "National Park Service Rustic," to make sure the structures blended seamlessly with their surroundings.

GIRL OF THE GOLDEN MIDWEST

Colter grew up in Minnesota in the late 1800s, when there were still many American Indians in the area. The arts of the local tribes intrigued her from an early age. When Colter was young, a friend gave her some Sioux drawings that she kept all her life.

When her father died and the family (all women) was thrown into financial difficulty, Colter enrolled in an art school in San Francisco so she could become an art teacher. She also worked in an architect's office while attending the California School of Design, and when she graduated, she moved back to the Midwest to support her family.

She eventually got a job with the Fred Harvey Company, which owned restaurants and hotels along railroad routes. Colter designed buildings out West for the company, using the Indian motifs she'd loved since childhood to help the structures fit into the landscape.

GREETINGS FROM THE GRAND CANYON

Just after the turn of the 20th century, when tourists started traveling west to see the Grand Canyon, the Santa Fe Railroad and the Fred Harvey Company asked Colter to design buildings where the visitors could stay, eat, and shop. She used local limestone for the walls and pine and juniper wood for ceiling beams. She decorated the walls with Indian paintings and drawings that had rarely been seen by non-Indians.

THAT LIVED-IN LOOK

Another way to make the buildings blend in was to artificially age them. At Hermit's Rest, originally a rest stop but now a snack bar and gift shop, Colter made sure the fireplace was sooty when the

---

Two future U.S. presidents fought at the Battle of Shiloh...

building first opened. She also let spiders build webs inside the building and placed a broken bell at the top of a stone entrance arch. When teased about the shabbiness of the place, Colter said, "You can't imagine what it cost to make it look this old."

Extensive research into American Indian towers in the Grand Canyon area inspired the design for the Watchtower, a 70-foot structure overlooking the canyon. Colter studied the ruins of towers to be sure hers looked just like the real thing—only bigger. Seventy feet was higher than any known American Indian tower, so she built hers with a hidden skeleton of concrete and steel, covered by native stones.

Other important Grand Canyon structures designed by Colter include Hopi House, a shop that displayed and sold American Indian arts; Lookout Studio, a gift shop and observation station that, from a distance, looks like part of the canyon wall; Phantom Ranch, a cluster of cabins 5,000 feet below the canyon's rim; and Bright Angel Lodge, a complex of cabins and a hotel that includes Colter's famous "geological fireplace," which re-creates the different geologic strata of the canyon in miniature from floor to ceiling.

SHE DID IT HER WAY

Colter was famous for being demanding and independent-minded. She made masons tear down walls if they didn't look the way she wanted them to. She insisted that her elderly sister accompany her on the miles-long mule ride down the trail to Phantom Ranch for its grand opening. She even had her own style in dress, boldly wearing pants at a time when "proper" women didn't. She was a character who never quite fit in, which makes it ironic that the architectural movement she put in motion was all about fitting buildings seamlessly into their surroundings.

ARIZONA

Grand Canyon National Park
Grand Canyon, AZ 86023

Founded: 1893
Area: 1,218,375 acres
Average annual visitors: 4,000,000

www.nps.gov/grca

WHAT A SHOCKER

Shenandoah National Park ranger Roy Sullivan was struck by lightning an unbelievable seven times between 1942 and 1977 . . . and lived to tell all the tales!

Strike #1 (1942): While on duty in one of Shenandoah's fire lookout towers, Sullivan took his first hit. The lightning bolt hit his leg, and he lost a big toenail.

Strike #2 (1969): This time, he was driving on a country road. The lightning hit his truck, knocked him out, and singed off his eyebrows.

Strike #3 (1970): People started calling Sullivan the "human lightning rod" after the third strike, which injured his shoulder.

Strike #4 (1972): He took this hit while on duty at one of Shenandoah's ranger stations. The lightning set his hair on fire, so Sullivan started carrying a bucket of water around with him—just in case he needed to put out a blaze.

Strike #5 (1973): This one also set his hair on fire (thank goodness for that water bucket!). And it knocked him out of his car and blew off one of his shoes.

Strike #6 (1974): Lightning hit Sullivan at a park campground, and he hurt his ankle.

Strike #7 (1977): This might have been his most dangerous strike. The lightning hit him while he was fishing and burned his stomach and chest, requiring a hospital stay. (He recovered.)

Honorable Mention: Sullivan's wife was also hit by lightning once while she and Roy were hanging up clothes on a line in their backyard.

Michigan's Keweenaw National Historical Park is the site of an early "copper rush."

TALES OF THE TRAIL: PART II THE ORIENT EXPRESS

Bill Irwin—accompanied by his faithful guide dog—
was the first blind thru-hiker to trek the Appalachian Trail.

Bill Irwin was 50 years old when he made it to the base of Mt. Katahdin on November 21, 1990. But he didn't do it alone; he was accompanied by Orient, a German shepherd guide dog. Blind since age 28, Irwin believed that hiking the entire Appalachian Trail was a calling from God.

THE EXPRESS LEAVES THE STATION
He began his hike in Georgia on March 8. Since Irwin couldn't use the detailed official maps of the trail to keep him on track, his son Billy made a set of audio tapes that would supply his dad with information about the trail from Georgia to Delaware, measuring out the miles between landmarks and streams and giving the locations of primitive park shelters and huts along the trail. The tapes also told Irwin where he could leave the trail to find hotels, restaurants, and post offices. A staff member of the Appalachian Trail Conference taped an audio description of the rest of the trail— from Delaware to Maine.

ORIENTING TOGETHER
It took Irwin eight months to accomplish his goal. He carried a ski pole to help him feel his way, but most important to him was Orient. As the days passed, Orient seemed to develop a sense of what the trail was all about. He appeared to recognize the white markers on trees and lead Irwin in the right direction. Inevitably, Irwin sometimes lost the trail, but Orient could pick up the scents of other hikers and lead him back to the trail. He even learned to recognize the trail markers—piles of stones, or cairns—that tell disoriented hikers where to go. Orient could also sniff out drinking water when the team got thirsty.

Some birchbark canoes used on the Great Lakes could've carried the weight of two cars.

Occasionally, both man and dog got lost; when that happened, Irwin pulled out a whistle he'd brought along to signal to other hikers who would help lead him back to the trail. Irwin used his sense of touch to trace the lettering that was cut into wooden signs, so he could read the names of the trails and mountains and also feel out the arrows that told him which way to go.

THE FOOT OF THE PROBLEM
Irwin and Orient climbed, waded, and slogged an average of about eight miles a day. Every five days, they left the trail for a short rest, to refresh their gear, and to pick up packages of tapes or new supplies at post offices along the way. Irwin went through seven pairs of boots on the trek because he often stepped on sharp rocks, in water, or on ice that other hikers easily avoided. Orient had some foot problems, too: the ice in the Smoky Mountains cut his feet until he was lame. As soon as Irwin realized the problem, he stopped at a trail lean-to, where the pair stayed for days until Orient was healed.

BILL TAKES A SPILL
All long-distance hikers fall once in a while, but for Irwin the slips and slides were particularly difficult. Orient prevented plenty of falls by slowing or hesitating when the footing was treacherous so that Irwin knew to feel his way carefully. If Orient himself started to fall, Irwin felt it through the dog's harness and saved him from a tumble with a strong jerk. But the joint effort didn't always work. Irwin fell thousands of times, including an incident in Pennsylvania when he fell on some rocks and broke a rib. The injury slowed the team down, but it didn't stop them. Irwin left the trail to call a friend who carried his heavy backpack in her car for a few days, until the rib healed enough for Irwin to resume the burden.

THE EXPRESS ARRIVES
The hardest part of the trek was the last three weeks, which involved hiking the final 432 mountainous miles in New Hampshire and Maine. By that time, Orient had become so trail-hardened and tough that he started out eagerly in the morning, but Irwin had a lot more to deal with. It was already October, cold and windy, and his pace slowed dramatically as he coped with frostbite

Pipe Spring National Monument is a water source and ranch museum in the Arizona desert.

and hypothermia. But when he and Orient finished the trail on the day before Thanksgiving in 1990, Irwin became one of only 120 out of 1,450 aspiring hikers that year who completed the journey.

Every hiker who tries to conquer the Appalachian Trail takes a trail nickname: Irwin and Orient were the "Orient Express." In the close-knit hiking community, the name became an expression of the respect and admiration the pair had earned.

See page 382 for another true-life tale from the trail.

Appalachian National Scenic Trail
Harpers Ferry, WV 25425

Founded: 1925
Length: 2,175 miles
Annual average visitors: 3,500,000

www.nps.gov/appa

* * *

WHAT ARE THOSE STREAMERS UNDER CLOUDS?
Ever been driving along and noticed wispy streamers hanging down from rain clouds in the distance? Those thin dark streaks are called virga. They can occur anytime but are most common during winter or in desert areas, when air is dry. Because of the low humidity, precipitation often evaporates before it reaches the ground, creating those "hangers" under the clouds.

Cenizo, often called "barometer bush," tends to bloom when rain is coming.

LET'S GO PARKING

National parking, that is. All 58 of the officially designated national parks are here. Feel free to visit them all— if you can find 'em in this dense forest of letters!

```
V D D U A C A D I A M T A K J Y I G Q A V V Q Z R R Y Z
N E T Y U W O S L M C R U E H H X S G N D N D K H J H A
M A A B E O V A J O S H U A T R E E N O T S W O L L E Y
B E M C W L K Q Y U P E T R I F I E D F O R E S T A T O
Y M S D N A L S I N I G R I V O Y A G E U R S N Y K H S
G N E A E U A A O T X S D J R R V V S E Q U O I A E Q E
N R O L V V M T V R E C I N A C L O V N E S S A L C E M
E A A Y V E E R S A G U T R O T Y R D W I K G T S L E I
P H E N N T R D K I G T U R K S S P Z N P W N N D A R T
Z W L S D A I D G N N O G E T D I J N I C R I U R R A E
S I I N E C C L E I J Q H A N G T U S L O A R O O K G U
K A A N R O A S X E G I M A T U G F Y A T N P M J G N F
C R G O D C N N G R M K L C Y E D I E N W G S Y F H O S
G D X U I C S A Y N L S R H H U S D U E E E T K I E C L
S J A E A F A D C O I O M T L D C O N D R L O O A D R L
Z E R L J R M V N L N K F H V N M I F A J L H M N Z A X
K T H E O D O R E R O O S E V E L T P T S S O S E Y T M
B R Y C E C A N Y O N V B I P B F Y S M H T C T K D E T
A F I G R M N O T O Z K I U E G I E Y T Y E A A I Q R F
D C S P Q A X I Y S Y T L I L I F L L A B L A E Y P L T
L I L E H F S N R E V A C D A B S L R A C I O R R V A N
A M E C T H A N D W D M H P D W N A A B I A S G C G K C
N O R T H C A S C A D E S Z Y S A V P B A S Q C S T E I
D R O C K Y M O U N T A I N T N H H G R E A T B A S I N
S K Y C B D C G D G N H M A M M O T H C A V E A O Y X C
D H A O D N A N E H S H A Y E L L A V K U B O K J Y N U
Z L L V E H M O Q D G B N Y A B R E I C A L G G F Y R E
B Y E H H I G E V E R G L A D E S D N A L N O Y N A C S
```

Mission San Antonio de Valero, a top tourist destination, is better known as the Alamo.

ACADIA

AMERICAN SAMOA

ARCHES

BADLANDS

BIG BEND

BISCAYNE

BLACK CANYON OF THE
GUNNISON

BRYCE CANYON

CANYONLANDS

CAPITOL REEF

CARLSBAD CAVERNS

CHANNEL ISLANDS

CONGAREE

CRATER LAKE

CUYAHOGA VALLEY

DEATH VALLEY

DENALI

DRY TORTUGAS

EVERGLADES

GATES OF THE ARCTIC

GLACIER

GLACIER BAY

GRAND CANYON

GRAND TETON

GREAT BASIN

GREAT SAND DUNE

GREAT SMOKY
MOUNTAINS

GUADALUPE
MOUNTAINS

HALEAKALA

HAWAII VOLCANOES

HOT SPRINGS

ISLE ROYALE

JOSHUA TREE

KATMAI

KENAI FJORDS

KINGS CANYON

KOBUK VALLEY

LAKE CLARK

LASSEN VOLANIC

MAMMOTH CAVE

MESA VERDE

MOUNT RAINIER

NORTH CASCADES

OLYMPIC

PETRIFIED FOREST

REDWOOD

ROCKY MOUNTAIN

SAGUARO

SEQUOIA

SHENANDOAH

THEODORE ROOSEVELT

VIRGIN ISLANDS

VOYAGEURS

WIND CAVE

WRANGELL ST. ELIAS

YELLOWSTONE

YOSEMITE

ZION

For answers, turn to page 389.

The Kelso Dunes in California's Mojave National Preserve tower over 600 feet high.

TO RAZE OR NOT TO RAZE

The White House (part of the NPS site President's Park) wasn't always a national treasure. A number of presidents once seriously considered tearing it down or turning it into a museum and building a new residence somewhere else. Here's why.

NOT ENOUGH SPACE

At first, most Americans didn't think there was anything particularly special about the White House. Few had seen it or had any idea what it looked like, and even the families who lived there found it completely inadequate.

When it was built, the White House was the largest house in the country (and it remained so until after the Civil War). But it served so many different purposes that little of it was available for First Families to actually live in. The first floor, or "State Floor," was made up entirely of public rooms; and half of the second floor was taken up by the president's offices, which where staffed by as many as 30 employees. The First Family had to get by with the eight—or fewer—second-floor rooms that were left. By Lincoln's time, the situation was intolerable. There was no privacy. Anyone could walk in on the president doing official business.

THE LINCOLN WHITE HOUSE

Lincoln was so uncomfortable with the situation that he had a private corridor (which has since been removed) constructed. This allowed him to get from the family quarters to his office without having to pass through the reception room, where throngs of strangers were usually waiting to see him.

Lincoln also received $20,000 in federal money to improve the furnishings of the White House, which had become, as one visitor put it, "bare, worn and spoiled," like "a deserted farmstead," with holes in the carpets and paint peeling off of the walls in the state rooms.

The president was busy with the Civil War, so he turned the matter over to his wife, who spent every penny and went $6,700

Fort Larned (KS) protected mail coaches, freighters, and others on the Santa Fe Trail.

over budget. Lincoln was furious and refused to ask Congress to cover the balance. "It would stink in the nostrils of the American people," he fumed, "to have it said that the President of the United States had approved a bill overrunning an appropriate [amount] for flubdubs for this damned old house, when the soldiers cannot have blankets."

The new furnishings did not last for more than a few years. When Lincoln was assassinated in 1865, the White House fell into disarray. "Apparently," writes the White House Historical Society, "no one really supervised the White House during the five weeks Mrs. Lincoln lay mourning in her room, and vandals helped themselves."

SAVING THE HOUSE

However, at the same time the White House was being ransacked, it was gaining a new respect with Americans, attaining an almost shrinelike status. National tragedy turned the White House into a national monument. It wasn't just the White House anymore—it was the place where the great fallen hero, Lincoln, had lived. Photography had been invented about 30 years earlier, and for the first time, photos of the White House circulated around the country. It became a symbol of the presidency . . . and of America.

The Founding Fathers had assumed that future presidents would add to, or even demolish and rebuild the official residence as they saw fit. But after 1865, no president would have dared to suggest tearing it down.

To read about building the White House, turn to page 191.

President's Park (White House)
Washington, D.C. 20242

Founded: 1790
Area: 82 acres
Average annual visitors: 1,200,000

www.nps.gov/whho

Looking for a Karner blue butterfly? Try the 25-mile Indiana Dunes National Lakeshore.

NAME THAT PARK!

Can you match the park to its description?

1. Effigy Mounds National Monument

2. Ice Age National Scenic Trail

3. Alibates National Monument

4. Ala Kahakai National Historic Trail

5. Weir Farm National Historic Site

6. Aniakchak National Monument and Preserve

7. Ebey's Landing National Historic Reserve

A. Located on the Big Island of Hawaii, this site includes petroglyphs, temples, and shrines sacred to the Hawaiian people. It's also a haven for sea turtles and threatened or endangered animal species.

B. One of the least-visited units of the national parks system, this Alaskan site boasts a six-mile-wide, 2,000-foot-deep caldera that formed more than 3,500 years ago. The caldera erupted most recently in 1931, when ash fell on villages nearly 40 miles away.

C. This preserved site in northeast Iowa includes the largest collection of ancient Native American burial mounds in the United States and the only ones made to look like mammals. In 1949, President Harry Truman signed legislation making this a protected area.

D. Most of the land that makes up this Washington site is privately owned, and it was established in 1978 to protect the area's historic and natural resources, including wetlands, roads, and buildings. The site also still includes a military fort and an airstrip that U.S. Navy pilots use for training.

E. This Connecticut site was once the home of a painter who turned it into a haven for artists of all kinds. More than 120

Kansas's Tallgrass Prairie National Preserve commemorates a vanishing treasure.

years later, the 60-acre site continues to inspire visiting painters.

F. Located in Texas, this site requires that visitors take a ranger-guided tour to its most popular attraction: flint quarries.

G. This site uses a mammoth on its official logo and is entirely contained within the state of Wisconsin. It also gives visitors the opportunity to hike in an area once populated by mammoths and saber-toothed cats.

For answers, turn to page 390.

* * *

AN ARTIST'S LIFE

Take a look at at these two National Park Service sites dedicated to American artists:

Saint-Gaudens National Historic Site
Established: 1977
This site in Cornish, New Hampshire, preserves the gardens, home, and studios that once belonged to Augustus Saint-Gaudens, one of America's most famous sculptors. Saint-Gaudens summered on this estate from 1885 to 1897 and lived here year-round from 1900 until his death in 1907. More than 100 of his sculptures are on display at the site.

Weir Farm National Historic Site
Established: 1990
J. Alden Weir was an impressionist painter who owned this Connecticut farm from 1882 to 1919. (He traded a painting he'd purchased for the deed to the farm.) First, he created his own paintings there, but soon after, he turned his home into an artists' retreat for family and friends. Among the artists who worked and lived at the farm over the years were painter Sperry Andrews and sculptor Mahonri Young, grandson of Mormon church president Brigham Young. Today, the farm is still a working artists' colony and educational center. Visitors can tour the studios and farm buildings and stroll through the rural landscape that has been inspiring artists for more than a century.

Tallgrass Prairie once covered 400,000 acres of North America; only 4% remains.

LONELY PHONE BOOTH

In the 1960s, some miners put a phone booth in the middle of the
Mojave Desert National Preserve. Long after they left, the booth
remained . . . waiting for someone to call.

HELLO? ANYBODY THERE?
Miles from the nearest town, the old phone booth stood at
the junction of two dirt roads. Its windows were shot out;
the overhead light was gone. Yet the phone lines on the endless
rows of poles still popped and clicked in anticipation—just as
they'd been doing for nearly 30 years. Finally, in 1997, it rang.

A guy named Deuce had read about the booth and called the
number . . . and continued to call until a desert dweller named
Lorene answered. Deuce wrote a story about his call to nowhere,
posted it on his Web site, and the word spread through cyberspace.
Someone else called. Then another person, and another—just to
see if someone would answer. And quite often someone did. Only
accessible by four-wheel drive, the lonely phone booth soon
became a destination. Travelers drove for hours just to answer the
phone. One Texas man camped there for 32 days and answered
more than 500 calls.

REACH OUT AND TOUCH SOMEONE
Someone posted a call log in the booth to record where people
were calling from: as close as Los Angeles and as far away as New
Zealand and Kosovo. Why'd they call? Some liked the idea of two
people who have never met—and probably never will—talking to
each other. Just sending a call out into the Great Void and having
someone answer was reward enough for most.

Unfortunately, the National Park Service and Pacific Bell tore
down the famous Mojave phone booth in 2000. Reason? It was
getting too many calls. The traffic (20 to 30 visitors a day) was
starting to have a negative impact on the fragile desert environment. The old stop sign at the cattle grate still swings in the wind.
And the phone lines still pop and click in anticipation. But all
that's left of the loneliest phone on earth is a ghost ring. So if the
urge strikes you to dial (760) 733-9969, be prepared to wait a very,
very long time for someone to answer.

West Virginia's Bluestone National Scenic River has carved a gorge 1,000 feet deep.

MORE IN MOJAVE

The phone booth is gone, but there's a lot to see and do at the Mojave Desert National Preserve. Eleven hiking trails (both established and rough paths) ranging from 1/4 mile to eight miles in length are open to visitors. There are also horseback riding trails, four-wheel-drive routes, and three campgrounds (one of which makes room for horses). And every spring (especially in March and April), Mojave's wildflowers come into bloom, a dramatic and colorful natural show that attracts hundreds of visitors each year.

CALIFORNIA

Mojave National Preserve
Barstow, CA 92311

Founded: 1994
Area: 1,600,000 acres
Average annual visitors: 630,000

www.nps.gov/moja

* * *

MNEMONICS FOR THE GREAT OUTDOORS

Directions on compass (north, east, south, west):
NEVER EAT SHREDDED WHEAT

Great Lakes (Huron, Ontario, Michigan, Erie, Superior):
H O M E S

The order of the planets according to their distance from the Sun (Mercury, Venus, Earth, Mars, Jupiter, Saturn, Uranus, Neptune):

MY VERY EDUCATED MOTHER JUST SENT US NICKELS.

The biological groupings used in taxonomy (domain, kingdom, phylum, class, order, family, genus, species):

DANISH KINGS POSSESS CROWNS OF FINE GEMSTONES.

DETERGENT IN THE DESERT

Twenty-Mule Team Borax was America's most popular hand and laundry soap during the early and mid 1900s, and its mule team icon is a tribute to one of the most arduous journeys ever taken.

EUREKA! IT'S ... BORAX?

In 1881, prospector Aaron Winters was living near the California/Nevada border in what is now Death Valley National Park in the hopes of unearthing a vein of silver or gold. Instead, he found another "gold mine"—the hard white crystal balls he scraped away each day while mining at his claim were borax, a rare crystal used in detergents. Winters quickly capitalized on the find and sold his claim to William T. Coleman, a San Francisco businessman who created a company called the Harmony Borax Works.

Coleman hired workers to dig up the Death Valley borax. They labored in the desert heat (temperatures sometimes reached 130 degrees) and made little money (most were paid just $1.50 a day), extracting more than 2 million tons of borax per year. All that borax then had to be transported to the nearest railroad stop, which was more than 160 miles away in the town of Mojave. Coleman employed mule teams to handle the chore. Between 1883 and 1889 (when a railway was built to access the borax mines), the mules hauled more than 20 million pounds of borax out of Death Valley.

MULE MUSCLE

Technically, these teams, called "twenty-mule teams," were made up of 18 mules and two horses. The mules—sure-footed, fast, and sturdy—supplied the muscle. The horses were the "wheelers," the animals closest to the wagon. Wheelers could weigh as much as 1,800 pounds. They had to be large and tall because it was their job to direct and turn the wagons.

The wagons themselves were enormous. Each one weighed 7,800 pounds empty and was built to haul at least 24,000 pounds of

---

Rosie the Riveter National Historical Park is in Richmond, CA, a wartime boom town.

borax through Death Valley's sand and over rock-strewn mountain trails. The wagons' front wheels measured five feet high, and the rear wheels seven feet high; the tires were made of iron.

Each team pulled three wagons. The first two carried the borax, and the third carried a 500-gallon water tank and enough hay, grain, and provisions to feed the men and animals during the 10-day trip to the railroad stop (where they could stock up on supplies). When on the trail, the wagons weighed more than 70,000 pounds.

PULLING WITH BELLS ON

The mules and horses wore thick collars and were latched together by an 80-foot chain fastened to the first wagon. A leather rope called the "jerk line" ran through the collar ring of each animal on the left side of the line. Drivers used this rope to control the team: a hard yank on the line turned the animals to the left; a series of jerks turned them right.

The mules also wore bells on their collars. Not only did this announce their arrival at the end of the journey, company officials thought that the bells created a rhythm that helped the team walk faster. At full speed, the mules pulled the wagons approximately two miles per hour.

WANNA BE A COWBOY?

Three men worked the team: a driver, skinner, and swamper. They could make up to $150 a month, which was a hefty sum in the late 19th century.

The driver sat atop the lead wagon; he controlled the jerk line and the brake straps. (One of the most famous drivers of the time was Bill Parkinson, called "Borax Bill." Parkinson was renowned for efficiently extricating his wagon trains from whatever perilous terrain they encountered and for keeping his animals in top condition.)

The skinner rode one of the wheeler horses. The skinner, also called a "teamster," was charged with keeping the wagons moving and the mules under control.

The swamper rode on the last wagon and controlled the brake when the team was going downhill. He was also the cook, blacksmith, and handyman on the trip.

That famous Gateway Arch is at the Jefferson National Expansion Monument in St. Louis.

THE ROAD TO MOJAVE

The trip to the railroad stop took the teams over some of the area's most treacherous terrain and took 20 days round-trip. It began in Death Valley at 190 feet below sea level, climbed to an elevation of 2,000 feet in the steep Funeral and Panamint mountains, and then descended into another desert to reach Mojave.

There was not a single house or building along the route, and during one stretch, the teams had to walk 60 miles to find water. The mule teams could travel 16 to 18 miles a day, even in temperatures that sometimes reached 140 degrees.

On arrival at the railroad station, workers unloaded the borax, the team rested overnight, and they set out on their return trip the next morning. Five teams of men and mules followed this schedule over the nearly six years that Coleman's company used the twenty-mule teams to extract borax from Death Valley.

TODAY

Remnants of the mine, plant, and company settlement can be found about one mile north of the Furnace Creek visitor center in Death Valley National Park. A 3/8-mile interpretive trail circles the area and includes pictures and descriptions of life at the site when the mine was in operation. There is also one underground borax mine still operating in Death Valley National Park. It's called the Billie Mine and can be found along the road to Dante's View.

CALIFORNIA

Death Valley National Park
Death Valley, CA 92328

Founded: 1994
Area: 3,400,000 acres
Average annual visitors: 800,000

www.nps.gov/deva

Alligator hunting isn't allowed in Florida's 720,000-acre Big Cypress National Preserve.

LODGER THAN LIFE

Whether you pitch a tent beneath the stars or slip between the sheets in a fancy hotel, an overnight stay in a national park is a memorable experience.

THE AHWAHNEE: YOSEMITE NATIONAL PARK
Nestled next to the granite cliffs that surround Yosemite Valley, the Ahwahnee is the most luxurious and expensive lodge in the National Park System. That's because the first National Park Service superintendent, Stephen T. Mather, spearheaded construction of the Ahwahnee for well-heeled visitors who didn't go for the tents and cabins that were the only options during the park's early years. Attracting upscale guests would ensure more federal funds, which, when the hotel opened in 1927, were tied to park visitation numbers. Mather also hoped the guests would be influential enough to lend political support to the park system. Mather also instructed the lodge's architect, Gilbert Stanley Underwood, to build the Ahwahnee to resist fire. Even though it looks like a log and stone lodge, it's actually made of stone and concrete that was stamped with real timbers and then colored to resemble wood.

Named after the Native American word for the Yosemite Valley, the Ahwahnee continued to attract the rich and famous, including John F. Kennedy (who brought his own rocking chair with him for his chronic back pain), Franklin and Eleanor Roosevelt, and Queen Elizabeth II. And although he was never an overnight guest, famous Yosemite photographer Ansel Adams used to drop by to play the piano in the lobby.

During World War II, the U.S. Navy commandeered the Ahwahnee to use as a convalescent hospital for the 7th Fleet. By the time the navy moved out in 1945, the hotel was in such bad shape that it had to be extensively renovated. These days the hotel attracts nobility of the Hollywood kind: before their public split, Brad Pitt and Jennifer Aniston were frequent guests.

BRYCE CANYON LODGE: BRYCE NATIONAL PARK
Perched on the rim of the colorful canyon it's named for, the Bryce Canyon Lodge was designed in the prevailing "parkitecture" style

of the early 20th century to fit in with its natural surroundings. Architect Gilbert Stanley Underwood designed the lodge a few years before the Ahwahnee, using local sandstone and indigenous ponderosa pine to create a color palette that would blend in. The Bryce Canyon Lodge was completed in 1925.

In the early years of national park tourism, visitors made a circuit through the western parks, shuttled by train from one lodge to another. To make Bryce Canyon Lodge stand out from all the rest, hotel employees lined up in front of the building and sang goodbye to the guests as they left for the railroad station, a custom the lodge continued well into the 1950s.

Visitors of today aren't sung to anymore, but they can still get a feel for the comfort of the lodge's historic cabins, which have been restored to their 1920s splendor. They feature fireplaces, log-beamed ceilings, reproductions of period furniture, and authentic quilts. The only thing that isn't historically accurate is the indoor plumbing.

EL TOVAR HOTEL: GRAND CANYON NATIONAL PARK

Built by the Santa Fe Railway in 1905 to promote its tourism services, the El Tovar Hotel on the Grand Canyon's South Rim is named for Pedro de Tovar, who led an expedition through the area in 1540. Architect Charles Whittlesey's design, using native stone and Douglas fir shipped in from Oregon, helped fit the structure into its majestic surroundings.

From its early days, the El Tovar had a reputation for excellence. Somewhat isolated by limited road access, the hotel kept its own chickens and cows so that its restaurant always had fresh eggs and milk.

Among the luminaries who've stayed there is Paul McCartney, who, in 2001, checked in under an assumed name and asked the staff to keep his visit a secret. But late one night, he wandered into the lounge and started playing the piano. Sleepy hotel guests—not realizing who was causing the ruckus—complained about the "noise," and the hotel staff had to ask McCartney to be quiet.

KETTLE FALLS HOTEL AND RESORT: VOYAGEURS NATIONAL PARK

On the banks of a remote lake near the Minnesota-Canada border, Kettle Falls Hotel is so remote that you can only get there by boat

California's Mojave National Preserve is a big desert area, covering 1.6 million acres.

or seaplane. The small complex of wooden structures is listed on the National Register of Historic Places. The hotel was constructed between 1910 and 1913 to house construction workers and lumberjacks working on the nearby Kettle Falls Dam, allegedly with money that the owner, W. E. Rose, got from local madam Nellie Bly (not to be confused with the famous journalist of the same name). Legend has it that Bly's "fancy ladies" plied their trade at the hotel. But that wasn't the only illegal activity going on. During Prohibition in the 1920s, bootleggers distilled and sold whiskey near the hotel. Today the small lodge offers more family-friendly pleasures: you're apt to find more fishermen than felons.

MANY GLACIER HOTEL: GLACIER NATIONAL PARK

On the banks of Swiftcurrent Lake and surrounded by the northern mountains of Montana, Many Glacier Hotel looks like a Swiss chalet. Building began on the hotel in 1914, but severe weather during construction made supply roads nearly inaccessible and delayed the project; soon the hotel was well over budget. It took almost five years to finish, and by the time it was complete, Louis Hill, president of the Great Northern Railway and sponsor of the hotel, regretted his investment. As many as 20 years after Many Glacier opened, Hill still hadn't recovered the millions he'd invested in this hotel and other Glacier Park buildings. In 1936, when hotel employees successfully fought off a wildfire and cabled the good news to headquarters saying, "We have saved the hotel!" Hill telegrammed back, "Why?"

The hotel fell into disrepair in the late 1950s, so to distract visitors from the peeling paint and rickety furnishing, the employees produced what they called "a program of evening diversions" from 1961 to 1983. These elaborate Broadway musicals, concerts, and variety shows starred the maids, waiters, and busboys. The idea apparently worked, because the hotel became increasingly popular in the mid-1980s and profits rose to the point where the needed repairs could be made.

OLD FAITHFUL INN: YELLOWSTONE NATIONAL PARK

One of the largest log structures in the world, with massive timbers that stretch up 77 feet in the lobby, the Old Faithful Inn doesn't actually look out on the geyser from which it takes its name.

You can visit a lava tube cave at Lava Beds National Monument in Tulelake, California.

Instead, architect Robert Chambers Reamers situated the entrance of the 1903 structure so that visitors got great views of Old Faithful as they stepped out of their carriages and prepared to enter the lodge (they couldn't see it from the inside).

Thanks to the soaring ceilings, the grand entrance is spectacular—though if you're squeamish, the bats that fly around in the upper rafters might be a distraction. There's a ghostly legend here, too. The story goes like this: A newlywed couple checked in shortly after the inn was opened. They toured the geysers, dined, and then retired for the evening. The next morning, the bride's headless body was found on her bed—and her soul was left to haunt the corridors. Too bad the story is a hoax: George Bornemann, the inn manager at the time, admitted to making it up to entertain the guests.

HONORABLE MENTION
CINNAMON BAY CAMPGROUND: VIRGIN ISLANDS NATIONAL PARK

The north shore of St. John in the U.S. Virgin Islands is the site of a national park lodge that isn't really a lodge at all. It's a complex of outdoor facilities—"cottages" made with two concrete walls and two screen walls, preassembled tents, and "bare sites" where you bring what you need and live off the land. These primitive accommodations are a far cry from the luxurious resorts elsewhere on the island—and they're a lot cheaper. A bare site will run you $27 a night year-round; a cottage around $125 during peak season (the average hotel room goes for about $400).

Cinnamon Bay is awash in history, too. The campground was built on the site of an old sugar plantation and rum distillery that dates back to the early 1700s. You can still see the large grinding stones they used to crush the cane before it was distilled into rum. So why isn't this place called Rum Bay? Legend has it that the name comes from the island's bay rum trees, the leaves of which smell like cinnamon when you crush them.

* * *

The Great Smoky Mountains were named for the smoky, bluish mist that often engulfs the area.

Philadelphia's Deshler-Morris House is the oldest official presidential residence.

MARCH OF THE MORMONS

If they'd had their druthers, the followers of Joseph Smith would probably have stayed in New York . . . and Ohio . . . and Illinois. Instead, they were run out of all those places and traveled 1,300 miles west before they finally found a home in Utah. The Mormon Pioneer National Historic Trail follows the route of that 19th-century migration.

CALLING ALL ANGELS

Joseph Smith said he saw his first angel in 1820 when he was a teenager. Seven years later, an angel showed him where to find some inscribed gold plates that he then transcribed into *The Book of Mormon*—the bible of the Mormon faith. And in 1830, Smith officially founded the Mormon religion in Fayette, New York.

His followers considered him to be a prophet, but a lot of other people thought he was dangerous and sacrilegious. So the Mormons were forced out of New York. They traveled west to Illinois where, in 1839, they bought a section of vacant land and named it Nauvoo (anglicized Hebrew for "to be beautiful").

The town of Nauvoo prospered, but over time, the Mormon practice of polygamy and the large number of new members the religion was attracting led to a growing feeling of fear among non-Mormons in the area. Then in 1844, Joseph Smith was attacked and killed by an angry mob. His followers stayed in Nauvoo for a time, but eventually—after hundreds of their houses and farm buildings were burned to the ground by angry neighbors—they decided to leave.

THE TREK WEST

It was up to Brigham Young, Smith's successor, to lead them somewhere safe. He decided on Utah. Before Joseph Smith died, he'd been considering moving the entire church membership there, to an area near the Great Salt Lake; he'd read a report written by John C. Fremont that included detailed maps of the area, and the fact that Utah was, at the time, beyond the boundaries of the

Capulin Volcano (NM), a national monument, last erupted around 60,000 years ago.

United States seemed a way to ensure the group's religious freedom.

On February 4, 1846, Brigham Young and 3,000 Mormons left Illinois for Utah. They expected to reach Salt Lake by the following winter, but rough trails and nasty winter weather in Iowa slowed them down. So they broke up the large wagon train into bands of 10, 50, or 100 people who would go on in waves and improve the trail, build bridges, and establish ferry services and way stations for the coming migration.

The first leg of the trip was the hardest. It took 120 days for the first group to reach the Missouri River, 265 miles from Nauvoo. Once there, they split in half: One group stayed on the east side of the river and established a settlement called Kanesville (now Council Bluffs, Iowa) as a way station. The others set up a small village called the Winter Quarters on the west side of the river in what is present-day Omaha, Nebraska.

There they stayed. Even though it was June, winter was coming, and Young didn't want his followers to struggle with unknown terrain and bitter weather during the harsh winter months. So the group dug in and waited for spring.

SPRINGING FORWARD

The next leg of the journey began in April 1847. The first wagon train to leave the Missouri river settlements consisted of 148 people (only three of whom were women), 72 wagons, and a large collection of livestock. They followed the established Oregon Trail, also known as the Great Platte River Road, through Nebraska and then along the North Platte River to Fort Caspar in Casper, Wyoming. There, they set up a ferry service and continued on across Wyoming to Fort Bridger, a fur trading post.

ARE WE THERE YET?

It was July. The Mormons had 116 miles left to travel before they reached the Great Salt Lake. On July 9, they set out again, this time leaving the Oregon Trail and following part of the route that the ill-fated Donner-Reed party had traveled the year before on its way to California.

The new trail was steep and crowded with brush. But the Mormons forged ahead, and on July 24, 1847, the first group arrived in the Great Salt Lake Valley. It had been a rough trip.

More than 200 species of birds have been sighted at Cabrillo National Monument (CA).

Four hundred people had died along the way; others were weak or sick. But most of them had made it.

They immediately started building a town and planting crops in preparation for the migration that would follow. From 1847 to 1869—when the first transcontinental railroad was completed—70,000 Mormons made the journey to Utah.

THIS IS THE PLACE
Today, the 1,300-mile-long Mormon Pioneer Trail is part of the National Park Service. It was established in 1978 and spans five states: Illinois, Iowa, Nebraska, Wyoming, and Utah. There are many sites for tourists to visit along the way. Some that the National Park Service recommends are the Nauvoo National Historic District in Illinois, the Winter Quarters Complex in Nebraska, the Ancient Bluff Ruins in Nebraska (these three buttes were named by British Mormon converts who thought they resembled ancient castles and ruins), the Fort Bridger State Historic Site (which features a reconstruction of the original trading post), and the This Is the Place Heritage Park in Salt Lake City, a 500-acre park with a visitor center and a reconstructed pioneer village.

To read a story of rescue and survival along the Mormon Pioneer National Historic Trail, turn to page 361.

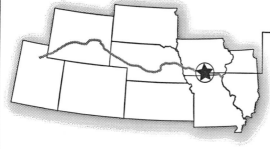

Mormon Pioneer National Historic Trail
Salt Lake City, UT 84111

Founded: 1978
Length: 1,300 miles

www.nps.gov/mopi

The Delaware & Lehigh National Heritage Corridor traverses five Pennsylvania counties.

SLAVES OF NEW YORK

One of the newest national park sites, the African Burial Ground National Monument in New York City is dedicated to the forgotten story of Africans in the New World.

In 1991, excavators working on a new federal building site in Manhattan found the skeletal remains of more than 400 people who'd been buried hundreds of years ago—Africans who helped build the young city from the 1600s on. The five-acre burial site, a few blocks from where the twin towers once stood, is believed to contain the skeletal remains of as many as 20,000 Africans who lived during the 17th and 18th centuries.

Before the Revolutionary War, New York was second only to Charleston, South Carolina, as the New World's slave-trading center. The slaves began arriving in 1626 and eventually made up nearly 40 percent of the population of what was then New Amsterdam.

THE FINDINGS

While studying the burial site, Howard University researchers found that 40 percent of the interred Africans were children under 12. Defects in tooth enamel indicated that many died of malnutrition and suffered more metabolic illnesses (like diabetes, sickle cell anemia, and hemophilia) than children who grew up in Africa. The skeletons of older slaves showed bone lesions, breaks, spinal fractures, and evidence of disease, malnutrition, and overwork. The researchers also found beads, pottery shards, and pins attached to burial shrouds.

A PLACE OF THEIR OWN

Barred from the cemeteries of most New York churches, both enslaved and free Africans buried their dead outside the early city, beyond the wall the Dutch built to defend themselves against the British and the Native Americans (the wall for which Wall Street was named). That land was owned by free blacks and was called the African Burial Ground.

In 1794, when New York City expanded beyond its colonial walls, city officials closed the African Burial Ground. In 1827, the

Mission Concepción has San Antonio's only mission church that has never collapsed.

State of New York abolished slavery. By then, the burial site was covered by 25 feet of landfill.

RISING FROM THE RUBBLE—AGAIN

After archaeologists discovered the burial ground in the early 1990s, they established a library and research office in the World Trade Center. Both were destroyed on September 11, 2001, but most of the artifacts from the project were found intact in the rubble.

In 2003, the remains were reinterred at the burial ground, and in February 2006 the African Burial Ground became a national monument (and part of the Manhattan Sites/National Parks of New York Harbor) by presidential order. Construction on a memorial at the site is scheduled to continue through 2008.

African Burial Ground National Monument
New York, NY 100007

Founded: 2006
Area: .345 acres

www.africanburialground.gov

NEW YORK

* * *

The African Burial Ground National Monument is one of three African American NPS monuments. The other two are the Booker T. Washington National Monument in Virginia and the George Washington Carver National Monument in Missouri.

* * *

"I expose slavery in this country, because to expose it is to kill it. Slavery is one of those monsters of darkness to whom the light of truth is death."

—Frederick Douglass

BURROS ON THE LOOSE

The lone prospector walking beside his overloaded burro is an icon of the Old West. But when the animals were no longer needed, they were abandoned and left to fend for themselves. In many areas, they flourished and, later, created problems in the national parks.

The first burros came to the Southwest in the 1500s with the Spaniards. By the 1800s, the animals had become the preferred beasts of burden for early prospectors because they were hardy and could trek many miles across the deserts in search of gold and silver. Burros carried water, supplies, and machinery to the mines and hauled out the ore and rock; they also turned the mill wheels that ground the ore.

Native to the Egyptian desert, these animals thrived in the harsh American wilderness, and by the mid-20th century, approximately 20,000 wild burros populated Western canyons and caverns.

BURROS AND BUREAUCRATS

All these loose burros became an ecological problem for America's national parks. The trouble became particularly acute at Grand Canyon National Park, Bandelier National Monument, and Death Valley National Park, where the burros overgrazed vegetation and endangered native animals (especially the bighorn sheep) that depended on it. The burros' wallowing, urination, and defecation in creeks and springs contaminated many of the parks' water sources. And the burros inadvertently created paths that were mistaken for trails, leading hikers off of regular passageways.

So in the 1950s, the National Park Service and the Bureau of Land Management, the government agency in charge of overseeing public lands, tried to remove the burros from the parks. It was a daunting task. Burros are solitary animals that do not spend much time in herds, so catching them was hard.

The government tried a couple of things. Officials attempted to corral the animals at water sources, but the burros were too quick and got away. Then agents used nonlethal net guns to try to trap

---

There are eight lighthouses along the New Jersey Coastal Heritage Trail.

the animals. That didn't work either, and the public was outraged at how many burros were actually killed with the "nonlethal" weapons. Finally, in 1971, wild burros gained some legal protection; Congress passed Wild Free-Roaming Horses and Burros Act, which required that the National Park Service devise humane ways of rounding up the burros and finding new places for them to live.

NEW HOMES ON THE RANGE
In the early 1980s, the National Park Service and animal advocacy groups (most notably, the New York–based Fund for Animals) devised a plan to remove most burros from the Grand Canyon and Death Valley parks in relatively short order. Helicopter pilots chased the animals up three-sided canyons until they ran out of room. Then, the trapped burros were easy for riders on horseback to capture. Over the years, this process has been simplified, and today rangers use traps baited with treats to lure the animals into captivity.

Bandelier National Monument was more problematic because of its open-ended canyons. After several frustrating years, park officials used herding dogs to hold the burros at bay until cowboys could rope them and load them into carriers. The captured animals from all three sites were then put up for private adoption.

In addition, the Fund for Animals purchased and released more than 2,000 animals onto their Black Beauty Ranch, a 2,000-acre sanctuary in eastern Texas. The Peaceful Valley Donkey Rescue program in Acton, California, also helped to find permanent homes for rescued burros and provided medical treatment and care—even microchip identification implantation—to those that live on their ranch. Animals that were deemed "unadoptable" went to government sanctuaries, where they lived out their lives roaming the prairie. All of these programs continue today. Finally, the wild western burros have safe places to call home.

BURRO BASICS
- Burros are also known as donkeys, which are domesticated asses. The term *burro* is Spanish for "ass."
- Burros are smaller than horses and excel as pack animals because they are sure-footed, patient, and smart.
- They're also hardy. Burros can live twice as long as horses and

need less food and water. They can lose 30 percent of their body weight before dehydration sets in and need to drink for just 5 minutes to replenish themselves. By comparison, most humans lose consciousness when they lose 10 percent of their body weight due to dehydration, and it takes them at least 24 hours of hydration to rebound.

* * *

MANZANAR NATIONAL HISTORIC SITE

On February 9, 1942, just months after the Japanese attack on Pearl Harbor, President Franklin D. Roosevelt signed Executive Order 9066, which gave U.S. authorities the legal right to relocate Japanese Americans living in Western coastal cities to inland internment camps. The officially stated rationale behind the plan was to prevent espionage. But some people (Eleanor Roosevelt included) thought it smacked of racism.

The army's Wartime Civilian Control Administration leased an old farm called Manzanar (Spanish for "apple orchard"), in Owens Valley, California, east of the Sierra Nevadas. A civilian staff working 10 hours a day, 7 days a week, constructed several structures initially, but after the detainees arrived, the Japanese built more buildings themselves. Eventually, eight guard towers went up around the perimeter of the camp, staffed by military police armed with submachine guns.

On March 21, 1942, the first 82 Japanese-American detainees arrived. By July, it topped 10,000. In total, some 120,000 Japanese Americans of all ages were held at Manzanar and at nine other camps around the country. Over the years, the residents found ways to personalize their surroundings, constructing elaborate gardens, ponds, and even digging out dirt basements under their barracks to increase their living space. When the Manzanar Relocation Camp closed in November 1945, some detainees were reluctant to leave; they had no homes to go back to. Most returned home to find they'd lost everything.

Only a few buildings remain in what's now the Manzanar National Historic site. But the Eastern California Museum, five miles north of Manzanar (in the town of Independence), maintains an extensive collection of oral history exhibits, historic photographs, and artifacts from the camp.

ALL ROADS LEAD TO CHACO

Can a bunch of old buildings and some rock art in New Mexico be considered an endangered species?

The civilization that flourished in Chaco Canyon (now a national historic park in New Mexico) parallels the Aztecs, Maya, and Incas of the ancient Americas. The people of Chaco were the Anasazi (an anglicized Navajo word meaning "ancient ones" or "ancient enemy"), and they were the ancestors of the modern-day Pueblo Indians, a group that includes 19 nations (among them the Hopi and the Zuni).

LOST AND FOUND

At the center of the Chaco Canyon ruins is Pueblo Bonito ("beautiful town"), a complex that was constructed between AD 850 and 1130, and named by the Spaniards who visited the area in the 16th century. Built of local sandstone, Pueblo Bonito is five stories high and includes about 800 rooms, 37 kivas (sacred spaces set aside for ceremonial purposes), and several spacious plazas that cover three acres. It's the largest prehistoric Native American building ever excavated in the Southwest and one of the most thoroughly explored sites in North America.

An American military expedition led by Lieutenant James Simpson discovered Chaco in 1849. Simpson later published a detailed description that launched modern archaeological expeditions to the site.

DIGGING UP THE EVIDENCE

Experts have long debated Pueblo Bonito's purpose. At first, they thought it was a kind of ancient apartment building, but there's a lot of evidence against that theory:

- Many of the rooms were too enclosed to have had fires, which would have been essential for cooking and warmth. Infrared photography also shows low levels of charcoal in and around

---

Once close to extinction, bighorn sheep are now relatively common in western parks.

the buildings, proving that there weren't enough fires to support a population.

- Fewer than 300 buried bodies have been found around Chaco, far too few for the compound to ever have been a thriving community.

- There isn't enough garbage to show that people lived there year-round. In fact, the trash that archaeologists did find was in layers, suggesting that people came for a short while and then went on their way.

- The weather in the canyon is extreme, making for a short growing season. Food would have been too scarce to support a large community. And even though water diversion systems were found, there wouldn't have been enough water for crops.

All this evidence—and the fact that the canyon is at the center of a vast network of ancient roads leading to outlying sites—finally convinced the experts that Chaco Canyon was a meeting place. During certain times of the year (though they aren't sure which times exactly), large numbers of people came to Chaco to build the structures, trade goods, harvest crops, and participate in ceremonies (the size of the kivas suggest that thousands of worshippers could gather at one time).

ANCIENT OBSERVATORIES

It also appears that the area was home to a series of simple and ingenious clockworks and calendars. Pueblo Bonito (and some of the other major buildings nearby) are oriented on a north-south axis. Inside the pueblo, the placement of doorways and steps and the shadow of one lonely Ponderosa pine tree—which may have been used as the gnomon of a sundial—indicate that the Anasazi used the site to monitor the movements of the sun.

Outside the pueblo, on nearby Fajada Butte, two slabs of sandstone catch a sliver of sunlight that identifies the summer and winter solstices. Another sliver of light shows the equinox. This calendar also marks the 18.6-year cycle of the moon.

FACING THE FUTURE

In 1989, rangers had to close Fajada Butte to tourists because the sandstone slabs had shifted, possibly from increased erosion due to too many visitors. And therein lies Chaco's problem.

The park attracts about 90,000 people a year even though its facilities include nothing more than a visitor center and campsite and it's accessible via two long dirt roads (one of which is only slightly less rough and dusty than the other). All visitors are free to explore the ruins. There are plans to pave one of the access roads, which will surely increase traffic to the park. Archaeological societies, citizen groups, and the Sierra Club oppose that plan; they consider Chaco to be endangered, just as an animal becomes endangered when civilization invades its habitat, and believe it should be protected, not made more accessible.

At least one ranger at the park does think that when the road is fully paved, it's likely that Pueblo Bonito and other sites will be declared off-limits to foot traffic and Chaco will become more like a museum than a living piece of history. So if you enjoy poking around ancient ruins rather than looking at them from a distance, plan your visit to Chaco sooner rather than later.

NEW MEXICO

Chaco Culture National Historic Park
Nageezi, NM 87037

Founded: 1907/1980
Area: 32,840 acres
Average annual visitors: 45,000

www.nps.gov/chcu

* * *

LONG LIVE THE LIZARDS!
Dinosaurs became extinct 65 million years ago, but lizards are still a common sight at Dinosaur National Monument on the border of Colorado and Utah. The small, inquisitive reptiles have endured on Earth for more than 300 million years, far outlasting their giant cousins

Idaho's tallest pinyon pines—more than 55 feet—are in City of Rocks National Reserve, in Almo.

ROADS LESS TRAVELED

We asked some national park rangers to give us the inside scoop on the best drives in the parks. Here are what they suggested—six little-known drives from gator country to canyon land. Fasten your seat belts!

KINGS CANYON NATIONAL PARK

Drive: From Grant Grove to Cedar Grove (one hour east of Fresno, California, on Highway 180)

Length: 44 miles round-trip (takes about two hours)

What you'll see: The drive follows the base of Kings Canyon, where you'll see caves, waterfalls, and, in the spring, rapids on the Kings River. Just don't go swimming. "It's raging," says park dispatcher Daniel Gibler. The river "comes down out of the mountain with enough force to move buildings. We pull people out of there every year."

THEODORE ROOSEVELT NATIONAL PARK

Drive: The park's South Unit loop road

Length: 36 miles total (takes about 1-1/2 hours)

What you'll see: This park in North Dakota is where the bison really roam . . . and other animals too—elk, wild horses, 180 species of birds, and lots of prairie dogs. There are many fields "with hundreds and hundreds of holes," says National Parks spokeswoman Kathy Kupper. It's "like that Whack-a-Mole game. They're just popping up constantly." (For an even more remote drive with the baddest Badland views, try the 28-mile scenic drive in the park's North Unit, off Highway 85 south of Watford City.)

EVERGLADES NATIONAL PARK

Drive: State road 9336 from Homestead to Flamingo, Florida

Length: 76 miles round-trip (takes about two hours)

What you'll see: Birds, panthers, alligators, and crocodiles often appear on this trip through an obscure corner of the Everglades' marshes and swamps. The area of the park gets few visitors because a hurricane decimated the campground and hotel. So the animals are thriving. Kupper says, "You'd think the park had put the alligators and crocodiles there on display. They're just sitting there with their mouths open, sunning themselves."

COLORADO NATIONAL MONUMENT

Drive: Rim Rock Drive off I-70, four miles south of Fruita, Colorado

Length: 23 miles total (the loop takes about 45 minutes)

What you'll see: Forget the Rockies and take in Colorado's canyon-and-plateau country instead, says National Parks spokesman Jeffrey Olson. Deep cliffs and rock towers greet you here. Keep an eye out, too, for lines of cyclists testing their mettle on the loop road, a climb of 2,300-vertical feet.

KENAI FJORDS NATIONAL PARK

Drive: Off of Glacier Road in Seward, Alaska

Length: 16 miles round trip (takes about 30 minutes)

What you'll see: This drive takes you into Alaska's rugged backcountry, past bald eagles and bears along Resurrection River to the base of Exit Glacier, a 3,000-foot ribbon of ice that spills out between mountain ridges. If you're game for a longer drive, try the 120-mile trip from Anchorage to Seward along the Phoenix Highway, a national scenic byway from the coast through mountain peaks (keep an eye out for goats, bears, and moose) and hemlock forests before returning to the sea.

GREAT SMOKY MOUNTAINS NATIONAL PARK

Drive: Parson Branch Road near Chilhowee, Tennessee, at the western end of the Cades Cove loop

Length: 8 miles one way (takes about 30 minutes)

What you'll see: This gravelly road was repaired in 2006 after storms washed it out. It's still bumpy, though, similar to riding along a hiking trail through old hardwood forests, past creeks, and over ridges.

For hikes, turn to page 343.

NATIONAL PARK RANGERS

"People expect rangers to know just about everything, and they usually do. The typical park ranger works as a historian, resource manager, law enforcement officer, curator, teacher, and sometimes paramedic and rescuer."
Vice President Dick Cheney, April 21, 2001

T he park ranger motto is "Preserve and protect our natural resources." Today's ranger does this—and so much more.

RANGER DUTIES

Typical ranger responsibilities include leading guided tours, maintaining nature trails, operating campgrounds, overseeing cultural activities, and teaching visitors about fire safety. But sometimes they perform atypical, even dangerous, jobs. Rangers lead search-and-rescue operations, are often the park's first defenders against fire, and perform park maintenance in hazardous areas (avalanche-prone mountains, backwoods, or rivers of white water). They also serve as the park police, issuing tickets and arresting criminals.

Park rangers are also often in charge of large areas within a national park; if an emergency should arise, backup or medical assistance may require 60 minutes or more to reach them.

In 2003, national park rangers were assaulted 106 times, and they're twice as likely to be attacked as are DEA agents. In 2006, in California alone, park rangers seized 20,000 marijuana plants, with an estimated street value of $50 million.

SO, YOU WANT TO BE A RANGER?

Despite the danger, obtaining a job as a national park ranger has become extremely competitive. Currently there are only 1,545 permanent and 1,400 seasonal park rangers. These rangers are spread among 390 major park sites in all states except Delaware, plus Washington, D.C., Guam, Puerto Rico, Samoa, and the Virgin Islands. Yellowstone, Yosemite, and the Great Smoky Mountains national parks have the largest contingents of rangers, but most sites have only one or two rangers. Most open positions result from the retirement of long-serving rangers, who must log at least 20 years before obtaining a pension. Rangers must be at least 18 years old and U.S. citizens.

Starting salaries for permanent employees range from $20,908 to $31,680 per year, depending on the position, its location, and the applicant's experience and education. The unofficial ranger motto is "We take our pay in sunsets." Temporary and summer hires with a college degree start at $18,687. (On the other hand, starting salary for the United States Park Police, part of the National Park Service, is $42,086.) Rangers cannot be promoted from a temporary or seasonal position to a permanent position, though; they must go through the full hiring process again. Once a ranger is hired, he or she is assigned to one of five divisions: law enforcement, resources management, interpretation, administration, and maintenance.

Although some rangers have just a four-year college degree (usually in wildlife management, parks and recreation, or any of the other natural sciences), most hires since 2004 have had master's degrees. All park rangers must also have current first-aid and CPR certificates and a clean driving record.

HOW TO APPLY
Applications are available through the U.S. Office of Personnel Management (www.opm.gov), in the "Administrative Careers with America" program. Applicants must compete for open positions through placement on an examination.

Information on the Seasonal Employment Program can be obtained from the Human Resources Office, National Park Service, P.O. Box 37127, Mail Stop 2225, Washington, D.C, 20013-7127; (202) 208-5074 or 877-554-4550; waso_pers_seasonal@nps.gov.

* * *

The most recognizable item of the park rangers' uniforms—the brown felt "Smoky the Bear" hat—not only protects them from rain, sun, and falling objects, but it's also designed to be used to carry water and fan campfires in a pinch.

...ducks, geese, and swans that have been sighted at Utah's Zion National Park.

WE'RE OFF TO SEE THE WIZARD

The Wizard of Menlo Park, that is.

Nearly everyone knows that Thomas Edison invented the lightbulb, but what most people don't know is that one of his greatest inventions was figuring out a better way to invent things—the research laboratory. Today, his laboratory and home make up the Edison National Historic Site in West Orange, New Jersey.

A BRIGHT STAR IS BORN
Thomas Alva Edison was born on February 11, 1847, in Milan, Ohio. It was soon apparent that Al (as he was called) was very bright because he was one of those kids who was always taking things apart to see how they worked.

The family moved to Michigan when Al was seven, and by the age of 12, he was selling newspapers and snacks on a train that ran between his hometown of Port Huron and Detroit. At 15, he was publishing the newspaper he sold, the first paper ever to be published aboard a moving train.

PATENTS PENDING
He got off the train, but he stayed in motion. After learning telegraphy, he traveled the country as a telegraph operator. It was during this time that he created his first important invention, a telegraphic repeater that automatically transmitted messages over a second line.

In 1868, he invented an electrical vote counter and got his first patent for it. In 1869, he designed an improved stock ticker and then set up a company to manufacture it. In 1874, he invented the quadruplex telegraph, which could send up to four messages simultaneously. By 1877, he had earned $40,000 from his inventions and decided it was time to expand—and refine—his invention process.

The chuparosa plant, common in the Sonoran Desert, is a favorite of hummingbirds...

MUCKING ABOUT IN NEW JERSEY
To that end, Edison built his first laboratory in Menlo Park, New Jersey. He was all of 30 years old. He wanted to bring together the people and materials that he needed to tackle more difficult challenges. Edison called his assistants "muckers," and they referred to him as the "Chief Mucker."

They usually had several projects going at once, and it wasn't long before they started churning out one invention after another—including such revolutionary devices as the phonograph and the electric light, no less. To ensure the commercial success of his electric light, Edison and his muckers also invented all of the generating and delivery systems to make electric power available to businesses and homes.

During this time, Edison filed more than 400 patents and became known around the world as "the Wizard of Menlo Park."

THE RIGHT INGREDIENTS
The lab was successful because of Edison's inventive genius, his dogged determination, and his ability to inspire his assistants' loyalty and dedication by working hard alongside them—and relaxing with them. The lab even had a pipe organ, and often after a long day of work Edison would sit down to play it while the gang sang along. The people who worked with him during those years have said that those were the happiest days of their lives.

Edison's goal was to create a small invention every ten days and a big invention every six months. His most important consideration when deciding on a project was to determine the ultimate practical commercial application—in other words, how he could make money from it. Edison once said, "I always invented to obtain money to go on inventing." For him, the money wasn't really the goal; it was just a way to ensure that he could continue his work.

THE WIZARD OF WEST ORANGE
Eventually the gang (and Edison's ideas for the future) outgrew the lab at Menlo Park, so the Wizard began building a new laboratory complex in West Orange, New Jersey. He hired a much larger and diverse staff, consisting of more than 200 machinists, scientists, craftsmen, and laborers. One associate recalled that when a new employee asked him if there were any rules, Edison replied, "There ain't no rules around here. We're trying to accomplish something."

Edison divided the staff into 10 to 20 small teams. Each worked simultaneously for as long as necessary to turn an idea from a prototype to a working model that could be manufactured.

Edison himself moved from team to team, advising and motivating them. When an invention was perfected, he quickly patented it. With such extensive facilities and a large staff, Edison managed to turn out new products on a timetable and scale that dwarfed his earlier accomplishments at Menlo Park. At the West Orange complex, they invented an alkaline storage battery, the movie camera, the first talking pictures, the mimeograph, the fluoroscope, and made major improvements to the phonograph.

SHOW ME THE MONEY!

Rather than sell the patent rights or royalties to his inventions, Edison knew that the real money was in selling products. So he built large factories next to his laboratory complex to mass-produce them. Not only did he manufacture movie cameras and projectors, but he even built a movie studio for making motion pictures. The building had a roof that opened up to let the sun in and the entire structure was on a turntable that could be rotated to keep the sun pointed at the stage throughout the day.

The laboratory and factory complex eventually employed nearly 5,000 people. Edison's research and development labs were the first of their kind anywhere—they revolutionized the process of technological research. His vision led to a new era in which innovation proceeded at an unprecedented rate; it brought with it great improvements in the quality of life and sweeping changes to society.

In 1892, the Edison General Electric Company merged with another small research and development company to form General Electric. Since then, GE has grown into a diversified technology, manufacturing, and service corporation with 250 manufacturing plants in 26 countries. GE employs 307,000 people worldwide and in 2005 had revenues in excess of $149 billion.

THE LATE, GREAT WIZARD

Edison worked at his West Orange laboratory complex for 44 years. He died in 1931 at the age of 84, and millions of people from around the world mourned his passing. Among the many awards he received during his lifetime was the Congressional Gold Medal "for development and application of inventions that have revolutionized civilization in the last century." They called him a genius, but as he was fond of saying, "Genius is one percent inspiration and ninety-nine percent perspiration."

NEW JERSEY

Edison National Historic Site
West Orange, NJ 07052

Founded: 1962
Area: 21 acres
Average annual visitors: 11,500

www.nps.gov/edis

* * *

THE JOKE'S ON . . . YOU!

In 1996, Taco Bell took out an ad in the *New York Times* and announced that the company had recently purchased the Liberty Bell (on display at Philadelphia's National Historic Park). The company compared the purchase to the popular "adopt-a-road" programs in the United States in which companies sponsor a highway and finance its upkeep. In the ad, Taco Bell wrote, "we hope our move will prompt other corporations to take similar action to do their part to reduce the country's debt."

The National Historic Park offices were flooded with calls from angry Americans protesting the park service's decision to sell off the Liberty Bell—a national treasure!—to a corporation. But Uncle John (and others) was on to the hoax: the ad ran on April Fool's Day and was, said Taco Bell in a later press release, "the best joke of the day."

It wasn't the only joke of the day, however. White House spokesperson, Mike McCurry, also announced that the government planned to sell the Lincoln Memorial to Ford and intended to change the memorial's name to the "Lincoln-Mercury Memorial." April Fool's!

Tupelo, Mississippi's, Brices Cross Roads Battlefield was the site of a Confederate victory.

ALONG THE OLD SPANISH TRAIL

Over the course of three centuries, a hodgepodge of priests, merchants, slaves, and fur trappers forged this almost 1,200-mile route from Santa Fe to Los Angeles. Six states' worth of high mountains, remote deserts, and deep canyons stood in the way. But eventually, several expeditions conquered the foreboding terrain and connected the dots. The end result is that the Old Spanish Trail amounts to much more than just one trail. It's a network of more than a dozen paths that combine native footpaths and European trading routes.

A MAN AND HIS MISSION

Every trail has to begin somewhere, and this one starts in Italy . . . sort of. That's where a Jesuit priest named Father Eusebio Kino began his journey. In 1687, Kino traveled from Italy to the city of Pimeria Alta—in what was then northern Mexico and is now southern Arizona. From there, the priest explored the Southwest in an attempt to find an overland passage to the Catholic missions in Monterey, California. On several expeditions, he built additional missions and ministered to Native American groups along the way. In turn, they shared their geographic knowledge, pointing the path-seeking padre along local trails. Father Kino kept detailed maps documenting his progress west but died in 1711 before he made it to California.

ANOTHER MAN, SAME MISSION

Sixty years later, a Franciscan missionary named Father Francisco Garces followed Kino's path, though he had some trouble. Twice on ventures into the desert, his Indian guides deserted him. Alone and sometimes lost, Garces persevered and pioneered westward past the Colorado River before he turned around.

Then, in January 1774, Father Garces guided an expedition to the Gila River and across the Colorado. From there, a Native American farmhand named Sebastian Tarabal took over. Although the group meandered a bit, Tarabal eventually recognized some landmarks, and that March, the group marched into the Spanish California coastal settlements of Mission San Gabriel near Los Angeles. They didn't continue on to Monterey, but they did prove that an overland route connecting Santa Fe and California was possible.

A KEY FAILURE

In 1775, two more clergymen—Atanasio Dominguez and Silvestre Velez de Escalante—set out from Santa Fe to find a more northerly route connecting modern-day New Mexico to Monterey. In late July 1776, Dominguez and Escalante headed northwest toward California. Aided by Ute Indians, they made their way to Utah and then turned south. But by October, the party was struggling: water was scarce, and winter was threatening. The leaders wanted to turn back from the cold weather, even though a dissenting group backed by the expedition's cartographer, Captain Don Bernardo Miera, pushed to keep going. After drawing lots to decide their fate, the group decided to turn back. But the trip wasn't fruitless: many future travelers used Miera's maps of this northern leg of the Old Spanish Trail.

A MOUNTAIN MAN FINDS THE MISSING LINK

Fifty years later, a 27-year-old fur trapper named Jedediah Smith led an expedition to appraise the trapping potential south and west of Great Salt Lake. Smith and his party began on the established Dominguez-Escalante route. But unlike their predecessors, they continued through Utah, along the Virgin River to its confluence with the Colorado River. Then, in October, they arrived in California. Low on resources and having lost half of their horses, the voyagers feared for their survival. But finally, they reached a Mojave village near present-day Needles, California.

After recuperating for a couple of weeks and trading with the Mojaves for fresh supplies and horses, the men picked up Garces's path to cross the menacing Mojave desert. Smith and his group reached southern California in the autumn of 1826 and were the first to connect the Garces and Dominguez-Escalante trails.

THERE CAN BE MORE THAN ONE

Other routes were forged, too. New Mexican merchant Antonio Armijo led the first commercial caravan round-trip along the northern Arizona border at the end of 1829. And for the next

...because of its rugged terrain and lack of water. They called it Mako Sica, or "land-bad."

20 years, various travelers sought to improve on the trail, searching for shorter paths or ones that were easier to traverse. American mountain man William Wolfskill found one of the most popular routes through Utah and the Great Basin; other trails stretch as far north as central Colorado.

OUT WITH THE OLD . . .

Given how long it took to forge, the Old Spanish Trail flourished for a relatively short time. By the end of the 1840s, stagecoaches and freight wagons replaced mule trains as the preferred method of travel along overland routes. But coaches and wagons couldn't navigate the trail's rough terrain and found alternative routes. Likewise, gold seekers and emigrants rushing to California were willing to face both the hot desert and hostile Native Americans in exchange for taking quicker routes. Thus, by the mid-19th century, the Old Spanish Trail had become obsolete.

In 2002, Congress named the route the Old Spanish National Historic Trail. Historical markers and educational exhibits were set up along the way—including signs along U.S. 160 in Colorado and U.S. 191 in Utah—to commemorate the trail throughout six states: New Mexico, Colorado, Arizona, Utah, Nevada, and California. Today, very few hiking trails exist along the Old Spanish Trail, but hiking is allowed in many areas around it. Still, the best way to travel the trail is by car: a long stretch of I-15 through Las Vegas, Nevada, follows the main route.

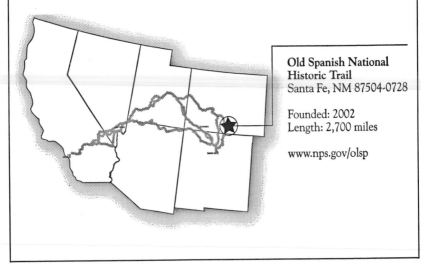

Old Spanish National
Historic Trail
Santa Fe, NM 87504-0728

Founded: 2002
Length: 2,700 miles

www.nps.gov/olsp

Hyde Park, NY, is home to three national historic sites: the home of...

RESTORING
YELLOWSTONE'S
<u>WOLVES</u>

Once upon a time, gray wolves flourished in Yellowstone National Park, but by 1940, there were almost none living there. What happened, and how did NPS officials help the wolves make a comeback?

PELTING PACKS

In 1872, when Yellowstone was established, several hundreds wolves lived in the park. They were the park's top predator. From the late 1800s until about 1940, though, park officials and local ranchers participated in a practice called "predator control." This meant that the park's wolves could be hunted in an effort to keep them away from local farms and populations. Wolf hunters received bounties of $20 a pelt, a hefty sum at the time. By the mid-1940s, few visitors or ranchers reported seeing wolf packs in Yellowstone, and by the 1970s, scientists could find no evidence that any wolves still lived in the park.

CANINE CONFEDERATES

In 1987, the government decided to look into reintroducing wolf populations to Yellowstone. Since the animals were indigenous to the region, many environmentalists believed they should remain a part of the park's population. Much debate and investigation followed—nearby ranchers, in particular, worried that a wolf population would wreck havoc on their livestock—but by 1995, wildlife biologists were ready to send a group of wolves back to Yellowstone.

Fourteen wolves were captured in Canada and transported to the park. Catching an entire pack is difficult, so the scientists took lone animals from different packs. A year later, 17 additional wolves were brought from Canada and released into Yellowstone.

AT HOME IN THE PEN

On arrival, the wolves were placed into one-acre acclimation pens for eight to ten weeks in an effort to keep them confined to a lim-

---

ited range. Three chain-link fence pens were positioned at different locations in northern Yellowstone—at Crystal Creek, Rose Creek, and Soda Butte Creek. The fences had an overhang and a skirt at the bottom to discourage the wolves from climbing over or digging under the pen. There were also plywood security boxes in each pen to provide shelter for the animals. Biologists wanted the wolves to form new packs, so the scientists placed a dominant male wolf, a dominant female, and several young subordinate wolves into each acclimation pen to mirror the natural pack structure. Within about 24 hours, the wolves began acting like packs do in the wild, and in two of the three cases, the newly formed "alpha" pairs eventually had pups.

While they were living in the acclimation pens, the wolves were fed only once every seven to ten days to mimic the waxing and waning eating habits of wild wolves. A typical pack of six in the wild consumes, on average, 800 pounds of meat per month. That averages out to two adult elk and a small deer.

FREEDOM!

At first, when scientists opened the enclosure gates, the wolves wouldn't venture into the park. Instead, they avoided the gate and spent most of their time at the rear of their pens. But when those back gates were finally removed, the wolves moved out. Before they did, though, each wolf was outfitted with a radio collar so that scientists could follow their movements and study their behavior.

Yellowstone's new wolf populations have fared surprisingly well. The first 14 animals quickly bore two litters, totaling nine pups. By the spring of 1997, 13 litters totaling 64 pups had been born. In addition, 10 young orphaned wolves were released into the park in early 1997. Today, more than 700 wolves live in Yellowstone.

WYOMING

Yellowstone National Park
Yellowstone National Park, WY 82190

Founded: 1872
Area: 2,212,789 acres
Average annual visitors: 3,000,000

www.nps.gov/yell

Appomattox Court House, where Lee surrendered in 1865, is a national historical park.

BADLANDS UXO

*Visitors who venture to the Stronghold Unit of Badlands National Park
have a special reason to follow the National Park Service's
advice to leave things as they are.*

BOMBS AWAY!
In the summer of 1942, United States war department officials knocked on the doors of 125 homes scattered across a
remote stretch of southwestern South Dakota. Residents were told
they had to leave their homes, farms, and ranches because their
land was being claimed for the war effort. The government leased
or bought the land, made promises that the residents would someday be able to return, and shooed folks out of the area. The
300,000-acre parcel of land also included ancient fossils, geological
formations, and sacred Native American sites.

As displaced residents watched from nearby towns and temporary tent shelters, the military fired on the land the residents used
to call home. The area became an air-to-air and air-to-ground
target practice range for the nearby, newly established Rapid City
Army Air Base. Old car bodies, painted drums, 250-foot plowed
bulls-eyes, flying drones, and geological features—including fossil
beds—were all used as targets.

For three years, planes flew low overhead and soldiers shot off
rounds of ammunition. Occasionally, shells dropped outside the
targeted area, and residents had to take cover. People also collected
discarded parachutes to make tablecloths and curtains. In the town
of Interior, six-inch shells hit a church and the post office. But
there are no records of any civilians being killed.

CLEANING UP THE MESS
The guns mostly went quiet shortly after World War II—part of
the area continued to be used for target practice by the South
Dakota National Guard until the early 1960s—but the military left
behind remnants of the 100- to 500-pound sand-filled practice
bombs, antitank and practice rockets, artillery projectiles, and
howitzer rounds. In addition, the area also contained dangerous
UXO (unexploded ordnance)—bullets, bombs, and other military
ammunition that was fired but never exploded. The residents,

Camp Sumter, GA, is the site of a Civil War prison site commonly called Andersonville.

who'd hoped to return to their homes after the war, had to stay away.

In the 1960s, the government began a clean-up effort. Officials said that with the exception of a 2,500-acre parcel of land known as the Impact Area, the area had been thoroughly searched and cleared. The fact that hikers and farmers in the area continued to find military debris was ignored.

BECOMING BADLANDS

By the 1970s, the area's former homeowners and a nearby Oglala Sioux tribe had successfully petitioned the government for much of the land to be returned to civilian use. In particular, the tribe received 133,000 acres of land—called the Stronghold Unit after a nearby area known as the Stronghold Table—which included part of the former gunnery range. The Stronghold Unit became part of the Badlands National Monument, and later Badlands National Park. But empty shell casings and other debris remained because the tribe didn't have the money to clean up the site.

Finally, in 1996, the tribe and the Department of Defense formed an agreement: members of the Oglala Sioux tribe would survey the area and mark any UXO. Then, the Army Corps of Engineers and specialized contractors would take it away. The agreement remains in place today.

BEWARE OF UXO

Today, the part of the former gunnery range that lies inside the boundaries of Badlands National Park still contains remnants of the war, including spent shells and possibly UXO. (The Impact Area remains under military control and is off limits.) So visitors to the Stronghold Unit of Badlands National Park should begin their journey at the White River visitor center, where they learn about UXO and how to avoid it.

SOUTH DAKOTA

Badlands National Park
Interior, SD 57750

Founded: 1939
Area: 244,000 acres
Average annual visitors: 900,000

www.nps.gov/badl

Crepuscular animals (cats, dogs, deer, mice, and some birds) are active at dawn and dusk.

ARCH NEMESIS?

On May 7, 2006, professional climber Dean Potter scaled Delicate Arch, an icon for the state of Utah and for Arches National Park. In a statement released after the climb, Potter said that getting to the top gave him "a chance to commune with the arch through expressing my own art of climbing." Other people were just plain mad.

IT'S MY BAG

Climbing arches, also called "arch bagging," has its roots in a 1982 self-published pamphlet titled *Arch Bagger*, written by a climber named Gerry Roach. People had climbed arches before Roach, of course—Harvey T. Carter and Fred Ayers climbed most of the biggies in the 1950s and 1960s. But Roach first used the term when he wrote about different routes that baggers could take to climb some of Arches' arches.

Since the early 1980s, the sport has mostly stayed under the radar, with arch baggers scaling only remote arches—out of the sight of tourists and park employees. That all changed with Potter's climb.

EVEN THE BEST OF INTENTIONS

Although Potter saw his climb as a way to get closer to nature, others considered it a desecration of a natural landmark. Many of these detractors found it odd that a guy looking for a little time alone with nature had brought along a camera crew to film the event. They accused him of self-promoting, a claim to which Potter responded, "As a professional athlete, recognition of what I do is part of the job."

That didn't quiet the critics. Soon after the climb, editors for the Web site Outside Online published a story about the Delicate Arch "incident" in which they implied that Potter had damaged the arch during his ascent. The article ran alongside pictures showing grooves in the top of the arch that looked like they could have come from a safety rope grinding across its crumbly sandstone. Potter was galled by the accusation and recounted his climb in detail, explaining why he was sure he hadn't caused the damage. He explained that his team had used a rope but had made sure to pad it with his jacket and thread it through an existing crack. They also used a specialized climbing device to prevent the rope from rubbing the rock. Any rope damage, Potter asserted, had been caused by someone else.

BAGGING AT ARCHES NO MORE

Whether or not the damage was Potter's fault, the National Park Service wasn't taking any more chances with climbers at Arches. They reworded the park's rock climbing rules to make it absolutely clear that bagging any of the major arches was forbidden. Unlawful arch baggers face fines and up to six months in prison.

But for those who still yearn to bag arches, here's a tip from Roach: look outside Arches National Park. They're around.

Arches National Park
Moab, UT 84532

Founded: 1929
Area: 76,518 acres
Average annual visitors: 800,000

www.nps.gov/arch

UTAH

* * *

EIGHT PHASES OF THE MOON

The moon completes the following cycle every four weeks:

- New moon
- Waxing crescent
- First quarter (half moon)
- Gibbous
- Full moon
- Gibbous
- Last quarter (half moon)
- Waning crescent

The Gila woodpecker and gilded flicker are among birds that nest in saguaro cacti.

MAUD OF GREEN GABLES

The young adult novel, Anne of Green Gables, *has been translated into more than 20 languages and has sold more than 50 million copies worldwide—good reason to honor author Lucy Maud Montgomery . . . and the girl and the house she conjured up.*

Anne of Green Gables was rejected by five publishers before American L.C. Page and Company accepted it in 1908. The book was an instant success for Canadian author Lucy Maud Montgomery. Set in the fictitious town of Avonlea, it's the story of a young orphan girl who is adopted by an elderly brother and sister. Montgomery (1874–1942)—known to friends as Maud—made $12,000 a year in royalties in the book's first few years in print, as much as the prime minister of Canada earned in those days.

THE REAL AVONLEA

After Montgomery's death in 1942, the Historic Sites and Monuments Board of Canada recognized her as a "person of historic significance." The real-life house that was the inspiration for Anne's fictitious house has been honored, too. In the early 1900s, it was owned by Montgomery's cousins and was just down the road from Montgomery's own home. Every year, more than half a million visitors tour the Green Gables National Historic Site in Canada's Prince Edward Island National Park.

Inside the green-shuttered white house is a re-creation of Anne's room, furnished with an iron-frame bed, a tiny dresser, and a wash pitcher and basin. Down in the parlor, Montgomery's typewriter is on display. Outside in the barn, you can see an exhibit of farm life in the 1800s and watch a film about Montgomery's life. (If you're looking for the restrooms, they're in the old woodshed.) Visitors can also hike through Anne's "Haunted Wood" and follow an interpretive trail that points out highlights from the novel.

Nez Perce National Historic Park has 38 sites in Idaho, Montana, Oregon, and Washington.

PRINCE EDWARD ISLAND

Visitors can also venture beyond the Green Gables House and visit the larger Prince Edward Island (PEI) National Park. According to many environmentalists, this park is one of the most endangered in the world because it's also one of the most popular parks in Canada. During the summer, so many people visit that the park has begun showing signs of stress: diminished natural habitats and coastal erosion are two examples.

Yet, the park remains one of the best places in Canada to see wildlife . . . especially birds. More than 300 species of birds live in the woods and along the shores of Prince Edward Island. This includes the endangered Piping Plover. And red foxes also make dens in the park's sand dunes. Beware: the foxes are cute, but they're also dangerous. Parks Canada warns visitors not to try to get too close.

Prince Edward Island National Park also offers a wealth of cultural activities. Remnants of early farms and civilizations dot the island and historic sites tell the stories of the Canadian confederacy.

PRINCE EDWARD ISLAND

Anne of Green Gables
National Historic Site
Charlottetown, PE C1A 5V6

Founded: 1937
Area: 4,497 acres (18.2 sq km)
Average annual visitors: 200,000

www.pc.gc.ca/lhn-nhs/pe/greengables

* * *

PRINCE EDWARD ISLAND STATS

Established: 1937
Area: 8.5 square miles (22 square kilometers)
Things to do: Eleven hiking trails snake throughout the island, and three campgrounds offer visitors a place to say overnight.

All 229 cannons at Tennessee's Shiloh National Military Park are original Civil War pieces.

WHAT IN THE
BLUE BLAZES?

*Maryland's Catoctin Mountain Park boasts a number of things: great
hiking, camping, and trout fishing; a presidential retreat, Camp David
(for invited visitors only); and the Blue Blazes whiskey still.*

MAKING MOONSHINE

Turning corn and rye into whiskey was a profitable occupation and a favorite hobby for locals living around northwestern Maryland's Catoctin Mountains, located in the eastern Appalachian range. But in 1791, Congress placed a federal tax on selling liquor. Most mountain folk couldn't afford to pay it (or didn't like such government interference), so they camouflaged their backyard stills and made whiskey illegally when the taxmen (known as "revenuers") weren't around. At night—by the light of the moon—"moonshine" was born.

During the late 19th and early 20th centuries, liquor found another foe: people who supported temperance lobbied the U.S. government to ban the sale and consumption of alcohol. They succeeded in 1919, with passage of the 18th Amendment. From 1920 to 1933, Prohibition was in full force; all distilleries were banned, and no one could sell alcohol legally. Moonshining on Catoctin Mountain and in other secret locales became a huge, illegal business. Before Prohibition, the price of whiskey depended on two things: the quality of the ingredients and the skill of the distiller. After Prohibition, quantity became more important than quality, and the price of the illicit liquor jumped from $2 a gallon to more than $20.

LIQUID GOLD

There were moonshine stills all over Appalachia, but the Catoctin Mountains provided a particularly good site. The mountains had an abundant supply of freshwater needed to power the stills, but more important, they were secluded yet close to several large cities. A fresh batch of Catoctin moonshine could reach Washington D.C., Baltimore, Philadelphia, or New York in a matter of hours.

Passionate about petroglyphs? New Mexico's El Morro National Monument has tons of 'em.

According to legend, a gang of two locals and several experienced North Carolina moonshiners owned Catoctin's Blue Blazes, one of the largest moonshine stills on the East Coast. It was nestled along Harman's Creek, about five miles from the town of Thurmont, and was a "steamer still," which meant that its power came from a huge boiler taken off of a steam locomotive. At its peak, Blue Blazes distilled enough mash (the mixture of "mashed" grain, yeast, and hot water that ferments into whiskey) to fill thirteen 2,000-gallon vats. This single still produced enough alcohol to meet the liquor needs of most of the East Coast.

RAID!
No matter how secluded the Catoctin Mountains, the constant flow of heavily loaded trucks into and out of the hills soon caught the eye of the locals and lawmen. On July 31, 1929, federal agents and local police officers surrounded and raided the still. Rumor has it that Charles Lewis, a moonshiner who was the jilted third wheel of a love triangle, went to the feds and told them how to get past the lookouts hidden in the woods around the still. Someone also tipped off the moonshiners to the raid (though no one is sure who). When the agents and police arrived, the moonshiners were ready—with guns drawn.

During the gun battle and the aftermath, more than 25,000 gallons of moonshine—worth more than half a million dollars on the black market—were found and destroyed. A deputy sheriff and several still workers were killed. Two moonshiners were eventually convicted for the deputy sheriff's death, but no one was ever charged with owning or operating the still.

GONE BUT STILL REMEMBERED
In 1954, Congress established Catoctin Mountain Park, and 1970 the National Park Service built a moonshine exhibit on the site where Blue Blazes once stood. No part of the original still survived the 1929 raid, so rangers erected a working model of a 50-gallon still in its place. This one was no nowhere near the size of the Blue Blazes; it was more like the stills individual farmers might have had in their yards. The contraption included a large pot that was directly heated by a flame below. Untaxed and unlicensed distilleries are still illegal in the United States, and the one on display came from a raid in the Great Smoky Mountains in the 1960s;

Trail ruts can still be seen along the Oregon National Historic Trail.

federal agents seized it from a local farmer, disassembled it, and then reconstructed it at the Catoctin site.

Today, the NPS welcomes visitors to the still. An easy, quarter-mile interpretive hiking trail begins at the visitor center on Park Central Road and goes right past the still. On Sundays in June and September, rangers give talks that detail the history of the area. Catoctin Mountain Park also offers 25 miles of hiking trails, numerous waterways for fishing, and many cross-country skiing trails in the winter.

Catoctin Mountain Park
Thurmont, MD 21788

Founded: 1954
Area: 5810 acres
Average annual visitors: 550,000

www.nps.gov/cato

MARYLAND

* * *

FACT OR FICTION?

Myth: Officials at Ellis Island often changed the names of immigrants because they couldn't pronounce or spell the foreign names.

Fact: This is a common misperception. Although some immigrants undoubtedly changed their names when they entered the United States, most were not the result of ignorant Ellis Island employees. Ellis Island (now a national monument) employed hundreds of translators throughout the island's tenure as America's premier immigration station. The translators spoke Yiddish, Russian, Italian, Lithuanian, and many more languages. Most were either immigrants themselves or the children of immigrants and, thus, could easily converse with the new arrivals. Records and travel documents were also thoroughly inspected, and shipping companies, which were in charge of drawing up the documents, took great pains to make them accurate since immigrants whose documents were incomplete or incorrect were deported at the shipping company's expense.

DINING AT BRACEBRIDGE MANOR

In the mood for a piece of peacock pie? How about some boar's head?
Better make your dinner reservations in advance.

When Yosemite's luxurious Ahwahnee Hotel opened in 1927, the owners—the Yosemite and Curry Company—tried to think of a good way to publicize the new hotel and offer something special to their upscale guests. So they hired Garnet Holme, the country's most famous outdoor dramatist (yes, there are such things) to create a pageant. Inspired by the description of a 17th-century Christmas feast in Washington Irving's *Bracebridge Hall*, Holme wrote and staged a musical extravaganza in which the Ahwahnee guests act out the roles of Squire Bracebridge's guests—while dining on seven courses based on 17th-century dishes.

Actors from Yosemite Valley and elsewhere played the parts, and most of them returned every year for decades. Garnet Holme and his wife acted in the pageant until his death in 1929.

PHOTO OP
Yosemite's resident photographer, Ansel Adams, became the event's organizer after Holme passed away. (Adams had played a supporting role as the Lord of Misrule in earlier performances.) Adams had also trained as a classical pianist before becoming a photographer, so he was more than qualified to take over.

Adams tweaked the pageant a bit. He rewrote the script, designed new sets, reworked the costumes, and added more music. He also cast himself in the lead role of Squire Bracebridge and his wife, Virginia, in the most important female role as the housekeeper.

LIFE IN THE THEATER
When Adams retired in 1973, Eugene Fulton took over. Fulton and his family had been involved in the Bracebridge Dinner for years. His daughter, Andrea, started acting in the pageant in the 1950s, when she was five years old.

Sunray venus, lion's paw, apple murex, calico scallops, slippersnails, dark cerith?

Today, little Andrea Fulton is all grown up and in charge of the three-hour pageant. In 2000, she hired a designer to update the costumes and set and, in 2003, had a writer revamp the script, changing the setting from Victorian to Elizabethan England.

DINNER'S READY!

But the event isn't just about the acting, music, and period costumes. There's that seven-course meal, too. The book *Bracebridge Hall* described the squire's dinner as including "peacock pie," "wassail," and "boar's head." But modern guests needn't fear: the Ahwahnee's chef reinterprets those dishes for the modern palate. The menu has included eggplant and artichoke strudel, Maine lobster, duck confit (standing in for the peacock pie), beef tenderloin (instead of boar's head), and plum pudding served with hot mulled wine. Each course is introduced with music, and the kitchen staff, waiters, and performers plan the show so the dishes are ready when the actors announce them.

CHRISTMAS IN FEBRUARY

The Ahwahnee holds eight performances throughout the Christmas season, but tickets go on sale more than ten months in advance. Even though admission is costly—about $350 each—the 300-plus seats for each night usually sell out quickly. So if you're interested in experiencing a Yosemite Christmas, you'd better starting planning around Valentine's Day!

CALIFORNIA

Yosemite National Park
Yosemite National Park, CA 95389

Founded: 1890
Area: 761,266 acres
Average annual visitors: 3,300,000

www.nps.gov/yose

As shell-hunters know, they're all types of seashells.

WHERE IN THE WORLD?

Here at the BRI, we know that Canada and the United States have
just a few of the world's greatest national parks. So we sent
Uncle John off to find the best ones around the globe.
But . . . where in the world are they?

1. JIM CORBETT NATIONAL PARK

Originally called Hailey National Park, this area was renamed in
1956 to honor a tiger hunter and pioneer conservationist. Today,
the park provides a protected haven for tigers and other endangered species. Visitors can ride an elephant into the park's grasslands and jungles to photograph tigers, leopards, jackals,
Himalayan black bears, and even wild elephant herds.

Uncle John was last seen on the shores of the Ramganga River
coaxing a "mugger" crocodile to smile for a photo. Where in the
world can he be?

A. India

B. Malaysia

C. Indochina

2. ROYAL NATIONAL PARK

Established in 1879, Royal National Park is the world's second-
oldest national park, founded seven years after Yellowstone. It was
originally dubbed "national park" but was renamed a "royal park"
after Queen Elizabeth visited in 1955. Visitors can hike on Royal's
coastal cliffs and heathlands or swim at the beaches; there's even
good surfing at Gairie Beach.

Uncle John was last seen gulping down a picnic lunch on the
grassy meadows of Audley before hopping in his canoe to glide
along the Hacking River. Where in the world is Uncle John?

A. Hong Kong

B. New Zealand

C. Australia

What was life like on the Santa Fe Trail? Check out Fort Larned National Historic Site.

3. FIORDLAND NATIONAL PARK

At nearly 5,000 square miles, Fiordland is one of the world's largest national parks. With its stunning glacial lakes and 14 rugged fjords, it's also one of the most spectacular—you won't want to miss its thundering waterfalls, lush rain forests, and deep caves. Running through the center of the park is a trail called the Milford Track; in 1908, a London newspaper called it "the finest walk in the world," and Milford Track hasn't lost the title yet. Movie lovers will recognize locations in Fiordland that were used to film *The Lord of the Rings*.

Uncle John went off looking for hobbits and hasn't come back. Where in the world is he?

A. Norway

B. New Zealand

C. Greenland

4. SAGARMATHA NATIONAL PARK

Established in 1976, this park contains three of the world's 10 highest peaks: Everest, Lhotse, and Cho Oyu. The park begins at 9,335 feet and rises to 29,035 feet at the top of Everest, the high point on the planet. However, this park's rugged terrain includes glacier peaks and gorges, requiring that visitors be fit, experienced hikers. Travelers to Sagarmatha are often guided by the area's indigenous natives—the Sherpas—who are the most respected climbers in the world.

Uncle John is still in training, preparing to huff and puff his way up the trails of Sagarmatha National Park. If he reaches his goal of sitting on top of the world, where will he be?

A. Tibet

B. Nepal

C. India

5. KILLARNEY NATIONAL PARK

The country's first national park was a gift in 1932, presented by a wealthy aristocrat and his in-laws in memory of his late wife and their daughter. The 25,000-acre park is famous for its sandstone mountains, three interlinked lakes (Upper, Lower and Middle lakes), the largest forest in the country, and the last native herd of

Blowin' in the wind! Fort Larned's flags last only about three months in the Kansas wind.

red deer. Visitors can also bike, fish, tour a castle, or hike to an overlook called Ladies View, where Queen Victoria's ladies-in-waiting came to admire the mountains, lakes, and greenery.

Uncle John was last seen fishing in Lower Lake for brown trout and Killarney shad before he fell in. Where in the world is he?

A. Ireland

B. Scotland

C. Iceland

6. ISE-SHIMA NATIONAL PARK

This park covers the entire Shima Peninsula that juts out into the Pacific Ocean. Two of its major attractions are Shinto religious shrines and Pearl Island, where Mikimoto Kokichi first produced cultured pearls in 1893. Today, visitors to Pearl Island can observe the processing of pearls, gaze at pearl rafts floating on the sea, or watch a woman diving for pearls.

Uncle John sent a postcard from Ise-Shima, saying that he'd become nearly as cultured as a Mikimoto pearl. Where in the world could that happen?

A. Indonesia

B. Fiji

C. Japan

7. CORAL BEACH RESERVE

The sights at Coral Beach Reserve are under Eliat Bay where, summer or winter, the water always hovers at around 70 degrees. Straddling the equator, the Coral Beach Reserve protects the northernmost coral reef in the world: it's 3,900 feet long, lies less than seven miles offshore, and includes more than 100 types of stony and soft coral that resemble trees, shrubs, cabbages, and mushrooms. The coral provides shelter and food for 650 equally colorful and unusual marine species, including black-quilled sea urchins, goatfish, and scorpion fish.

At Coral Beach Reserve, Uncle John donned swim trunks, a snorkel mask, and flippers and was last seen trying to smell the flower-shaped coral. Where in the world is he now?

A. Israel

Spectacular colors are a feature of Vermilion Cliffs National Monument in Arizona.

B. Greece

C. Australia

8. CORCOVADO NATIONAL PARK
Corcovado National Park is home to 10 percent of its continent's mammals; 139 species of mammals, 400 species of birds, and 116 of amphibians and reptiles live in the park's 160 square miles. These critters inhabit a park that is a tropical wilderness combined with beautiful beaches. In a nation famous for ecotourism, Corcovado is a high point.

Uncle John has been treading softly as he explores some of the park's protected habitats—especially the mangrove swamp and jolillo palm groves. He's gotten some good photos of the glass frog with its transparent skin but hasn't been seen since he started tracking jaguar paw prints. Where'd he go?

A. Peru

B. Costa Rica

C. Argentina

9. AMBOSELI NATIONAL RESERVE
The gleaming, snowcapped peaks of Kilimanjaro dominate the view from the grassy plains of Amboseli National Reserve. This legendary park area was made famous in Ernest Hemmingway's stories of big-game hunting. From Observation Hill, tourists can glimpse a preserve that is home to more than 50 mammal species, including lions, leopards, cheetahs, rhinos, and elephants. The park is surrounded by nomadic villages belonging to the tall, proud native people known as the Masai, who now control the reserve.

Part of Amboseli Reserve is composed of a dried-up lake bed, where Uncle John was last seen chasing the mirages that form in the shimmering heat. Where in the world is he?

A. Kenya

B. South Africa

C. Morocco

For answers, turn to page 390.

THE ACCIDENTAL EXPLORER

*A conquistador looking for a shortcut from Mexico to Asia found
southern California instead—and ended up finding a
place in the history books.*

LAND HO!

Juan Rodriquez Cabrillo is the first European of record to set foot on what's now the West Coast of the United States. He sailed up the coast from Navidad, Mexico (now called Manzanillo), looking for a trade route between Mexico and the Spice Islands in Asia.

In September 1542, he landed at Point Loma, a peninsula in San Diego Bay. He named the city San Miguel, after the saint whose feast day had just passed. Years later, another Spanish explorer—Sebastian Vizcaíno—came along and renamed the city after a different Catholic saint: San Diego de Alcalá.

After only six days in San Diego, Cabrillo's expedition pushed on, still searching for the elusive trading shortcut. The expedition sailed north, close to present-day Monterey, and then turned south when the seas got rough. On the return trip, they stopped in the Channel Islands, off the coast of Santa Barbara. There, Cabrillo slipped and fell—some say during a skirmish with natives. He broke his leg, and on January 3, 1543, he died from complications. He's buried on the islands, but no one knows exactly where.

WAS HE OR WASN'T HE?

That should have been the end of the story, but it's not. Instead, Cabrillo's trip raises two questions:

Was he really the first European to step foot in the western United States? His ship's log says that on landing in San Diego Bay, the crew met a band of Kumeyaay Indians, who seemed to be familiar with Europeans. The Kumeyaay treated the Cabrillo party cordially and came prepared to trade with them. Some historians speculate that this is because earlier European explorers came to California from the east, while exploring the Colorado River. But

Adam Swarner, a New York soldier, was the first prisoner to die at Andersonville, GA.

no one knows for sure if those explorers actually made it to the coast.

There's also the question of Cabrillo's national origins. He was sailing under the flag of Spain when he landed in San Diego, but some scholars think he was actually a Portuguese explorer named João Rodrigues Cabrilho (the names *are* similar). Others maintain that he was Spanish. In fact, the first historic mention of his name is as a captain of crossbowmen in the ranks of conquistadors who served with Spaniard Hernán Cortés against the Aztecs in 1519.

A FITTING MONUMENT . . . EVENTUALLY

Either way, the Portuguese claimed him. In 1913, at the prompting of a group of Portuguese-Americans, a half-acre on Point Loma was set aside to host a statue of Cabrillo. Due to a lack of money, the statue was never made. Again, in 1926, a statue was planned but never erected (money problems again). Finally, in 1939, Portuguese sculptor Alvaro de Bree carved a 14-foot sandstone statue of Cabrillo. De Bree intended to display it at the 1939 San Francisco World's Fair, but the statue was shipped too late and missed the exhibition. A California state senator heard about the statue and decided he wanted to exhibit it in San Diego. It took several years to procure the piece, but in 1949, de Bree's statue was moved to the current site: the Cabrillo National Monument.

Because the statue was damaged from the start and then salt air and pollution slowly eroded it over the years, the city of San Diego hired a Portuguese sculptor to make a replica out of a harder stone. In 1980, that piece replaced the original on the point overlooking San Diego Bay. The first Cabrillo statue is in storage.

CALIFORNIA

Cabrillo National Monument
San Diego, CA 92106-3601

Founded: 1913
Area: 159.94 acres
Average annual visitors: 900,000

www.nps.gov/cabr

Tonto National Monument (AZ) has the ruins of two cliff dwellings about 800 years old.

WHAT LIES BENEATH

From holes in the ground that can blow your hat off to caverns that preserve the dead, the national parks are home to some amazing caves.

MAMMOTH CAVE NATIONAL PARK (KENTUCKY)

What's so special: Mammoth Cave is far and away the most extensive underground passage system on earth. It includes 365 surveyed miles of underground passageways, and new ones are still being discovered. Some geologists estimate that another 600 miles of passages await discovery.

The caves lie under Kentucky's wooded hills, a subterranean world complete with its own rivers, canyons, lakes, and waterfalls. The caves are aptly named: an immense 192-foot-high vertical shaft is called Mammoth Dome, and what better to call a 105-foot-deep shaft than Bottomless Pit? The passageways are studded with "rooms" filled with stalagmites and stalactites like the Frozen Niagara, which spills down the walls like a giant rock waterfall. In the Snowball Room, visitors can gaze at walls and ceilings covered with snowball scoops of gypsum—while having a nosh at the snack bar.

Mammoth's remarkable residents—eyeless fish, eyeless shrimp, blind cave beetles, and white spiders—are just a few of its 130-plus species. And as fascinating as the living creatures are, the consistent 54°F temperature and dry air preserve the dead: some of the mummified human bodies and their artifacts that have been found in Mammoth are more than 4,000 years old. Even the cave walls tell ancient tales—from ages-old charcoal petroglyphs to early 19th-century ceiling graffiti written in candle soot! (Back then, it was an accepted practice for tourists to write their names on the walls.)

Making Mammoth: About 350 million years ago, the hillsides above Mammoth Cave were part of a warm, shallow seabed. Over millennia, the water dropped, and the layers of limestone it left were topped by sandstone. Cracks and holes in the sandstone exposed the limestone; carbonic acid carried in rainwater that dissolved the limestone under the surface and raised the water's acidity level. The acidic water and the great force of rivers then carved ever-deeper passages through the rock.

Mammoth's amazing cave formations were created over millions of years as the water picked up calcite from the limestone, then slowly seeped through the limestone ceiling, leaving behind what's called "precipitated calcite" to form stalactites. Fast-moving drips from the ceiling that splashed to the floor deposited calcite that grew into stalagmites.

A bit of history: Native Americans mined salt in Mammoth Cave for more than 4,000 years ago, abandoning it 2,000 years later for reasons no one has yet figured out. Then, so the legend goes, in 1798, a Kentucky homesteader named John Houchins went hunting, followed a wounded bear into an enormous cave, lost the bear, and found Mammoth.

The caves soon came under private ownership; by 1816, people flocked to see their mineral formations and ancient Indian artifacts. Mammoth became the country's second-oldest tourist attraction (Niagara Falls was the first) with guided tours that lasted up to 12 hours. It also attracted celebs of the day like the "Swedish Nightingale" (singer Jenny Lind) and Shakespearean actor Edwin Booth, both of whom performed in Mammoth's Star Chamber.

By the time President Calvin Coolidge set aside Mammoth Cave as a national park in 1926, it rested beneath about 600 small family farms. More than a decade passed before Kentucky—using state funds and private contributions—bought those farms and the more than 50,000 acres of land above the caves. The park now hosts nearly two million visitors annually.

CARLSBAD CAVERNS NATIONAL PARK (NEW MEXICO)

What's so special: More than 100 limestone caves are scattered across the Chihuahuan Desert of the Southwest's Guadalupe Mountains. Inside Carlsbad Cavern, the park's show cave, is North America's largest single underground chamber—the Big Room, which is nearly 4,000 feet long, 1.2 miles in circumference, and 350 feet high. Even sophisticated cavers have been caught gaping at the ornate nature-made decorations in Carlsbad Cavern: rock formations that look like soda straws, clouds, and talon-shaped chandeliers hang from the ceilings. From the floors rise columns as immense as the Giant Dome: 62 feet high, 16 feet in diameter, and off-kilter like the Leaning Tower of Pisa.

One million Mexican free-tail bats live near the cave's entrance from May to October, before leaving to winter down south. Tourists gather at sunset to watch the bats fly out of the cave, first in small numbers and then in the hundreds of thousands.

Making Carlsbad: Like other limestone caves, Carlsbad Caverns was once part of a sea floor, but the similarity ends there. Most limestone caves are carved out by water carrying carbonic acid, and they remain wet. Carlsbad Caverns was formed in a desert landscape without underground water, rivers, or streams.

In the 1970s, geologists realized that sulfuric acid had created the caverns. Ages ago, when the area was cooler and wetter, rainwater seeped into cracks in the earth's surface, and oil deposits in the subsoil brought the rainwater (which was rich in oxygen) into contact with hydrogen sulfide gas. The oxygen and the hydrogen sulfide combined with microbes in the soil to make sulfuric acid, a corrosive substance that cut large holes into the limestone.

A bit of history: Native Americans who lived in the Guadalupe Mountains for more than 1,200 years took shelter in Carlsbad Cavern, but probably never ventured deeply into it. The cave's first credited explorer was a teenage cowboy named Jim White.

At the turn of the 20th century, Carlsbad Cavern was being mined for bat droppings, or guano, to make fertilizer. White quit his ranching job to work in the mine. He explored the caves in his time off and tried to get others interested, but few people bought his weird tales of a wonderland under the ground. (It didn't help matters that the only way into the cavern was to have White take you down in an empty guano bucket!)

Then in 1918, White guided a photographer through the caves; the resulting black-and-white photos caused a sensation. Suddenly, many people were willing to hop in the bucket, and the former cowboy was guiding awestruck Washington officials through Carlsbad. Finally, in 1923, Calvin Coolidge created Carlsbad Cave National Monument, and in 1930 Congress made it official, creating Carlsbad Caverns National Park.

John Muir nicknamed the Sierra Nevada "Range of Light"...

WIND CAVE NATIONAL PARK (SOUTH DAKOTA)

What's so special: Beneath the Black Hills lies Wind Cave, the fourth-largest cave in the world and, at 320 million years and counting, one of the oldest. A complex subterranean maze with more than 80 miles of known passageways underneath one square mile of surface area, Wind Cave is constantly expanding as new passageways are still being discovered. Geologists estimate that only 5 percent of it has been explored so far.

Wind Cave features knobbed formations of "cave popcorn," silvery "frostwork" that looks like frosted Scotch pines, and rare "helictite bushes" (bushy growths of calcite that are gnarled and twisted like dried twigs and stems). But the cave is most famous for an immense network of honeycombed calcite formations called "boxwork."

Wind Cave is also famous for the phenomenon that gave it its name. In 1881, two brothers (and suspected horse thieves), Jesse and Tom Bingham, heard a loud whistling noise. They followed the sound to a hole in the ground where the wind blew out with such force that Jesse's hat sailed off his head. Winds still rush in and out of the cave entrance and have been measured at as much as 75 miles an hour.

Making cave winds: The winds are a result of atmospheric pressure inside the cave adjusting to atmospheric pressures aboveground. When outside weather is clear and calm with high atmospheric pressure, air currents are pulled into the cave. When low pressure brings in storms, winds in the cave are expelled. Wind Cave is one of earth's largest natural barometers, as the wind blasts, which indicate changing air pressure, predict precipitation.

Wind Cave's other unique feature, its mass of honeycomb-like boxwork, is still something of a mystery, though some geologists think calcite was deposited in the cave walls' fissures and cracks long ago. Then, limestone and dolomite deposits covered up the calcite. Over millions of years, as the cave aged, the limestone and dolomite wore away, leaving behind the more durable honey-combed veins of calcite.

A bit of history: The Lakota people told stories of a trickster spirit living in Wind Cave who convinced humans to leave the underground and live on the surface of the earth, a story that parallels

Adam and Eve's banishment from the garden of Eden. The cave was sacred to the Lakota, the white settlers weren't as reverential. Once Wind Cave was discovered, locals dug open its small entrance, and newspapers started running articles about it.

By 1890, the South Dakota Mining Company had assumed control over the cave and hired businessman J. D. McDonald to manage the property. That's when J.D.'s son Alvin, Wind Cave's pioneering explorer, began mapping the cave and keeping a diary of his discoveries. The diary entry stating that he'd "given up finding the end of Wind Cave" is still quoted by modern explorers.

Squabbles over Wind Cave's ownership brought attention from Washington, and in January 1903, Theodore Roosevelt signed the bill to create Wind Cave National Park, the first national park that protected a cave.

* * *

A PLACE TO RELAX

Parks like Yellowstone, Yosemite, and Banff are often packed year-round, making it difficult for visitors to have a relaxing park vacation. So we've compiled a list of 10 lesser-traveled park sites where you can take in the glory of nature without the hassle of crowds.

1. Gwaii Haanas National Park (British Columbia)
2. Tallgrass Prairie National Preserve (Kansas)
3. Arches National Park (Utah)
4. Badlands National Park (South Dakota)
5. Cape Breton Highlands National Park (Nova Scotia)
6. Ivvavik National Park (Northwest Territories)
7. Dry Tortugas National Park (Florida)
8. Big Bend National Park (Texas)
9. Congaree National Park (South Carolina)
10. Kenai Fjords National Park (Alaska)

Honorable Mention:
Grand Canyon: North Rim (Arizona)

Number of national monuments managed by the National Park Service: 74.

INTEGRATING
CENTRAL HIGH

*The year 1957 was pivotal in the fight for equality in American schools.
That fall, nine African American students began classes at Central High
School in Little Rock, Arkansas. They were met by angry segregationists
determined to keep the state's schools all white, but the teenagers
persevered and became heroes of the civil rights movement. Today, the
school of that historic confrontation is a national historic site.*

BROWN COMES TO LITTLE ROCK
In 1927, the American Institute of Architects called Little
Rock's Central High "America's most beautiful high school,"
and it was certainly state of the art. The school cost $1.5 million
to build (a king's ransom in 1927), was two city blocks long, had
an auditorium that seated 2,000 people, and was a media marvel
from the start. Local newspapers even covered its opening. It was
also segregated, as most Southern schools were at the time. Only
white students attended Central High; black students went to a
different school in another part of the city.

In the 1950s, though, school segregation was becoming hot
news. In 1954, the Supreme Court outlawed it with the *Brown v.
Board of Education* ruling. All American public schools had to be
integrated, said the court; it was up to the states to carry out the
order. In some places, integration began in earnest. But elsewhere,
especially in Southern towns and cities where racial prejudice
flourished, officials made little effort to enforce the court's ruling.

THE LITTLE ROCK NINE
In Little Rock, the school superintendent tried to follow the
Supreme Court ruling. He laid out a plan for integrating the city's
schools that would begin with the 1957 school year. In response,
the NAACP found nine black students ranging in age from 14 to
17 who were willing to enroll in all-white Central High. They
were Ernest Green, Terrence Roberts, Elizabeth Eckford, Jefferson
Thomas, Carlotta Walls, Minnijean Brown, Gloria Ray, Thelma
Mothershed, and Melba Pattillo. Collectively, they were called the
"Little Rock Nine."

Wilson's Creek was the first major Civil War battle fought west of the Mississippi River.

TWENTY DAYS IN SEPTEMBER

Integrating Central High School wouldn't be easy. Throughout the summer, community groups and state leaders had been trying to find a way around it. The Mother's League of Central High School, a group that wanted to uphold segregation, filed a court petition to have the nine students barred from entering the school, arguing that admitting them could "lead to violence." The county granted the order, but a federal judge overturned it. As the first day of school approached, tensions rose. Extremists threatened violence. Finally, on September 2 (Labor Day), Governor Orval Faubus made a decision: he defied the federal government and called in the Arkansas National Guard to bar the black students from entering the school.

The next day, eight of the nine gathered at one of the high school's side entrances. They were to be escorted by two local ministers. But the National Guardsmen refused to allow them entry. Finally, they and their chaperones went home.

Elizabeth Eckford was the ninth student. Her family didn't own a phone, so she didn't know that she was supposed to meet her classmates and guides at the side entrance. Eckford simply walked up to the main entrance and tried to enter the school. There, she was met by an angry mob of white students and parents. They shouted at her, threatened her, and refused to let her inside. (One of the most famous photographs of the day shows Eckford walking toward the school, holding her books to her chest, as a white student yells from behind her.) Finally, Eckford left, getting a reprieve from the mob only after she boarded a city bus to take her home.

Two weeks passed before the Little Rock Nine tried again. On September 23, they tried to enter the school secretly, through a back entrance. They made it inside, but when word got out that they were there, a riot began outside and city police officers had to escort them out of the building for their own protection.

EISENHOWER LENDS A HAND

Word of the riot made the national news. People outside the South were appalled by the events in Arkansas, and President Dwight D. Eisenhower decided that the federal government needed to get involved. On September 24, 1957, Eisenhower deployed U.S. Army troops to Little Rock. The soldiers were charged with the task of keeping the local populace under control and making sure

What does Keystone, South Dakota, mean to you?

the Little Rock Nine got to class. The next day, under armed military guard, the nine students walked through the front doors of Central High School and attended their first full day of classes. It was the first time since Reconstruction that a U.S. president had used federal troops to protect African Americans' civil rights.

Inside the school, things weren't much better. The threats and harassment continued, so soldiers escorted the students to and from class. A few white students befriended the Little Rock Nine, but most stayed away out of either fear or prejudice. Over the course of the next year, the black students and their handful of supporters received death threats and were attacked by fellow students. Most of the nine adhered to Martin Luther King's theories of nonviolence, but one student—Minnijean Brown—decided to fight back. When white students cornered her in the cafeteria, she poured chili on them. When a classmate hit her with a purse, she called the girl "white trash." Eventually, Brown was suspended.

The remaining eight students finished out the school year at Central High School. They were still protected by soldiers. In October 1957, Eisenhower brought the Arkansas National Guard under federal control. The Army troops went back to their bases, and the National Guardsmen, now commanded by the president and not Governor Faubus, protected the students for the rest of the year. In May 1958, Ernest Green graduated from Central High School, the first black student to do so. Martin Luther King attended the ceremony.

IN THE YEARS THAT FOLLOWED

The segregation battle in Little Rock didn't end with the school year. Rather than integrate the city's high schools, the school board closed them the next year. The schools stayed closed until the fall of 1959, when federal courts ordered the city to reopen and integrate its public high schools.

In the decades since, the Little Rock Nine have found much success. They all graduated from high school: in addition to Green, Carlotta Walls, Thelma Mothershed, and Jefferson Thomas got their diplomas from Central High. Most of them went on to college, and they became lawyers, civil-rights activists, accountants, and teachers. They also received numerous awards, including the Congressional Gold Medal, the highest honor the U.S. government can bestow on civilians.

It's the town near Mount Rushmore National Memorial.

Central High School became a national historic site in 1998. It's also still a high school—one of the best academically in the country. Visitors to the site today can follow the Little Rock Nine's journey from the visitor center across the street (a refurbished gas station). A movie and an exhibit chronicle the 1957 crisis. Tours of the school are by reservation only.

Little Rock Central High School National Historic Site
Little Rock, AR 72202

Founded: 1998
Average annual visitors: 45,000

www.nps.gov/chsc

* * *

WE SALUTE THEM

- The *Brown v. Board of Education* ruling has its own national historic site in Topeka, Kansas. Located inside a building that once housed the Monroe School (which young Linda Brown—the case's namesake—attended), the Brown v. Board of Education National Historic Site includes five rooms (including a bookstore) in which videos and exhibits educate visitors about the historic Supreme Court ruling that brought integration to American public schools.

- After the Civil War, an all–African American squadron of military men called the Buffalo Soldiers took on many tasks throughout the United States; one was patrolling and protecting western national parks. Mark Matthews, the last surviving Buffalo Soldier, died in September 2005. He was 111 years old and is buried at Arlington National Cemetery in Virginia.

Arizona's Montezuma Castle National Monument is built into a sandstone cliff.

ROOSEVELT'S TREE ARMY

*FDR's Civilian Conservation Corps (CCC) gave millions of
Depression-era young men a helping hand—and they returned the favor
by rejuvenating the National Park System.*

THE BOYS OF THE GREAT DEPRESSION

The CCC was integral to Franklin D. Roosevelt's 1930s New Deal program of economic recovery. The government agency provided work and vocational training for unemployed single men between the ages of 17 and 25 as a way to alleviate poverty and unemployment during the Great Depression. "The boys," as those men were called, worked in six-month stints and could reenlist for a total of two years. They were paid $1 a day and given room and board (or as they called it, "three hots and a flop"). They were allowed to keep only $5 of their monthly wages for themselves; they sent the rest back home to help support their families.

FROM CALIFORNIA TO THE NEW YORK ISLAND

The Labor Department farmed out the CCC enrollees to other federal departments, and the National Park Service was one of the major beneficiaries. From 1933 to 1942, more than $9 million in permanent improvements were made to national parks, thanks to the CCC. The bulk of the work was replanting deforested areas (where the young men earned the nickname "Roosevelt's Tree Army"), building roads, and controlling erosion. But the boys also cleared more than 13,000 miles of hiking trails and built 4,000 acres of campgrounds. It's estimated that they planted between two and three billion trees in both national and state parks across the country. And you can still see a lot of their work in national parks today.

CATOCTIN MOUNTAINS PARK (MARYLAND)

CCC workers originally built Camp David—the vacation home to the president and first family since 1942—in the 1930s as a vacation spot for federal employees. But when FDR finally gave in

At 13,796 feet, Hawaii's Mauna Kea is the world's highest island mountain.

to pressure from the Secret Service to find a safe place to vacation, he adopted the camp for his own use, naming it Shangri-La. Later, President Eisenhower renamed it Camp David, after his grandson. It's not open to visitors, of course, but Catoctin Mountains Park is. The CCC also replanted the mountains around Camp David, which had been devastated by overzealous logging.

DEATH VALLEY NATIONAL PARK (CALIFORNIA)
Working in Death Valley—one of the most inhospitable environments in the world—the CCC graded 500 miles of roadway, installed water and telephone lines, built 76 buildings for park employees, cut trails throughout the Panamint Mountains, established five campgrounds, installed restroom and picnic facilities, and even created and installed signs so visitors wouldn't get lost in the desert.

DENALI NATIONAL PARK (ALASKA)
Speaking of inhospitable places, CCC improvements made visiting what was then called Mt. McKinley National Park a lot easier. They laid water and sewer lines, installed telephone lines, and built dog kennels for the sled teams that have always been the traditional mode of winter transportation in the park. To help the two-legged staff, they built the Wonder Lake ranger station, as far into the interior of the park as the road stretches.

OREGON CAVES NATIONAL MONUMENT (OREGON)
The CCC turned this relatively inaccessible site into an easy-to-reach tourist destination by building viewing platforms in the caves at Oregon Caves National Monument. They cleared and cut stairway routes and removed "headache" rocks (where heads might get bumped). They also strung telephone lines, built retaining walls, and planted trees.

PETRIFIED NATIONAL FOREST (ARIZONA)
Most of the CCC men weren't skilled craftsmen, but there were a few. These men built the beautiful Painted Desert Inn, a former lodge that's now a museum and bookstore. The building can still be admired for its expert construction, hand-painted glass panels, and hammered tin chandeliers. All are courtesy of the CCC boys.

SHENANDOAH NATIONAL PARK (VIRGINIA)

If you've ever driven the curvy Skyline Drive in Shenandoah National Park, imagine driving it without guardrails. Before the CCC recruits came along, drivers navigated that road at their own risk. The boys installed wooden guardrails throughout the park, regraded Skyline Drive, installed nearly 70 scenic overlooks, cleared 500 miles of trails, and built stone gutters for drainage.

YOSEMITE NATIONAL PARK (CALIFORNIA)

Californians treasure Yosemite in part because it's one of the few heavily forested areas left in the state. But the park's mountains wouldn't be as lush if it hadn't been for the CCC boys who sprayed, pruned, and removed dying trees in the park, preventing the spread of the diseases and pests that ran rampant in the 1930s. Without them, the forests of the Sierra Nevadas—including the Mariposa Grove, home to the famous giant sequoias—might have been lost forever.

A PUBLIC WORKS PROJECT THAT WORKED

During the nine years that the CCC was active, it employed almost three million men—5 percent of the U.S. population at the time. In 1935, at its peak, there were 500,000 members in more than 2,500 camps throughout the country and in Puerto Rico and the Virgin Islands.

FDR wanted to continue the CCC indefinitely, but Congress cut funding in 1941 in response to the pressures of World War II, and the program closed the next year. Instead of planting trees for FDR, young men were encouraged to fight for Uncle Sam.

Former CCC camps were later used as Civilian Public Service camps, where conscientious objectors to the war performed "work of national importance" as a substitute for military service. Other old CCC camps were turned into Japanese-American internment camps and POW camps for captured German soldiers.

Today, there are several CCC museums across the country. The most well known is in St. Louis, Missouri, and displays lots of memorabilia: uniforms, mess kits, work-record cards, and even programs from holiday dinners and celebrations—a good way to learn about how these young men lived and about how their work continues to enrich the country they served.

SLIMED!

*Many people come to Great Smoky Mountains National Park hoping
to see a bear—from a distance, of course. But we came across a
group of researchers who were even more excited to find
bugs and a little yellow blob of slime mold.*

4,666 AND COUNTING

The nonprofit group Discover Life in America has organized
hundreds of taxonomists (people who differentiate and
classify plants and animals), biologists, botanists, and ecologists
who, along with volunteers, work to identify and inventory all the
forms of life in Great Smoky Mountains National Park . . everything from bears to myxomcetes (slime mold). In size and scope,
it's the first scientific survey of its kind.

The project is called the All Taxa Biodiversity Inventory
(ATBI for short), and it began in 1998 with the goal of finding,
identifying, and sorting all the species of life in the park. Eight
years later, the ATBI had identified 4,666 species not previously
known to inhabit Great Smoky Mountains National Park. Even
more remarkable, the researchers also discovered more than 650
types of plants and animals that were previously unknown to science—including 20 new forms of slime mold! And the tally
keeps rising.

The researchers do most of their collecting, photographing, and
releasing work from April to October in what's called a "bioblitz," a
rapid assessment of what lives in a particular area at a given point
in time. For example, they participated in a four-day Beetle Blitz to
study the park's beetle population and a Fern Foray to study . . .
well . . . ferns.

WHAT'S SO GREAT ABOUT THE SMOKIES?

The reasons for so much biodiversity lie in the Smoky Mountains'
landscape and climate. The range formed about 200 to 300 million
years ago, and it was relatively undisturbed by ice-age glaciers and
rising oceans. So the 500,000-plus acres that would become the
park became a refuge for thousands of plants and animals.

The mountain elevation, from 875 to 6,643 feet above sea level,
and the resulting wide range of weather conditions, also helped.

President Lyndon Johnson flew to his Texas ranch 74 times during his five years in office.

Plants and animals common to the southeastern United States live in the lowlands; those common to the northeast are found at the higher elevations. The high rainfall and humidity (as opposed to drier mountain climates like the Rockies) makes for lush tree and plant growth, providing plenty of food and cover for the more than 200 varieties of birds, 66 types of mammals, 50 native fish, 39 reptile species, and 43 different kinds of amphibians that live in the park.

SO FAR, SO GREAT

Researchers have documented over 10,000 plant and animal species in the park so far. And some scientists believe that there are more than 100,000 species living in the park. For its part, Discover Life in America has proved so successful in the Smokies that its supporters hope to institute similar projects in every national park in the country.

TENNESSEE

Great Smoky Mountains National Park
Gatlinburg, TN 37738

Founded: 1934
Area: 521,085 acres
Average annual visitors: 9,000,000

www.nps.gov/grsm

* * *

THE BOTTOMLESS POGUE?

Not really. But the Pogue, a 14-acre pond in Vermont's Marsh-Billings-Rockefeller National Historic Park, is rumored to be bottomless. How the pond got its name (and its reputation) is up for debate, but the National Park Service offers two theories:

- It's derived from a Native American word (though no one seems to know the original word).
- It's derived from a Scottish word (again, no one seems to know the original word).

No matter. Today, the boggy Pogue is a favorite spot for day hikers and visitors who want to take in Vermont's spectacular fall foliage.

He spent about one-fourth of his presidency there, and it's now a national historic park.

BILL AND JOHN'S EXCELLENT ADVENTURE

The story of the only two men to swim the Grand Canyon . . .
and the trials they faced along the way.

Bill Beer wrote in his book *We Swam the Grand Canyon*, it was a "cheap vacation that got a little out of hand." In 1955, 26-year-old Beer and his buddy, John Daggett, 27, two Southern California surfers, swam the length of the Colorado River through the Grand Canyon . . . and lived to tell the tale.

BEER FLOATS
On April 10, 1955, they got into the water at Lees Ferry, where the Grand Canyon officially begins; the water was 51 degrees. They wore swim fins, goggles, thin rubber jackets, and life jackets. They carried four rubber bags packed with food for a month, movie equipment, cooking gear, and sleeping bags.

Soon after they embarked on the journey, word of their stunt got out, and the National Park Service and the local sheriff's office conducted an aerial search for the two men. The authorities found nothing and gave them up for dead.

THE OUTLAWS OUTWIT THE LAW
Beer and Daggett were still very much alive, though, and when they realized they were out of film for their movie camera, they decided to take a break. The men hiked up the seven-mile Kaibob Trail to the El Tovar Hotel on the canyon's South Rim. It was their first taste of civilization in days, and they were surprised by the newspaper headlines they saw: "Fear Pair Lost in Colorado Swim Try." They were famous, but they were also in a lot of trouble. Their swim was so dangerous that it was illegal. So they were hauled into the park superintendent's office to face the consequences.

They argued their case, saying that unless they were allowed to finish, others would try until the river had been swum. Finally, they managed to persuade the superintendent, who gave them permission to continue their trip.

RAPIDS TRANSIT

The men still had 192 miles to go—a distance that included some of the roughest rapids on the river, most notably roaring Lava Falls. They pushed on anyway and were cut, banged, and bruised by the river. Daggett was nearly killed when he was sucked under a rock in one stretch of rapids. When the river threw him up, he was barely conscious and was bleeding badly from a scalp wound. After a short break, he kept going. The men also had a lot of trouble with strong winds. They wore their swim goggles around camp in order to keep the blowing sand out of their eyes. Then, finally, 26 days after they began, they arrived at Pierce's Ferry in Lake Mead, 280 miles downriver from Lees Ferry.

They were heralded by the public, and people wanted to learn more about their adventure. The footage they filmed during the trip (which included shots of them braving the rapids) was shown on television, and they gave lectures about the journey. They were the 219th and 220th persons to swim the Colorado River through the Grand Canyon—and the only ones to do it without a boat. When the publicity wore off, Daggett disappeared from public life. Beer wrote his book and remained an outdoor enthusiast all his life. He died in a small plane crash in 2000 at the age of 71.

ARIZONA

Grand Canyon National Park
Grand Canyon, AZ 86023

Founded: 1893
Area: 1,218,375 acres
Average annual visitors: 4,000,000

www.nps.gov/grca

PARANORMAL PARKS

America's national parks are full of ghostly tales; here are four that might send you running for cover.

MELISSA: MAMMOTH CAVE NATIONAL PARK (KENTUCKY)

When it comes to haunted parks, Mammoth Cave probably takes the cake. But whether the ghosts of slave tour guides or lost explorers, few spooks at Mammoth frighten more people than Melissa. According to legend, in 1858 this young woman made a deathbed confession to having killed a suitor in Mammoth Cave. It was an accident (of course!), a cruel joke gone bad. Melissa had fallen in love with her tutor, but when he didn't return her feelings, she lured him into Mammoth Cave under the pretense of giving him a tour and then sneaked out of the labyrinth when he wasn't looking. Melissa was a local who knew the cave well, but the tutor was from Boston and had no experience with the cave's underground cavernous maze. Melissa waited topside for him to emerge frightened and contrite, but he never did. Hours passed, and then days, and the tutor remained inside the cave. Melissa claimed to have gone back after him; she looked for him and called out to him, but to no avail. No one ever saw the tutor again. After she became sick with consumption (tuberculosis), Melissa fessed up to her crime and then died, still feeling guilty over the tutor's disappearance.

That might have been the end of it, but over the next 100 years, visitors to Mammoth Cave reported odd encounters that many people attribute to Melissa. One man spoke of hearing a woman calling out to someone in the deep recesses of the cave. And another visitor, while venturing deep into the cave, reported hearing what sounded like a woman's ghostly cough . . . Melissa had died of consumption, after all. Talk about a woman scorned!

PLANE CRASH VICTIMS: GRAND CANYON NATIONAL PARK (ARIZONA)

In 1956, two planes collided over the Grand Canyon and crashed into the cliffs. Both were flying off course—many flight experts believe that the pilots were trying to give their passengers better views of the canyon. More than 120 people died, and at the time, the crash was called the worst accident in aviation history. The site was so remote that rescue and clean-up crews couldn't reach some of the debris or bodies, so there they remained in an area that park rangers later called Crash Canyon.

Almost 50 years after the crash, a ranger named KJ Glover was camping at the floor of Crash Canyon near the Colorado River. In the middle of the night, Glover awoke to confused voices and footsteps traipsing through the brush outside her tent. When she peeked outside, she saw a group of people passing by her campsite. The people were dressed up: the men in button-up shirts, and the women in skirts that hung past their knees. The fashions weren't modern, and they certainly weren't appropriate for a midnight hike through the Grand Canyon. Glover kept watch as the group passed her and continued up the canyon toward the site of the 1956 crash. In the morning, Glover replayed the incident in her head, and although she realized she *could* have been dreaming, she believed herself to have been fully awake and seeing the ghosts of the people who died in those plane crashes five decades earlier.

OLD GREEN EYES: CHICKAMAUGA AND CHATTANOOGA NATIONAL MILITARY PARK (GEORGIA AND TENNESSEE)

From Gettysburg to Antietam to the Great Smoky Mountains, Civil War ghosts abound in the national parks. But none is so eerie as "Old Green Eyes," the bodiless spirit of a Confederate soldier who haunts Chickamauga Creek in Georgia. Chickamauga and the nearby town of Chattanooga, Tennessee, were strategic strongholds for the Union during the Civil War. If Confederate soldiers had captured the area, they'd have easily been able to push into Union territory.

In September 1863, the Confederates managed to take Chickamauga, but two months later, the Union proved victorious at Chattanooga and prevented the rebels from moving into Tennessee. More than 40,000 soldiers died in the battles; one of those was Old Green Eyes (no one seems to know the name he had while he was alive). The soldier was decapitated during the battle at Chickamauga; only his head was ever found. It was buried on the battlefield and, according to residents, continues to haunt the area. Locals and visitors claim to have seen the spirit and head—recognizable by its glowing green eyes—moaning and wandering the battlefield searching for its missing body.

A slot canyon is a deep, narrow canyon, often with water or mud at the bottom.

THE AITU: NATIONAL PARK OF AMERICAN SAMOA

In Samoa, locals have long feared ghostly creatures called *aitu*, or evil spirits. The aitu are said to meet at the park's To'aga beach at noon and after sunset and to frighten people who venture into their territory. When National Park Service officials started scouting the site during the early 1900s, Samoans warned them of the aitu, but one man—a pharmacist with the U.S. Navy—learned about the spirits the hard way.

In 1924, while the pharmacist was living in Samoa, he encountered ghosts that continuously knocked on his front door; his wife had run-ins with similar spooks that wandered through her house and moved the furniture. And one evening, the pharmacist, his wife, and several other people encountered a party of headless revelers on To'aga beach. The pharmacist ultimately left the island, and the park offices were moved into town. But the threat of an aitu haunting remains, so if you're visiting Samoa, be sure to stay away from To'aga beach during prime aitu haunting hours!

* * *

WORLD'S LARGEST LAKES

The United States and Canada share two of the five largest lakes in the world. Here are the top five largest lakes in area (including two "seas" that are actually misnamed; they have no outlet and thus are really lakes):

1. Caspian Sea (Asia):
169,000 square miles

2. Lake Superior (Canada and the United States):
31,820 square miles

3. Lake Victoria (Africa):
26,828 square miles

4. Aral Sea (Kazakhstan and Uzbekistan):
26,166 square miles

5. Lake Huron (Canada and the United States):
23,010 square miles

THE TRAVELING PROFESSOR

Loyola Marymount University travel and tourism professor
Alan Hogenauer is the only living person known to have visited all
390 U.S. national park sites.

Visiting every national park, even over the course of many years, seems like a lifetime project. But in the early 1960s, college professor Alan Hogenauer decided to do it. He'd already bagged a few, starting with the Statue of Liberty in 1953 (when he was just 12). And over the last four decades, he's planned trips where he could see a few parks at a time. Gradually, his to-do list got shorter.

WHAT?!? WHAT?!?
There were times that Hogenauer thought he might not finish his project, like the time President Jimmy Carter declared several remote areas in Alaska to be national parks. Hogenauer imagined that the only people who would see these parks would have to be dropped in by helicopter and then clear a path to get there. When he did a bit more research, though, he found out that along almost every lake in Alaska lives a person with a seaplane who can be hired to fly into a remote area for a few hundred dollars an hour. Expensive, yes, but better than hiking 20 miles over the tundra.

Hogenauer was once again dismayed when congressman Phil Burton announced a plan in which a new park would be named every month. Fortunately, that never happened.

KEEPING SCORE
Hogenauer first ran the entire gamut of parks by 1980, when there were about 320 sites. Since then, he's visited 70 more as they joined the system. With that goal completed, he decided on a new challenge: to visit all the separate pieces of the parks as well. (For instance, some parks, like the Indiana Dunes, are made up of several noncontiguous areas.) As of this writing, he has only one more to go.

The Santa Fe Trail is about 753 miles from Kansas City to Santa Fe.

He didn't stop at the park system either. Hogenauer has also visited all the state capitals, all 436 congressional districts, and every U.S. city with more than 100,000 residents.

* * *

HOW TO COLLECT THE NATIONAL PARKS

When you visit a National Park Service site, you can document your visit by getting a rubber-stamp cancellation. They're a bit like the stamps you'd get from foreign countries in a passport. And the NPS even offers a special passport book to keep them in.

It's a great way to keep your memories of travel adventures over a lifetime. An NPS Passport project is especially fun for kids, who enjoy collecting the stamps; and, of course, the younger you start, the longer you have to build up an impressive collection of NPS sites. The stamps are similar to what you'd see on a letter over a postage stamp—a circular cancellation that gives the name and place of the site, plus the date. For instance, the stamp might say "Petroglyph National Monument, Albuquerque, NM" and the date you were there.

These cancellation stamps are available not just at national parks but at nearly all NPS units—national memorials, historic sites, national seashores, scenic trails, battlefields, and more. Sometimes it takes a bit of searching to find out just where to get the stamp, but the search itself can be part of the fun. (Hint: if there's a visitor's center or NPS bookstore anywhere near the site, try those first.)

The NPS Passport book is a 6-inch by 3-inch, spiral-bound 104-page guidebook that includes spaces for the rubber passport stamps, notes, a list of all official NPS sites, maps, illustrations, and photos. The basic Passport book costs $7.95. A fancier version called the Passport Explorer Edition comes in a zip-up, weatherproof portfolio and is pricier, at $44.95.

How many stamps can you collect? More than most lifetimes allow. Remember, from the White House on down, there are 390 NPS sites, including 58 national parks, 74 national monuments, 77 national historic sites, 10 national seashores, 14 national cemeteries, and 12 national recreation areas. Within those parks, there are hundreds of monuments.

Louisiana's Outback is home to more than 3,000 alligator nests.

THE JOHNSTOWN FLOOD

The Johnstown flood was one of the greatest disasters in American history. Today, the site of that tragedy is a national memorial.

Johnstown, Pennsylvania, in the western Appalachian Mountains not far from Pittsburgh, was a thriving steel town in 1889. The city had a population of about 30,000 and sat in a narrow valley at the fork of the Little Conemaugh and Stony Creek rivers.

The townspeople knew that they lived in a floodplain; it was obvious every spring when heavy rains poured down the mountain and overran the rivers' banks; floodwaters seeped into nearby buildings and homes. Fourteen miles upriver and 450 feet higher in elevation was the man-made Lake Conemaugh. Situated on the side of a mountain and held in place by the South Fork Dam, the lake was two miles long and home to the exclusive South Fork Fishing and Hunting Club, where successful Pittsburgh businessmen went for vacation. No one in Johnstown gave much thought to the lake's old, earthen dam—except to joke about it collapsing someday.

THE DELUGE

During the night of May 30, 1889, one of the worst rainstorms in history dumped 10 inches of rain on Johnstown. By noon the next day, the South Fork Club's engineer took a nervous look at the rising lake waters and sent a messenger to telegraph a warning of possible flooding to the Johnstown authorities. He and the club's president also gathered a work group and desperately tried to bolster the dam.

At 3:10 p.m., they lost the battle. At first, the lake started to seep over the dam; then, with an awful roar, the entire dam collapsed. Within 45 minutes, the lake was completely emptied, its contents on a disastrous journey. Twenty million tons of water gushed through the narrow valley toward Johnstown at speeds of 40 miles an hour, tearing up, crushing, and carrying along everything in its path: whole trees, houses, train cars, boulders—and bodies.

WATER, WATER EVERYWHERE
The whistles at the mill sounded shortly after 4 p.m., but people didn't know why (though most historians believe it wouldn't have done any good if they had because it all happened so fast). The first sign of disaster was a deafening roar that grew louder with each second. Some said it sounded like hail or a cyclone or thunder. One man remembered the crunching sounds of houses torn apart by the water. Then, shrieks and screams became part of the uproar.

At 4:07 p.m., a 60-foot-high wall of water slammed into Johnstown. People on the streets were swept away. Some residents climbed to their rooftops only to be carried off when their houses splintered beneath them. Others floated on rafts of debris and were dashed into buildings or bridges or sucked underwater by whirlpools.

IT'S NOT OVER YET
The water moved through the city as one mass until it came to a railroad bridge, where most of the debris started piling up. Then, the wave split in two and slowed as it continued down the valley. The survivors who'd been swept toward the bridge clung there or became trapped in the wreckage, which was piled 40 feet high.

As night fell, the huge pile of rubble caught fire. Eighty Johnstowners died in the fire.

TRIUMPH OVER TRAGEDY
Some Johnstown residents did survive the disaster. One was 16-year-old Victor Heiser who clambered to the roof of his family's stable. As he watched the wall of water rush toward him, he saw it splinter other structures and expected the same. But instead, the stable was lifted off its foundation and began to roll like a barrel in the water, crashing into other houses in its path. Victor jumped from one piece of house to another, finally landing on a piece of barn roof. He rode along on it, eventually jumping onto the roof of a brick building that was still standing. Victor had looked at his watch when the terror began. He remembered that it had said 4:20. It wasn't quite 4:30 when his wild ride ended.

Looking for Cutthroat Castle? You'll find it in Colorado's Hovenweep National Monument.

HELPING HANDS . . . AND HAMS

In all, 2,209 people—almost 10 percent of Johnstown's population—lost their lives in the flood. Four square miles of the city no longer existed. Sixteen hundred homes were destroyed, and 99 whole families died. Hundreds of missing people were never found.

Donations of money, food, and clothing poured in to Johnstown. The citizens of Cincinnati sent 20,000 hams. Prisoners in Pittsburgh baked and sent bread. Standard Oil donated a carload of kerosene for light and heat. Emergency shelters, tents, and prefab houses were erected. More than $3 million was donated from around the world. And the American Red Cross, led by Clara Barton herself, carried out its first major peacetime venture.

COMMEMORATION

The South Fork Dam was never replaced, and today, the Johnstown Flood National Memorial preserves the ruins of the dam, part of the old lake bed, and some of the buildings of the South Fork Fishing and Hunting Club. The visitor center regularly shows a park service–produced film that re-creates the flood. Every May 31, a ceremony is held in remembrance of the victims of the Johnstown flood, and people light 2,209 candles on the remains of the South Fork Dam.

PENNSYLVANIA

Johnstown Flood National Memorial Park
South Fork, PA 15956

Founded: 1895
Area: 178 acres
Average annual visitors: 112,000

www.nps.gov/jofl

* * *

HIDDEN HIKE

Visitors to Harper's Ferry National Historic Park can trek a portion of the Appalachian Trail and pass through two states all in a matter of minutes. Catch the Appalachian Trail as it runs through the park near the lower town. Walk to the C&O Canal, and you'll have crossed from West Virginia into Maryland.

THE EVERGLADES BY THE NUMBERS

Florida's Everglades National Park is North America's only subtropical preserve, a collection of islands, waterways, mangrove forests, and ponds that are known for being home to an abundant array of wildlife (especially mosquitoes).

1/3
Amount of the park that's covered with water

2
Major Native American tribes (the Seminoles and the Miccosukees) that once called the Everglades home

4
Number of poisonous snake species that live in the Everglades: eastern diamondback rattlesnakes, dusky pygmy rattlesnakes, cottonmouths, and coral snakes. A total of 26 snake species live in the park.

5 feet
Wingspan of the endangered wood stork. In the 1930s, 4,000 mating pairs of wood storks lived in the Everglades; today, only 250 pairs remain.

8 feet
Highest elevation in the park

15 feet
Minimum "safe distance" the NPS recommends for alligator viewing. If the animal hisses or opens its mouth, back off!

36
Species of threatened or endangered animals that live in the park. These include Florida panthers, American alligators, and West Indian manatees.

43
Number of different mosquito species found in the Everglades; 13 of these bite humans, so be sure to keep your can of Off handy.

The first female Native American doctor in the U.S. was Susan LaFlesche Picotte...

60 inches
Average annual rainfall. Most of it falls during the rainy season, which runs from May to October.

90° F
Average summer temperature in the Everglades; the average humidity hovers around 90 percent.

120 miles
Length of the Everglades' "River of Grass," water that flows out of Lake Okeechobee and travels over fields of saw grass. The River of Grass is also 50 miles wide and, in most places, less than a foot deep.

350
Number of bird species that live in or migrate through the Everglades. Two—the smooth-billed ani and the short-tailed hawk—live nowhere else in the United States except Florida.

1947
Year Everglades National Park was established

10,000
Number of islands that make up Everglades National Park

800,000
Number of football fields that would fit in Lake Okeechobee

FLORIDA

Everglades National Park
Homestead, FL 33034

Founded: 1947
Area: 1,398,617 acres
Average annual visitors: 1,200,000

www.nps.gov/ever

OREGON OR BUST

You've heard its name, you learned about it in school, but how much do you really know about the Oregon Trail?

1. How many modern states can be found along the Oregon Trail?

   A. Two
   B. Four
   C. Six
   D. Eight

2. On what date did the first Oregon Trail wagon train set out for the West Coast?

   A. May 16, 1842
   B. June 3, 1840
   C. March 13, 1850
   D. November 13, 1849

3. What prompted most early pioneers to travel to Oregon?

   A. The weather was better than in the Midwest.
   B. They wanted free land.
   C. They wanted to move away from Native American settlements.
   D. They wanted to live closer to the ocean.

4. What was the most essential supply needed on the trail?

   A. Food
   B. A gun
   C. A wagon
   D. All of the above

5. What was the average travel time from Missouri to Oregon?

   A. Two to three weeks
   B. Two to three months
   C. Four to six weeks
   D. Four to six months

At 136.64 miles, South Dakota's Jewel Cave is the second-longest cave in the world.

6. What was the most dangerous hazard the pioneers faced on their way to Oregon?

    A. Attacks by Native Americans
    B. Cholera
    C. Sunstroke
    D. Runaway oxen

7. Why did travelers circle their wagons?

    A. To protect themselves from attacks by Native Americans
    B. To keep children under control
    C. To corral livestock
    D. To protect themselves from bad weather

8. What caused traffic on the trail to diminish?

    A. The Civil War
    B. Attacks by Native Americans
    C. The transcontinental railroad
    D. The invention of the telegraph

9. About how many people traveled over the Oregon Trail?

    A. 350,000
    B. 500,000
    C. 875,000
    D. 1,000,000

10. When did the Oregon Trail become part of the National Park Service?

    A. 1900
    B. 1935
    C. 1954
    D. 1978

For answers, turn to page 391.

But it will get longer. Airflow studies suggest that most of the cave is yet to be found!

FAR OUT

In a remote Alaskan outpost, the Bering Land Bridge National Preserve memorializes human migration over a vanished subcontinent.

GRAND CROSSING

Archaeologists believe the first human inhabitants of the Americas arrived about 20,000 years ago via a land bridge called Beringia that connected Siberia and Alaska. It was about 1,000 miles wide; plants, animals, and even humans lived on it. The settlers migrated across Beringia from Asia and carved out new homes in the new land. But as the earth's temperature rose, the ice and glaciers surrounding the bridge melted and caused sea levels to rise and cover Beringia, isolating the migrants from their original homelands. Today, the 56-mile-wide Bering Strait separates Alaska from Siberia.

LONG DIVISION

One of the core purposes of Alaska's Bering Land Bridge National Preserve is to provide archaeological research on the early Asian migrants. Representatives from the park safeguard identified archaeological sites and protect the area's natural environment so that unidentified sites will still be intact when someone finds them in the future. Archaeologists have already found many interesting artifacts on the preserve, including 9,000-year-old pieces of sharpened stone that were used as blades, early chisels, and pottery fragments.

WHAT A LONG, STRANGE TRIP

If you want to visit the preserve, you'll need to be a hardy sort. There are no roads leading there, so most people take small planes or boats. In the winter, you can get there by snowmobile or dogsled, but you'd better be ready for some serious cold: the average January temperature is 6 degrees Fahrenheit, and lows sometimes dip down to 40 below. The preserve is so remote (many call it the most remote park site in the United States) that only a few thousand people visit every year. (By comparison, the Grand Canyon's annual score is about 4 million.)

Alligators aplenty inhabit the marshes of Canaveral National Seashore in Florida.

Once you arrive, you'll find that the area is sparse and unpopulated. There's a hot springs where a barracks and a bathhouse have been operating off and on since the days of the Alaska gold rush, catering to the area's few tourists and to the Inuit who use the hot springs for spiritual and healing purposes. There are a few emergency cabins spread around the preserve to provide shelter for campers or other people who get into trouble out in the wilderness during the winter. The cabins are primitive, however—they include just a fireplace and a cot, no bathrooms or water. Even the park administration finds the area too cold and remote to spend much time there; the administrative offices are based in Nome, more than 50 miles away.

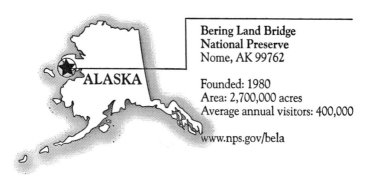

Bering Land Bridge
National Preserve
Nome, AK 99762

Founded: 1980
Area: 2,700,000 acres
Average annual visitors: 400,000

www.nps.gov/bela

* * *

THE HAUNTED LAKE

Galen Clark became America's first park ranger in 1867, and he spent much of his time—before and during his service—exploring Yosemite's forests. During one of his walks near the park's Grouse Lake, he heard a wailing cry coming from the forest. He assumed it was a lost dog, but later that night, after he met up with a group of Native American hunters, he learned otherwise. When Clark told them of the cry, they said it was no dog: a boy from the tribe had drowned in the lake many years before, and anytime anyone passed by, he wailed. Furthermore, none of the tribesmen would go into the lake because they believed that if they did, the boy's spirit would grab them by the legs and pull them under. Clark later said he came to believe a bird must have made the noise but that the Native Americans were convinced of the legend.

The largest recorded American gator measured 19 feet in length.

CAN'T WE
JUST BE FRIENDS?

Canada and America may be allies now, but relations weren't always so friendly. On November 13, 1838, Canadian rebels and American forces attacked the Great White North and sparked a brief war with the Canucks. Today, that firefight is memorialized at Ontario's Battle of the Windmill National Historic Site.

FALSE INTELLIGENCE

During the mid-1800s, Canada was still a British colony. Great Britain won Canada after defeating France in the French and Indian War, and the Canadians had been living under British rule ever since. Some rebel Canadians and a handful of Americans wanted to oust the British and introduce an American-like democracy to Canada. In 1838, they decided to act.

The rebels conducted border raids for several months, sneaking into Canada from New York State and attacking British military stations. But in November 1838, they decided to mount a full-scale attack, enter Canada through northern New York, cross the St. Lawrence River, and take the town of Prescott, Ontario. Why Prescott? It was there, it was close, and the rebels believed that once they were entrenched in the town, angry Canadians would rise up and join the cause.

Most Canadians just weren't that upset with the British, though. Yes, they endured taxation without representation like the American colonists had, but Great Britain made many concessions to the Canadians when they came under English rule. Catholicism was still allowed, and French (most Canadians at that time had French ancestors) was still an official language. Whatever their problems with England, most Canadians weren't ready to take up arms against the crown.

A SPY IN THEIR MIDST

The rebels were unaware of this as they planned their invasion. It was supposed to be a secret attack—and an easy one at that; the rebels believed that Prescott was only lightly defended by the British army. In looking for good strategic points around the town,

---

California's Trona Pinnacles (porous rock spires) have been featured in many movies...

the rebels settled on a 60-foot-tall stone windmill that stood on a slope overlooking Prescott. Taking control of the windmill, they believed, would give them the high ground and a strategic advantage over the British.

But the British were on to them. Great Britain had known about the rebels for some time and had planted a spy in their ranks. So when the 250 rebels crossed into Canada on November 13, 1838, they were greeted by 1,000 British troops. It was a setback, but the rebels fought anyway, still certain that the angry Canadian populace would join them at any moment.

THE COSTS OF WAR

In the end, Canada's general public never rose up. The rebels battled British troops for four days, holed themselves up in the windmill, and even managed to inflict some damage. But on November 16, the British regrouped and launched a full-scale assault. They drove the rebels out of the windmill, chased off some, and killed or captured the ones who remained. In the end, 13 British soldiers were killed and 78 were wounded, but 50 rebels were killed and more than 100 were captured. Some of the captured were executed, but most were pardoned or sent to Australian penal colonies.

The United States and Canada never warred again, but the little-known Battle of the Windmill helped pave the way for Canadian independence in 1867. The rebellion encouraged others to denounce British rule, and eventually, even the complacent populace decided they no longer wanted to be a colony.

Today, the site of this historic battle is part of Parks Canada and is located just east of the town of Prescott. The windmill still stands, and park officials lead visitors on tours to the top, where they can stand as the rebels did more than 100 years ago and take in dramatic views of the St. Lawrence River.

ONTARIO

Battle of the Windmill
National Historic Site
Prescott, ON K0E 1T0

Founded: 2004

www.pc.gc.ca/lhn-nhs/on/windmill

...including *Star Trek V, Planet of the Apes,* and *Lost in Space.*

WHERE THE
BISON ROAM

*Millions of bison once played alongside the deer and the antelope
of Yellowstone—but in the early 1900s, there were only a
few dozen left in the park.*

BISON BASICS
Yellowstone National Park is the only place in the
continental United States where bison have lived continuously since prehistoric times. They are the largest mammals in the
park: males can weigh up to 1,800 pounds; females weigh close to
1,000. Both stand six feet tall. But don't let their size fool you into
believing they're slow: they can run up to 30 miles per hour.

Before the 19th century, bison numbered in the tens of millions
in North America, and for thousands of years, Native Americans
relied on them for survival—using the meat for food, hides for
clothing and shelter, sinews for bows, dung for fires, and grease for
cooking. The natives even boiled down the hooves for glue, and
when food was scarce, they ate marrow from bison bones.

RAILROADS AND RUGS
The arrival of settlers on the plains changed everything. They
wanted to raise their own cattle on the bisons' grazing lands, and
railroad companies wanted the bison off their tracks. Plus, when
the settlers got a look at Native American "buffalo coats" and rugs,
they couldn't get enough; bison hunting became an industry.

In the mid-1800s, bison hunters earned between $3 and $5 per
head. With a good rifle and a reliable horse, a hunter could kill as
many as 100 animals a day. Buffalo Bill Cody earned his name by
killing thousands of bison, supposedly within just a few months. As
many as 1,000 different companies employed bison hunters in the
1800s, and sometimes more than 100,000 bison were killed in a
single day. Some of the meat was harvested, but most of the animals were skinned and their carcasses were left to rot. The 30 to 60
million bison that roamed the plains in the early 1800s were
reduced to fewer than 200 by 1890.

If you hear an owl hooting at night in the Everglades, it's most likely a barred owl.

A BIG COMEBACK

At the turn of the 20th century, with only about 50 bison left within the borders of Yellowstone National Park, park officials realized that the animals were in danger of extinction. So they imported about 20 bison from elsewhere and started to interbreed them with the Yellowstone herd. By the 1950s, the number of bison in the park had grown to nearly 1,500.

Today, bison are neither threatened nor endangered in Yellowstone . . . as long as they stay within the park borders. It's a different story if they cross into Montana.

NOT IN MY BACKYARD!

Ranchers in Montana have long dueled with the state's free-roaming bison. After the U.S. bison herds started making a comeback in the mid-20th century, they started having run-ins with ranchers. Admittedly, bison are big animals that can trample fences, devastate cattle grazing land, and generally destroy private property. But the most worrisome thing for ranchers is that some bison in Yellowstone carry a disease called brucellosis, which makes the animals unable to carry their offspring to term. Because it can be transmitted from bison to domesticated cattle, brucellosis is a serious threat to cattle ranchers. That's why the three states bordering Yellowstone Park—Wyoming, Montana, and Idaho—have long-standing (since the 1970s) boundary-control agreements with the National Park Service. The agreements allow states to come up with ways to control animals that wander onto private property.

In 1982, Montana acted on this border agreement by passing a law that allowed ranchers to shoot bison that wandered out of Yellowstone. The public was so upset about the law, though, that after seven years bison hunting was put on hold. The hold lasted 23 years, but as more and more bison contracted brucellosis (and posed a threat to cattle), Montana again reinstated the bison hunting law in 2005, allowing people to hunt bison that wandered beyond the park's borders.

OTHER SOLUTIONS

The federal and state governments still want to protect the animals, so they're doing what they can to keep the bison from leaving the park in the first place. NPS officials use helicopters, ATVs, and snowmobiles to chase strays back into Yellowstone. And if the bison do manage to cross the border, they're captured and tested for brucellosis. Those that test positive are destroyed; the rest are returned to the park.

STUCK IN A (BISON) JAM

Thanks to these efforts, nearly 4,000 bison live in the park today. In fact, there are so many bison living in Yellowstone that visitors driving through the park's backcountry are more likely to be waylaid by a "bison jam" than a traffic jam. Large numbers of bison often cross the roads, and vehicles can be stopped for several minutes or even hours.

The best places to see these big groups of bison depend on the season. In the summer, Hayden Valley near the Yellowstone River is prime bison-watching territory. In the winter, the animals hang out near the geyser basins, where the heat keeps them warm and melts the snow that covers their food.

WYOMING

Yellowstone National Park
Yellowstone National Park, WY 82190

Founded: 1872
Area: 2,212,789 acres
Average annual visitors: 3,000,000

www.nps.gov/yell

* * *

A BISON BY ANY OTHER NAME . . .

Bison are often mistakenly called "buffalo." Though the two species are distantly related genetically, the only true buffaloes are the Asian water buffalo, which lives in southeast Asia, and the African buffalo. The American bison—most often mistaken for buffalo—is the largest land mammal in North America and one of the largest types of wild cattle in the world.

AMERICA'S FAVORITE DRIVE

A drive on the Blue Ridge Parkway transports
22 million visitors a year to an earlier, less complicated time.

The 469-mile scenic highway from Virginia to North Carolina known as the Blue Ridge Parkway—and "America's Favorite Drive"—is the longest rural parkway in the country. It's surrounded by more than 80,000 acres of national park land and was conceived as a way to connect Shenandoah National Park in the north to Great Smoky Mountains National Park in the south.

But the parkway wasn't dreamed up just for R & R. It was authorized by President Franklin D. Roosevelt in the 1930s as a Depression-era public works project and was built primarily by the Civilian Conservation Corps (CCC): local architects, engineers, and workers from North Carolina and Virginia who badly needed the employment. Builders broke ground at Cumberland Knob, North Carolina, on September 11, 1935. All but 7.5 miles were completed after 32 years of work.

THE MISSING LINK

Those last 7.5 miles were supposed to skirt North Carolina's Grandfather Mountain—the highest peak in the Blue Ridge Mountains—but the steep terrain and controversy over the environmental harm the road would cause delayed things. Finally, in the mid-1980s, the National Park Service and the Federal Highway Administration engineers designing the project came up with a better idea: elevate the road using a series of bridges so they could avoid unnecessary blasting and extensive cutting into the mountain. The final 7.5-mile segment was completed in 1987 and now includes 13 bridges, the most famous of which is the Linn Cove Viaduct.

That 1,243-foot-long S-shaped bridge is made of concrete tinted with iron oxide to better blend with its surroundings. It was built offsite in 50-ton segments to minimize the environ-

---

Seashell hunting is best after a storm, when debris and shells wash onto the beach.

mental impact and make construction at the top of the mountain easier.

FLORA AND FAUNA BY THE SEASON

The parkway traverses a rural setting that takes visitors back to a time before the congestion and noise of the 21st century (except during autumn, when the arrival of tourists known as "leaf peepers" flock to the parkway and slow traffic down to a crawl). The big attractions are the deciduous varieties of 100 or so species of trees, including black gum, birch, oak, hickory, and maple.

Visitors in April and May come to see the wildflowers (more species of wildflowers than can be found throughout the entire continent of Europe!) and the blooming trees and shrubs: tulip and dogwood trees, flame azaleas, and Catawba rhododendrons.

At any time of year, visitors can catch sight of the 54 kinds of mammals that live along the parkway, including whitetail deer (an ever-expanding population, so be careful as you drive), black bears, squirrels, raccoons, possums, and skunks. Fifty kinds of salamanders and 40 kinds of reptiles live here, too. And more than 100 bird species make their home here for at least part of the year.

BILBO CATCHERS AND WHISKEY STILLS

The park service has also preserved some authentic pioneer cabins and imported others. A 19th-century working farm is the main attraction at the Mountain Farm Self-Guiding Trail at Humpback Rocks. Docents and rangers in period costumes give living-history demonstrations, making soup on a wood-burning oven or knitting with homespun yarn dyed with natural pigments like bark and berries. Kids can play with toys from the era—like the bilbo catcher, a wooden ball attached to a cup by a string, the object of which is to toss and catch the ball inside the cup.

At the Peaks of Otter stop, the park service maintains another working 19th-century farm that's more hands-on: visitors can pull weeds in the garden or harvest green beans in season. Less industrious types can sit in the rocking chairs that line the back porch of the farmhouse. At the same stop, a visit to Polly Wood's Ordinary—an 1830s cabin that was the first lodging in the area for travelers—gives visitors a look into what it was like to be a tourist in the 19th century. (You'll find out, for example, that sheets were washed every few weeks rather than between guests.)

Indians carve sacred pipes from the stone at Pipestone National Monument (MN).

Farther south, the Mountain Industry Trail at Mabry Mill has a self-guided tour among original and restored farm buildings, a whiskey still, blacksmith shop, and a working grist mill on a scenic pond. Depending on the season, visitors can watch demonstrations of blacksmithing and leather tanning, help make a batch of apple butter, or learn to make their own soap.

The Blue Ridge Parkway
Asheville, NC 28803

Founded: 1936
Length: 469 miles
Average annual visitors: 20,000,000

www.nps.gov/blri

* * *

MAKING BEAUTIFUL MUSIC

In 1986, San Francisco artists Peter Richards and George Gonzales completed work on the Wave Organ, a sculpture that makes music when it's hit by ocean waves. Richards got the idea while visiting Sydney, Australia. The sounds that came up through a vent pipe attached to a floating concrete dock led him to wonder if he could create an "acoustic sculpture" that would include several pipes to catch and transmit the sounds of the lapping waves. Over the next six years, Richards and Gonzales (a master stone mason and sculptor) made a prototype of the Wave Organ and then the organ itself.

Today, the Wave Organ stands on a jetty at the eastern edge of San Francisco's Golden Gate National Recreation Area. Visitors can find it by going past the Golden Gate Yacht Club and the Exploratorium science museum to the very end of Yacht Road. The stone sculpture is made of carved marble and granite. Many of the stones are headstones from an old cemetery that was demolished to make way for new housing. There are also 25 pipes installed at various heights to catch the rising and falling tides. According to Richards, the best time to visit the organ is at high tide, and be sure to listen carefully. The sounds the organ makes are subtle and quiet.

Only hand tools are used in the physically challenging task of quarrying the stone.

WAX AND WANE AT GLENN SPRINGS

Building ruins, a long-abandoned cemetery, and a spring are all that remain of the south Texas settlement of Glenn Springs, located in what became Big Bend National Park.

DESERT OASIS

The springs in south Texas were the focus of activity long before the first settlers arrived. In the arid desert, where these springs were few and far between, water was a much-sought commodity and came to be known as "liquid gold." The Comanches regularly stopped in the area during trading missions to and from Mexico. But the first recorded white person to come upon Glenn Springs was Edward L. Hartz, a lieutenant with the U.S. Army, who found the springs in 1859 as he explored the Comanche Trail.

Over the next 22 years, the land was bought and sold several times, but the area finally got a name in 1881 when rancher W. J. Glenn surveyed the area and settled there. Over the next few decades, the area around Glenn Springs slowly grew into a desert village.

THE WHOLE BALL OF WAX

The springs would sustain the community, but what would make life in the Texas desert worth the hardship of living there? The answer was the candelilla plant, which grew in abundance in the stark countryside and could be turned into another "liquid gold" . . . wax.

In 1914, businessmen C. D. Wood and W. K. Ellis built a factory and started manufacturing candelilla wax, which was a major component of soaps, candles, and varnish and was also used to waterproof army tents. Wood and Ellis hired a Texan named C. G. Compton to manage the factory and its workers. The factory employed about 60 Mexican wax makers, known as *candelilleros*, who cut stacks of the plant by hand and then boiled it to extract the wax. In the evenings, those men retired to their side of Glenn Springs, which had become a segregated village.

Some of the scenes in *Easy Rider* were filmed at Arizona's Wupatki National Monument.

NOT SO FRIENDLY FIRE

The segregation was just one example of the deep hostilities that existed in the town. As early as 1911, U.S. troops had started protecting the area. Raiders often stormed into town, and the Mexican Revolution—which lasted from 1910 to 1920—triggered violence on both sides of the border.

But the U.S. soldiers weren't enough. On May 5, 1916, as the villagers slept, Mexican bandits raided Glenn Springs. Accounts vary, but estimates put the number of outlaws at 60 to several hundred. The posse, led by a Pancho Villa loyalist named Rodriguez Ramirez, rode into Glenn Springs armed with pistols and bravado, shouting "Viva Villa" and "Viva Carranza," to show their support for two leaders of the Mexican Revolution.

Nine U.S. soldiers from the 7th Cavalry were stationed in Glenn Springs at the time and were sleeping in their tents when the marauders arrived. They managed to find shelter in a nearby adobe building and traded fire with the bandits for three hours. But they couldn't save the town. The bandits set fire to the building and raised general mayhem. Three soldiers were killed, and five others were critically burned or wounded. Many residents—both Mexican and Anglo—were also wounded. The general store was looted, two other buildings were burned, and the much of the wax factory was destroyed.

STARTING OVER AIN'T EASY

The raiders left, but there was always the threat that others could return. So when news of the Glenn Springs raid hit Eastern newspapers, President Woodrow Wilson mobilized the Texas National Guard to join federal forces along the border. Another military camp was established at Glenn Springs in 1916 and remained until 1920, when the Mexican Revolution ended and the border violence quelled.

For its part, the town rebuilt and tried to persevere, but finding skilled workers who were willing to toil 12 hours a day in the fiery summer heat —for just $1 a day—was hard. Then, after World War I, the price of wax plummeted because the U.S. government (the industry's biggest customer) no longer needed it for the war effort. Finally, the wax factory's owners sold the property to a local rancher, most of the remaining villagers moved away, and Glenn Springs lay deserted. The property changed hands for several years

---

You can see a 100-room pueblo, ball court, amphitheater, and pottery at Wupatki.

until 1943, when the State of Texas bought it and the surrounding land (a total of 801,163 acres). The state handed over the deed to the federal government, and President Franklin D. Roosevelt dedicated Big Bend National Park the next year.

NO LONGER ALL DRIED UP

The spring that was the lifeline of the village temporarily dried up during a drought in the early 1950s, but it has revived and remains active today. Ruins of the rifle pits, adobe buildings, a small cemetery, and the boiler and water tanks of the factory are all that remain of Glenn Springs village. Eleven known burial sites are marked with a single headstone.

Most of the people who come to Glenn Springs today are tourists at Big Bend. Adventurers can access the site via the Glenn Spring Loop, a series of dirt and gravel roads that are passable only by four-wheel-drive vehicles, motorcycles, or mountain bikes. The site can also be reached by hiking 11 miles from the Basin ranger station between October and April (it is too hot the rest of the year).

TEXAS

Big Bend National Park
Big Bend National Park, TX 79834

Founded: 1944
Area: 801,163 acres
Average annual visitors: 400,947

www.nps.gov/bibe

* * *

IN THE NEIGHBORHOOD

Thomas Jefferson's father, Peter, was among the original group who surveyed the land surrounding the Blue Ridge Parkway in 1749. Jefferson's beloved family home, Monticello, is in Charlottesville, Virginia, only about 30 miles from the northern entry to the parkway.

Ohio's Hopewell Culture National Historic Park includes several earthen mounds.

TRAILS LESS TRAVELED

On page 272, we told you about the little-known drives park rangers recommend. Here we share their favorite hikes.

BIG BEND NATIONAL PARK (TEXAS)
Trail: Hot Springs Trail

Where to start: Pick up the trailhead at the end of the road leading to the Rio Grande campsite.

Description: 3 miles round-trip; some steep ups and downs.

What you'll see: This cactus- and mesquite-studded trail climbs a steep mountain and then follows a plateau, affording great vistas to the canyons and deserts beyond. At the end of the trail, you'll run into a hot spring, the waters of which are still collected in the remains of an old bathhouse pool adjacent to the Rio Grande. Water temperature in the hot springs is a comfortable 105 degrees, and guests are free to take a soak. If you want a real wildlife treat, keep your eyes out for javelina, small wild boars that forage in the area and pose little threat to people. According to Big Bend's Steve McAllister, "They look like prehistoric hairy little pigs."

GLACIER NATIONAL PARK (MONTANA)
Trail: Bowman Lake

Where to start: Catch the trail at the end of Bowman Lake Road, near the lakeshore.

Description: 14 miles round-trip; gentle ups and downs.

What you'll see: This trail follows the northwestern shore of the narrow Bowman Lake. Although it's a heavily wooded trail, ranger Kyle Johnson says that hikers can peek through the trees and underbrush and "get little snapshots across the lake" to glacier-sculpted Square Peak, Rainbow Peak, and Mt. Carter. The area along the trail is also a bald eagle habitat, which makes this one of the best places in the park to spot the birds. You're also likely see loons, osprey, and sandpipers.

Hovenweep, as in Hovenweep National Monument, means "deserted valley."

LASSEN VOLCANIC NATIONAL PARK (CALFORNIA)
Trail: Brokeoff Mountain

Where to start: Catch the trail near the southwest entrance to the park, at the Brokeoff Mountain parking lot.

Description: 7 miles round-trip; 2,600-foot elevation gain.

What you'll see: This strenuous trail heads straight up the mountain through forests and open meadows until it passes the tree line. At the summit, you'll get fantastic views that include Mt. Shasta and the dormant Brokeoff Mountain volcano caldera. Because of the high elevation (more than 9,000 feet at the end of the trail), there's often no one on the pathways even into mid-August. And if you like a remote hike, this one is for you. Ranger Russell Virgilio says that's because Lassen gets "less visitors in a year than Yosemite gets in a busy month."

REDWOODS NATIONAL PARK (CALIFORNIA)
Trail: Damnation Creek

Where to start: The trailhead is just north of False Klamath Cove on Highway 101.

Description: 4.5 miles round-trip; strenuous terrain descends 1,000 feet.

What you'll see: Some of the tallest trees in the world make up the old-growth forest of redwoods that surrounds this rugged trail, which was used centuries ago by the Tolowa tribe as a route to gather food. The steep pathway descends all the way to the ocean. Look for a stone arch on the beach, which was carved by years of waves and wind.

YELLOWSTONE NATIONAL PARK (WYOMING, WEST THUMB AREA)
Trail: Riddle Lake

Where to begin: The trail marker is just south of the Continental Divide, about 3 miles south of Grant Village Junction.

Description: 5 miles round-trip; mostly flat.

What you'll see: The trail meanders through a dense pine forest

Four hurricanes and a tropical storm hit Gulf Islands National Seashore in 2004–2005.

and briefly breaks into open marshy meadows. After 2.5 miles, you'll see the lake, a pristine watering hole where you aren't likely to find many other folks, but according to ranger Ivan Kowski, "you might see the occasional moose." You're even more likely to see bears, though, because this trail cuts through a grizzly management area, which means humans aren't allowed until after July 15 (and then only until the first autumn snows fall). So if you hike Riddle Lake, be sure to make noise to avoid surprising the animals.

ZION NATIONAL PARK (UTAH)
Trail: Middle Fork of Taylor Creek

Where to begin: 2 miles east of the Kolob Canyon visitor's center.

Description: 5.4 miles round-trip; 400-foot elevation gain.

What you'll see: The trail follows a small drainage creek into a box canyon and is surrounded on two sides by sheer 1,500-foot cliffs. Hikers will cross the creek several times (although the pass is narrow enough that you may not even get your feet wet) and will pass two historic pioneer homes—the Old Fife Cabin and the Larson Cabin. The hike ends at the Double Arch Alcove, a colorful grotto carved in the cliffs that includes a large blind arch (an arch without an opening) above it.

* * *

LEAVE THE LOGS ALONE!
In California's Redwoods National Park, thieves regularly make off with one of the area's richest natural resources: the redwood logs themselves. Downed redwoods have long been easy pickings for poachers, but taking the trees harms the forest's already delicate ecosystem. It can take up to 500 years for a downed redwood to decompose, and during this time, the logs provide homes for animals and invertebrates and fertilizer for the new redwoods that take root nearby.

Taking the downed trees has always been a crime, but recently, California state officials have become more strict with enforcement. In 2006, five people were convicted of poaching the trees—logs that were more than 750 years old—from Redwoods National Park. And the government shows no sign of letting up anytime soon.

Most areas have reopened now as a result of recovery efforts in Florida and Mississippi.

THOSE CRAZY MIXED-UP PARKS!

Here's an easy way to visit four U.S. national parks—just find 'em in this puzzle. Unscramble the anagrams, and you'll have them right away. Or solve all the other clues and the parks will appear.

ACROSS

1 Rugged rock
5 Fixes copy
10 Trace of smoke
14 Therapist's 55 minutes
15 ___ the Hedgehog
16 "... baked in ___"
17 Boy or girl preceder
18 CAREER TALK in a scrambled Oregon park?
20 Girl in a Beach Boys song
22 New Rochelle, NY, college
23 Bottom line
24 Grief
26 Shut in
28 Milan opera house

Did you know that the White House is part of the National Park System?

31 The Thin Man dog
32 Seltzer starter
33 Dumb ___ (stupid heads)
35 Owner of Harpo, Inc.
39 Quick drive
40 What this puzzle has four of
42 "___ Rock" (Simon & Garfunkel song)
43 Some TVs
45 Fossil fuel
46 End-of-week cry
47 Other, in 25-Down
49 Good-for-nothin'
51 Hebrew title of reverence for God
54 Romance novelist Danielle
55 TV Chihuahua
56 Terminate with extreme prejudice
58 À la King?
62 ICY ALGEBRA in a scrambled Alaskan park?
65 Slaughter of baseball
66 Southwestern stewpot
67 Labor leader's cry
68 Fashion Emergency host
69 Like Yao Ming
70 Did a gondolier's job
71 Apparently Fosdick had none

DOWN

1 Blacken
2 *Goodbye Columbus* novelist Philip
3 Mercury or Saturn
4 CANNY DRAGON in a scrambled Arizona park?
5 Bake in a sauce, often with crumbs on top
6 Palme ___ (Cannes award)
7 "... bombs bursting ___
8 Grammy winner Puente
9 Shots on lots
10 ___-Mart
11 Bucky Beaver's brand
12 Bill ___, one of Fagin's gang
13 Calvin of golf
19 Approached rapidly
21 1988 Dennis Quaid thriller
25 Mexican state, or its capital
27 POLITE FARCE in a scrambled Utah park?
28 Maiden
29 Boxer's fare
30 Deer hide
31 One way to look (not a good one)
34 Ranch add-on
36 Big name in tomato sauce
37 "I ___ no mood for this!"
38 Sword handle
41 Like some sirens
44 East German secret police
48 Nettle
50 Epcot center?
51 Jargon
52 Street of mystery
53 ___ fours (crawling)
54 Actress Danning
57 *New Yorker* cartoonist Peter
59 "Didn't know I had it ___!"
60 ___ Prieta (1989 earthquake site)
61 River through Belgium
63 Shortstop Ripken
64 Had a little lamb

For answers, turn to page 393.

The White House's official park name is President's Park.

THE GRAND CANYON MULES

Mules have been hauling people and cargo up and down the Grand Canyon for more than a century. Here are some fun facts about those industrious pack animals.

- Mule trips into the Grand Canyon are so popular that reservations are taken as many as 23 months in advance—and trips always sell out.

- For day-trippers, it takes about 2-1/2 hours to get down the 10-mile Bright Angel Trail to Plateau Point, a good stopping point along the canyon route. But if you want to go all the way to the canyon floor, it will take a full day.

- President Teddy Roosevelt took a mule ride down when he visited in 1903. He was one of the first public figures to do so.

- Mule rides aren't cheap. A one-day ride up and back is about $140—but it includes a boxed lunch!

- The first person to offer mule rides was Captain John Hance, the first white settler in the Grand Canyon. He began his business in 1887. Today, private companies are licensed to offer the rides.

- The mules have a nearly perfect 100-year safety record—an impressive feat considering the steep switchbacks and crumbling shale on the trails.

- To ride to the bottom of the canyon on a mule, you must weigh less than 200 pounds, be taller than 4 feet 7 inches, not be pregnant, and speak English well enough to understand your wrangler's commands.

- Mules are not just for fun in the Grand Canyon. Five days a week, the U.S. Postal Service uses mule trains to deliver mail to Supai, Arizona, in the Havasupai Indian Reservation, located at the bottom of the canyon. Mules carry all forms of mail, including letters, food, and even mattresses. They haul an average of one ton of cargo down the canyon each day.

Menoceras, a pony-sized rhinoceros, once roamed in what is now Nebraska...

THE PILFERED PETRIFIED PARK

The National Park Service has closed 19 parks over the years, usually for routine administrative reasons. But there's one exception.

The world's greatest concentrations of fossilized cycads (pronounced *SIGH-kads*) were discovered in South Dakota's Black Hills in 1892. Ranging from the size of a fist to an oversized prize-winning pumpkin, the dinosaur-era plants resembled pineapples with palm fronds on the top. Soon after the cycads' discovery, Yale University researcher George Reber Wieland became so fascinated with them that he bought all the plants and the 320 acres they were on so that they "might not fall into unworthy hands." Two years later, he offered the land and cycads to the federal government. President Warren G. Harding signed a proclamation in October 1922 declaring the area a national monument.

WHO'S MINDING THE STORE?
Despite the cycads' protected status, there's no record of any federal employees guarding them. Local ranchers were entrusted with day-to-day surveillance of the site, and the superintendent of nearby Wind Cave National Park was asked to look in occasionally. No wonder, then, that when the National Park Service director wrote to Wind Cave in 1933 asking for a specimen to display at the Chicago World's Fair, there were none to be found. The cycad field had been looted.

BURIED TREASURES
In 1935, Wieland and a crew of 13 Civilian Conservation Corps workers started digging, and found many more cycads—together they weighed more than one ton. But the park service didn't see much sense in investing in the area or building a visitor center when the public couldn't actually see the cycads anymore because they'd either been looted or were underground. So Wieland collected the cycads and left. Although the site's scientific importance

---

...its fossil remains can be seen at Agate Fossil Beds National Monument.

was clear, one report declared, "The subject of fossil cycads does not have a broad appeal." So Congress abolished the monument in 1956.

Today, thanks to Wieland, Yale University has his collection of fossil cycads, the largest collection in the world. The National Park Service, on the other hand, has none.

* * *

HOW WELL DO YOU KNOW YOUR MOUNTAINS?

Match each mountain or mountain range to its appropriate type.

1. Mauna Loa (Hawaii)
2. Sierra Nevada (California)
3. Devils Tower (Wyoming)
4. Black Hills (South Dakota)
5. Appalachians (eastern United States)

A. Dome: Formed when flat-lying sedimentary rock is bowed up into dome shape.

B. Fault block: Possesses uplifted segments along a linear fracture zone and is characterized by high escarpments and tilted blocks (in the United States).

C. Fold: Occurs near basins of sedimentary rock layers and is formed by uplift and lateral compression.

D. Volcanic: Created by an active volcano and typically in fault zones and subduction zones.

E. Volcanic: Created by the residual products of a volcano.

Answers
1. D; 2. B; 3. E; 4. A; 5. C

Hampton National Historic Site in Maryland offers a look at a 19th-century slave estate.

SPLASHING AROUND

These four national parks are all wet.

CHANNEL ISLANDS NATIONAL PARK (CALIFORNIA)

Located just 90 miles north of Los Angeles, Channel Islands is one of the least-visited national parks in the United States. That's because it's accessible primarily by boat (one island does allow landings by small planes), so only about 30,000 people per year actually visit.

Channels Islands National Park was established in 1980 to protect five of eight islands off the coast of Ventura, California. The islands are so remote that they've evolved without much interference from humans. More than 195 species of plants and animals found nowhere else in the world live on the islands, which are also home to the largest breeding colony of seabirds in Southern California. Once-endangered brown pelicans roost on the islands' steep cliffs, and Channel Island foxes, the smallest foxes in North America (they're the size of housecats), roam the park.

Each of the islands boasts its own unique history and treasures for visitors:

- Anacapa Island offers a 1.5-mile trail through the island where hikers can see morning glories, bright yellow sunflower trees, and the largest breeding colony of endangered brown pelicans in the world. The island also has the Anacapa Lighthouse, constructed in 1932 and the last permanent lighthouse built on the West Coast.

- Santa Cruz is the park's largest island; it's three times the size of Manhattan. It's also home to the first bald eagle chicks to hatch on the islands in more than 50 years. In July 2006, those chicks took to the air for the first time.

- Santa Barbara is the smallest island; it's only one square mile. It's also home to the island night lizard, a threatened species that lives only on Santa Barbara and two other islands off the California coast (San Clemente and San Nicholas).

- San Miguel was used as a bombing range after World War II. Rangers advise visitors not to stray off the trails because live

---

In 1790, the Hampton mansion was the largest house in the United States.

ammunition still litters the island and is occasionally uncovered by shifting sands. Also, the island's Point Bennett is home to one of the largest concentrations of wildlife in the world.

- Santa Rosa boasts 500 different plant species, including a subspecies of the Torrey pine, one of the rarest pine trees in the world. Archaeologists on Santa Rosa have also found remains from Chumash Indians, a tribe that lived on the island until 1820, and their ancestors. The artifacts uncovered show that humans lived on Santa Rosa thousands of years ago. In fact, the oldest human remains in North America (dating from 13,000 B.C.) were found there.

Channel Islands National Park also protects one nautical mile of ocean habitat surrounding the islands. Living in those waters is a variety of marine life—dolphins, seals, sea lions, whales, and sharks are common sights. The waters off the Channel Islands are also home to the largest aggregation of blue whales in the world.

BISCAYNE NATIONAL PARK (FLORIDA)

Just south of Miami, within sight of the skyscrapers, is Biscayne National Park, the largest marine park in the National Park System. Ninety-five percent of the park is covered by water, and it was created in 1968 to protect 50 undeveloped coral keys and the surrounding coral reefs. The park also contains part of the third largest coral reef in the world, mangrove shorelines, and an abundance of marine life that includes endangered manatees, the American crocodile, and many varieties of sea turtles.

The area was made famous by pirates who roamed the Caribbean during the 18th and 19th centuries. The most famous (or notorious) was Black Caesar, who often pretended to be adrift in an open boat near the islands. When passing ships anchored to help him, Caesar's band of cutthroats would attack. Caesar and other pirates also hide their treasure in Biscayne Bay. Pirate booty was found on Elliot Key as recently as 1965; a storm uprooted a tree and a chest containing Spanish money was found beneath it. Biscayne's subversive history continued into the 1930s, when the area became a haven for gamblers and rum bootleggers.

Visitors who want to travel to Biscayne's outer keys should be prepared for a long journey. The keys are ten miles offshore and there is no bridge or ferry service. You'll need a personal boat—motor or sail—to get there. Visitors who don't have their own

Longfellow National Historic Site (including his house) is located in Massachusetts...

boats can rent canoes or kayaks to explore the mainland shore or take snorkeling or glass-bottom boat trips to the offshore coral reefs.

APOSTLE ISLANDS NATIONAL LAKESHORE (WISCONSIN)

The Apostle Islands lie in the cold waters of Lake Superior off the far northwestern tip of Wisconsin. Named for the 12 apostles by 17th-century Jesuit missionaries, there are actually 21 islands in Apostle Islands National Lakeshore. They range in size from three to 14,000 acres, and 12 miles of mainland are also included in the park. Established in 1970, the park is known for its sandstone cliffs and wild, undeveloped islands. The islands are accessible only by motorboats or kayaks. Visitors can hike, camp, and fish in the park. Blueberry picking is popular in July and August, and a local business offers cruises around the islands. The Apostle Islands also boast six lighthouses, the largest collection of lighthouses of any national park and some of the nation's finest. And Stockton Island, located in Lake Superior northeast of the park's visitor center, has one of the greatest concentrations of black bears in North America; approximately 35 bears live on only 10,054 acres.

DRY TORTUGAS NATIONAL PARK (FLORIDA)

In 1513, explorer Ponce de Leon was the first European to uncover this cluster of islands located 70 miles west of Key West. He also gave the islands their name. Leon and his men noted the large populations of sea turtles in the area and called the islands *las Tortugas*, Spanish for "the turtles." In later years, explorers added "Dry" to the name, noting that there wasn't any freshwater on the islands.

In 1846, the U.S. military began building a massive fortress in the Tortugas. Construction continued for 30 years, ebbing and flowing as funding came and went, but it was never completed, thanks to the invention of the rifled cannon, which made it easier to attack ships at sea and made such a fortress unnecessary. Then, during the Civil War, the completed portion of the fortress served as a Union military prison for captured deserters. (The fort remained in Union hands throughout the war.) It also held four of the men convicted of participating in President Abraham Lincoln's assassination, including Dr. Samuel Mudd, who treated John Wilkes Booth for a leg injury sustained during the escape.

...the house served as George Washington's headquarters during the Siege of Boston.

Through the end of the 19th century, Dry Tortugas was used as a quarantine station and as a naval installation during the Spanish-American War. Eventually, the military abandoned the site. President Franklin D. Roosevelt visited in 1935 and decided to turn it into a national monument. (Dry Tortugas became a national park in 1970.)

Today it's home to an abundance of wildlife—most notably wild birds and several types of turtles, including the endangered green sea turtle, the threatened loggerhead turtle, and the world's largest turtle (the leatherback) which can grow to be 7 feet long. Dry Tortugas is also one of the National Park System's smallest, most remote, and least-visited sites. Visitors arrive by boat or seaplane from Key West and can tour the fort and old prisons. Other activities in the park include swimming, camping, sport fishing, and scuba diving.

* * *

SAY WHAT?

Bison, bears, alligators . . . these animals are common in America's national parks. But here are three creatures you might have to see to believe:

Eyeless fish: Mammoth Cave National Park
It's dark inside Mammoth Cave, so several species of animals have adapted to life underground. In particular, the cave's eyeless fish are white and . . . well . . . eyeless, since they have no need for sight or camouflage in the cave's dark waterways.

Water ouzel: Yosemite National Park
John Muir described the water ouzel as a "joyous and lovable little fellow"; perhaps the description came from the birds' ability to skim over streams, lakes, even waterfalls as though they can walk on the liquid surface. Water ouzels can also stay underwater for up to 10 seconds and sometimes walk along the lake or river bottom to feed.

Pupfish: Death Valley National Park
This prehistoric fish species is a remnant of the last ice age, when Death Valley was underwater. Pupfish are small and have adapted to life in the park's shallow, hot Salt Creek.

First monument authorized by the federal government: Yorktown Monument (VA).

THE WILD LIFE OF GREY OWL

For more than 70 years, visitors to Manitoba's Riding Mountain National Park have stopped by a little log cabin along the shore of Beaver Lodge Lake. Although modest in scope, the cabin was once home to a formidable figure named Grey Owl, Canada's greatest— and some say, most infamous—conservationist.

HIS LEGACY TAKES FLIGHT

A trapper by trade, Grey Owl's life changed in 1925 when he discovered a pair of beaver kittens whose mother had died in his traps. Touched by the animals' plight, Grey Owl raised them for a year and a half before he released them back into the wilds of northern Quebec. The experience made Grey Owl rethink his profession, and by 1929, he and his wife, a Mohawk woman named Anahareo (a writer who also went by the name Gertrude Bernard), moved to Cabano, Quebec, to establish a protected beaver colony.

The colony was a good start, but Grey Owl recognized that Canada's dwindling beaver population needed more of his help. So he wrote an article about the issue for a British magazine called *Country Life*. The piece proved immensely popular in Canada and abroad, and Grey Owl was soon flooded with requests to write more articles and to lecture on the topic. He complied and within two years had earned the nickname "Beaver Man." It was a title he relished, and he even played up the persona by adopting another beaver, which he tamed and named Jelly Roll.

MOVING INTO THE PARKS

The Canadian government also took notice of Grey Owl's reputation and, in February 1931, offered him a position at Riding Mountain National Park. He was a media draw, and officials hoped his stories and colorful personality would attract more visitors to the park. He was also charged with the task of revitalizing Riding Mountain's ailing beaver population. Eight months later, though, frustrated by a drought that made it difficult for him to do much

---

Washington's Yorktown victory marked the end of the American Revolutionary War.

for the parks' beavers, Grey Owl requested a transfer. On October 26, 1931, he, his wife, and their ever-growing family of beaver kittens relocated to Ajawaan Lake in central Saskatchewan's Prince Albert National Park.

The new park was a perfect fit, and Grey Owl continued his work on the part of Canada's beavers. Over the next five years, he wrote and published three best-selling books about frontier life: *Pilgrims of the Wild* (1935), *Sajo and her Beaver People* (1935), and *Tales of an Empty Cabin* (1936). The volumes were acclaimed by critics and environmentalists as being among the finest works on Canadian wilderness conservation. To promote the books, Grey Owl embarked on a two-year-long lecturing tour across North America and England, where he entertained commoners and royalty with tales about his exotic Ojibway heritage.

This hectic schedule took its toll, though, and Grey Owl died of pneumonia on April 13, 1938. He was buried in Prince Albert National Park on a hillside overlooking Ajawaan Lake. His story should have ended there.

THE TRUTH SURFACES
Soon after his death, a number of Canadian and international publications ran extensive exposés about his past. According to the *North Bay Nugget*, the *Times* in London, and other papers, Grey Owl wasn't an Indian at all. Rather, he was born Archibald Stansfield Belaney on September 18, 1888, in Hastings, England. The son of a farmer, young Archie grew up hoping to one day leave his European home to explore the wilds of North America.

He got the chance in 1906 when he immigrated to Canada to study agriculture. After a year in Toronto, he moved to Temiscaming, a small town in northern Ontario. It was there that he met a local trapper named Bill Guppy who took Belaney under his wing and taught him about the great outdoors.

THE MAKING OF AN INDIAN
Guppy shared his trapping and survival skills with Belaney and also introduced him to a number of Native Americans who lived on nearby Bear Island. From the start, Belaney admired the native lifestyle, and over time, he learned the local Ojibwa dialect and adopted many of their customs and beliefs. He also created a new history for himself, telling others that he had

grown up in the American Southwest, the son of a Scottish father and an Apache mother.

In 1910, he married a young Ojibwa woman named Angele Eguana. Her family embraced him, and it was Angele's uncle John Eguana who gave Belaney the inspiration for his new identity when he called him "the young owl who sits taking in everything."

WANDERLUST
Grey Owl's restless spirit eventually got the best of him, though, and he left his wife and newborn daughter one year later to work as a trapper, guide, and forest ranger in Biscocasing, a small community 100 miles west of Temagami.

Over the next few years, Grey Owl joined the Canadian army, fought in World War I, was injured, and then was sent home to recover. Through it all, his new identity was in full effect. Grey Owl was treated as a native by his fellow soldiers. He returned to Canada in September 1917 with an honorable discharge.

He went back to hunting and trapping in northern Ontario. He also occasionally returned to Temagami to visit the family he left behind. On one of those visits in 1925, he met and fell in love with Anahareo. It was during his early years with her that Grey Owl became interested in the plight of Canada's beavers, and it was she who convinced him to leave his life as a trapper behind and stand up for Canada's wildlife and Native American population.

HERO OR LIAR?
It has been more than 65 years since Grey Owl's true life story was exposed, yet people around the world still debate the merits of his contributions. For some, he was simply a liar who abandoned his family and lived under a false identity. But for others, he was a heroic conservationist who left a lasting impact on the environmental movement. His efforts helped save Canada's beavers from the brink of extinction, and the Ontario government honored him in 1959 with a commemorative plaque at Findlayson Provincial Park in Temagami. His story has also been told in books like *Devil in Deerskins: My Life with Grey Owl*, by his wife Anahareo, and films like 1999's *Grey Owl*, starring Pierce Brosnan.

And then there's his log cabin in Riding Mountain National Park. Grey Owl lived there during the eight months in 1931 that he spent working as a naturalist in the park. The cabin is located on Beaver Lodge Lake at the end of a marked trail that begins at Highway 19 (near the junction with Highway 10). It is a lengthy but pleasant 17-kilometer (11-mile) round-trip. Inside the cabin, visitors can see photos, letters, and correspondence from Grey Owl's brief stay in Riding Mountain National Park.

MANITOBA

Riding Mountain National Park
Wasagaming, MB R0J 2H0

Founded: 1933
Area: 735,879 acres (2978 sq km)
Average annual visitors: 400,000

www.pc.gc.ca/pn-np/mb/riding

* * *

A PATRIOTIC MINE

Underground at South Carolina's Ninety Six National Historic Site is the Kasciuszko Mine, a manmade passageway that was intended to be used as a means of attacking British troops during the American Revolution. Slaves and Patriot (pro-American) ditch diggers forged the mine; they used pick axes and shovels and worked by candlelight—visitors can still see the niches in the mine's walls where the Patriots set their candles. They were digging underneath the British position, and the goal was to fill the mine with explosives and attack the enemy troops. But the builders were caught before Patriot soldiers could execute the plan, and the nearby battle ended before the Americans could get back underground.

For almost 200 years, the mine was abandoned. Local kids even played inside it. Finally, in the 1970s, the National Park Service took over the site. Archaeologists found that most of the mine had been well preserved; only one section had collapsed.

As for the name, that comes from Colonel Thaddeus Kasciuszko, the Patriots' chief engineer.

The Missouri boyhood home of George Washington Carver is a national monument.

CAUTIONARY TALES

If you spend a lot of time in the backcountry, there are a few things you should know.

GONE IN A FLASH

Flash floods are the number-one weather-related killer in the United States, claiming about 200 lives every year. And during the monsoon months—July, August, and September—the Grand Canyon, like much of the desert in the American Southwest, is prone to them.

In August 1963, a short downpour dropped 1.5 inches of rain on the canyon rim. After sitting out the rain about halfway down the canyon, a man and his son resumed their trek on Bright Angel Trail. Suddenly a 10-foot wall of muddy water carrying rock, sand, gravel, and desert vegetation burst out of a side canyon onto the trail, washing the two away.

Since that tragedy, four other hikers have been killed by flash floods in the Grand Canyon, and many more in the various narrow slot canyons of northern Arizona. The gorges of Utah's Zion National Park have been the scene of flash flood tragedies, too.

Even under blue skies, hikers have been killed by flash floods generated by thunderstorms as far as 25 miles away. Because desert soil can't absorb large amounts of rainfall, the canyons of the deserts in the Southwest can funnel huge walls of water downhill in minutes. The only warning is a deep roaring sound that gives a hiker a few seconds to scramble to higher ground.

BOLTS OUT OF THE BLUE

On July 27, 1985, five hikers climbed the cables (which the park service puts up in the spring and takes down in October) up the sheer rock slope of Yosemite's Half Dome. In their excitement to get there, they ignored the thunderstorm brewing over the Sierra Nevada and a National Park Service warning sign at the base of Half Dome that read: "Danger: If a thunderstorm is anywhere on the horizon DO NOT PASS BEYOND THIS SIGN. Lightning has struck Half Dome during every month of the year."

Two blinding bolts of lightning struck the granite rock that day; two young men were killed, and three were injured—one of the worst accidents in Yosemite's history. Lightning also killed a hiker

50 miles to the south in Sequoia National Park.

Lightning is the number-two weather-related killer in the United States; an average of 67 people are killed and 300 injured every year. Outdoorsy types are at greatest risk, of course, especially along high mountain trails on exposed rocks in areas of frequent thunderstorms. (The safest place to be during a thunderstorm is in an enclosed building or in a hard-topped vehicle.)

Rocky Mountain National Park, with lots of trails higher than 10,000 feet above sea level, has been the scene of 10 lightning deaths. Two have occurred on Mt. Whitney, one on Moro Rock in Sequoia National Park, and five in Yellowstone. The good news is that 90 percent of people struck by lightning live to talk about it.

HOT STUFF

Lassen Volcanic National Park in northern California has a geothermal area of boiling mud pots, steam vents, and hot springs colorfully named Bumpass Hell. The story goes that Kendall Bumpass, a local cowboy, stepped through the thin crust surrounding one of the mud pots, badly scalding his leg. When he showed a newspaperman the site of the accident, he did it again, this time burning his leg so badly that it had to be amputated. So "Bumpass Hell" is an apt warning.

Yellowstone National Park has more geysers, hot pools, mud pots, and boiling springs than any other place on earth. Not surprising, then, that it's had more than 19 deaths and 100 burn injuries due to visitors stepping, falling, or diving into hot water. In fact, hot springs deaths in Yellowstone are more common than grizzly bear kills. One young man died when he dove into a hot pool to try and save a dog that had jumped in. Both man and dog died. Now pets are forbidden in the thermal areas.

Warning signs about the danger are abundant in Yellowstone and visitors are warned to stay on the boardwalks, to keep a close watch on children (who account for a high percentage of the injuries and deaths), and not to step on the thin crust around the thermal pools.

And in case you're wondering, at Yellowstone's altitude, water boils at 198°F; most springs are hotter than 150°F, and some get as hot as 205°F.

So be careful out there. Read the signs the park service has put up for you, watch the skies for storms, don't go where you're not supposed to, keep a close eye on the kids, and don't say we didn't warn you.

GIMME A HAND

All of the people who traveled the Mormon Pioneer Trail to Utah were resilient, but one group was particularly hardy: the men and women who made the journey with handcarts.

The handcart movement lasted from 1856 to 1860 and was a way for pioneers to immigrate to Utah even if they didn't have the money or livestock to travel in a wagon train. Most of the handcart immigrants were poor people from Europe, especially Scandinavia and Great Britain. They took ships to East Coast ports, trains to Iowa City, and, from there, traveled the Mormon Pioneer Trail on foot, lugging the large, two-wheeled handcarts behind them. Brigham Young himself designed the carts: they were 4-1/2 feet wide and weighed 60 pounds. The immigrants added about 250 more pounds of weight—this included bedding, supplies, even young children. (Several wagons pulled by oxen usually followed the group, carrying additional supplies.) The journey was long, the handcarts were heavy, the weather was usually bad, and settlers often heckled the pioneers as they walked. But surprisingly, most of the handcart travelers (some 3,000 people) made it to Utah without incident.

MARTIN AND WILLIE

Two groups, though, had a difficult time. In the summer of 1856, two handcart companies—the Martin and Willie companies—set off for Utah. The groups were comprised of about 930 people from Britain who had arrived in Iowa City a few weeks before. Local church groups were unprepared for the immigrants' arrival and quickly threw together enough handcarts for them to take on their journey. The Martin and Willie companies were scheduled to leave for Utah at the end of August, and though many people debated leaving so close to the start of winter, the companies set out anyway.

The first major setback came in September, when a wild bison herd in Nebraska frightened the travelers' cattle and caused a stampede. Without the animals, the pioneers had to abandon their wagons and load additional supplies onto their handcarts. This made the carts harder to pull and the journey more tedious. In October, they arrived in Wyoming and discovered that they

---

...at more than 1,100 square miles, it's about the size of Rhode Island.

couldn't restock their supplies; no one was expecting them, so there were no supplies available. Still, they pressed on, rationing food and abandoning excess baggage (including wool blankets that they'd need later on).

Then the blizzard started. As the pioneers lugged their handcarts along the trail, snow swirled around them; bitter winds bit at their exposed skin. Many got frostbite. Most were starving. All they could do was hope for rescue.

BRING THEM IN!
Fortunately, word of their plight had reached Mormon president Brigham Young. An Englishman named Franklin D. Richards and his group of missionaries had also been traveling the Mormon Pioneer Trail and passed the Martin and Willie companies on the way to Salt Lake. After assessing the group's situation, Richards and his company rode hard for Utah and reported that the two handcart companies were stranded in Wyoming and desperately needed help. Young immediately mobilized his congregation for a rescue. He said, "Many of our brethren and sisters are on the plains with handcarts, and probably many are 700 miles from this place, and they must be brought here. We must send assistance to them . . . the subject matter for this community is to send for them and bring them in before the winter sets in."

Three days later, 27 men and 16 wagons carrying food, blankets, and other supplies set off in search of the beleaguered Martin and Willie companies. Ultimately, more than 200 wagons and teams joined the effort. It took about two weeks to find the travelers; winter storms made the rescuers' trip difficult as well. When the wagon teams finally arrived, they discovered that more than two weeks of cold and hunger had taken a toll on the companies. About 100 people had died, and most of the survivors were suffering from frostbite and were near starvation.

HOME FREE . . . ALMOST
The rescuers had food, warm clothes, and blankets for the weary travelers, but they still had to get back to Utah. The weather wasn't getting any better, and crossing the plains and the Rocky Mountains wasn't easy. Still, they followed the Mormon Pioneer Trail, heading for Salt Lake. They traveled in waves—the strongest went first, the weakest followed behind.

Where'd those oranges come from?

On November 4, the first groups arrived at the Sweetwater River in central Wyoming. Typically, arriving at the Sweetwater was a joyous occasion for pioneers. The thousands of people who traveled the Oregon and Mormon trails welcomed the river's clear water after spending weeks on the dusty plains. For the Martin and Willie companies, though, the Sweetwater was just another obstacle. It was only two feet deep and 90 to 120 feet wide, but it was clogged with broken ice. Many travelers just didn't have the energy to slog through the freezing water. Fortunately, rescuers were there to help.

C. Allen Huntington, Stephen Taylor, David Kimball, and George Grant took on the task of ferrying the travelers across the river. The men were all from Salt Lake and had answered Brigham Young's call for rescue volunteers. Kimball and Grant were just teenagers; the other two were adults. They spent the entire day pulling handcarts and carrying men, women, and children to safety on the south side of the Sweetwater. About crossing the river, a woman said that one of the men "stayed so long in the water that he had to be taken out and packed to camp, and he was a long time before he recovered, as he was chilled through."

DIVINITY ON THE TRAIL

By November 30, the rescue teams and all of the surviving members of the handcart companies had arrived in Salt Lake. They were greeted with an overwhelming welcome from the people living there. Residents offered their homes, clothes, food, and any assistance they could to the travelers.

The expedition came under harsh criticism from many sides, including Brigham Young himself, who chastised the handcart company organizers for allowing the groups to leave so late in the season. But most of the travelers viewed the experience as divine. One man said, "I was in that company and my wife was in it. We suffered beyond anything you can imagine and many died of exposure and starvation. But we became acquainted with God in our extremities." Another told of identifying a spot on the trail beyond which he couldn't pull his cart. When he reached that spot, he said his cart began to push him. He concluded that "the price we paid to become acquainted with God was a privilege to pay, and I am thankful that I was privileged to come in the Martin handcart company."

The Spanish introduced the citrus fruit to the Americas in 1513.

AFTERMATH

In the end, almost 200 people died during the Martin and Willie companies' exodus to Utah. But the events of the winter of 1856—and the stories of the pioneers who survived it—were inspirational to the Mormon people.

In 2006, the Mormon Church honored the 150-year anniversary of the Martin and Willie tragedy and rescue. They also continue to recognize the perseverance of the entire group of handcart pioneers. Many Mormon youth groups reenact the handcart treks every year over a two- or three-day period. The participants wear traditional 19th-century clothing, pull handcarts similar to the ones their ancestors would have used, and travel rough trails all over the western United States.

To read more about the Mormon Pioneer National Historic Trail, turn to page 261.

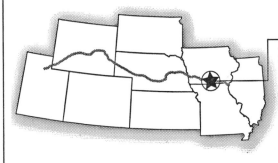

Mormon Pioneer National Historic Trail
Salt Lake City, UT 84111

Founded: 1978
Length: 1,300 miles

www.nps.gov/mopi

* * *

WE GOT OUR OWN WINSOR CASTLE

Note the spelling: Winsor, not Windsor. Winsor Castle is a fortified ranch house at Pipe Spring National Monument in Arizona. It was built by the Mormon Church and named after Ansor P. Winsor, the first superintendent of the large cattle ranch established at the site in 1870. Several stone buildings from that pioneer era remain, along with an orchard, garden, farm animals, ponds, and a Paiute Indian camp.

Northeastern Nevada's spectacular Lamoille Canyon is called the "Yosemite of Nevada."

FORTIFYING TALES

Here are sagas of war and peace as told at NPS sites across the country.

YE OLDEST FORT:
CASTILLO DE SAN MARCOS (FLORIDA)

Why it's important: The Castillo de San Marcos was built to protect Spanish settlements in the New World and Spanish ships sailing with gold, silver, gems, spices, and other treasures from South America to Spain. Its thick rock walls have stood above the harbor of St. Augustine, Florida, for more than three centuries—making it the oldest masonry fort in continental North America.

Still standing: Castillo San Marcos flew many different flags over the years: Spanish, British, Confederate, and Union. But the fort's stone walls still stand. In 1933, the fort became part of the National Park Service (it had been managed by the War Department until that time). Today, visitors can tour the ancient fort, stand in the watchtower where soldiers kept a lookout for pirates, and, on weekends, see and hear the firing of 18th-century bronze cannons that bear a Spanish coat of arms.

THE COLONIAL SUPERHIGHWAY:
FORT STANWIX (NEW YORK)

Why it's important: In 1756, colonists could travel from the Great Lakes to the Atlantic Ocean or from Canada to New York City by water—except for a few miles of land between the Mohawk River and Wood Creek near what is now Rome, New York. This overland hike, called the "Oneida Carrying Place" (after the Oneida Indians who'd pulled their canoes over it for thousands of years) was a highway for everyone who ventured there during colonial times: Native Americans, traders, and settlers. In 1756, the British, under General John Stanwix, built Fort Stanwix to protect the route. Over the next 20 years, the fort was neglected, abandoned, and then resurrected as a patriot stronghold during the Revolutionary War. In August 1777, British and American forces fought a fierce battle at Fort Stanwix; at first, it looked like the British would prove victorious, but in the end, a hardy and determined American force pushed the British out of the area and back into Canada.

Alaska-bound? The Charley Wild River offers whitewater thrills and exceptional clarity.

Still standing: Named a national monument in 1935, Fort Stanwix is the only colonial fort continuously occupied by patriot forces during the American Revolution. There are three trails that encircle the fort: one follows part of Oneida Carrying Place; the other two trails include historical markers and artifacts to teach visitors about the history of the siege of 1777. Ranger-led programs throughout the fort also illustrate 18th-century military life, showing visitors what the soldiers ate, what kinds of camps they lived in, and what kinds of weapons they used.

TAKING A BITE OUT OF CRIME: FORT SMITH (ARKANSAS)

Why it's important: Fort Smith was established on Christmas day in 1817, but its history was anything but merry. The fort was on the border of—and was the gateway to—Indian Territory (in what's now Oklahoma). The territory had been set aside for Native Americans forcibly removed from their homes, and the soldiers at Fort Smith were charged with the task of trying to keep peace between the different tribes who'd been forced to live there. Later, they also acted as a buffer between the western settlements and raids by Native American tribes.

Later, Fort Smith wore a variety of hats, including that of a commissary building that was a major supply center for explorers, gold seekers, and cavalry expeditions. And during the latter half of the 19th century, it was the seat of the U.S. Court for the Western District of Arkansas, a role that earned it the nickname "Court of the Damned." Outlaws ran wild in Arkansas and in Indian Territory until 1875, when President Grant appointed Isaac C. Parker to the Federal bench at Fort Smith. For the next 21 years, Judge Parker held court six days a week for up to ten hours a day in an effort to restore law and order to Indian Territory. During Parker's first summer on the bench, juries convicted 15 people of murder. All of the convicts received the death penalty, and the hanging of six convicted men that September made headlines and earned Parker the nickname the of "Hangin' Judge." In all, the U.S. government executed 86 men during the 23 years Fort Smith was a courthouse and jail.

The fort's dingy jail had a nickname, too—"Hell on the Border"—because the cells were dirty, hot, and very uncomfortable.

There are more than 250 species of North American crawfish; Louisiana's harvest...

Still standing: Fort Smith became a National Historical Site in 1961 and, in 2000, underwent a $7.5 million restoration to give visitors a better taste of what life (and justice) in Indian Territory during the 19th century was really like. Outside, trails lead to a reconstruction of Fort Smith's infamous gallows and a portion along the Arkansas River of the Trail of Tears—the route taken by the Cherokee during relocation in 1838. Inside the fort is the commissary, the courtroom of "Hangin' Judge" Isaac Parker, and those "Hell on the Border" jail cells. Talks by rangers tell of the history of the fort and give visitors a feel for life and justice in the Wild West.

* * *

MEET DR. MUDD

After shooting President Lincoln at Ford's Theatre on April 14, 1865, John Wilkes Booth jumped approximately 11 feet from the president's box to the stage below. He landed badly and snapped the fibula bone in his left leg above his ankle. Despite the injury, he managed to escape and make his way to the Maryland home of Dr. Samuel Mudd, who set the leg and even had a pair of crutches made for Booth to use on the run.

The assassin and his band of conspirators didn't get far, though. On April 26, they were captured and, soon after, put on trial. Mudd was accused, too, charged with aiding the conspiracy to kill the president. Although Mudd protested his innocence and claimed to have met Booth and his accomplices only that one time (despite evidence to the contrary), he was convicted and sentenced to life in prison. Soon, he found himself imprisoned at Fort Jefferson on the Dry Tortugas off the Florida Keys.

Mudd proved to be a model prisoner and even an asset. In 1867, an outbreak of yellow fever killed the prison's doctor and Mudd took over. He contracted the disease himself but recovered and spent the next two years doctoring sick inmates. In 1869, at the urging of soldiers at Fort Jefferson, President Andrew Johnson pardoned Mudd.

Today, many people think the expression "his name is mud" stems from the doctor's association with Lincoln's assassination. But the phrase was actually in use long before that event.

A REVOLUTIONARY RIVER

The John H. Chafee Blackstone River Valley National Heritage Corridor comprises 24 Massachusetts and Rhode Island towns that were the birthplace of one of the most explosive revolutions in U.S. history—the American industrial revolution.

T**HAT'S PROGRESS!**
Blackstone history starts with Samuel Slater, a one-time superintendent at an English textile mill who immigrated to America in 1789. In Pawtucket, Rhode Island, Slater built the first cotton-spinning factory in the United States. The mill was powered by the Blackstone River; rushing water—the result of a spectacular drop of 438 feet in just 46 miles—poured onto a waterwheel that ran the machinery at the Slater Mill. For the first time in American history, cotton thread could be produced by machine rather than by hand—and that changed everything. The once predominantly agricultural society became more urbanized.

In the late 1700s, the demand for cloth was high and so was Slater Mill's profit margin. Soon the banks of the Blackstone River—from Worcester, Massachusetts, to Pawtucket—were crowded with cotton, wool, and textile mills. The sound of the whirring shuttles and banging looms in the factories nearly drowned out the roar of the Blackstone—then known as the "hardest working river in America."

The people who worked long hours in the factories had to live somewhere, so mill towns sprung up in the river valley. Slatersville, the village built around Slater Mill, was the prototype for the other mill towns. It included a company store, housing for workers, churches, schools, libraries, and community halls.

The first mill towns were populated by former farm families from New England. But later, immigrants flooded into the valley from Canada, Ireland, Poland, Sweden, and Portugal, giving the Blackstone River Valley one of the most diverse ethnic populations in the country.

The Upper Delaware Scenic River area includes Pennsylvania's Zane Grey Museum.

A NEW KIND OF NATIONAL PARK

The factories of the Blackstone River Valley churned out products for more than 100 years—everything from monkey wrenches to space suits to Mr. Potato Head (which is still manufactured in Pawtucket). But by the 1970s, most of the valley's industry had moved away. Costs (both for wages and operations) were lower in other cities. And the "hardest working river" became "one of America's most polluted rivers," according to a 1971 *Audubon* magazine article. By the 1980s, it looked like most of the mills would be torn down.

In 1986, Congress decided to preserve the valley and its history. The 24 cities, towns, and villages along the river became the John H. Chafee Blackstone River Valley National Heritage Corridor (named after the late Rhode Island senator). The government doesn't own the land; instead, the National Park Service works in partnership with Rhode Island and Massachusetts businesses, schools, organizations, and private citizens to manage the preserve.

FROM PERSPIRATION TO RECREATION

Today, the Blackstone River Valley is humming with history. Visitors can tour museums, see restored mills, and hike along the Blackstone Canal towpath, where they'll see parts of the canal on which barges transported cloth from the mills to seaports. Diners are also a big draw in Worcester, Massachusetts—home of the Worcester Lunch Car Company, the first lunch wagon and diner manufacturing company. And the Blackstone River Coalition, a group dedicated to preserving the river and valley, is in the process of cleaning up the river and making it safe for swimming and fishing by 2015. Meanwhile, 10 passenger riverboats take visitors on sightseeing tours of the river's most scenic locations, including a 20-foot waterfall in the town of Valley Falls, spectacular fall foliage, marshes, and abundant wildlife populations.

MASSACHUSETTS

RI

John H. Chafee
Blackstone River Valley
National Heritage Corridor
Woonsocket, RI 02895

Founded: 1986
Area: 400,000 acres

www.nps.gov/blac

Vermont's Smugglers' Notch is a ski area now, but it was once a smuggling route.

UNCLE JOHN'S
TIME-TRAVEL GUIDE

*In science fiction, people use time machines to visit the past,
but in the national parks, all you need is a living-history program.
Here are some of our favorites.*

RELIVE THE REVOLUTIONARY WAR

During the summer, Saratoga National Historical Park in New York offers visitors a chance to experience a Revolutionary War camp, where the women make mouthwatering meals of pork roast (with apple pie for dessert) in pots heated by coals and soldiers demonstrate how muskets and cannons are fired.

Oneida guides (like the Native American allies who led early colonists on scouting missions) in traditional warrior dress take tourists on walking tours through the area's woods and tall grasses and demonstrate how their ancestors used guerrilla tactics (like making a stealth attack and then retreating) to fight the redcoat army.

EXPERIENCE A HOMESTEADER'S LIFE

At the Lincoln Boyhood National Memorial (open from April to October) in Spencer County, Indiana, visitors can see the homestead where President Abraham Lincoln lived from ages 7 to 21. Volunteers dressed in period clothing do all the chores that made up a 19th century homesteader's day: chopping firewood, cooking, cleaning, feeding farm animals, milking cows, spinning, sewing, quiltmaking, and plowing, planting, cultivating, and harvesting crops.

SHOP AT A FRONTIER MALL

Bent's Old Fort National Historic Site in the town of La Junta is the home of Colorado's first shopping mall, a reconstructed adobe fur-trading post on the Santa Fe Trail. The site's events are seasonal. At various times throughout the year, trappers haggle with Native Americans and pioneers over everything from guns and buffalo robes to medicines and soap. (Reproductions of some of

---

The Champlain Canal, designed and built from 1819–1825, was America's first canal.

these items are sold in the general store.) Visitors can also take a wagon ride or take a look at a herd of (now rare) Spanish Barb horses, the ancestors of the West's wild mustangs. In December, the fort is filled with volunteers in traditional outfits; they sing carols and share taffy and other Christmas treats that were popular in the 1800s. They also participate in traditional holiday activities, including a Yule log hunt and breaking a Mexican piñata. Everyone is invited!

HANG OUT WITH CIVIL WAR SOLDIERS

At Gettysburg National Military Park and in the nearby town of Gettysburg, Pennsylvania, thousands of living-history participants arrive every year in the spring and summer months to reenact the Civil War's bloodiest (51,000 casualties) and most important battle (the Union victory at Gettysburg foretold the Confederate defeat).

But living history at Gettysburg is more than just the battle. Visitors can watch reenactors participate in traditional drills like reveille and taps and see what life was like off the battlefield. Volunteers display the weapons the Civil War soldiers fired, the camps they slept in, and the foods they ate. They also participate in regimental bands and fife and drum corps and sing the songs soldiers wove about their families and homes. Sometimes, visitors can even meet the medical corps (the women who tended the wounded) and watch a (fake!) amputation as it would have been performed back then. Ouch.

RIDE A TRAIN PULLED BY A STEAM ENGINE

At Steamtown National Historic Site in Scranton, Pennsylvania, visitors can ride trains pulled by a steam locomotive built between 1917 and 1935 or a diesel electric locomotive built in the 1950s. The rides are either round-trips from the Steamtown station to Moscow or Tobyhanna, Pennsylvania, or short trips to the Scranton train yard. You can even buy a ticket that lets you ride in the cab with the crew . . . if you're willing to sign a release that absolves the U.S. government of liability for any personal injuries you may incur while rubbing elbows with the engineer and the fireman who shovels the coal. Watch out for cinders!

Steamtown's living-history program can be found at the station, too. Here, Depression-era hoboes take breaks from riding the rails, and yard workers stop to chat.

The 60-mile canal connects the south end of Lake Champlain to the Hudson River.

MAKE MOONSHINE
The Big South Fork National River and Recreation Area in Kentucky gives visitors a chance to meet up with a 1930s-era moonshine maker who will demonstrate the finer points of making whiskey out of corn. Travelers can see a whiskey still up close and learn the ingredients for the "mash" that ferments into moonshine: water, cornmeal, corn malt, and sugar. During Prohibition, a "good" moonshiner could produce an eight-gallon batch of whiskey in about six hours; lesser moonshiners often blew up their stills or poisoned themselves from drinking bad corn whiskey. So the NPS—and Uncle John (hic!)—say, "Don't try this at home!"

* * *

FUN FESTIVALS
If it's a festival you want, America's national parks are for you. Take a look at these wacky festivals found in parks around the country:

Railroaders Festival: Golden Spike National Historic Site
When: August
What: You can see a reenactment of the driving of the golden spike (which connected the transcontinental railroad in Utah in 1869), participate in handcart races and buffalo chip throwing, and listen to a concert of fiddle music.

Batfest: Carlsbad Caverns National Park
When: Summer
What: This New Mexico festival celebrates the hundreds of Mexican free-tailed bats that swarm out of Carlsbad Caverns every evening. The festival lasts from 9:30 p.m. to 5:30 a.m.; visitors can use telescopes to take in the night sky, listen to astronomy presentations, and then enjoy a breakfast the next morning.

Sand Sculpture Contest: Point Reyes National Seashore
When: September
What: It's California's premier sand castle–building contest. Both adults and kids can compete (in separate contests), and previous entries include a Mr. Potato Head, a giant Mickey Mouse, African animals at a watering hole, and of course . . . castles.

During the 1770s most people owned only one or two changes of clothing.

SUNKEN TREASURES

When you think "national park," you might think of grassy meadows or geysers or mountains, but there's plenty of park land that's underwater, and there's a crack team of divers who take care of it all.

The millions of underwater acres of national park land include everything from kelp forests in California's Channel Islands to pirate shipwrecks in the Dry Tortugas off the Florida Keys. The full-time team of five divers (four archaeologists and one photographer) who make up the Park Service's Submerged Resources Center (SRC) are in charge of exploring and documenting these underwater treasures. They conduct surveys, raise shipwrecks, and have even recovered long-ago drowning victims. Here are some of their more notable projects.

NEW YORK WELCOME WAGON

About 40 percent of Americans trace their lineage to ancestors who entered the United States through New York's Ellis Island. And many of those rode a steam ferry called *Ellis Island* that operated in New York Harbor from 1904 until the station closed in 1954. In its day, the ferry carried more than 120,000 immigrants from the island to their new home on the mainland.

After sitting idle and abandoned in the harbor for 14 years, the ferry sank at her slip in 1968. In 2002, as the National Park Service prepared a massive restoration project on Ellis Island, the SRC began an underwater archaeological assessment and documentation of the partially submerged ferry and the slip. (No word yet on their findings.)

AMERICAN ATLANTIS

Beneath the rambling 250 square miles of Lake Powell in the Glen Canyon National Recreation Area in Arizona and Utah, there are hundreds of submerged pictographs and prehistoric sites once occupied by the ancient cliff-dwelling Anasazi people. The SRC began several investigations of the sites between 1975 and 1980, taking an archaeological inventory and excavating and filming the sunken Pueblo ruins.

MYSTERY SOLVED

In 1929, locals Russell and Blanch Warren disappeared while driving on Washington's Olympic Peninsula. The authorities suspected that the couple had drowned in chilly Lake Crescent in what's now Olympic National Park, but it wasn't until 2002 that there was any evidence of this. That's when divers found the couple's 1927 Chevrolet 170 feet down and 66 feet from shore. The SRC investigated the site and recovered the remains of one body, which was believed to be that of Russell Warren.

ADVENTURES FOR YOU

Underwater park areas aren't just for the SRC, though. There are more than 60 sites that are open to the public.

The waters around Michigan's Isle Royale National Park are particularly interesting. This is the resting place of many ships sunk between about 1870 to the early 1900s, a busy time for shipping on Lake Superior. Experienced divers (who have a recommended minimum experience of 50 open-water dives) can explore the wrecks; swim through engine rooms, along companionways, and into staterooms; and see and photograph artifacts—anything from bottles to lanterns to shoes.

Less experienced divers and snorkelers can also take to national park waters. Florida's Biscayne National Park is the largest marine park in the system, with 95 percent of its 173,000 acres covered by water. And it's a boon for snorkelers. Dolphins, more than 512 species of fish, and a variety of ocean plants live in this underwater environment.

* * *

CRATER LAKE NATIONAL PARK

At 1,943 feet, Crater Lake in southern Oregon is the deepest lake in the United States, but it's not actually a meteor crater. It's the caldera of a long-dead volcano called Mt. Mazamathat, which erupted 7,700 years ago.

The lake and national park that contains it are also subject to some of the most extreme winter weather in the continental United States. On average, 533 inches of snow fall at Crater Lake every year, and snow often remains on the ground until June.

Who's buried at Grant's Tomb? Technically, no one is buried there.

OUTCAST ISLAND

Visitors say it's like visiting the Hawaii of 50 years ago. But 50 years ago, Kalaupapa was still officially a place of exile for people suffering from leprosy, or Hansen's disease.

The Kalaupapa Peninsula on the Hawaiian island of Molokai juts into the ocean like a fat finger pointing north. Its boundaries are the Pacific Ocean on three sides and an enormous mountain, the world's tallest sea cliff, on the fourth. In 1865, the Board of Health for the kingdom of Hawaii began sending lepers to the eastern side of Kalaupapa in an effort to isolate them from healthy populations on the other islands and hopefully curb the spread of the disease. But the peninsula was no place for convalescence. It has the coldest, wettest climate on the island; in the winter, the sun sets behind the 3,000-foot cliff by 3:00 p.m., ushering in a cold, damp evening. Even when researchers discovered that warm, sunny climates helped slow the progress of the disease, the Hawaiian monarchy (and later the United States) continued to use Kalaupapa as a dumping ground for its leprosy patients.

A SUSCEPTIBLE POPULATION

Isolated for most of their history, the Hawaiians had little resistance to foreign diseases. A population estimated at more than 250,000 when the first Europeans—led by the British Captain James Cook—arrived in 1778 sank to about 31,000 by 1896, decimated by a variety of diseases that included smallpox, cholera, influenza, and leprosy.

Officially called Hansen's disease after Gerhard Armauer Hansen, the Norwegian scientist who discovered the bacteria in 1873, leprosy attacks the body's peripheral nerves, affecting the skin, eyes, and other tissues. It can result in loss of muscle control and shrinking bones in the hands and feet. This damage to nerves, skin, and tissue leads to the disfigurement that marks leprosy patients.

No one knows for sure who brought leprosy to the islands. During the 19th and early 20th centuries, it was called *mai pake*, the "Chinese sickness," based on a general suspicion by Hawaiians of Chinese immigrants to the islands, and *mai alii*, the "chief's sickness," referring to the Hawaiian chiefs who traveled to other countries and may have brought it back. Later, researchers discovered that Hawaiians had a particular susceptibility to the disease, as did people with French bloodlines. In fact, the leading leprosy hospital on the mainland—the Louisiana Leper Home in Carville—was in a state largely populated by people of French descent.

THE FIRST "SETTLERS"

Initially, Hawaii's leprosy victims weren't ostracized or quarantined, and there were no specific medical institutions to care for them. But as the disease spread during the 1850s and 1860s, Hawaiian health officials and King Kamehameha V established Kalihi Hospital in Honolulu, on the island of Oahu, to diagnose patients. The hospital was more of a way station, a place patients passed through before being exiled to Kalaupapa. Within weeks of Kalihi's opening in 1865, doctors at the hospital banished the first group to Molokai: nine men and three women, the sickest of the hospital's 43 leprosy patients (this group also included a young stowaway, the son of one of the patients).

The patients arrived on Molokai to find that they'd be living in an abandoned village with few amenities. The village consisted of a few cottages and thatched huts; each man had been given a shovel, an axe, and a wool blanket; and the women had been given only a blanket. Since they arrived on a January afternoon, the sun was already setting behind the cliff. The only things they had to eat were salted beef and bread. For the first years, the outcasts were mostly left to fend for themselves.

A HERO IN BELGIAN CLOTHING

Over the next 103 years, about 8,000 patients—mostly Hawaiians, but also Asians and caucasians—were sent to Molokai. During that time, the settlers formed a community. They built schools, churches, orphanages, and a hospital. And they made the best of their situation. Writers like Robert Louis Stevenson, Jack London, and Ernie Pyle visited the colony and described the peninsula as a surprisingly cheerful place where the residents entertained themselves with games, music, and parties.

The patients at Kalaupapa also had help from outsiders, mostly clergymen and nuns who came to assist the sick. The most famous of these was Father Joseph de Veuster of Belgium. Known as Father

Damien, the Catholic priest came to Kalaupapa in 1873, when he was 33. He was supposed to be one of four priests who worked in a three-month rotating system on Molokai, but two days after his arrival, Damien wrote to his superior: "I am willing to devote my life to the leprosy victims." So Damien stayed, and the rotating system was dropped.

Working 19 hours a day, Father Damien threw himself into the roles of priest, nurse, confidant, disciplinarian, judge, peacekeeper, and grave digger. By one account, Damien dug 1,300 graves. (This is probably not an exaggeration: the death rate at the time was one patient a day.) Eventually, though, Damien succumbed to leprosy himself. He was diagnosed in 1884 and died on April 15, 1889.

During Damien's time on Kalaupapa, the health board finally assigned a resident physician to the colony. And gradually, the patients and facilities moved to the west side of the peninsula, where the weather was warmer and drier.

THE CURE

In the early 1940s, researchers at the Louisiana Lepers Home in Carville found a cure for Hansen's disease: an antibacterial drug called sulfonamide. The treatment found its way to Kalaupapa in 1946. But even though their health improved and only 32 new patients were sent to Molokai between 1949 and 1969, the people living on Kalaupapa remained physically separated from the rest of the world. Their visitors had to stay behind fences, and their mail was fumigated well into the 1960s.

Finally, in 1969, Hawaii reversed its isolation laws, and the Kalaupapa residents were free to go wherever they wanted. But most were reluctant to begin a new life elsewhere. Some had been there from childhood and knew no other life; others were so disfigured that they didn't want to face the outside world.

THE NEXT STEP

In the early 1970s, a government report described the peninsula as having "potential for future recreational and resort use." This spurred the 100 or so people who still lived in Kalaupapa into action. To protect their colony, they started working with Representative Patsy Mink to have their town declared a National Historical Site. Then, in 1980, President Jimmy Carter signed a law that made Kalaupapa part of the National Parks system; it would preserve the settlement and allow for limited visitation by the public.

Today, Kalaupapa remains a residential colony. About 30 former patients live there, and as of the summer of 2006, their average age was 78; the youngest resident was 65. Most residents spend their time like senior citizens anywhere: fishing, gardening, reading, and watching television. The most exciting day for them is "barge day"; once a year, usually in July when the ocean is at its most calm, a barge brings in oversized items they've ordered for themselves: television sets, furniture, refrigerators, cartons of canned goods, and cars.

THE PARK

Tourists who want to visit Kalaupapa can do so, but the ways in and out are limited. The only way to get to the park is by air or by hiking or riding mules down the steep, three-mile-long Kalaupapa Trail that links Molokai proper (called "topside" because it's on the top of the mountain) to the colony. At the bottom of the trail, visitors connect with Father Damien Tours, owned and operated by a Kalaupapa resident and the only tour company to the settlement. Tours operate Monday through Saturday, except Thanksgiving, Christmas, and New Year's. The park is never closed, and there's no entrance fee. All visitors have to receive a permit from the State Department of Health to enter Kalaupapa, and no children under the age of 16 are allowed.

There are no restaurants, no hotels, and no campgrounds in the park. The nearest campsites and hotels are on topside Molokai.

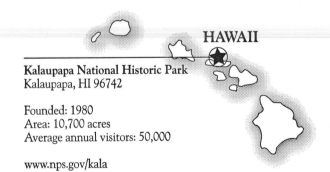

HAWAII

Kalaupapa National Historic Park
Kalaupapa, HI 96742

Founded: 1980
Area: 10,700 acres
Average annual visitors: 50,000

www.nps.gov/kala

GRAND DISASTER

In 1956, two planes crashed into the Grand Canyon. The tragedy spurred Congress to make some changes to the way air travel was monitored in the United States.

STORMY WEATHER AHEAD
On June 39, 1956, two planes took off from the Los Angeles airport only three minutes apart. One was a TWA flight headed for Chicago; the other was a United flight going to Kansas City. They were flying at different altitudes: United at 21,000 feet and TWA at 19,000 feet.

As the planes approached the Grand Canyon, the TWA pilot, Captain Jack Grady, asked if he could change altitude to 21,000 feet. The weather over Nevada and Arizona was choppy; thunderstorms were brewing. Grady wanted to give his passengers a smooth ride.

The air-traffic controller in Los Angeles denied Grady's request because he knew that the United flight was nearby and flying that altitude. In the 1950s, individual airlines kept in contact with their pilots only by radio. The airlines, in turn, kept in contact with air-traffic controllers who monitored air travel over major cities. Pilots flying over rural areas relied on scheduled flight plans and what they could see. Air-traffic controllers did, however, continue to assign altitude, and then the airlines relayed that information to pilots in the air.

Grady's next request was that he be allowed to fly 1,000 feet above the weather. This meant that he'd pull above the clouds and take a look around. It would be up to him to keep an eye out for other planes. That request was granted.

COLLISION
At about 10:30 a.m., the TWA plane ascended through the clouds. At the same moment, the United flight was passing just overhead. The clouds were thick, so it's likely that neither plane saw the other. The two collided when TWA's tail fin scraped into United's left wing; the contact pierced's TWA's fuselage and sent the plane spiraling to the ground. The TWA flight crashed into the Grand Canyon's Temple Butte.

No. Translations of the names of some of the 54 bridges along Maui's Hana Highway.

The United plane flew for a few more minutes and even managed to radio in a garbled distress call to an air-traffic controller in Salt Lake City. But pilot Robert Shirley couldn't keep his plane aloft, and the United flight crashed into the Grand Canyon's Chuar Butte about 1.2 miles away from where the TWA flight went down.

On impact, the TWA plane exploded into flames. Tourists at the Grand Canyon's South Rim, about 10 miles away, reported seeing smoke from the canyon. The United flight hit the ground so hard that it disintegrated. There were no survivors.

LOST AND FOUND

Without radar monitoring systems, air-traffic controllers had no way of knowing that the two planes had crashed. Both flights were scheduled to radio in their positions when they passed over Arizona's Painted Desert, just east of the Grand Canyon. When neither did, air-traffic controllers got nervous. When neither plane arrived at its destination, worry turned to panic.

While the airlines tried to locate their planes, a pair of tour pilots discovered the wreckage of the TWA flight. Palen and Henry Hudgin were brothers who ran Grand Canyon Airlines, a company that flew tourists over the canyon. Around dusk on June 30, they passed over Temple Butte and saw the tail section of the TWA plane. They also found the main crash site—about 500 feet away. The next day, they returned to the site and found the wreckage of the United flight.

The Hudgin brothers alerted authorities, and within two days, Army helicopters were surveying the site and looking for a way to remove bodies and debris. The cliffs where the planes had crashed were isolated and difficult to access. Helicopters, expert climbers, and even Swiss mountaineers participated in the recovery effort. Eventually, 96 of 128 bodies were recovered and identified. Many of the unidentified were buried at the United Airlines Accident Memorial in the Grand Canyon; others were buried at a TWA memorial in Flagstaff, Arizona.

AFTERMATH

At the time, the United/TWA crash was the worst accident in aviation history. Both planes had clean safety records, and air travel was still new enough that mass loss of life was rare. Both the horror of the accident and calls by the public to make air travel more safe galvanized the U.S. Congress. Within two years, Congress had allocated more than $810 million to modernize America's air-traffic control system. Long-range radar was put into place, and a single organization—the Federal Aviation Administration (FAA)—was created to monitor air travel over the United States. Flying paths were no longer just left up to pilots and what they could see. It took almost two decades for all the new equipment and flying rules to be put into place, but by 1971, air travel over the United States had become the complex, closely monitored system it is today.

Wreckage from the 1956 crash still litters the Grand Canyon; by some estimates, 85 percent of United's wreckage and 40 percent of TWA's remain on the steep cliffs. Despite National Park Service rangers' warnings against exploring the sheer and dangerous cliffs near the crash site, hikers and climbers still investigate the area. Many have found artifacts from the crash, including seat belt buckles with the TWA logo, wallets, watches, and even sticks of gum.

ARIZONA

Grand Canyon National Park
Grand Canyon, AZ 86023

Founded: 1893
Area: 1,218,375 acres
Average annual visitors: 4,000,000

www.nps.gov/grca

* * *

FOR THE LOVE OF SPORT

Looking for adventure? Check out the Alaska Survival Slalom Challenge, held ever summer in Denali National Park.

As part of the Nenana River Wildwater Festival, this challenge is like no other. Its creators describe it as a "kind of slalom, adventure, scavenger hunt, kayak-a-thon." The goal: be the first team of two to finish the 100-yard course, which includes an obstacle course on the Nenana River (Denali's eastern boundary), dragging an inflatable kayak up the beach, and tossing three rocks into your team's bucket.

Thirty-six fish species live in Shenandoah National Park's streams.

TALES OF THE TRAIL: PART III THE "ONE-LEG" WONDER

Scott Rogers was the first above-the-knee amputee to become a 2,000-miler.

Scott Rogers of Washburn, Tennessee, lost his left leg in a shotgun accident in 1998. Five years later, he decided to take on a personal challenge: at the age of 36, Rogers would hike the Appalachian Trail.

An amputee like Rogers can have a tough time learning to walk because of the lack of a knee to move an artificial leg forward. Rogers was lucky to have an insurance company that would pay for a state-of-the-art, $47,000 bionic leg (called a C-Leg) that enabled him to walk almost as well as he had on his own two legs. The leg is computerized and battery operated, and it monitors and adjusts its position and movement 50 times per second to keep its wearer stable. The German manufacturer of the C-Leg developed special solar-powered battery rechargers for Rogers when it learned of his decision to tackle the Appalachian Trail. The batteries didn't always work, but Rogers brought along a crutch to help him when he had to power the leg with his own muscles. He also had to cover the leg with its own specially made raincoat when necessary, since water would destroy its components.

LOTS OF HELP ALONG THE WAY

The technical aspects out of the way—or so he thought—Rogers began his hike in Georgia on March 22, 2004. His wife, Leisa, and their six children followed his route in a motor home so they could meet at different campsites along the way and provide help or supplies. But the ultimate assistance came from a fellow hiker. At one point, Rogers was having trouble with his solar recharger and often had to hike on a dead leg . . . until he met a hiker with the trail name "Gadget," who just happened to have brought a high-powered recharger with him. The next time Rogers saw his wife, he asked her to get the same recharger for him. He said later that he couldn't have gone on without it.

HALFWAY THERE
Rogers made it to the West Virginia midpoint before fall set in but knew he wouldn't make it to Mt. Katahdin before it closed for the year. So he left the trail to do a flip-flop—hiking from Katahdin back to West Virginia. Even with relatively decent weather, the trail was treacherous: littered with slippery rocks and boulders the size of cars. In one 13-mile stretch, Rogers fell 28 times. Still, he kept going.

In Pennsylvania, after 230 days on the trail and with 300 miles to go, Rogers learned of his brother's death. So Rogers left the trail, needing to be with his family but thinking that his trek was over. He had hiked 1,865 miles.

THE FINAL 300
Eighteen months later, on September 18, 2005, Rogers returned to the point where he'd left the trail. He finished the last leg of his hike on September 21 and described his trip as a mixture of joy and sadness. On September 22, he visited the Appalachian Trail Convention office in Harper's Ferry, West Virginia, and officially completed his paperwork to become a 2,000-miler. It had taken longer than he'd expected, but Scott Rogers—trail name: "One-Leg"—had achieved his goal.

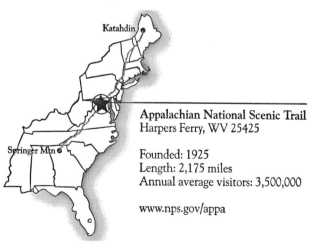

Appalachian National Scenic Trail
Harpers Ferry, WV 25425

Founded: 1925
Length: 2,175 miles
Annual average visitors: 3,500,000

www.nps.gov/appa

...poisoning by milk from cows that had eaten the white snakeroot plant.

ANSWERS

PARK STATS (PAGE 5)

1. **B** – Although it was the first U.S. state, Delaware still has no National Park Service sites.

2. **C** – The 390 primary park sites include everything from forests to historic houses to Hawaiian volcanoes.

3. **C** – Alaska's Wrangell-St. Elias comprises a whopping 13.2 million acres.

4. **A** – This Pennsylvania house, which takes up only 0.2 acres, belonged to freedom fighter Thaddeus Kosciuszko, a Polish immigrant who sided with the colonists during the American Revolution.

5. **A** – Crater Lake in Oregon is 1,943 feet deep and is the seventh-deepest lake in the world.

6. **B** – Talk about contradiction. It can get chilly at the Gates of the Arctic National Park and Preserve. Sometimes, temperatures dip below freezing even in the middle of July. But at Kobuk Valley, summer temperatures can reach a steamy 100°F!

7. **C** – Hot Springs National Park in Arkansas was the first site to be called a national park. Congress set the area aside as a national park in 1832, 40 years before Yellowstone.

8. **C** – The U.S. Congress established the National Park Service on August 25, 1916, as part of the United States Department of the Interior.

9. **B** – There are 11 major designations: national parks, monuments, historical parks, historic sites, memorials, historic trails, outdoor recreation areas, wild and scenic rivers, lakeshores, seashores, and battlefields.

10. **A** – Collectively, the NPS sites take up about 84.4 million acres, but 4.3 acres of that is privately owned.

UNCOVERING PARKS CANADA (PAGE 52)

1. **G** – Canada's transcontinental railroad led to the creation of Glacier National Park in 1886, but before the railroad could be completed, engineers had to find a way through the Selkirk Mountains. The solution was Rogers Pass, found in 1881 by Albert Bowman Rogers, an employee of the Canadian Pacific Railroad Company. Laying the tracks through the gap in the mountains was difficult: avalanches plagued the area, average annual winter snowfalls were 40 feet (12 meters), and the gorges over which the railroad had to pass were steep. But eventually the railroad workers laid the track through the pass and completed the railroad in 1885. A year later, the Canadian government established Glacier National Park, hoping to bring tourists (and money) to the area.

2. **B** – In the Cree language, the word *wapusk* means "white bear." It's fitting, then, that the largest known polar bear denning area in the world is Wapusk National Park, which covers an area of 4,429 square miles (11,475 square kilometers).

3. **A** – About 300 kilometers (185 miles) long, Cabot Trail is named for Englishman John Cabot, the first European to visit Nova Scotia's Cape Breton Island. The road hugs the island's north shore and passes magnificent scenery, including views of the Gulf of St. Lawrence, bogs, tundra, and woodlands. Keep an eye out for whales in the gulf, and moose lingering near streams, and bald eagles overhead.

4. **F** – The only wilderness national park in Ontario (meaning it's a park designated specifically to protect an ecosystem), Pukaskwa contains the least-developed shoreline on the Great Lakes—the northeastern stretch of Lake Superior between Hattie Cove and Michipicoten, Ontario.

5. **C** – Grasslands National Park protects an area that is one of Canada's last remaining swatches of prairie. The park was established in 1981 and is home to prairie dogs, lizards, antelope, and many other animals. It also includes the

...to navigate their way across the Pacific Ocean.

Kildeer Badlands, the site where western Canada's first dinosaur bones were found (in 1874 by scientist George Mercer Dawson), and is the place to which Sitting Bull and approximately 5,000 Sioux warriors fled after George Armstong Custer's defeat and death at the Battle of the Little Big Horn.

6. **H** – Founded in 1914 and encompassing 100 square miles (260 square kilometers), Mt. Revelstoke contains a portion of the only inland temperate rain forest in the world.

7. **I** – Established in 2003, Ukkusiksalik includes 7,913 square miles (20,500 square kilometers) and is located just south of the Arctic Circle. It's also home to 500 archaeological sites and a host of animals, including polar bears, grizzly bears, wolves, and seals.

8. **E** – Mt. Logan in Kluane National Park is not only the highest peak in Canada, it's the second-highest peak in North America (Alaska's Mt. McKinley is first).

9. **J** – Point Pelee is still the southernmost tip of Canada's mainland (and at the same latitude as northern California), but it's lost its point. In March 2006, high winds and storms washed away the sandy point. A "no swimming" sign that once stood on the point turned up on a beach in Ohio . . . about 38 miles (100 kilometers) across Lake Erie.

10. **D** – One of the most remote parks in Canada's system, Aulavik is accessible primarily by plane. It's located in the far north Northwest Territories on Banks Island, one of the Canadian Arctic islands. The park is also home to the highest concentration of muskoxen in the world. (Muskoxen are known for their . . . ahem . . . musky odor.) More than 68,000 muskoxen live on Banks Island, and about 20 percent of those call Aulavik National Park home.

Puffins, which visit Alaska every summer, are better swimmers than fliers.

THE LAZY MAN'S WAY TO SEE PARK FEATURES
(PAGE 96)

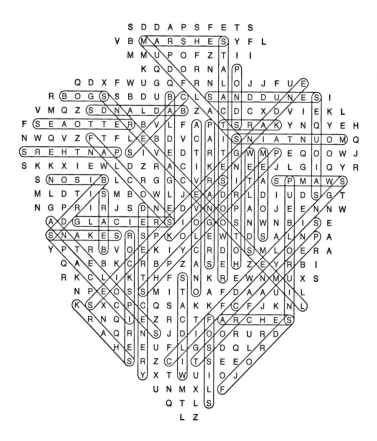

NATIONAL PARK IQ TEST (PAGE 148)

1 I	5. L	9. B
2. D	6. F	10. E
3. A	7. K	11. G
4. C	8. J	12. H

St. Croix Island National Historic Site: first French settlement in North America.

PARK LINGO (PAGE 164)

L	E	S	S		R	I	D	E		P	L	E	B	E
O	N	E	A		E	D	I	T		R	A	M	E	N
E	D	G	Y		P	U	N	T		A	C	I	D	S
B	O	O	G	I	E	B	O	U	L	D	E	R	S	
	R	N	A				A	A	U					
S	O	D	A	S	T	R	A	W	S		P	E	R	T
N	A	A	C	P		A	S	H	E	S		N	I	N
O	S	T	E	O		S	C	I		T	A	N	G	O
W	E	E		T	I	T	A	N		I	Q	U	I	T
E	S	S	O		G	A	P	E	R	G	U	I	D	E
	T	I	O			O	M	E						
	I	R	O	N	R	U	N	G	L	A	D	D	E	R
O	T	T	O	S		T	I	L	L		U	R	E	Y
K	N	E	L	T		A	T	E	E		C	A	R	E
D	O	S	E	S		H	E	E	D		T	W	O	S

There are more pronghorn antelope living in Wyoming than there are people.

LET'S GO PARKING (PAGE 246)

```
V D D U A C A D I A M T A K J Y I G Q A V V Q Z R R Y Z
N E T Y U W O S L M C R U E H H X S G N D N D K H J H A
M A A B E O V A J O S H U A T R E E N O T S W O L L E Y
B E M C W L K Q Y U P E T R I F I E D F O R E S T A T O
Y M S D N A L S I N I G R I V O Y A G E U R S N Y K H S
G N E A E U A A O T X S D J R R V V S E Q U O I A E Q E
N R O L V V M T V R E C I N A C L O V N E S S A L C E M
E A A Y V E E R S A G U T R O T Y R D W I K G T S L E I
P H E N N T R D K I G T U R K S S P Z N P W N N D A R T
Z W L S D A I D G N N O G E T D I J N I C R I U R R A E
S I I N E C C L E I J Q H A N G T U S L O A R O O K G U
K A A N R O A S X E G I M A T U G F Y A T N P M J G N F
C R G O D C N N G R M K L C Y E D I E N W G S Y F H O S
G D X U I C S A Y N L S R H H U S D U E E E T K I E C L
S J A E A F A D C O I O M T L D C O N D R L O O A D R L
Z E R L J R M V N L N K F H V N M F A J L H M N Z A X
K T H E O D O R E R O O S E V E L T P T S S O S E Y T M
B R Y C E C A N Y O N V B I P B F Y S M H T C T K D E T
A F I G R M N O T O Z K I U E G I E Y T Y E A A I Q R F
D C S P Q A X I Y S Y T L I L I F L L A B L A E Y P L T
L I L E H F S N R E V A C D A B S L R A C I O R R V A N
A M E C T H A N D W D M H P D W N A A B I A S G C G K C
N O R T H C A S C A D E S Z Y S A V P B A S Q C S T E I
D R O C K Y M O U N T A I N T N H H G R E A T B A S I N
S K Y C B D C G D G N H M A M M O T H C A V E A O Y X C
D H A O D N A N E H S H A Y E L L A V K U B O K J Y N U
Z L L V E H M O Q D G B N Y A B R E I C A L G G F Y R E
B Y E H H I G E V E R G L A D E S D N A L N O Y N A C S
```

About 100 antelope live at the state's Fossil Butte National Monument.

NAME THAT PARK! (PAGE 250)

1. **C** – Effigy Mounds National Monument is made up of three sites: the North Unit, the South Unit, and the Sny Magill Unit. The monument preserves 206 burial mounds; 31 of these are effigies.

2. **G** – The Ice Age National Scenic Trail is 1,200 miles long, and people who hike its entire length are called "thousand milers."

3. **F** – Early Native Americans prized and made arrowheads from the multicolored alibates flint because it's strong and holds a sharp edge. At the park today, there are 736 flint pits, the only place in the world where alibates flint is exposed aboveground.

4. **A** – The Ala Kahakai Trail is 175 miles long and was established in 2000.

5. **E** – In 1882, Julian Alden Weir traded a painting he'd bought for $560 for the Connecticut farm, which he used as a summer retreat and artist's colony for 37 years.

6. **B** – Aniakchak offers some of the best white-water rafting in the world. The Aniakchak River drops 1,000 feet over the first 15 miles out of the caldera (about 75 feet per mile). The last 12 miles before the river empties into the Pacific Ocean are gentle and make for a leisurely float . . . perhaps to contemplate the first 15.

7. **D** – In 1851, Colonel Isaac Neff Ebey was one of the first settlers to homestead on the island that now bears his name. He became a prominent local politician but was killed in 1857 by Native Americans avenging the death of a chieftain.

WHERE IN THE WORLD? (PAGE 296)

1. A	4. B	7. A
2. C	5. A	8. B
3. B	6. C	9. A

Dangerous plants, animals, and diseases in Shenandoah National Park...

OREGON OR BUST (PAGE 328)

1. **C** – There are six states along the Oregon Trail: Missouri, Kansas, Nebraska, Wyoming, Idaho, and Oregon.

2. **A** – The first wagon train left Elm Grove, Missouri, on May 16, 1842. Approximately 1,000 pioneers made the journey. Although they were the first organized group to make it from Missouri to Oregon, they weren't the first travelers along the Oregon Trail. Fur trappers had been using the trail since the early 1800s.

3. **B** – In 1843, residents living in the area that became Oregon decided to offer free land to anyone who would farm it. Single people could claim 320 acres; married couples, 640. Land claims remained free until 1854, when Oregon Territory officials changed the laws. New residents couldn't just walk in and claim a farm, but they could buy one cheaply; Oregon's fertile fields went for $1.25 per acre. (If you were thinking gold in California was the main reason, you weren't far off; the 1849 gold rush was the second most important force driving people west via the Oregon Trail.)

4. **D** – Pioneers on the trail had to pack smart and bring along only the essentials. Most travelers carried the following: flour, cornmeal, sugar, bacon, coffee, dried fruit, salt, tea, rice, baking soda, and beans. They brought a gun to stave off bandits and for hunting fresh game, and they packed it all into a prairie schooner, the most modern wagon of the time. But even with all these packing tips, most travelers overloaded their wagons and thus walked all the way to Oregon.

5. **D** – The 2,170-mile trek took an average of four to six months to complete. Travelers needed to leave Missouri in April or May so they would be sure to avoid winter weather in Oregon's Cascade and Blue mountain ranges.

6. **B –** Wagon accidents, drownings, bad weather, and many other hazards awaited travelers on the Oregon Trail, but the most disastrous was cholera. At the time, there was no cure for the disease, and cholera killed more people on the trail than anything else. Some wagon trains lost as many as two-thirds of their people to cholera.

7. **C –** Contrary to popular belief, attacks by natives were rare on the Oregon Trail. In fact, many travelers reported friendly encounters with Native Americans—the Cheyenne and Pawnee often helped round up loose cattle or pull wagons out of ditches. Losing one's oxen, however, was a real possibility. So the pioneers circled their wagons in an effort to keep their livestock from wandering off.

8. **C –** Completion of the transcontinental railroad in 1869 made the Oregon Trail obsolete, as rail travel replaced wagon trains as the preferred method of transportation to the West.

9. **A –** Between 1841 and 1867, approximately 350,000 people made the journey from the Midwest to Oregon's Willamette Valley; it was one of the largest migrations in American history.

10. **D –** Congress established the Oregon National Historic Trail in 1978. Today, U.S. Highway 26 follows much of the route of the Oregon Trail.

Alligators can tolerate salt water only briefly because...

THOSE CRAZY MIXED-UP PARKS! (PAGE 346)

C	R	A	G		E	D	I	T	S		W	I	S	P
H	O	U	R		S	O	N	I	C		A	P	I	E
A	T	T	A		C	R	A	T	E	R	L	A	K	E
R	H	O	N	D	A		I	O	N	A		N	E	T
			D	O	L	O	R		E	N	C	A	S	E
L	A	S	C	A	L	A		A	S	T	A			
A	L	K	A		O	X	E	S		O	P	R	A	H
S	P	I	N		P	A	R	K	S		I	A	M	A
S	O	N	Y	S		C	O	A	L		T	G	I	F
		O	T	R	A		N	O	C	O	U	N	T	
A	D	O	N	A	I		S	T	E	E	L			
R	E	N		S	L	A	Y		E	E	R	I	L	Y
G	L	A	C	I	E	R	B	A	Y		E	N	O	S
O	L	L	A		U	N	I	T	E		E	M	M	E
T	A	L	L		P	O	L	E	D		F	E	A	R

...they do not have salt glands.

INDEX

Z

Zion National Park

PARK INDEX BY LOCATION

UNITED STATES

Alabama

Alaska

Arizona

Arkansas

California

THE LAST PAGE

Sit down and be counted!
    Become a member of the Bathroom Readers' Institute! No join-up fees, monthly minimums or maximums, organized dance parties, quilting bees, solicitors, annoying phone calls (we only have one phone line), Spam—or any other canned meat product—to worry about . . . just the chance to get our fabulous monthly newsletter (and if you want) some extremely cool Uncle John stuff.

So send us a letter:

> Uncle John's Bathroom Reader
> Portable Press
> 5880 Oberlin Drive
> San Diego, CA 92121

Or email us at unclejohn@advmkt.com

Hope you enjoyed the book—and if you're skipping to the end, what are you doing reading this page? Go back and finish!

This book was printed by Banta Book Group on 55# Dorado Opaque Stock.

Waste wood recycling
One hundred percent of the fiber used in manufacturing Dorado Opaque
is recycled from saw mill waste.

High Yield Pulping
Dorado Opaque is made from high yield, state of art mechanical pulp.
This process has a yield factor of 90%, meaning that only 10% of the
wood weight is lost in processing.

Conversely the traditional chemical pulping process used to make other offset
papers has a yield factor of only 50%.

Sustainable Forestry Practices and Protection of Fragile Forests
70% of the fiber used in the production of Dorado Opaque is harvested
from forests managed in accordance with CSA
(Canadian Standards Association) sustainable forestry standards.
The objectives of these standards are to maintain biodiversity in the forests,
encourage private landowner support of sustainable forest management,
protect water quality and prevent land erosion.
Banta's mill partner works closely with the World Wildlife Fund (WWF)
to identify, set aside and preserve blocks of HVCA or High Value Conservation
Area wood lands that are deemed to be fragile or at risk.

Chorine bleaching
Dorado is totally chlorine free or TCF.

Waste Paper Reclamation
Banta's mill partner is one of the largest processors of waste paper
in North America. They annually convert over 2,000,000 tons of waste paper
to recycled fiber. This fiber is typically reused in the production of
newsprint and phone directory paper.